TO SAVE HEAVEN AND EARTH

TO SAVE HEAVEN AND EARTH

Rescue in the Rwandan Genocide

Jennie E. Burnet

CORNELL UNIVERSITY PRESS ITHACA AND LONDON

First published 2023 by Cornell University Press

Library of Congress Cataloging-in-Publication Data

Names: Burnet, Jennie E., author.
Title: To save heaven and earth : rescue in the Rwandan genocide / Jennie E. Burnet.
Description: Ithaca [New York] : Cornell University Press, [2022] | Includes bibliographical references and index.
Identifiers: LCCN 2022007252 (print) | LCCN 2022007253 (ebook) | ISBN 9781501767104 (hardcover) | ISBN 9781501767111 (paperback) | ISBN 9781501767135 (pdf) | ISBN 9781501767128 (epub)
Subjects: LCSH: Rwandan Genocide, Rwanda, 1994. | Genocide—Rwanda—History—20th century. | Tutsi (African people)—Crimes against—Rwanda—History—20th century. | Rwanda—History—Civil War, 1994—Atrocities. | Rwanda—History—Civil War, 1994—Civilian relief. | Rwanda—Ethnic relations—History—20th century.
Classification: LCC DT450.435 B88 2022 (print) | LCC DT450.435 (ebook) | DDC 967.57104/31—dc23/eng/20220816
LC record available at https://lccn.loc.gov/2022007252
LC ebook record available at https://lccn.loc.gov/2022007253

For those who died trying to assist others
In memory of Tayo Jolaosho

Contents

MAP 1. Rwanda, 1994 administrative boundaries and field sites, with genocide start dates. Created by Dr. Dajun Dai.

MAP 2. Rwanda, 2006 administrative boundaries and field sites, with genocide start dates. Created by Dr. Dajun Dai.

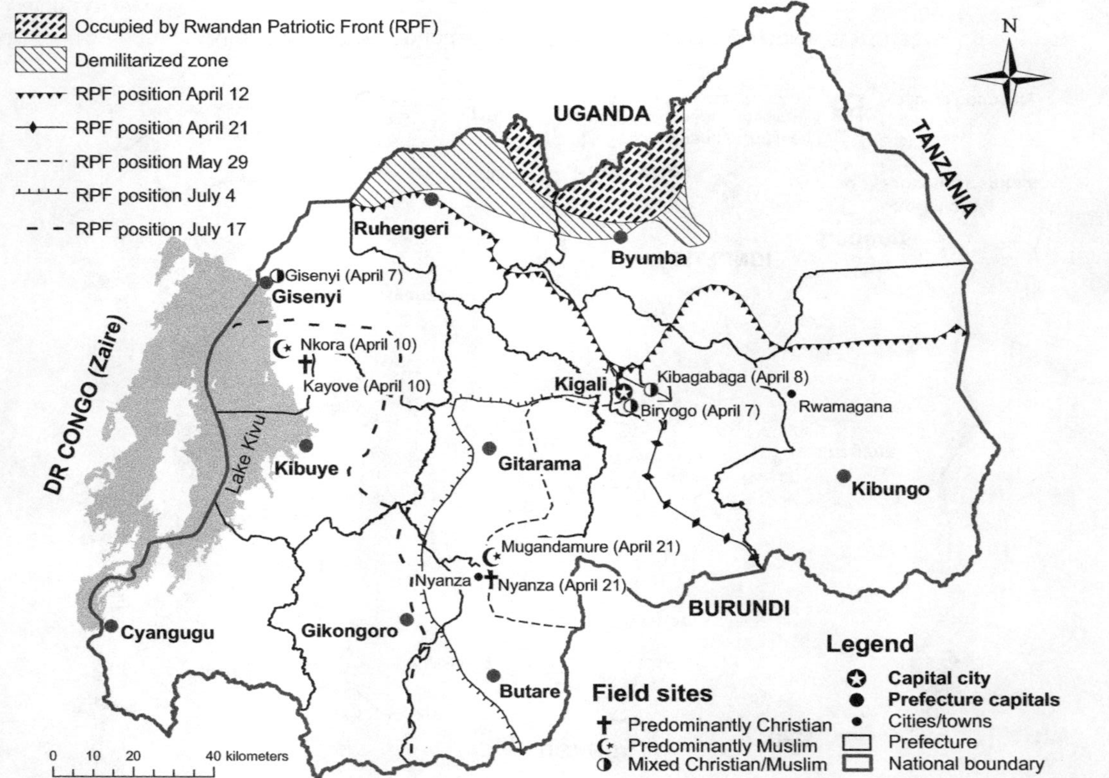

MAP 3. Rwandan Patriotic Front positions and advance, April 6–July 17, 1994. Created by Dr. Dajun Dai. Adapted from Kuperman (2001, 43; 2004, 67), Viret (2010), Davenport and Stam (2014), and interview data.

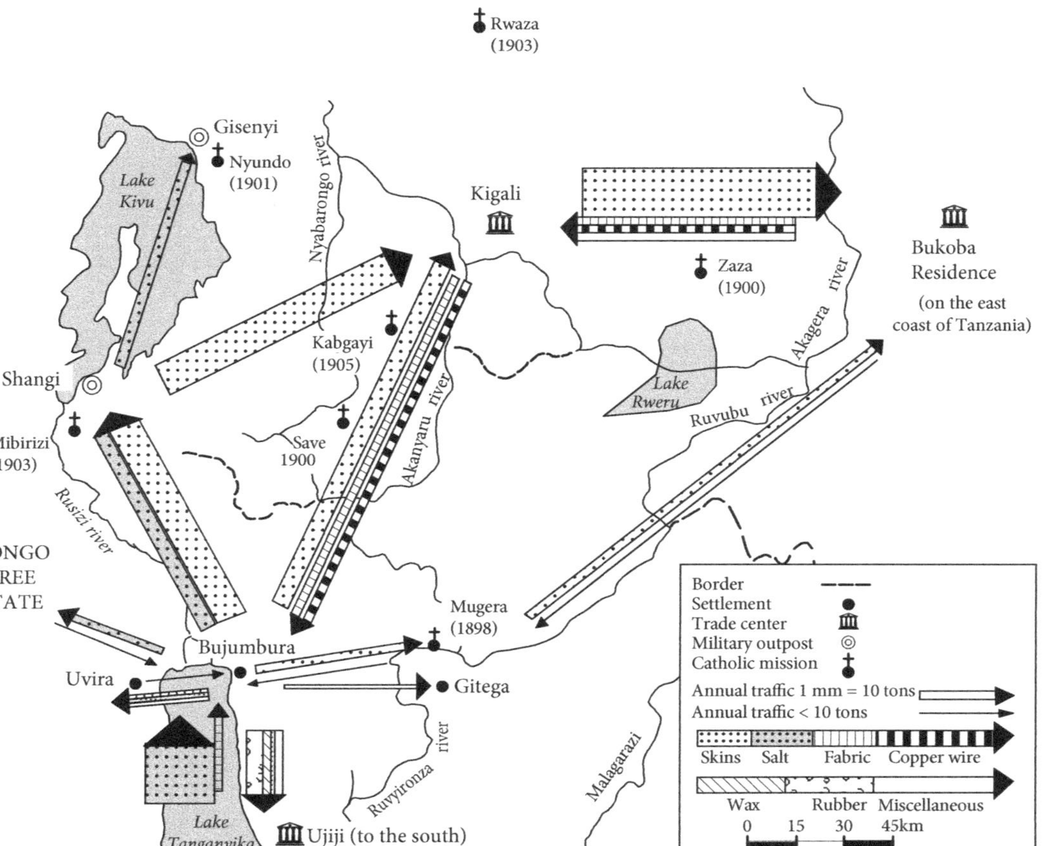

MAP 4. Major trade routes in Ruanda-Urundi, German East Africa, 1912, with German military outposts, settlements, and Catholic missions marked. Created by Dr. Dajun Dai. Adapted from Sirven (1984, 283).

Preface

In the one hundred days between April 6, 1994, and July 14, 1994, 77 percent of Tutsi in Rwanda (and a total of five hundred thousand to eight hundred thousand Rwandans of all races) lost their lives in a state-sponsored genocide.[1] Inside Rwanda, these events are formally known as "the 1994 Genocide against Tutsis"; outside, they are commonly referred to simply as the Rwandan genocide. At its core, the Rwandan genocide was a short, intense period of mass murder largely perpetrated by ordinary civilians. A growing body of research has examined the decision making and motivations of "ordinary" perpetrators.[2] Few scholars have examined the decision making or motivations of bystanders or rescuers.[3] Perpetrators, bystanders, and rescuers in Rwanda all faced the same chaotic context, deciding how to act and react to the suddenly abnormal situation. Many people hid or fled. Some participated gleefully and passionately in the killing. Many others acted as required to save themselves and their families—understanding their actions as morally justifiable acts of self-defense. Why, then, did some people risk their lives to save others?

My interest in the question of rescue grew out of more than twenty years of ethnographic research in Rwanda, much of which focused on the aftermath of the genocide, the politics of memory, women in politics, gender, and reconciliation. In the 1990s and early 2000s, I often encountered a trope about the 1994 genocide: Muslims did not participate in killing. Non-Muslim Rwandans, especially those living outside Rwanda, often told me that Muslims offered protection to Tutsi and did not participate in the genocide. The new Rwandan government reinforced these ideas, and international media eventually took up this message. My curiosity about this belief and its foundations eventually grew into skepticism. The International Criminal Tribunal for Rwanda (ICTR) indicted four Rwandans who had Muslim names.[4] During interviews I conducted in Nyamirambo, a well-known Muslim neighborhood in the capital city, residents told me about Muslim genocide perpetrators. Clearly, some Muslims had participated in the genocide. Whether they had done so less frequently than Christians or for different reasons was unknown.

Beyond the myth of Muslim nonparticipation, genocide survivors regularly told me about people who had helped save their lives. Friends, neighbors, relatives, or even strangers hid them for months, gave them food or water, warned them of approaching militiamen, or offered other temporary forms of protection. Yet these acts of rescue were rarely discussed in Rwandan public forums in the late 1990s or early 2000s. Rather, state practices of national memory politicized victimhood and maintained a racialized dichotomy, with "victim" or "survivor" standing in for "Tutsi," and "perpetrator," "*genocidaire*," or "prisoner" standing in for "Hutu" (Burnet 2009, 2012). In my earlier research, I came to understand that acts of rescue during the genocide—by all kinds of people, not just Muslims—were far more common than government-sanctioned discourse allowed. My curiosity about those acts and what motivated them eventually led to this project.

Research Ethics and Methods

As I elaborated at length in my first book, conducting ethnographic research in post-genocide Rwanda poses numerous ethical and logistical challenges, as well as political risks and occasional safety concerns (Burnet 2012). Conducting research in conflict and post-conflict zones is a risky proposition in terms of personal safety for researchers, short- and long-term safety for research participants and interviewees, and the potential for politicization of the research process, findings, or outcomes.[5] I made research, work, or other trips to Rwanda in 1997, 1998, 2002, 2003, 2007, 2009, 2011, 2013, 2014, 2016, 2017, and 2019. From 1999 though 2001, I lived in a middle-class neighborhood in Kigali, the capital city, and in a rural community in southern Rwanda.[6] I also made frequent, relatively short visits to hills, hamlets, and towns in all regions of the country. I arrived in Rwanda fluent in French and English; during my time there, I completed an eight-month, intensive Kinyarwanda course.

Over two decades, I conducted more than three years and nine months of ethnographic research in the country. Through these years of experience, I have navigated challenges ranging from finding adequate, safe lodging in deeply rural areas, to transporting research team members where roads are impassable or nonexistent, to making decisions about security following a nearby brutal attack on a schoolteacher in her home. Throughout, I have followed American Anthropological Association guidance on professional responsibility and research ethics, including its 1971 Principles of Professional Responsibility and subsequent statements on ethics in 1998, 2009, and 2012. Thus, I placed the safety and security of research participants first, my research team's safety second, my own safety third, the research fourth, and my responsibilities to the public, discipline, and students after that.

This book draws on over two hundred interviews with a wide variety of actors, conducted in ten communities in Rwanda between 2011 and 2014, as well as ongoing ethnographic research conducted since 1997. The majority of the 232 formal interviews at the heart of this book were gathered by a small team I led in 2013 and 2014.[7] The team included anthropologist Hager El Hadidi, my coinvestigator; Ildéphonse Nkiliye, associate director of the Research Center of the Catholic University of Kabgayi; and five interpreters. The team worked in deep collaboration during fieldwork, and team members contributed to the inductive process of interpreting results in the field (a standard practice in ethnographic research). As author, I bear sole responsibility for the opinions, findings, and conclusions in this book. Team members conducted interviews in ten communities: Nyamirambo sector, Nyarugenge district and Kibagabaga sector, Gasabo district in Kigali Province; Nyanza town and Mugandamure hamlet in Nyanza district, South Province; Gisenyi sector, Rubavu district, West Province; and the rural communities of Kayove, Ngabo, Vumbi, Kinunu and Boneza sectors, Rutsiro district, West Province.[8] Twenty formal interviews from pilot research in other communities in 2011 were included in the data analysis.

Although this project was grounded primarily in semi-structured interviews, the research team deployed participant observation on a limited basis in each community and engaged in a "dialectic of experience and interpretation" (Clifford 1988, 38). Whenever possible, team members participated in prayers in churches or mosques and attended Eid al-Fitr or Eid al-Adha celebrations or other community events while we resided in each community. While the team did not spend enough time in these locales to conduct full-scale ethnographic research, they recorded field notes each day and conducted informal ethnographic interviews outside formal interviews.[9] As my field experience has shown, these are a vital tool for gathering information in highly politicized research contexts and for confirming data from formal interviews. My prior ethnographic research enhanced the data analysis by providing a large corpus of cultural and linguistic data for comparison where relevant.

The communities where we conducted interviews were selected to capture varying degrees of geographic proximity to political power at the time of the genocide, different start dates of genocidal violence targeting Tutsi, and regional differences in the prevalence or relative strength of the Hutu Power movement (see maps 1 and 2). Scott Straus (2006), Lee Ann Fujii (2009), and Timothy Longman (2009) all concluded that human social connections to political power and geographic proximity to political power—whether manifested in a government administrative office, police station, military barracks, or political party office—were relevant factors in the speed, intensity, and thoroughness of genocide policy implementation in communities. The geographic sample included three sites where the Muslim community—as opposed to individuals—mobilized to mount active resistance to the genocide or to rescue Tutsi and other targeted people: Mugandamure hamlet, Nyanza district; Kibagabaga, a peri-urban community on the outskirts of Kigali at the time of the genocide (now a sector in Gasabo district of Kigali Province); and Nkora, a rural community on the shores of Lake Kivu (now part of Rutsiro district, West Province). Nearby predominantly Christian communities were selected for purposes of comparison to investigate the role religion may have played in rescue activity. The initial geographic sample of eight communities became ten during research, as we sought interviewees and developed a more complete understanding of regional dynamics during the genocide.

In each community, the team interviewed current and former government officials, representatives from Ibuka (the national genocide survivors' association), judges from the Gacaca courts, Muslim and Christian religious leaders, genocide survivors, convicted genocide perpetrators, rescuers identified by other interviewees, rescuers (*indakemwa*) identified in a 2009 pilot study by Ibuka, and community members.[10] Often, interviewees fell into multiple categories. For example, a government official may also have been an Ibuka representative and a genocide survivor, or a convicted perpetrator may also have been a government official in 1994.

The interviews, which consisted of open-ended questions, were conducted in Kinyarwanda, Swahili, Arabic, French, or English, depending on the interviewee's preference. When needed, Rwandan interpreters who were trained for the project provided simultaneous translation from Kinyarwanda to French or English. Dr. El Hadidi conducted a handful of interviews in Arabic. When interviewees consented, we recorded interviews with digital recording devices. We always took detailed handwritten or typed notes. Interviewees were offered anonymity and confidentiality. To protect anonymity, we assigned codes to all interview recordings and transcripts and deleted interviewees' names from recordings, interview notes, and field notes. Daily, team members recorded detailed ethnographic field notes comprising their observations of everyday life and interactions with Rwandans outside of formal research settings. Before leaving each field site, the research team, including interpreters, met to summarize results, construct timelines of local events, and note important themes emerging from the data.

For digitally recorded interviews, a team of native Kinyarwanda speakers created English-language transcripts. In the first round of data analysis, the interview transcripts, field notes, and archival documents were manually coded by me and two graduate research assistants. In the second round of data analysis, a software package was used. Themes in the data were identified by searching the same materials for repetitions, similarities and differences, word lists, key words in context, and word co-occurrence (Bernard and Ryan 2010, 69). Then, the team generated themes based on research literature, indigenous typologies, and *in vivo* coding of the transcripts (2010, 69). After these themes were defined and elaborated in a codebook, a team of US student research assistants under my close supervision coded the data with the software.

Feminist and Antiracist Methodologies

This book and the research on which it is based are grounded in feminist and antiracist theory, praxis, and epistemology. My use of actor-network theory in this project embraces three foundational assumptions grounded in feminist theory. First, I decenter "liberal humanism" (Weedon 1987, 173) and a Cartesian concept of knowing the self. Second, I reject the notion of a person as the sole author of their thoughts and actions.[11] Third, feminist theory recognizes that human agency emerges from unique subject positions produced by fields of power that emerge from structures, discourses, and praxis.

In this book, I bridge scientific and humanist modes of inquiry. The research project departed from a positivist, scientific desire to uncover fundamental truths about the human condition: this stance drove much of the research design. Yet throughout the project I embraced the feminist stance that all knowing—even scientific ways of knowing—is partial (Haraway 1988). In the book, I have adopted a mode of ethnographic writing that Lila Abu-Lughod (1991) calls "tactical humanism." Abu-Lughod critiques anthropological knowledge production as it risks participating in and perpetuating "global inequality along the lines of 'cultural' difference" (159). Given anthropology's colonial origins and the ongoing dominance of scholars based in anthropology departments in Europe and North America, the discipline's knowledge production is grounded in Western epistemology (Mudimbe 1988). Nonetheless I have taken steps to mitigate these effects. First, I have deeply contextualized local social conditions and histories to communicate the ways that transnational, "extralocal and long-term processes are . . . manifested locally . . . produced in the actions of individuals living their particular lives inscribed in their bodies and words" (Abu-Lughod 1991, 150). Second, I have attempted to decolonize my scholarship by citing Rwandan or African scholars, Black scholars of all genders, women scholars, and LGBTQI+ scholars whenever possible. Third, I have adopted a humanist stance and tried to make the lives, actions, and motivations of ordinary Rwandans during extraordinary circumstances intelligible to anyone who reads this book. Finally, I entered this study with the assumption that all humans can participate in genocide or engage in acts of rescue regardless of nationality, race, ethnicity, class, or gender.

In short, I rejected explanations of behavior, motivation, or agency predicated on cultural determinism.

I have embraced feminist methodologies from the conception of this project to the manuscript completion. Anthropologist Faye V. Harrison writes that "methods . . . in and of themselves . . . are not feminist or non-feminist" (2007, 25). Yet there are feminist methodologies "because methodologies articulate conceptual, theoretical, and ethical perspectives on the whats, whys and hows of research and the production of knowledge" (25). Feminist scholarship has long emphasized that knowledge is "situational and grounded in particular dynamics of the research situation" (Lewin 2006, 20). In this research, I have considered the ways that "privilege and disempowerment" affected ordinary Rwandans' lives and paid special attention to the ways the "determinants of social status—caste, class, race, . . . sexuality," and gender impacted the choices they felt they had as the 1994 genocide unfolded (2006, 19). I grounded this intersectional methodology in the scholarship of Kimberlé Crenshaw (1991), Patricia Hill Collins (1990, 1998), bell hooks (1982), and other scholars who used their ideas. In my analysis, I have included my own social positions in the text, especially in contexts where my presence may have wielded power. In both data collection and data analysis, I have followed "a doctrine and practice of objectivity that privileges contestation, deconstruction, passionate construction, webbed connections, and hope for transformation of systems of knowledge and ways of seeing" (Haraway 1988, 584–85).

I have also foregrounded feminist ethnography in this project through my emphasis on polyvocality (Abu-Lughod 1991, 138; Strathern 1987, 289). The importance of polyvocality drove the strategic sampling strategy for interviewees in each community and undergirded data analysis. In writing the book, I carried polyvocality through the text. Each chapter opens with an extended vignette focused on a single person or small group of people that I constructed from multiple interviews, texts, ethnographic observation, and primary and secondary sources. These vignettes are, in effect, "fictions," as Clifford Geertz (1975) described the technique of thick description, but they are not "fictitious." They are fictions because I have changed names, filled in gaps, smoothed out narratives, and described scenes in poetic language. Yet they are not fictitious, because they hew closely to empirically established facts, reflect multiple voices rather than a single point of view, and capture the underlying cultural logics that made some actions more or less possible than others. Additional voices appear in the chapters themselves; and wherever ordinary Rwandans disagreed about the unfolding of events or specific individuals' actions, I have rendered these contentions in the text.

Drawing on my earlier feminist research praxis, I trained research team members in the technique of "deep empathy" to encourage interviewees to share their stories (Burnet 2012, 34).[12] This technique often posed difficulties for interviewers, especially when speaking with genocide survivors or perpetrators. Using deep empathy during interviews with genocide survivors sometimes impacted research team members' mental health by exposing them to narratives that could provoke secondary psychosocial trauma or trigger symptoms for those living with the mental health effects of trauma. Interviewing genocide perpetrators was difficult in a different way. Most perpetrators were reluctant to say much of anything about their actions during the genocide. At times, deep empathy coaxed a few to speak at length about what they did. At other times, convicted perpetrators continued to insist they had "done nothing" during the genocide, and research team members adopted a more antagonist stance. Interviewers began with established probes, asking what crimes they had confessed to in exchange for a reduced sentence or for what crimes they had been sentenced. In addition to deep empathy, team members "listened to silence" during interviews (Burnet 2012, 34). In Rwandan culture, the most important information is often left unstated and instead communicated silently. This silent communication can come through omissions: not stating the obvious, leaving the listener to capture commonsense ideas, or leaving out what Michael Taussig (1999, 50) called "public secrets," meaning the things that everybody knows but nobody talks about. Facial expressions, body language, and coded language are other ways silence imparts meaning in Rwandan culture. Interviewers and interpreters recorded these nonverbal communications in notes.

In data analysis and the writing of this book, I continued my commitment to feminist research praxis through reflexive, intersubjective, and dialectic interpretation of data. This data included interviews, field notes related to participant observation, primary sources (such as ICTR judgments), and secondary sources. For each community, I constructed chronologies of events using these sources to triangulate facts or to highlight significant differences in various accounts of events. When conducting research with conflict-affected individuals, regardless of their roles in violence, interviewers need to tread lightly, listen with empathy, and respect research participants' account of events in the moment. In data analysis, however, people's testimony must be triangulated with the testimony of others and what can be known about events from other sources. This practice is an ethical and methodological minimum to produce scientifically valid accounts of chaotic and potentially traumatic events. In writing this book, I have maintained "a commitment to mobile positioning and to passionate detachment" (Haraway 1988, 585) by situating Rwandans who engaged in acts of rescue as knowers of their own lives.

During my early fieldwork in the years immediately after the genocide, I intended to examine the everyday life of civil war and genocide instead of their aftermaths. However, I discovered that ordinary Rwandans were reluctant to speak in formal interviews about the civil war and genocide. During extensive ethnographic fieldwork in two communities between 1997 and 2001, I came to understand that this reluctance was enmeshed in micro- and macro-level politics of memory about the genocide, the civil war, and killings perpetrated by the Rwandan Patriotic Front (RPF) (Burnet 2012). This interpretation was founded on feminist theory and ethnographic praxis. As I wrote, "the scientific validity of ethnography relies on long-term fieldwork because it is only through the accumulation of experience and interpretation along with involvement in local webs of power that the anthropologist is able to pass her own subjective interpretations and those of her interviewees" (2012, 35).

In contrast, this project on rescue relied on a comparative, case-study framework grounded in positivist social sciences instead of in long-term ethnographic fieldwork. Despite this key difference, my analysis and interpretation of rescue during the Rwandan genocide would not have been possible without the years of ethnographic research I had already done (2012). The data analysis required deep knowledge of Rwandan culture and society, especially the particularities of Rwanda's "terribly closed rural world," as Danielle de Lame (2005, 14) described it. Without this knowledge, I likely would have never gotten past the commonsense assumption that rescuers are good people who do good things to arrive at this study's most significant conclusion: successful rescue almost always entails morally ambiguous decisions conditioned by the moral gray zone of genocide.

Beyond deep knowledge of Rwandan culture and society, my long-term engagements with the country, whether professional or personal, have given me a network of informal research collaborators. Over the years, these collaborators have shown me strategies for conducting research in difficult contexts; challenged my analyses, pushing me to reconsider or examine them in more depth; and given me courage to publish unpopular yet valid research findings. I happily acknowledge their contributions to this research, but I alone am responsible for the findings and conclusions reported in this book.

Studying Genocide through Retrospective Narratives

Retrospective narratives are always grounded in the present context and thus have limitations for understanding human behavior, motivation, or decision making in the past, whether near or far. Given that most of the interviews for this book covered events more than twenty years in the past, this argument presents a cogent potential critique. Yet, there are few (perhaps no) other methods for studying behavior, motivation, or decision making during mass violence or genocide. Human behavioral experiments related to violent behavior, such as Stanley Milgram's (1974) now controversial "obedience to authority" experiments, have been rightfully deemed unethical because of their potential harm to research participants and their limitations in providing reliable results. Even if individual narratives about past events may be unreliable, multiple narratives about the past can collectively illuminate reliable accounts of micro- and macro-level phenomena. Narratives about the past can provide reliable accounts of behavior, motivations, or decision making when triangulated with each other and with other data.

Beyond their utility for understanding community- or national-level events, narratives about the past are memory-making endeavors. "Memory . . . captures simultaneously the individual, embodied, and lived side *and* the collective, social, and constructed side of our relations with the past" (Rothberg 2009, 4). These endeavors can be individual, connecting people to their pasts, present, and possible futures, but they are also collective. An individual's personal memories interact with other people's memories, and collective memory. Narrative as a form of memory making takes on additional emotional or political charges in the context of violent conflict, genocide, and torture. Pain and violence inscribe themselves in both personal and collective memory in myriad ways that are not always amenable to narrative or memory. As literary theorist Elaine Scarry wrote, "Physical pain does not simply resist language but actively destroys it" (1985, 4). Scarry asserts that the only way to make "radically private" experiences of physical pain real is by rendering them part of the "realm of public discourse" (6). In her critique of Scarry's approach, Joanna Bourke (2014) underscores the ways in which cultural, social, political, and historical contexts shape the embodiment and memory of pain. Anthropologist Victoria Sanford claims that bearing witness to mass violence, a form of "speaking truth to power" in certain contexts, serves not only to reconstruct the past but also to rebuild communities and seek redress (Sanford 2003, 211).

Survivor testimony is particularly fraught in this regard. In genocide studies, survivor testimony has been treated with both deference and respect (Greene and Kumar 2000; Langer 1991; Matthäus 2009); I give it a privileged position in this book and in my previous work. Yet the effects of torture and extreme stress on a survivor's ability to remember events precisely have been well documented by psychologists (Williams and Banyard 1999). Other factors may affect memory as well. I have written about the ways in which Rwandans' memories of and narratives about the past are shaped by dominant public discourses surrounding the country's history, the meanings of race, the civil war, and the 1994 genocide

(Burnet 2009, 2012). These factors must be considered in the analysis of narratives and their multiple possible truths, whether factual, forensic, emotional, social, or political. Nonetheless, survivor testimony demands a privileged position in the collective memoryscape. Through bearing witness and giving narrative form to their memories, survivors build their worlds anew. Documenting their testimony and sharing it with a broader audience offer redress by transforming their experiences into facts knowable by others.

Yet, in this book's analysis, I treat survivor testimony as another narrative to be triangulated—a narrative truth but not the absolute truth. To genocide survivor testimony, I add the testimonies of ordinary Hutu people who lived through the genocide and the civil war. In Rwanda, testimonies from people not classified as survivors are rarely heard. Adding their voices to the public memory of the 1994 genocide of Tutsi augments the narrative truths about the genocide and fills gaps in the absolute truth of it.

To account for the methodological problems of relying on retrospective narrative, I have used multiple techniques to triangulate information gleaned from interviews. For each community included in the study, I mapped events and constructed detailed timelines from published secondary sources and judgments issued by the ICTR. This information was used to generate questions about specific events or people in the communities we studied and confirm aspects of more contentious narratives. The hundreds of ethnographic interviews recorded in daily field notes by the research team, along with those I have recorded over the past twenty years, provided an additional dataset for triangulation. In my experience, the most important information is often revealed in the informal conversations before, after, and around formal interviews. Finally, narratives were triangulated with each other to validate empirical facts and identify themes or concepts. The net result is a well-validated analysis at the level of the community and the nation, even if individual narratives are only partially true or empirically untrue. Where I quote extensively from individual interviews, I am mobilizing them not as empirically true in and of themselves but rather to illustrate important points or themes that emerged from the data.

On Naming Research Objects

Whether to refer to the 1994 genocide in Rwanda by its official Rwandan name, "the 1994 Genocide against Tutsis," by the internationally accepted term "Rwandan genocide," or by some other phrase is a complicated and highly politicized issue. In earlier writings, I used terms such as "Rwandan genocide," "1994 genocide and massacres," or "genocide and massacres," following the neutral terminology in Kinyarwanda *itsembabwoko n'itsembatsemba* (genocide and massacres) preferred by the government between 1997 and 2002, when the bulk of my earlier fieldwork was completed (Burnet 2012, 20–21). This formulation avoided mention of race (*ubwoko*), repressed from public discourse in the interest of national reconciliation, but it still recognized that not all victims were targeted because of their race. In the mid-2000s, the government (then led by the RPF) shifted its preference to *jenoside* (genocide) or *jenoside ya 1994* (1994 genocide) in place of *itsembabwoko n'itsembatsemba* (Waldorf 2009, 104–5). In a 2008 revision of the 2003 constitution, the government introduced new terminology, *jenoside yakorewe abaTutsi muri 1994* (literally, "genocide that carried away the Tutsi in 1994"), usually rendered in English by the government as "the 1994 Genocide against Tutsis." The change in language was intended to clarify the precise target of the genocide. Yet this language shift played a less positive role as well: it further erased the many Hutu and Twa victims of the genocide and sublimated the civil war (1990–1994), which had created the context that made genocide possible. In this book, I use "Rwandan genocide," "the 1994 genocide," "the genocide," or the "1994 genocide of Tutsi" to refer to these killings. Although "genocide of Tutsi" risks erasing some victims of genocidal violence, including the Hutu and Twa who risked their lives to save others, I want to reflect the shift in language within the country and acknowledge the primary target of the genocide.

Much of the writing by social scientists and historians on Rwanda has referred to Hutu, Tutsi, and Twa as "ethnicity." Following this precedent, I used the terms "ethnicity," "ethnic," and "ethnic violence" in my previous book. Yet these categories do not correspond to differences in culture, language, religion, or national origin, which are all typical markers of ethnicity. In this book, I refer to these categories as "race," meaning social categories that *allegedly* correspond to distinct sets of biological characteristics, since race more accurately reflects how these categories operated in Rwanda during the 1990s. In Kinyarwanda, Hutu, Tutsi, and Twa are referred to as *ubwoko*, meaning literally "sort" or "type." The word *ubwoko* can be applied to trees or cattle as easily as humans (Burnet 2012, 48). In the precolonial period, Hutu and Tutsi were flexible categories and largely contingent on the local context.[13] Under colonial occupation, Europeans projected their own racist ideas on Rwandan society and placed Tutsi, Hutu, and Twa in a rigid hierarchy based on the pseudoscientific Hamitic hypothesis, later demonstrated as the myth it was (Sanders 1969). Over the course of the twentieth century, distinct sets of phenotypic attributes became associated with each category. As a result, Hutu, Tutsi, and Twa operate much more like racial categories in the United States than like ethnic categories elsewhere in Africa, even if race and ethnicity share much in common as social forces. For these reasons, I use the term "race" for these social categories and the dynamic discursive system they produced over time.

All names of people in this book are pseudonyms except where otherwise noted. In addition, the names of people mentioned in interviews have been changed except when the person is dead, was convicted of genocide crimes, or is a public figure.

Acknowledgments

First, I would like to thank the many Rwandans who have participated in, collaborated in, or otherwise supported my research over nearly three decades. I hope I have portrayed your lives, motivations, and experiences in the nuanced complexity they deserve. Thank you to those who have been steadfast friends. You have taught me so much about life and living in the wake of unthinkable tragedy.

I send gratitude to the research team that gathered the two hundred formal interviews at the heart of this book. The team included my co-investigator, the anthropologist Dr. Hager El Hadidi, associate professor of anthropology at California State University at Bakersfield; the sociologist Ildéphonse Nkiliye, associate director of the Research Center of the Catholic University of Kabgayi; and five interpreters, who wish to remain anonymous. They worked long days in difficult conditions without complaint.

This book was made possible thanks (in part) by funds granted through a J. B. and Maurice C. Shapiro Fellowship at the Jack, Joseph and Morton Mandel Center for Advanced Holocaust Studies, United States Holocaust Memorial Museum. The statements made and views expressed, however, are solely my responsibility. The research for this book was supported by the National Science Foundation under Grant Numbers 1230062 and 1550655. Any opinions, findings, and conclusions expressed in this material are my own and do not necessarily reflect the views of the National Science Foundation. The University of Louisville Research Foundation and Department of Anthropology supported pilot research conducted in 2011. The Georgia State University College of Arts and Sciences and Global Studies Institute funded teaching leave so that I could write this book. Over the course of my work on the book, dozens of students from Georgia State University, the University of Louisville, and the University of Wisconsin at Madison assisted with data mining, data coding, and other research activities: Michelle Fox, Joanna Thompson, Clay Voytek, Benjamin (Ben) Belisle, Britni Wright, Isabella Schiwy, Elliott Whiteside, Telesphore Kagaba, and Marko Kljajic.

Many thanks go to the editors, staff, and editorial board of Cornell University Press. Editors Roger Haydon and Jim Lance believed in this book over the years it took to bring it to this point. Thank you for your feedback and support. I also appreciate the helpful comments from the two anonymous readers who completed their reviews in the midst of the COVID-19 pandemic. Thank you for sacrificing your precious time and energy to bring this book to publication.

This manuscript would never have arrived at this point without the wonderful editorial assistance of MaryAnne Hamilton. Thank you for helping me figure out what I was trying to say and then guiding me to say it clearly in my own voice. My appreciation goes to Clay Voytek for his diligent copyediting and fact checking.

Many colleagues have provided helpful feedback and commentary on drafts, both early and near final. I would like to thank David Newbury for his detailed comments on an early draft of the manuscript and Catharine Newbury for her continued moral support. Tim Longman provided valuable feedback on the manuscript. The community of Holocaust studies scholars at the United States Holocaust Memorial Museum and Mandel Center for Advanced Holocaust Studies helped me broaden the comparative framework of the manuscript. Many thanks to Amos Goldberg, Bettina Brandt, and Carolin Lange for our stimulating conversations at Busboys and Poets and ongoing solidarity. I owe much gratitude to Antonius Robben for his detailed and thought-provoking commentary on an earlier application of Primo Levi's moral gray zone. His comments helped me refine my use of it here. The Georgia State University Humanities Research Center seminar pushed my thinking in new directions. Most of all, I am grateful for my colleagues in the Georgia State University Department of Anthropology. You offered me a haven after the four-year experiment of the Global Studies Institute came to an end. It feels good to be back among my people. I cannot forget my colleagues in the Department of Anthropology at the University of Louisville. Thank you for all you did to support the early stages of this book.

To the friends and colleagues enlisted in our networks of mutual assistance: thank you for keeping me afloat. Tayo Jolaosho accompanied me in writing, often daily, for nearly two years. Their sudden and early departure from this life left a raw hole in my heart. Dear Tayo, I will continue the struggle. Maggie Walker gave me deadlines, read drafts—rough, polished, bad, and good—and patiently helped me articulate the theoretical framework of this book. I have learned so much about Herbert Marcuse from you; I cannot wait to read your book! To Susan Thomson for her feedback on early drafts of chapters and pushing me to continue. To Susi and Maya for providing shelter and company during my fellowship in DC. To Susi and Debbie for their unwavering support through my move to Atlanta and for keeping up our regular video dates. To my neighbor friends who asked questions about my research and work, listened to me complain, and kept an eye on my house and family when I was away.

My heartfelt gratitude goes to my family. My parents always believed in me and taught me to believe in myself. They supported this book in ways large and small. I thank my husband, Theogene, and our sons, Hazen and Rene, for their love, support, and patience. They tolerated my long absences during research, gave me space to write, and provided solace when I needed it. Most importantly, they remind me every day that there is good in the world even when things fall apart.

Abbreviations

AMA	African Muslims Agency
AMUR	Association des Musulmans du Rwanda (Muslim Association of Rwanda)
CDR	Coalition pour la défense de la république (Coalition for the Defense of the Republic)
CND	Conseil National du Développement (National Development Council)
ICTR	International Criminal Tribunal for Rwanda
MDR	Mouvement démocratique républicain (Republican Democratic Movement)
MIGEPROF	Ministère du genre et de la promotion de la femme (Ministry of Gender and Women in Development)
MINALOC	Ministry of Local Government
MRND	Mouvement révolutionnaire national pour le développement, renamed Mouvement républicain national pour la démocratie et le développement (Revolutionary Movement for National Development, renamed Republican Movement for Democracy and Development)
PAREMHUTU	Parti du mouvement de l'émancipation hutu (Hutu Emancipation Movement Parti)
PDI	Parti démocratique islamique, Parti démocratique idéal (Islamic Democratic Party, Ideal Democratic Party)
PL	Parti libéral (Liberal Party)
PSD	Parti social-démocrate (Social Democratic Party)
RPF	Rwandan Patriotic Front
RTLM	Radio-télévision des mille collines (Thousand Hills Radio-Television)
UN	United Nations
UNAMIR	United Nations Assistance Mission for Rwanda (Mission des nations unies d'assistance au Rwanda)
UNAR	Union nationale rwandaise (Rwandan National Union)

Note on Transliteration, Language, and Interview Codes

Unless otherwise noted, all translations of texts in French or Kinyarwanda to English are my own. In general, I have used spellings for Kinyarwanda words as they appear in current Rwandan periodicals. Thus, spellings do not include markings for vowel length or the tonality of words. Words are cited with their prefix and augment, elements that change between the singular and plural (e.g., *umurima*, sing., "field," and *imirima*, pl., "fields"). The sequence *-li-* is always written *-ri-* except for a few proper names. When using Hutu, Tutsi, or Twa as nouns, I do not anglicize them by adding an *s* in the plural. I hope that this practice reminds the reader that these words are primarily adjectives that describe individuals instead of corporate groups.

The country today known as the Democratic Republic of the Congo—sometimes referred to as DRC, DROC, DR-Congo, Congo-Kinshasa, or simply "the Congo"—borders Rwanda to the west. The Congo has been known by a variety of names since it was first colonized by Europeans. From 1885 to 1908, it was known as the Congo Free State. From 1908 until its independence in 1960, it was called the Belgian Congo. From independence until 1971, it was known as the Republic of the Congo. In 1971, President Mobutu Sese Seko renamed the country Zaire, to renounce European colonialism and its ongoing influence in the country. In 1997, when Laurent-Désiré Kabila came to power after ousting President Mobutu through a military campaign, he renamed the country the Democratic Republic of the Congo. To reduce confusion, I generally refer to the country in this text as the Democratic Republic of the Congo or the Congo, regardless of the country's name at the time. In quotations referring to the Congo, I retain the terminology used by the speaker and clarify as needed.

Throughout the text, I have cited extensively from the more than two hundred interviews conducted as part of this project between 2011 and 2014. These citations appear in parentheses and contain a unique identifier of three letters and two digits that was assigned to each interview during research (for example, KIG21). A list of interview dates, locations, and interviewer can be made available on request.

TO SAVE HEAVEN AND EARTH

Introduction

How could I bear to lose heaven and earth in the same lifetime?

—Ismael Mugenzi, Muslim farmer who rescued his neighbors (NKO12)

One night in April 1994, Ismael Mugenzi heard a knock at his door.[1] It was his neighbor, Hitimana, who had come with his wife and brother-in-law. Mugenzi lived in a one-room house with wattle-and-daub walls and a thatched roof near the shores of Lake Kivu in rural northwestern Rwanda. Since he had not inherited sufficient farmland, he eked out a living fishing from his dugout canoe, which he powered with long paddles. He sometimes took his fish to sell in markets on the other side of the lake, in the Democratic Republic of Congo (then known as Zaire). Hitimana was an ordinary farmer who produced food for his family and a small cash income from coffee trees he cultivated. The drop in coffee prices on world markets a few years before had greatly reduced his income. Hitimana, a Catholic, and Mugenzi, a Muslim, were both Hutu. Hitimana attended Mass from time to time at the Roman Catholic parish church in their community. Mugenzi mostly prayed at home, except on Fridays, when he jogged thirty minutes to the nearest mosque at Nkora, a rural hamlet on Lake Kivu. Mugenzi and Hitimana had another connection as well: Mugenzi and Hitimana's wife had been classmates in primary school in the 1980s. On this night in April, in the midst of the 1994 genocide of Tutsi, Hitimana had come to beg Mugenzi for help. He wanted Mugenzi to take his wife and brother-in-law, who were Tutsi, across Lake Kivu in his small boat, to safety in the Congo.

The genocide had turned the Interahamwe, the youth branch of the president's political party, into a militia that roamed the hills hunting for Tutsi in hiding. Helping hide his neighbor's relatives would put Mugenzi in danger as well. As Mugenzi explained in a 2013 interview, "I accepted to take her and her brother.

I was very afraid. But because she had been my classmate, I took her" (NKO12). He took the woman and her brother across the lake under cover of darkness, returning early in the morning before anyone noticed his absence. A few weeks later, he also saved a mother with her newborn child, and the woman's sister, who was still a child. His Muslim cousin helped him despite the risk of being discovered by the cousin's brother, an Interahamwe member who participated avidly in killing Tutsi and pillaging. Mugenzi selflessly imperiled himself and his family, amid all the other hardships they endured, to save the lives of people he saw as innocent. Asked why he risked his life to paddle his neighbors to safety, Mugenzi replied, "As poor as I am, I must do good to merit heaven. How could I bear to lose heaven and earth in the same lifetime? A true Muslim should not get involved in such violence" (NKO12).

How do we explain Mugenzi's heroism? Should we accept his explanation, given twenty years after the fact? Can piety fully explain his actions? Did empathy for his childhood classmate push him to help? Do his character or personality traits set him apart from others who joined in killing?

Much of the research on rescue during genocide has assumed, implicitly or otherwise, that rescuers are exceptional people who have unique characteristics, such as an "altruistic personality" (Oliner and Oliner 1988) or a self-conception grounded in specific values.[2] Perpetration has been much more studied than rescue. The growing body of research on micro-level processes of violence during mass atrocities, however, has repeatedly demonstrated that most perpetrators are average, "normal," ordinary people.[3] Furthermore, the reasons people become involved in mass violence are complex and range far beyond the most common retrospective explanation perpetrators give—"I was following orders"—as Christopher Browning (1992) has shown for the Holocaust, Alexander Hinton (2005) for Cambodia, and numerous others for Rwanda.[4] If perpetrators are average, normal, ordinary people, should not rescuers also be? If the reasons for perpetration are varied and complex, should not the reasons for rescue also be varied and complex?

Singular explanations of motivation and action—whether of rescue or perpetration—do not align with the reality that genocide and mass atrocities are not singular events. They are complex processes that unfold over time and entail millions of discrete acts by thousands or hundreds of thousands of people. People caught in the machine of genocide do not decide just once how to act or react. Instead, they must repeatedly decide what to do or not do. As the context evolves, various options emerge or disappear. Prior decisions or actions shape present possibilities. The genocide machine is primed to produce individual and collective actions that are in line with genocidal policy and to inhibit actions counter to it. In this context, rescue is an exceptional behavior. Why, then, do some people defy the machine and risk their lives?

This book aims to answer this question by examining rescue during the 1994 genocide of Tutsi in Rwanda. Many books have examined the causes, processes, and consequences of the Rwandan genocide. Few have considered those people who risked their lives to try to save people from the slaughter or examined how individual people reacted to the violence and chaos around them. This book seeks to address that gap. In considering the many ways people acted during the genocide, it considers external factors, such as geographical features, the built environment, opportunity to rescue, the details of genocide policy, and genocide timelines; internal factors, such as the states of mind, characters, self-conceptions, moral orientations, and motivations of those who rescued or tried to rescue; and sociological factors, such as social networks, gender or social position, local power dynamics, political ideologies, cultural models, the power of crowds, and collective action. I examine these constellations of factors to understand how they shaped decision making, enabling some people to rescue while pushing others to participate in the killing. This analysis considers the innumerable "small gestures of support" and "ordinary everyday gestures" that constitute rescue in genocide, as French historian Jacques Sémelin wrote (2011, 2; 2019). Framed within the interdisciplinary scholarship of genocide studies and rooted in the methodologies of cultural anthropology, this book presents rarely heard stories of small gestures, heroism, and good done amid evil.

In the first weeks of April 1994, as the genocide began, most ordinary people reacted within the moral norms of Rwandan society: they acted to help their kin, neighbors, friends, and coworkers. As the genocide became nationwide policy, and intense violence spread throughout the country, morally correct actions became riskier and more difficult. The absolutist logic of the genocide—you are either with us (the government and Hutu extremists) or against us (and with the Rwandan Patriotic Front rebels, RPF sympathizers, and all Tutsi)—worked to destroy the social cohesion so vital to daily life in Rwanda. In this context, acting to help people targeted for killing—even in small ways—became exceptional and brave.

Previous studies of rescuers, in Rwanda and elsewhere, have tended to give partial answers regarding how and why some people risk their lives to save others.[5] Those studies have rarely considered the full complexity of human agency in the fraught sociopolitical context of genocide. Most studies of rescue assume that rescuers operate from positions of moral clarity, that they are saints. But rescuers, like perpetrators and bystanders, operate on the margins of, and sometimes deeply within, the "moral gray zone" of genocide (Levi 1989). Rescuers can also be complicit in the genocidal project or profit from it in some way, as Oskar Schindler did in the Holocaust. Some people participate actively in killing while simultaneously saving people. Even those rescuers who are motivated by deeply held moral convictions—whether around common humanity, renunciation of sin, or obedience to God's commandments—must continually make decisions from morally ambiguous positions. Rescuers often lie, bribe, steal, or beg to protect people. They sometimes deny assistance to ensure the protection of others. In genocide's moral gray zone, victims, perpetrators, bystanders, and rescuers alike face "choiceless choices," situations where no option is morally correct (Melson 2005).

I contend that no single factor or set of factors can accurately predict who will become a rescuer. Instead, I propose a more contextual, ephemeral explanation of rescue grounded simultaneously in macro-, meso-, and micro-level factors. The compulsion to help is the beginning but not the end of rescue. Rescue is a decision made repeatedly, in rapidly changing contexts, and sometimes under intense pressure. Not just anyone can become a rescuer. To succeed, rescuers must persist in their decision to help and remain courageous in the face of increasing risks to their kin's well-being and their own. They must also be willing to act in the face of moral ambiguity. Many rescuers who hew faithfully to paths of moral rectitude are killed along with those they attempted to save. Rescuers succeed because they have a combination of characteristics that allow them to confront the complex and dynamic circumstances of the genocide: a moral compulsion to help, the courage to risk everything, the persistence to continue making the choice to rescue in the face of great adversity and danger, and the willingness to engage in morally ambiguous decision making. Yet these characteristics on their own are insufficient to guarantee the outcome. Rescuers also need luck. Successful rescue, then, is the end result of thousands of moment-by-moment decisions unfolding over time in the dynamic context of genocide. In short, constituting a structural model of rescue grounded in positivistic social science that predicts or can be tested is impossible.

The theoretical heart of this book is a reexamination of the structure-agency problem in the social sciences. Within genocide studies, scholars tend to either focus on macro-level processes, institutions, politics, and economics, thus emphasizing structure, or they examine micro-level processes and individual actions, thus emphasizing agency. A few scholars have attempted to examine the intersections of these two approaches through dynamic sociopolitical models. All these approaches give human agency a determinative role in genocide and mass violence. My goal is to render visible the tangible effects of external forces, in the form of government policy, the landscape, local histories of interracial relations, hate media messages, and the perceived threat of invading rebel forces, in producing human action. I plumb the depths of genocide's moral gray zone to understand the factors that push or pull people toward acts of genocide or acts of rescue. I trace the often-elusive roles of social forces, ranging from the power of the mob to obligations generated by patronage and reciprocity. Focusing on the unique moral problems that arise in genocide and the acts that occur within it helps illuminate the complex interplay between internal dispositions, external constraints, and social configurations that produce genocide and allow some people, like Mugenzi, to act against it.

Understanding Rescue in Genocide

The vast majority of research on rescue during genocide emerged from studies of the Holocaust. Over time, this work has coalesced around three dominant paradigms for understanding the means and motives of rescuers. Samuel and Pearl Oliner's groundbreaking study of Holocaust rescuers designated as Righteous Among the Nations led to an understanding of rescue as emerging from altruism, defined as people risking "their lives and frequently those of their families to help Jews survive . . . without material rewards of any kind" (Oliner and Oliner 1988, 1). This paradigm, which emphasizes the intrinsic features of moral behavior, dominated the study of rescuer behavior for over a decade.[6] Further comparative study of rescuers led to the development of a second theoretical paradigm that focuses on extrinsic features that shape human agency.[7] A third paradigm developed from more recent studies emphasizes sociological or cultural factors.[8]

Research that falls under the intrinsic paradigm tends to seek stable qualities, character types, or traits that compel certain people to become rescuers. In their research on the Righteous Among Nations, Oliner and Oliner (1988) highlighted human social connection and empathy as universal motivators for rescuers and concluded that an "altruistic personality" set them apart from others in Nazi Europe and propelled these individuals to help save Jews. A number of researchers have followed their lead. Ervin Staub (2003), for instance, found that personality characteristics affect helping behavior; in particular, he suggested that a "prosocial orientation" primes some people to think about their own responsibility for other people's welfare (93). Likewise, Kristen Monroe (2004) argued that "ethical political behavior flows naturally from our perceptions of self" (241). Her theory posits that "ethical acts emanate not so much from conscious choice but rather from deep-seated instincts, predispositions, and habitual patterns of behavior that are related to our central identity" and "effectively preset for most adults" (241).

The second dominant paradigm for rescuer behavior focuses on extrinsic features that shape agency—things like geography, proximity to victims, presence of other minorities, details of genocidal policy, and opportunity. These structural factors make rescue more or less possible, regardless of an individual's compulsion to help. This perspective reveals the emergence of informal, underground networks of rescuers as soon as genocides get under way—no matter the geographical or social context (Sémelin, Andrieu, and Gensburger 2011). These networks are often extremely fragile and quickly destroyed by genocidal states with armed force at their disposition (Andrieu 2011, 496). Although cases of rescue have been identified in all genocides, it is impossible to distill or describe what makes an individual into a rescuer since they "do not necessarily have a stable 'personality'" (Andrieu 2011, 499). This approach acknowledges that people who rescue may share some innate or enculturated characteristics, but it emphasizes the external constraints that shape these motivations and actions.

The third prevalent paradigm, developed from more recent studies of rescuers in the Holocaust and other instances of genocide or mass violence, emphasizes the role of sociological factors in rescue. Scholars have examined the roles of social norms or cultural traits; social ties; political ideologies and religious beliefs, practices, or communities; membership in minority groups; and situational factors such as ambiguity or collective action.[9] This paradigm can account for cultural or national variability in rescue, the highly localized variability in ordinary people's responses to genocidal projects, and differing involvement in rescue between communities within the same country. Additionally, these studies begin to account for the paradox of individuals who simultaneously rescue people and kill. These "killer-rescuers," as Lee Ann Fujii (2011) called them, often helped people with whom they had social ties while killing others they did not know.

The question of how and why people act as they do in the face of mass atrocities is complex and delicate, engaging with many disciplines. Within the interdisciplinary field of genocide studies, historians, sociologists, psychologists, philosophers, anthropologists, and political scientists have tried to understand how and why people engage with genocidal projects in different ways.[10] Their work has created a fairly standardized set of categories to capture people's roles in genocide: victims, perpetrators, bystanders, and rescuers—or, in Staub's (1993) terms, "heroic helpers." This widely used typology has been productive in terms of social theory because it helps clarify the characteristics and motivations of people within a given category and lends itself to the development of theories of action and motivation.

However, these categories "can obscure as much as they reveal" (Fujii 2011, 145) by reducing a person, and their often-contradictory beliefs and actions, to a set of expected behaviors. Furthermore, this typology fails to capture the dynamic nature of genocide and obscures the reality that people may move from one category to another as they make new decisions based on changing situations, or even occupy multiple categories simultaneously (Fujii 2008, 8). The Rwanda case, in particular, challenges the paradigms about participants' roles during genocide. As Scott Straus demonstrated for average genocide perpetrators who were mostly subsistence farmers, decisions about what to do in the genocide were aimed at minimizing the potential negative outcomes for themselves or their kin (Straus 2006, 10–11). In the swift evolution of the genocide, as the civilian population was mobilized and enlisted in the state's killing machine, these decisions moved some people from altruistic behaviors (helping their neighbors, coworkers, or kin) to bystander behaviors (actively doing nothing) to perpetrator behaviors (participating in the genocide).

In other words, the dynamic context of genocide renders the idea of unitary, static categories unworkable. Genocide is a complex social, political, cultural, and economic process comprising hundreds of thousands of acts that unfold over time; decisions and behaviors emerge from millions of factors that coalesce into the complex whole that constitutes a genocide. People caught in the machine of genocide decide how to act or react not once, but over and over again, revisiting decisions and making new ones as the context evolves and various choices emerge or disappear. From this perspective, the categories quickly become less distinct. Bystanders can become perpetrators, perpetrators rescuers, victims perpetrators, and rescuers perpetrators. A momentary decision, or even an action taken without thought, can move a person from one category to another.

The categories can, however, illuminate one another. Understanding the dynamics of genocidal violence and perpetrator behavior is important to appreciate the alternatives of nonparticipation, rescue, and passive or active resistance. As Claire Andrieu (2011) explains, where genocide is state policy backed by the administration and implemented by the army, "resistance is not expected, and thus constitutes an exception" (495).

Many studies of the Rwandan genocide have classified Hutu and Twa who did not participate as bystanders.[11] In fact, most ordinary Rwandans avoided becoming involved in killing or participating in the genocide in other ways.[12] I take seriously Andrieu's proposition that we consider nonparticipation as potential resistance instead of bystander behavior.[13] Passive resistance to government administrators' orders has long been a feature of everyday life in Rwanda (Thomson 2013), which James Scott (1985) referred to as "weapons of the weak." As Alexis Kagame (1956) wrote about precolonial Rwandan culture, "Public authorities' orders do not require a moral conscience. If people can elude them intelligently so as not to be punished," the community will not condemn them

(399). Giorgia Donà (2018) explores this resistance to pressure to participate in genocide, calling certain forms "situated bystandership." She argues that "acts of nonintervention" place situated bystanders closer to the category of victim.

Passive resistance, acts of nonintervention, acts of genocide, and acts of rescue occurred, at times, in the same circumstances—some lives were spared while others were not. Ordinary Rwandans who resisted involvement in the genocide faced the same conditions as those who committed acts of genocide. Although acts of rescue are always possible, certain conditions make them more likely to occur or more likely to succeed. Each event or decision leads to new configurations that make some actions more or less likely than others. For example, a mayor ordering the population to "clear the brush" made it more likely that civilians looked for hiding Tutsi and turned them over to killing squads (Wagner 1998). Or, a young man reporting for duty at a roadblock made it more likely he would commit violence against someone. By shifting the focus away from categories and toward acts—acts of genocide and acts of rescue—we can better understand how complex decisions and behaviors emerge in the dynamic set of social, political, and economic processes that constitutes a genocide.

In this book, I reserve the term *rescuer* for those who tried to help or save Tutsi or others targeted in the genocide and did not also participate in the genocide in any way, whether by killing, raping, destroying property, or looting. My definition of *rescuer* is very similar to the meaning given by the national genocide survivors association, Ibuka, to the term *indakemwa*, a word unique to Rwanda (Kayishema and Masabo 2010). Indakemwa, meaning "those who are morally beyond reproach" or "righteous," is modeled after the designation "Righteous Among Nations," used by the state of Israel's Yad Vashem to recognize non-Jews who risked their lives, freedom, or safety to save Jews during the Holocaust without expectation of financial compensation or other reward (Tevosyan 2008, 186). Similarly, Ibuka defined indakemwa as people who (1) had saved one or more Tutsi during this genocide; (2) did not receive any compensation for their actions; (3) did not participate in the genocide by killing, physically assaulting, tracking or hunting Tutsi, denouncing or revealing Tutsi in hiding, or stealing or destroying property; and (4) testified about the genocide in legal proceedings and did not spread genocide ideology (Kayishema and Masabo 2010, 22–24). Because indakemwa is an official designation of Ibuka, and because this study did not include in its definition of *rescuer* all of the criteria established by Ibuka, I reserve its use for those indakemwa officially recognized by Ibuka.

Although the terminology I use in this book draws on the classic typology, referring to perpetrators, bystanders, and rescuers, I add terms to capture the focus on actions and behaviors: *acts of rescue*, *acts of genocide*, *rescuer behavior*, *bystander behavior*, and *perpetrator behavior*. I use the term *rescuer behavior* to refer to actions assisting Tutsi or other potential targets of the genocide, whether or not the individual also participated in the genocide in some way. The terms *acts of rescue* and *acts of genocide*, not meant to invoke any legal definitions, allow for a broader view of rescue that can encompass both straightforward rescuer behavior and the many ambiguous ways perpetrators sometimes helped save people.

Rescue in the Rwandan Genocide

Relatively few stories of heroic rescue have been documented in the Rwandan genocide. In the immediate aftermath of the genocide, some survivors wanted to recognize the courageous individuals who had helped save their lives, but the political context made such recognition too risky. In 2002, the human rights organization African Rights published *A Tribute to Courage*, a book that featured the stories of seventeen Rwandans and two expatriates who saved hundreds during the carnage. Seven of the rescuers documented perished during the genocide because of their courageous acts. The fates of the others illustrate the dangers of being identified as a rescuer. Three died before the book's publication, two of them murdered by unknown assailants. One later became implicated in the genocide during the Gacaca trials and served time in prison for his role in the violence. Outside of these stories, rescuers whose stories became widely known sometimes faced public opposition from the new government or were accused of genocide crimes. For example, Paul Rusesabagina, the hotel manager portrayed in the film *Hotel Rwanda* and featured in Philip Gourevitch's (1998) widely read book *We Wish to Inform You*, faced a campaign to smear his reputation in the years after the film's release. The complicated story of Rusesabagina, which is discussed in depth in chapter 7, and the fates of other rescuers who faced harassment discouraged genocide survivors from publicly recognizing the people who had helped save them.

Public discourse opened slightly on the question of rescuers in the late 2000s, after the completion of genocide trials in Rwanda. In 2006 and 2007, President Paul Kagame awarded medals for the Campaign against Genocide to soldiers, police, citizens, and foreigners who had helped rescue potential victims. Among the citizens receiving this recognition were several featured in *A Tribute to Courage*. Then, in 2009, Ibuka launched its pilot research project to identify indakemwa, and it still seeks support to continue this work in a systematic way.

Recognizing rescuers and understanding how and why they did what they did is important for many reasons. In Rwanda, the empathy, courage, and humanity demonstrated by those who rescued during the genocide have long-term impacts on the people they saved. Many genocide survivors who were rescued have an ongoing desire to recognize the people who saved them by telling their stories. Many survivors have maintained friendships or kin-like relationships with their rescuers. Tutsi genocide survivors who were helped by Hutu or Twa people can recognize that not all Hutu or Twa were perpetrators or heartless bystanders, despite the discursive practices of the current Rwandan government that reinforce these stereotypes. Survivors who were helped by people from other social categories tend to be more open to trust Rwandans from all backgrounds. In addition, these ongoing efforts to recognize rescuers formally and publicly have the potential to provide models of behavior and decision making to oppose genocide in both ideology and action.

For genocide survivors who were not helped by others, hearing stories of rescue, especially those told by survivors, can illuminate new ways of seeing their fellow Rwandans. An interpreter who assisted on the project explained how the stories gave her new hope. She and her family had saved themselves during the genocide. After several interviews with indakemwa and the survivors they had saved, the interpreter said, "Thank you for involving me in this research. I didn't know of stories like this. Knowing that people could sacrifice so much to try to save Tutsi. It brings a good feeling in my heart." Rescuers' stories can help restore some hope and trust in others. Outside Rwanda, stories about rescuers help undermine negative stereotypes of Africa and Africans and, in the case of Muslim rescuers, Islam and Muslims. These stories of the small glimmers of good amid evil humanize Rwandans for people who wrongly assume that what happened in Rwanda was due to a lack of modernity, civilization, education, or depth of religious conviction.

Moral Ambiguity, Agency, and Rescue

In this book, I consider internal, external, and sociological features of rescuer behavior to examine the diffused forms of agency that emerge in the moral gray zone of genocide. I contend that successful rescue in Rwanda emerged not from individual rescuers' altruism but from a network of relations between the rescuer, the rescued, and all the other humans involved, as well as the complex, localized unfolding of events in various contexts. The evolving dynamics of genocidal violence made rescuer behavior riskier, and thus less likely, over time. Rescuer behavior was widespread, but successful rescue was rare. Rescuers who succeed in saving people often wend a morally dubious path through the gray zone of genocide to achieve good outcomes.

k contributes to the interdisciplinary scholarship on mass violence e in several ways. First, it contributes to the growing interest within political science to understand the micro-level processes of conflict and violence that make up macro-level phenomena. Second, it proposes a theoretical framework that allows for the integration of micro-, meso-, and macro-level analyses. Third, it moves the empirical literature on the Rwandan genocide in a new direction by examining rescuer behavior, and it adds micro-level detail about the genocide from geographic regions not covered by other scholars. Finally, the book contributes to theory about rescue in comparative genocide studies by demonstrating that, because successful rescue is the end result of thousands of moment-by-moment decisions unfolding over time, no structural model can fully capture or explain rescuer behavior.

To explain how rescue emerges from the same moral gray zone as the evil of genocidal violence, I begin with macro-level phenomena and drill down to micro-level processes. Chapter 1 describes the macro- and meso-level conditions, policies, events, actors, and sociopolitical dynamics that shaped violence during the Rwandan genocide. The social categories Hutu, Tutsi, and Twa were a foundational condition that made genocide possible, but the country's history of racialized violence and competition for political power made these categories salient in ordinary people's lives. Rwandan historiography after the 1959 social revolution that brought Hutu to power created a national founding narrative that cast Tutsi political power as a menace to Hutu people and the nation.[14] The civil war that began in 1990, the proliferation of racist propaganda, and political polarization in the new multiparty system generated widespread uncertainty and made genocide possible. In the six days after President Habyarimana's assassination, the genocide of Tutsi and massacres of Hutu and Twa opposed to the new government had become national policy.

In chapter 2, I outline the theoretical framework at the foundation of my analysis. This analysis applies actor-network theory to illuminate the complex and diffuse origins of human agency in genocide. Both a method of analysis and a theoretical framework, it conceives of agency as an emergent property of networks of relations between heterogeneous network components. These components can include human and nonhuman actors, inanimate objects, and contextual factors. I merge actor-network theory with Primo Levi's concept of the moral gray zone of genocide to expose the moral ambiguity of the choices demanded of ordinary people in the extraordinary conditions of genocide.

Chapter 3 confronts the trope of Muslim resistance to genocide and examines the reasons why certain, but not all, predominantly Muslim communities engaged in collective acts of rescue. Muslim Hutu in the Biryogo neighborhood of Kigali and in the town of Gisenyi reacted to the genocide much like Rwandans of other faiths. Sometimes they opposed it. Sometimes they tried to ignore it. Sometimes they tried to save people. Sometimes they joined in genocide crimes. Muslims in Biryogo and Gisenyi were deeply enmeshed in actor-networks that coalesced into genocidal agency due to the particular, local histories of settlement, colonial apartheid policies, urbanization, and patronage ties entangled with business, trade, and politics. Yet religion still influenced Muslim actions in these neighborhoods, even if it did not result in collective rescue efforts.

Chapter 4 examines the unfolding of genocide at the micro level at three sites in and around Nyanza town in southern Rwanda. In Gitarama and Butare prefectures, regional government administrators and security forces resisted the nationwide genocide policy and contained anti-Tutsi violence for two weeks. Then a few pivotal events at the national level reconfigured regional and local leadership, and massacres engulfed Nyanza and communities across southern Rwanda. Nonetheless, hyper-local social histories, kinship ties, religious belief and practices, social cohesion, and decision making of local leaders produced collective rescue efforts at the Centre Saint Antoine, an orphanage run by Roman Catholic Rogationist monks; in Mugandamure, a former Muslim quarter during the colonial era; and at Rubona hill, a peri-urban community. These cases illustrate that even if religion was not a determining factor in rescue, it still influenced the options available to people and the choices they made.

Chapter 5 focuses on the opportunity for rescue presented by Rwanda's political borders. The chapter illustrates the rescue strategies enabled by proximity to the border through a detailed case study of Gisenyi, a town on Rwanda's northwest border with the Democratic Republic of the Congo. Drawing on actor-network analyses of international borders and migration, I argue that state sovereignty became synonymous with genocidal violence. As the demarcation of this genocidal sovereignty ended, the border became both salvation and snare to those fleeing genocide. Unlike in Nyanza in southern Rwanda, Gisenyi's dense patronage ties to President Habyarimana's family, military officers, and businessmen who founded the Hutu Power movement predisposed the town and region to genocidal violence immediately after the president's assassination. For many Hutu in Gisenyi—regardless of their religion—their first impulse was to help their Tutsi kin, neighbors, coworkers, or acquaintances. Yet their dense social ties to Hutu extremists made it difficult for them to persist in rescue efforts for long. These patronage ties increased the capacity of some people to save Tutsi from the genocide. The chapter concludes by considering cases where people leveraged their wealth or social capital to rescue Tutsi.

Chapter 6 examines the ways rural people engaged with the state's policy of genocide at the physical and symbolic margins of the state. Rwanda's vast water border with the Congo—an invisible line across the watery expanse of Lake Kivu—merged with local social histories in the rural communities along the lakeshore to shape agency during the genocide in varied ways. In Kayove, unique local histories of political authority, migration, and religion merged with its mountainous topography, its remoteness, Lake Kivu, and the border to produce distinct patterns of engagement with—or escape from—the state's genocidal sovereignty. Hutu Muslims in Nkora directly opposed the genocidal mobs early in April 1994. When open opposition became too dangerous, they shifted strategies to hide and then evacuate Tutsi across the lake through ephemeral networks of assistance.

Chapter 7 questions the common assumptions that rescuers are morally exceptional people and religious piety increases the likelihood of rescue by examining two cases where Hutu gave their lives while trying to save Tutsi from the genocide. The chapter explores how and why some people persisted in their rescue efforts even in the face of almost certain death. By comparing martyrs—meaning those who made the ultimate sacrifice in their attempts to save others—with people who save lives and lived, I demonstrate that martyrs refused the moral compromise necessitated by the genocide's gray zone. The chapter concludes by considering the immense symbolic potency of martyrs in the aftermath of genocide and considers why some martyrs are widely recognized while others are largely ignored.

The conclusion draws out the common elements shared by many rescuers in Rwanda. In the Rwandan genocide, individuals faced complex decisions about how to behave and what to do. Often these decisions were morally ambiguous or impossible, in the sense that all the options were terrible. Refusing to participate in the genocide or choosing to rescue someone was not a onetime decision driven by moral, ethical, or religious conviction, and the compulsion to help was the beginning, not the end of rescue. Rescue was a decision made repeatedly, in rapidly changing contexts, and sometimes under intense pressure. This repeated decision making reflects the way all ordinary Rwandans—whether Tutsi, Hutu, or Twa, whether victim, perpetrator, rescuer, or bystander—navigated the genocide. Rescuers who saved people succeeded in navigating the moral gray zone of genocide—the same gray zone occupied by perpetrators and bystanders—to achieve good outcomes. I explore the implications of this surprising conclusion: rescue itself is a morally ambiguous category.

1

DYNAMICS OF VIOLENCE IN THE GRAY ZONE

I was scared. I was bleeding [*long pause*]. I know I stabbed him with the spear. I don't know where I hit him. . . . I ran away immediately.

—Idi, genocide victim and perpetrator (RWA06)

In 1994, Idi was twenty-five years old and living in Rwamagana in eastern Rwanda. Born to Muslim parents, he had been forced by injury to retire from a professional soccer career. He lived with his Tutsi mother; his Hutu father had long ago left for work in Kenya and never returned. In Rwamagana, the genocide began shortly after daybreak on the morning of April 7, 1994. Upon hearing that President Habyarimana's plane had been shot down, Idi's mother cried, "My son, I saw what happened in 1959. People hunted other people down—now, I am about to die."

As the violence began, the family split up and hid with different neighbors and friends. Ten days later, on April 16, Rwandan army soldiers found and detained Idi and his friend as they went to buy sugar:

> They caught us and asked us where we were coming from and accused us of being Inyenzi [literally cockroaches, meaning RPF rebels]. They asked for our papers [identification cards], but we didn't have them. They said, "You are Tutsi!" but we denied it. There was someone else they had caught at a roadblock whose papers said that he was Tutsi. . . . The soldiers said, "We caught a Tutsi at the roadblock, and now we've met you crossing the road. You say you were going to buy sugar. We know how clever they [Tutsi] can be." They beat us in a terrifying way. They stabbed us in the legs with their bayonets and asked us to tell them if we were Inyenzi. Then they took us to the roadblock where people were. People at the roadblock said, "We know these children. They are

> Boniface's children. They are Hutu." But soldiers said, "No, we do not agree."
>
> . . .
>
> One soldier who had a bandaged arm spit in my face and shouted, "Keep quiet, you Inyenzi!" Then he said, "This is my order: if you know that you are not Tutsi, then kill him [the Tutsi man the soldiers had detained]." We said, "We have nothing [to use as a weapon]." He asked, "You do not have a club?" We said, "No." "No manly weapon you walk around with?" We said, "No." The people who were there begged for our lives, and the soldiers said that they will excuse us only after the man is dead.
>
> . . .
>
> The soldiers went to their vehicle and got two spears. They looked at me and said, "You don't look much like a Hutu. If you kill this man, we will know that you are not Tutsi." I refused straightaway. One soldier drew his Kalashnikov, and people scattered. Nobody had died there [at the roadblock] yet.
>
> . . .
>
> The soldiers handed us [Idi and his friend] the spears and threatened us, "Take these spears! You must kill him." [Idi's friend] begged, "Please, have mercy on me." They slapped my friend, and he dropped the spear. Then, they got an older man who was on duty at the roadblock and gave him the spear. The soldier asked him, "How many have you killed at this roadblock anyway?" The man replied, "But all of these people are Hutu." They spit in his face and retorted, "What about this one we've caught then? Look at his papers!" [They pointed at the Tutsi man they had detained]. Then they pointed the gun at me and ordered, "Stab him with the spear!" I was scared. I was bleeding [*long pause*]. I know I stabbed him with the spear. I don't know where I hit him. I don't know—I ran away immediately. . . . They didn't chase after me. (RWA06)

Idi eventually made his way back to the house where he had been hiding. He later learned that others at the roadblock killed the man he had stabbed.

A few days later, when the Rwandan Patriotic Front liberated Rwamagana, Idi became an RPF soldier and joined the fight to end the genocide. He served in the RPF through the rest of the war and then in the Rwandan Defense Forces (RDF), the new government army, for several years after. He was even deployed to the Democratic Republic of the Congo for several years during the RDF's involvement in the Congo Wars. During genocide trials in Rwamagana, Idi gave testimony about what happened at the roadblock. Because he was an RDF soldier, he was court-martialed for his genocide crimes instead of being tried in the civilian courts. When I interviewed him in 2011, he had completed his prison term, been discharged from the Rwandan Defense Forces, and released back to his home community.

This heartbreaking story from the first interviews conducted for this project illustrates the friability of the classic genocide studies typology of victim, perpetrator, bystander, and killer. Idi's impulsive action—stabbing the man—taken after hours of torture at the roadblock turned him instantaneously from victim into perpetrator. But Idi's act of genocide was simultaneously an act of survival. Even his victim's sister understood this. After the genocide, Idi went to her to ask for forgiveness and make amends, long before genocide trials began. She told him, "I honestly do not consider you guilty of anything. . . . I know you almost died, and forgiving is a must. You are a believer [meaning a Muslim], and you are a neighbor" (RWA06). Idi's story illustrates vividly how, in "the moral gray zone of genocide" (Levi 1989), few actions are morally pure, and few choices are clearly right.

Understanding the conditions, processes, and constellations of relations that produced the genocide is important because the people who resisted the call to kill or rescued others operated in the same conditions as those who perpetrated it. Yet rescuer behavior was more possible or more likely to succeed in some regions or communities than others. Macro- and meso-level structural factors produced local variability in genocidal violence because they articulated—in different ways at different places, owing to micro-level factors—local configurations of power, local histories of interpersonal relations, and differing local influences of distinct political parties. These local, regional, and national constellations of factors interacted in varying ways—at times facilitating one another and at others generating "friction" (Tsing 2015). This chapter is not intended to explain the causes of the 1994 genocide of Tutsi in detail.[1] Rather, it considers the interactions between national and local instigators of genocidal violence—the Hutu extremists who took control of the government—and the conditions, processes, and constellations of relations that transmitted the violence nationwide and then sustained it for several months. What emerges from this analysis is a complex picture of a phenomenon that defies understanding by the logics of rational choice—ordinary people joining in mass violence without clear motivation—and escapes the trope of innocent Tutsi victims attacked by evil Hutu perpetrators.

The 1994 Genocide of Tutsi in Rwanda

The 1994 genocide of Tutsi began on April 6 and ended on July 4, 1994. In those one hundred days, an estimated eight hundred thousand Rwandans lost their lives in the genocide and concurrent civil war (United Nations 1999).[2] Approximately a half million Tutsi living in Rwanda (77 percent of the country's Tutsi population) were annihilated in the state-sponsored genocide (Des Forges 1999, 15).[3] It is hard to overstate the devastation wrought by the genocide. Beyond the massacres of Tutsi men, women, children, and elders and killings of opposition political party members, the genocide comprised torture, sexual violence, destruction of property, and widespread looting and theft.

The genocide unfolded amid a protracted civil war that had started on October 1, 1990, when the RPF rebel group invaded Rwanda from Uganda with the intention to liberate the country from President Juvénal Habyarimana's dictatorship.[4] While the civil war was not the cause of the genocide, it contributed significantly to the context that made genocide possible. The triggering event for violence was the assassination of President Habyarimana on April 6, 1994. The president's plane, a midsize business jet, was approaching the national airport in Kigali, returning the president from ongoing peace negotiations in Arusha, Tanzania, when it was struck by a surface-to-air missile; the plane crashed at 8:25 p.m. local time (Guichaoua 2015b, 143). Everyone on board died in the crash, including senior officials from the Rwandan government, the army chief of staff, and the recently elected president of Burundi.

Precisely who shot down the plane has since been a matter of vigorous debate.[5] At the time, however, Rwandan military leaders and the president's family blamed the RPF. They used the crash to inflame the passions of young loyalists in the president's party and allied parties that had coalesced around the Hutu Power political movement, which had been spreading racist propaganda for years. The youth wings of these parties, known as the Interahamwe and Impuzamugambi, had been militarized over the preceding year. On the morning of April 7, 1994, members of these organizations, provoked by the president's assassination, attacked Tutsi civilians in Kigali, Gisenyi, and several other communities around the country where the Hutu Power movement dominated. Genocide became a national policy on April 12, 1994.

Many journalists, and some scholars with little knowledge of Rwanda's history, see the genocide as spontaneous, the renewed eruption of cyclical violence between Hutu and Tutsi or long-standing and atavistic "tribal," ethnic, or racial conflict. The dominant perspective, adopted by the post-genocide Rwandan government, views the genocide as the product of a carefully orchestrated plan whose foundations were laid many decades earlier, rooted in racialized political competition over the control of the state. While each of these approaches captures partial truths about the origins of the 1994 genocide of Tutsi, neither captures the dynamic forces; multiple competing factions; political, economic, social, and ideological structures; or individual and collective actions that coalesced into genocide. Although certain aspects of the violence were planned and even rehearsed in advance, the genocide of Tutsi did not begin as a fait accompli. Rather, it emerged over several days as Hutu-extremist politicians, military officers, and businessmen jockeyed for positions in the government.[6] These hard-liners pursued genocide as a strategy to maintain their hold on power. These national policies and events structured the unfolding of genocide in communities around the country.

The plane crash created power vacuums in the government, the military and security forces, and the president's political party, the Mouvement révolutionnaire national pour le développement (MRND, Revolutionary Movement for National Development). In the hours after President Habyarimana's assassination, retired colonel Théoneste Bagosora, members of the president's family, and political hard-liners from the MRND and the Coalition pour la défense de la république (CDR, Coalition for the Defense of the Republic)—all Hutu extremists—sought to install a military government (Guichaoua 2015b, 160–61). Military commanders, however, refused this plan, insisting that a civilian government be created instead. The hard-liners then pursued their coup through other means. Colonel Bagosora ordered the Presidential Guard, an elite unit of the Rwandan Armed Forces that was loyal to him, to assassinate political opposition members in the government. Before midnight on April 6, the Presidential Guard had fanned out across Kigali with lists of people to assassinate, both Hutu and Tutsi, including moderate politicians within the government, opposition political party leaders, human rights activists, and other critics of the Habyarimana government of all races.

Among the first to be assassinated was Prime Minister Agathe Uwilingiyimana, a Hutu from an opposition party, who was the rightful civilian leader of the country in the president's absence (Burnet 2019; Guichaoua 2015b, 161). By noon on April 7, the Presidential Guard had also murdered opposition party representatives and leaders in the cabinet, as well as prominent opposition politicians not in the government (Booh-Booh 1994). The earliest reports from the UN peacekeeping forces in Kigali confirmed the violence was being perpetrated by Presidential Guard troops, the national police, and the army (Booh-Booh 1994). The hard-liners then maneuvered to name an interim government comprising solely politicians aligned with the Hutu Power movement.

On the morning of April 7, what appeared to be spontaneous violence against Tutsi civilians erupted in Kigali and some communities in northwestern and southern Rwanda. Interahamwe and Impuzamugambi cadres attacked and killed anyone they believed to be Tutsi or RPF supporters, including Hutu and Twa supporters of opposition parties. They said they were seeking vengeance for the murder of "their father," as they called President Habyarimana.

At first, small groups of assailants "killed their victims where they found them, in their homes, on the streets" (Des Forges 1999, 209). Unknown numbers (at least scores, possibly hundreds) of civilians were killed throughout Kigali on this first day of violence. In other communities where MRND and CDR political parties dominated, such as Gisenyi in the northwest of the country, roving bands of Interahamwe erected roadblocks and began attacking people by 10 a.m. on April 7. Whether this early violence was locally organized or centrally ordered is unknown.

On April 8, 1994, an interim civilian government was formed after moderate military officers at the helm of the Rwandan army had refused retired colonel Bagosora's proposal of military government on April 6. The same day fighting resumed between the Rwandan army and RPF rebels. In public statements, Rwandan military leaders continued to call for calm, an end to killing, and a restoration of the rule of law. They also tried to establish a cease-fire with the RPF, which both the interim civilian government and the RPF rejected. During this time, Colonel Bagosora and the Hutu hard-liners allied with him struggled to outmaneuver the moderates at the helm of the Rwandan army. For several days, "the state's direction was ambiguous," and both Hutu and Tutsi political leaders were killed (Straus 2015, 307).

On April 12, Hutu Power hard-liners succeeded in consolidating control of the government and army, and the interim government fled to Murambi, a military training center in Gitarama prefecture. The same day, "mass killing shifted to an exterminatory campaign" (Straus 2015, 60); genocide became a coherent national policy. As the massacres by the Presidential Guard and militias spread to rural communities, which had been calm up to this point (Guichaoua 2015b, xlv), the interim government issued instructions to local authorities to "sensitize" residents to "civil defense" (Guichaoua 2015b, 243). Thus began the mobilization of ordinary Rwandans to hunt down RPF "infiltrators" and their "accomplices," in the parlance of government officials and Hutu Power operatives, meaning all Tutsi and supporters of opposition political parties. Tutsi were easily identified by their national identity cards, which indicated race. Although some Tutsi had changed the racial identification on their cards, their neighbors usually knew who was Tutsi. In addition, people were sometimes identified by physical features that were stereotypically associated with Tutsi.

The RPF, pressured by the interim government's actions against it, resumed its civil war against the government. President Habyarimana's government had signed peace accords with the RPF, known as the Arusha Accords, in August 1993. A tense armistice had reigned following their signing. Although the accords laid out a clear path to a transitional government and the integration of the RPF's military wing into the Rwandan army, President Habyarimana had delayed their implementation at every opportunity. The RPF, having withdrawn from positions within thirty kilometers of the capital city in early March 1993, occupied 5 percent of Rwanda (Prunier 1997, 174–77). In April 1994, one battalion of RPF soldiers was garrisoned in the parliamentary building in central Kigali, per the Arusha Accords. On April 8, Rwandan army troops surrounded the parliament building and began bombarding it. The RPF battalion inside returned fire to defend itself and the RPF politicians who were meant to join the government as part of the Arusha Accords.[7]

As the chaos unfolded, the RPF forces in the north resumed their military offensive, pushing southward toward Kigali. Advancing into eastern Rwanda, the RPF liberated territory and stopped the genocide as it went (see map 3). When the interim government relocated to Gitarama on April 12, RPF troops had already begun to approach the perimeter of the city (Guichaoua 2015b, 222). The civil war continued on multiple fronts as the genocide unfolded nationwide. The fierce battle for Kigali lasted until July 4, when the RPF finally routed the government troops. On July 14, the RPF seized control of the country and drove the genocidal government, along with the militias and army, into exile.

Local configurations of power and histories of violence, the varying strength of the MRND and CDR political parties in different communities, distance from the battle lines between the RPF and government army, social ties, and more shaped the unfolding of the genocide in each region. Not all regional and local administrators adopted genocide as local policy immediately. As a result, killings started at different times in different places (see map 2). In some communities, attacks on Tutsi civilians and opposition party members began on the morning of April 7. In others, they started on April 12, after Hutu extremists adopted genocide as national policy. In central and southern Rwanda, government officials refused to implement the orders to hunt down Tutsi. Instead, they worked to quell violence initiated by Interahamwe militias and Hutu Power operatives in their communities. They largely succeeded until the interim government replaced the governor of Butare prefecture, who had opposed the genocide, and launched a call to action.

On April 19, several high officials from the interim government, including the president, prime minister, numerous ministers, and all the burgomasters—commune leaders or mayors—from Butare Province gathered in Butare town in southern Rwanda for the swearing-in ceremony of a new governor in Butare. During the ceremony, the prime minister gave a fiery speech calling for a "final war" and denouncing "those who sympathized with the enemy," meaning those who refused to seek out and kill Tutsi and anyone else supporting the RPF (Des Forges 1999, 457–58). After the meeting, the burgomasters returned to their communes and began to order killings, looting, and property destruction. The interim government and national security forces bused in militiamen to help initiate the violence in communities that continued to resist.

The start date of killings made a difference in terms of rescue. Where massacres both started later and ended earlier, acts of rescue had greater likelihood of succeeding (see maps 2 and 3). Southern Rwanda's initial resistance to genocide, however, had the perverse effect of increasing the genocide's efficacy in the region. Tutsi civilians in that region had sought refuge from the violence in churches, schools, and government buildings, where they were initially protected by local police or soldiers under orders from local officials. When those officials changed their stance and joined the genocide, the targets, gathered in spaces they had understood as safe, were easy to locate and kill en masse. Where killings began early and continued longer, local authorities and violent instigators deployed strategies to entangle more and more people in the violence. As rescuer behavior entailed ever greater risks, many rescuers in areas where the genocide continued for months eventually abandoned their efforts.

These national events combined with macro- and meso-level structural factors to shape how the genocide unfolded at the local and micro level. Hutu extremist elites, faced with the RPF's military threat and the potential failure of their coup, mobilized the population by calling on a national founding narrative that cast all Tutsi (and not only the RPF) as a threat to the nation. These ideas had traction among ordinary Rwandans thanks in large part to years of polarized political discourse and racist propaganda, as well as a government system that reached deep into the countryside via an elaborate hierarchical system that spread down to governmental units of ten houses, known as *nyumbakumi*.[8] Many citizens, especially in rural areas, relied on information and guidance from local authorities, who consequently wielded significant power in everyday life. Thus, when local authorities gave orders to hunt down "RPF infiltrators" and their "accomplices," the people were primed to respond. The militarization of Rwandan society also facilitated the violence—the Interahamwe had been armed and trained, and civilians were accustomed to participating in security patrols. Once genocide became the national policy, the violence took on a life of its own: "The genocide was like a machine. Once it was turned on, it roamed everywhere" (NYA38).

Enabling Conditions for Genocide

Many conditions and events leading up to April 6, 1994, created the context that made genocide possible, including the existence of the social categories Hutu, Tutsi, and Twa, a history of racialized violence and competition for political power, a national founding narrative that cast Tutsi as dangerous to the nation, desperate economic conditions and extreme poverty, the civil war, and the proliferation of racist propaganda. These foundations for genocide were laid gradually, but they were activated by the civil war and the government's reaction to it. The civil war, combined with the return of multiparty politics in 1992, polarized Rwandan political space and reinforced an absolutist logic in which ordinary Rwandans had to be "for" President Habyarimana, his MRND party, and their Hutu Power allies, or be denounced as "against" the nation and "for" the RPF rebels and the return of Tutsi domination. The spread of racist propaganda condemning Tutsi, who were generalized as being clandestine RPF supporters, racialized this political polarization. The militarization of the MRND and CDR youth wings, known respectively as the Interahamwe and the Impuzamugambi, and the growing lawlessness and impunity with which they committed crimes against Tutsi or political opponents of President Habyarimana created a tense atmosphere, preparing the population for the worst.

Even if socially produced categories of race were not the cause of the Rwandan genocide, they were a foundational condition that made it possible. Many summaries of Rwandan history and society state that the population comprises three "races" (or "ethnic groups," "tribes," or "castes"): Tutsi at 15 percent of the population, Hutu at 85 percent, and Twa at less than 1 percent.[9] Yet the origin of these widely cited statistics is unclear. They form part of the mythico-histories that have structured reality in Rwanda (Malkki 1995). What scholars today call race or ethnicity in Rwanda has not been marked by differences in language, culture, religion, or territory in recorded history (Straus 2006, 129; Burnet 2012, 14). Historical, linguistic, and archaeological evidence indicates that the people who populated what today is Rwanda have shared similar ways of life, language, and culture since approximately 500 BCE (Schoenbrun 1998). This shared cultural heritage was what made them Rwandans.

Although the terms Hutu, Tutsi, and Twa predate the colonial era, their meanings and importance have changed significantly over time and varied by region (C. Newbury 1988). When German colonizers arrived at the end of the nineteenth century, they encountered a kingdom led by the Nyiginya dynasty—headed by the *mwami* (king), the *umugabekazi* (queen mother), their families, and the *abiru* (religious advisers to the mwami who performed important rituals)—and ruled via a system of chieftaincies with different responsibilities. While the Nyiginya lineage was Tutsi, many powerful chiefs and lineages were Hutu. However, European colonizers (first German, then Belgian) imposed their own nineteenth-century ideas about race on the country, profoundly changing the meanings of these social categories in Rwanda. At the time, Europeans understood humanity to be divided into biological races that existed in a hierarchy, with Caucasians at the apex. They believed Tutsi to be a lost tribe of Israel, biologically "closer" to Caucasians and superior to Hutu. German and Belgian colonizers perceived Tutsi as more intelligent, more refined, and biologically suited to political rule and the civilizing mission of the colonial project. The mwami and the Nyiginya dynasty took advantage of this opportunity to solidify their rule and allied themselves with the German colonizers. In the 1930s, the Belgians officially excluded Hutu from chieftaincies and formal education and exempted Tutsi of all social classes from corvée labor. Some chiefs exploited this corvée "to extract surplus from the common people, or forcibly to create a surplus where there was none" for their own benefit in the name of the colonial state (C. Newbury 1988, 128). In regions where former Hutu chieftaincies were handed over to Tutsi chiefs, the local population chafed against their new rulers who had no local kinship or social ties.

These racial divisions that emerged during colonialism were further reified during the transition to independence, 1959–1960. A small cadre of educated Hutu male elites called for creation of a popular democracy, transition of power to the Hutu majority, and rectification of the racist divide imposed by the colonizers and ruling Tutsi elite. Tutsi from the ruling class mobilized behind the Nyiginya lineage and advocated for a constitutional monarchy. Hutu and Tutsi peasants tried to make sense of the situation, so they could choose which party to back. Their choices were strongly predicated on local power structures, local histories of political rule and chieftaincies, and perceptions about local elites, whether Tutsi or Hutu (C. Newbury 1988, 199–206).

Racial violence was part of Rwanda's founding story. In November 1959, when the nation was on the verge of emerging from colonial rule, Hutu youth attacked Tutsi households and destroyed their houses, stole their livestock, and beat the men, provoked by rumors that a Hutu chief had been killed by Tutsi (C. Newbury 1988, 197; Prunier 1997, 49–53). Tutsi youth then engaged in reprisals against Hutu leaders. The violence continued through 1961, eventually targeting Tutsi ruling elites and their families (C. Newbury 1988, 197). In July 1960, the mwami, along with thousands of Tutsi chiefs and their families and clients, fled Rwanda to neighboring Uganda, Burundi, and the Belgian Congo (Thomson 2018, 47). The Belgians initiated a hasty transfer of power, with national elections planned for 1960. The postindependence government, which was dominated by Hutu, distilled a founding narrative that portrayed Tutsi political power as a threat to the nation and asserted the rightful place of Hutu as the majority ethnic group at the center of political power (Straus 2015, 285–86). Thus, this immediate postindependence period laid the groundwork for the Hutu nationalism that made genocide possible in the 1990s.

In 1994, most Rwandans were subsistence farmers living in rural, and often remote, communities spread across the country's hills.[10] These people—along with itinerant laborers, domestic workers, traders and small business owners, the unemployed, and the poor—are those I call "ordinary Rwandans." Ordinary Rwandans mostly lived in poverty and had low education levels. In 1994, almost 44 percent of the Rwandan population was illiterate, 40 percent had never attended school, just over 32 percent had completed primary school, and only 2.4 percent had completed secondary school (Republic of Rwanda 1994, 137–38). Average household landholdings were far below the threshold required to produce sufficient food and income for a family to thrive (André and Platteau 1998). The fall of coffee prices on world markets in the late 1980s, several years of drought, and the effects of the structural adjustment program plunged many rural families into new or deeper poverty in the late 1980s and early 1990s (Willame 1995, 109–32). Rwandan young men in particular faced an impasse; because they were overwhelmingly jobless and landless, they could not marry and be socially recognized as adults.

The ongoing civil war between government troops and the RPF rebel group was another enabling condition for genocide. The RPF's initial attack on October 1, 1990, came as a surprise; RPF troops took the Gabiro military camp, located sixty kilometers inside Rwanda, within a few days (Prunier 1997, 94; Melvern 2000, 29). Thanks to military help from Zaire (Congo), France, and Belgium, the Rwandan army pushed the RPF into northern Rwanda, but by late 1991, the RPF controlled 5 percent of Rwanda's territory (Kinzer 2008, 96). The war displaced approximately three hundred thousand people in 1991, as many Hutu fled areas captured by the RPF (Prunier 1997, 136). After an offensive in February 1993, the RPF gained even more territory in northern Rwanda, and the number of displaced reached one million (Guichaoua 2015b, 65). Peace negotiations eventually led to the Arusha Accords, but elites allied with the Hutu Power movement opposed the accords and the envisioned power-sharing arrangement with the RPF.

The prolonged civil war posed a direct threat to "the highest-level, decision-making elites" and thus featured prominently in their "strategic calculations" (Straus 2015, 62). The top Rwandan military and political officials stood to lose their prominent positions and the accompanying wealth and prestige if the RPF won the war or the conflict were resolved through a negotiated settlement. That external threat was compounded by an internal threat to the elites' hold on power—the emergence of opposition political parties in the late 1990s.

The war allowed President Habyarimana the chance to "consolidate [his] power base, which had been slipping," by casting the RPF as a common enemy (Des Forges 1995, 45). Elites allied with Hutu Power framed the civil war as a struggle against the return of Hutu subjugation to a Tutsi minority, reviving old ideas, largely dormant since the 1970s, about Tutsi domination under European colonialism. This founding narrative was used by the elites to foment anti-Tutsi sentiment and rally support behind the government and military (Straus 2015, 62). The RPF's military actions supported the narrative. Each time the RPF advanced, more civilians were displaced, ratcheting up the effect of the war on those far from the battle lines. Communities in south and central Rwanda received refugees fleeing the RPF; those refugees brought stories of atrocities committed by RPF rebels. These actions allowed political elites to frame the RPF and its sympathizers as simultaneously an external threat (in the form of RPF combatants and the Rwandan exiles who supported them) and an internal one (in the form of embedded RPF rebels, Tutsi inside Rwanda whom Hutu extremists presumed to be RPF accomplices or sympathizers, and Hutu members of the political opposition).

The results of this framing were immediate. Days after the RPF's initial invasion in 1990, local mobs attacked Tutsi in several communities in western and southern Rwanda, where attacks against Tutsi had been the most brutal in the 1960s. Local government officials blamed the attacks on unruly youth, but the government failed to investigate or bring the perpetrators to justice. Government elites used the situation to their advantage. Nationwide, the government arrested and held hundreds of businessmen, human rights activists, journalists, and political leaders who were critical of the government on suspicion of collaborating with the rebel army. The vast majority of those detained were Tutsi.

The proliferation of private media outlets in 1991 provided many new opportunities to spread this founding narrative and its underlying fears of a return to "Tutsi domination." Many new media outlets quickly evolved into hate-media channels that nurtured a culture of fear, suspicion, and terror in the Rwandan population. These outlets repeated the idea that all Tutsi and all members of opposition political parties supported the RPF rebels and thus were enemies of the nation. The Hutu-extremist media broadcast overt hate speech against Tutsi with such persistence that the hate was normalized, making all Tutsi people, not only the RPF, the enemy. As a result, when President Habyarimana was assassinated and the war resumed, ordinary (Hutu) civilians understood what they needed to do to protect themselves and defend Rwanda: attack Tutsi. These factors made murder and genocide intelligible as a reasonable form of self-defense (Thomson 2019).

All these conditions made genocide a possibility in 1994, but they did not make it inevitable. As Scott Straus (2015) demonstrates, similar conditions in other countries did not lead to genocide. Rwandan political elites still had to decide that the massive social, political, and economic costs of genocide were worth the results, or at least that genocide was better than the alternatives (Straus 2015, 321). It was a political and military decision with grave human consequences.

Instigators of Genocidal Violence and Systemic Forces

Even if the 1994 genocide of Tutsi was not meticulously preplanned, national institutions like the government security forces, political parties, and government administration collaborated in realizing a genocidal project once a national policy emerged on April 12. These institutions penetrated the countryside and interacted with regional and local institutions, such as political parties and the militias, as well as local elites who became the instigators of genocidal violence. Women also participated in organizing and implementing the genocide, despite the patriarchal nature of Rwandan society.[11] Perhaps more importantly, men in various positions of power were flanked by influential wives. These women organized parallel women's structures in political parties, led civil society organizations, and supported their husband's careers by expanding their influence. André Guichaoua (2015b) characterized this shadow sphere of influence as a "government of women" (52).

Hutu extremist elites in Kigali could transmit their extermination orders throughout the country despite the sparse communication infrastructure (Straus 2006, 8), but regional and local officials did not blindly follow orders from the interim government. "For local power holders and power seekers, the script [(or orders) did] not represent a set of instructions they must follow to the letter, but rather an opportunity to apply their own interpretation to the text" (Fujii 2009, 12–13). The interactions and frictions between national, regional, and local instigators of the genocide played out in different ways in different places, depending on distinct local histories of communal violence and social relations, as well as the dominance of various political parties locally. How the genocide became national policy and the roles played by key actors at the national, regional, and local levels influenced individual decision making during the genocide.

The Interim Government

The interim government took shape on the evening of April 8 after moderate military officers refused retired colonel Bagosora's proposed military government. Sworn in on April 10, the interim government fled Kigali and the battlefront between the national army and RPF rebels on April 11. Although most decisions were made by military commanders, Bagosora, or top MRND or CDR party officials and their affiliated militias, the interim government played a coordinating role and promoted cohesion among the new civilian authorities (Guichaoua 2015b, 247–48). While not necessarily in charge, the civilian authorities in the interim government were at the center of power and tasked with facilitating the death squads who sought to kill RPF rebels, or "Inyenzi," meaning literally "cockroaches" as Hutu-extremist propaganda referred to the RPF rebels, and RPF "accomplices," all coded language meaning Tutsi and opponents of the new political order.

While many ministers from the interim government later professed innocence during genocide trials, from the start their meetings focused on "the conduct and financing of the war," "diplomatic action," mobilizing "against the internal enemy," international arms purchases, and collaborating with the Hutu extremist political parties at the center of the genocide (Guichaoua 2015b, 241–42). Two women featured among the ministers in the interim government, both holdovers from the transitional government in power until the coup d'état on April 7: Pauline Nyiramasuhuko, minister of family and women's affairs, and Agnes Ntamabyaliro, minister of justice (Guichaoua 2015b). Nyiramasuhuko had a reputation for being "hotheaded and aggressive," and she was an ardent supporter of the Hutu Power movement (Guichaoua 2015b, 263). She played a key role in implementing the genocide in Butare prefecture and town, where she organized killings and ordered the rape of Tutsi women (258). The International Criminal Tribunal for Rwanda found her guilty of genocide and crimes against humanity. The ICTR sentenced her to life in prison, but the ICTR Appeals Chamber later reduced her sentence to forty-seven years. Ntamabyaliro was prosecuted for genocide crimes in the Rwandan courts and sentenced to life in prison in solitary confinement (Hogg 2010, 75).

Government Security Forces

Rwandan government security forces, comprising the army, the Presidential Guard, the national police (or gendarmerie), and the local (or communal) police, played key roles in implementing the genocide nationwide. Yet they did not always act uniformly in line with the genocidal project. Few women joined the Rwandan military or police forces (Hogg 2010, 95). Those few who did rarely rose to high ranks or positions of power. The tiny number of female officers in the national security forces in 1994 generally complied with orders within the command structure and participated in the genocide. For example, a female military doctor with the rank of major was convicted of genocide crimes by Rwandan courts (95–97).

Presidential Guard units were central to the army's command structure. Most of their members had been recruited from the president's home region in northwestern Rwanda, which was also the home of Bagosora and the president's widow. In the days after President Habyarimana's plane went down, in addition to eliminating key political targets, the Presidential Guard organized the system of roadblocks that played a crucial role in sorting Tutsi civilians from Hutu and Twa so that they could be killed (Booh-Booh 1994).

The Rwandan Armed Forces was among the first actors in the violence. In the early morning hours of April 7, government soldiers in the town of Butare began killing people after receiving the news of President Habyarimana's death at midnight on April 6 (Des Forges 1999, 438). They rounded up "young men," including Tutsi and opposition political party members, beat them, and tortured them (438–39). The local commander of the National Police and governor intervened to contain the violence before it spread to the local militia groups (439–41).

The army quickly focused its attention on battling the RPF, which resumed active combat on April 8, rapidly advancing from its position in far northern Rwanda toward Kigali. However, even as the army focused on the war with the RPF, military units participated in the genocide when needed and worked to purge their own ranks. Tutsi soldiers were executed, unless they managed to convince their comrades and commanding officers of their loyalty. Some military officers, however, rejected the genocide and tried to protect civilians. For example, in Butare, Lieutenant Hategekimana worked with Catholic leaders opposed to the genocide to try to escort civilians to safe shelters (Des Forges 1999, 445). Still, military officers and soldiers who resisted the genocide were not always successful.

Initially, the national police facilitated the genocide by ignoring violence perpetrated by the Interahamwe in many places. Over time, the national police became directly involved in organizing or directing killing, arresting or detaining high-profile Tutsi and opposition party members, and serving search or arrest warrants. At Nyange, Rwandan national police bulldozed a church where civilians had barricaded themselves, allowing militiamen and the local population to finish the killing (Mugwanya 2011, 85–86). Communal police, in contrast, tended to adopt the stance of the burgomaster, to whom they reported, and other local officials. Thus their responses varied by locale. Communal police participated actively in the genocide in some places, but in others they courageously defended burgomasters who resisted the violence.

Political Parties and the Hutu Power Movement

The 1994 genocide occurred during a transition to multiparty competitive politics. President Habyarimana had made Rwanda a single-party state under the MRND party, following the model of President Nyerere's Tanganyika African National Union in Tanzania. Just before the civil war began in October 1990, political leaders within Rwandan called for an opening of the political system and a return to multiparty politics. The parties that emerged had varying popularity in different regions (see table 1). The CDR attracted adherents from far northern and northwestern Rwanda and adopted anti-RPF and anti-Tutsi positions. The Mouvement démocratique républicain (MDR, Republican Democratic Movement), which was born from the remnants of the Parti du movement de l'émancipation hutu (PARMEHUTU, Hutu Emancipation Movement Party), attracted many Hutu from southern and central Rwanda. The Parti socialiste démocrate (PSD, Social Democratic Party) dominated in central and southern Rwanda, especially in the prefectures of Gitarama and Butare. The Parti libéral (PL, Liberal Party) attracted Tutsi from around the country, but it was strongest in eastern and southern Rwanda, where it also attracted many Hutu members.

The civil war quickly polarized political discourse. The MRND and CDR staunchly opposed negotiation with the RPF. The PL came to be seen as synonymous with the RPF, even though PL leaders often took positions different from those of the RPF. The MDR party came to occupy a centrist role, simultaneously opposing MRND and CDR and advocating for a negotiated settlement with the RPF. The sudden emergence in November 1993 of a new political force, the Hutu Power movement, aligned political conflict along racial lines (Thomson 2018, 73). Table 1 summarizes the realignment that occurred during this period, setting the stage for which parties supported the genocide in 1994. The birth of Hutu Power occurred at a political rally, where the vice president of the MDR addressed an audience drawn from all parties. Using racially charged language, he denigrated moderate MDR leaders (such as Prime Minister Uwilingiyimana and party president Faustin Twagiramungu) who advocated for negotiation with the RPF, and he called for a split in the MDR, naming the new wing MDR-Power. The PSD, which dominated in Gitarama and Butare prefectures, also split

TABLE 1 Major political parties and alliances, 1974–1994

1974–1990	**State party system**	
	MRND	
	Multiparty system	
1991–1993	**Presidential bloc** Party (youth wing)	**Opposition parties** Party (youth wing)
	MRND (Interahamwe)	MDR (Inkuba)
	CDR (Impuzamugambi)	PSD (Abakombozi)
	PDI	PL
1993–1994	**Hutu Power bloc** Party (militia)	**Opposed to genocide** Party
	MRND (Interahamwe)	MDR
	CDR (Impuzamugambi)	PSD
	MDR-Power (Inkuba)	PL
	PSD-Power (Abakombozi)	PDI
	PL-Power	

between moderate and Hutu Power wings in mid-1993. In the ensuing weeks and months, Hutu Power became a rallying call, mobilizing Hutu from all parties against the RPF and Tutsi. Hutu Power supporters "publicly and definitely labeled Tutsi the common enemy" (Thomson 2018, 73).

This labeling had devastating consequences. In everyday life, ordinary people paid little attention to race. Yet this polarized racial discourse resurrected prior moments of violent political crisis that had pitted Hutu against Tutsi. Anxieties rose among ordinary people regarding the likely cost of their political decisions. A Muslim Hutu man from Biryogo described the times: "It was in 1994 before the president was killed. They had started killing Tutsi [here in Biryogo, a neighborhood in Kigali]. That's when we recognized that they were going to start killing people because of their race or because of their adherence to the PL party, or any other party which didn't see eye to eye with the MRND or with the CDR about things" (BIR25). What he left unsaid was that Rwandans easily jumped to these conclusions because the events resurrected memories of prior episodes of racial and political violence at independence, during the 1960s, and in 1973–1974. By casting multiparty politics and peace negotiations in racial terms, the Hutu Power movement eliminated centrist solutions to the war and painted centrist Hutu politicians as naïve or as RPF pawns. A Muslim genocide survivor from Biryogo explained, "Political parties began putting people's names on lists. . . . The MRND, CDR, and Interahamwe started working on these lists months in advance" (BIR08). Thus, even if these lists were not part of a fully detailed genocide plan, they simultaneously reinforced the interweaving of race and politics and made it possible for government security forces and the militias to identify and find their targets immediately once violence began. After five months of racist slogans, ordinary people were primed to interpret President Habyarimana's assassination in April 1994 as an offensive move in a zero-sum game pitting Hutu against Tutsi (Straus 2015).

As elsewhere, men dominated the leadership of political parties. These leaders' wives often operated in concert with their husbands to further their careers and expand their sphere of influence. A few women rose to party leadership positions, including Agathe Uwilingiyimana in the MDR, Pauline Nyiramasuhuko in the MRND, and Agnes Ntamabyaliro in the PL, who all rose to prominence at the national level and became ministers. During the genocide, women in all leadership levels of parties in the Hutu Power bloc actively participated in organizing and implementing the genocide.

Interahamwe and Impuzamugambi Militias

The notorious Interahamwe and Impuzamugambi militias served as the primary instigators of violence during the genocide. Their zeal and strength provided the force needed when civilians were reluctant to attack Tutsi. The Interahamwe began as a youth wing of the MRND. The initial core group formed in 1991, from soccer fanatics who supported the Loisirs football club (Guichaoua 2015b, 125). The initial group included Hutu and Tutsi alike; its members became grassroots MRND party activists, spreading the party's message and recruiting members (126). The goal of the group was to encourage male youths to pledge their loyalty to the MRND party rather than newly formed, competing political parties. Over time, MRND party officials became more prominent at Interahamwe meetings, provided economic support for the group's activities, and guided the group's executive committee. In early 1992, the Interahamwe organized to extend its reach and created local chapters in Gisenyi and Butare (126–27). Both the CDR and MDR responded to the creation of Interahamwe by creating their own youth wings that energetically recruited grassroots activists. The CDR's youth wing, the Impuzamugambi, became particularly powerful in Gisenyi prefecture and in certain neighborhoods of Kigali where many migrants from Gisenyi lived.

By mid-1992, the Interahamwe had become the vibrant and violent muscle of the MRND party. On June 6, 1992, Interahamwe members arrived at an MRND rally "armed with machetes, hoes, axes, clubs, bows, arrows, and rocks" (Guichaoua 2015b, 131). They ransacked several neighborhoods, looting and physically attacking supporters of opposition parties. Following that incident, Interahamwe rallies frequently turned violent. Government authorities did little to prevent the violence, and they refused to prosecute anyone for it (132). By late 1993, President Habyarimana and MRND party officials had organized formal weapons training for the Interahamwe and Impuzamugambi, and the government issued rifles and grenades to leaders of regional and local chapters (139), effectively turning the organizations into militias.

The members of these organizations were well suited to this new role. The Interahamwe and Impuzamugambi had both been established to recruit young men to their respective parties. They were largely masculinist in their orientations and remained primarily male institutions (Guichaoua 2015b, 125–27). Nonetheless, some women joined them. In the years leading up to the genocide, female militia members regularly participated in political rallies, which often turned violent. During the genocide, women militia members often served as cheerleaders for the violence, searched bodies for valuables, or otherwise supported the killings (African Rights 1995, 2). One female Interahamwe member interviewed by researchers in prison in 2005 admitted to murdering people during the genocide (Adler, Loyle, and Globerman 2007, 216). She claimed that she was pressured by her husband to join the Interahamwe and participate in killing (223–24).

The Hutu Power youth wings recruited members from among the jobless and landless male youth who lacked opportunities to build a better life. These young men had nothing to do, ample time on their hands, and little to lose. When the president's assassination created an opportunity, they stood ready to wreak havoc; as genocide developed, they provided the muscle needed to instigate killings in communities where residents were reluctant to kill. Much of the Interahamwe militias' initial violence in April 1994 was spontaneous, triggered by the assassination, but it was not disordered. Years of polarizing political discourse and racist propaganda had clearly delineated the targets: RPF rebels, RPF sympathizers, Tutsi, and members of moderate political parties.

Hutu extremist political elites harnessed this spontaneous violence and channeled it into a policy to annihilate Tutsi. Yet at times elites lost control of the violence. For example, in early May 1994, Interahamwe in Gisenyi began attacking wealthy Hutu civilians and engaging in indiscriminate looting and extortion (GIS41). Regional and communal authorities in Gisenyi called a mandatory meeting to clarify who should be targeted and who should be spared. At other times, militia members took advantage of the chaos to work out personal vendettas. In rural Nkora, "an Interahamwe attacked a Hutu woman from a nearby family, accusing her of being Tutsi, and killed her" (NKO18). The woman's family, who were also in the Interahamwe, then killed the man and his entire family in revenge.

Local Government Officials

In 1994, the country's infrastructure was underdeveloped; many communities were remote, lacking direct communication by telephone and having only limited access via roads (Straus 2006, 202–3). Nonetheless, local government officials wielded considerable authority and respect. The government's administrative structure was divided into twelve prefectures, which were subdivided into 145 communes. Communes were further subdivided into sectors, cells, and *nyumbakumi*. Mayors led the communes, *conseillers* the sectors, and *responsables* the cells.

These local officials were the primary interface with the state for most citizens. Consequently, the reactions and actions of local government officials and local elites strongly shaped those of ordinary Rwandans. In some communities, regional and local government officials refused to implement the genocide orders from the central government. Instead, they interpreted the orders literally and focused on defending their communities against RPF rebels (not Tutsi civilians) and quelling militia violence against Tutsi civilians, delaying the onset of genocide in those regions and supporting rescue. In the next chapter, I discuss this pattern at length as it played out in Nyabisindu commune (Nyanza) in southern Rwanda.

In 1994, there were no female governors or mayors. As of 1990, women constituted only 1.2 percent of *conseillers* (Hogg 2010, 74, 94–95). More women served in lower levels of the local government such as *responsables*, but precise numbers are unknown (94). Once the genocide began, many of the women in local government launched "themselves into the killing campaign as a way to increase their importance" like their male counterparts (Des Forges 1999, 226). For example, the female *conseiller* of Muhima sector in Nyarugenge commune, Kigali, organized roadblocks and directed killings (Hogg 2010), and other women in the Nyarugenge commune government ordered militiamen to seize Tutsi men and women and kill them (Des Forges 1999, 229).

Beyond government officials, the rural elite, comprising teachers, doctors, nurses, the clergy, civic association leaders, international aid agency employees, businessmen, and political party leaders, also wielded significant influence and authority in rural communities (Straus 2006, 68). At times of crisis, such as the communal violence in 1959, attacks against Tutsi in 1963–1964, and renewed anti-Tutsi violence in 1973–1974, ordinary Rwandans in rural communities looked to these local elites, as well as governmental officials, for guidance in how to behave. Throughout the civil war, in particular after the assassination of President Habyarimana and during the genocide, ordinary Rwandans again relied on these local elites for cues about how to react. Thus, when local elites or government authorities asked them to engage in acts of genocide, they were socially primed to act outside moral norms, especially when these orders were given in the context of national security.

Few genocide perpetrators in Rwanda faced the extreme structural constraints, hours of torture, and direct threat of death that confronted Idi, with whom this chapter began. Local relations between people, histories of cohabitation or violence, and local configurations of power produced variability in genocidal violence and policy implementation. Yet the interactions between national and local instigators of violence against Tutsi sustained the terrible violence at the genocide's core. As genocide emerged to become a nationwide policy, ordinary Rwandans were forced to make very difficult decisions, often with limited information, about how to behave. In the midst of this chaos, the majority of them initially offered assistance to their Tutsi kin, friends, neighbors, and coworkers. Many of those who had offered help to Tutsi abandoned their efforts as risks increased. Others faced choiceless choices—where no option was morally correct. A few mustered the courage and persistence to continue to make the decision to help in the face of increasing risk. The next chapter considers the impact of these constraints and the dynamic context of the genocide on perpetrators who joined willingly in the violence—often without clear motivation. And some perpetrators also rescued Tutsi, troubling the popular trope of evil perpetrators.

2

AGENCY AND MORALITY IN THE GRAY ZONE

> **The genocide was like a machine. Once it was turned on, it roamed everywhere. People had to kill. Sometimes it was a moral, psychological obligation, but in others it was a physical obligation.**
>
> —Father Eros, Italian priest (NYA38)

I interviewed Kabera, a barrel-chested man in his fifties with immense hands and thick arms rippled with muscle, one afternoon in 2013. He was out of breath when he arrived at the schoolroom where I was conducting interviews. He had come running from his work as a day laborer loading freight for businesses next to the highway. He plopped down on the narrow wood bench across from me and declared, "Ask me anything you want. I have nothing to hide" (MUG34). He wanted to get back to work as quickly as possible, and he grew impatient as I went through the informed consent protocol. His faded, threadbare button-down shirt hung open to mid-chest; a grungy white singlet peeked out. A pale blue plastic rosary hung around his neck; the crucifix swung wildly when he gestured as he talked. Despite his intimidating strength and size, he had a gentle demeanor.

In the region, Kabera was widely known as a notorious killer during the genocide. By his own admission, he had killed or helped kill scores (perhaps even hundreds) of people with clubs, machetes, or farming implements like hoes. He had killed people who were like "brothers. People who gave me milk," as he put it (MUG34). He had killed so many people that he lost count. In 1994, Kabera was thirty-five years old, married with children, and living in prolonged poverty because he did not own farmland. In our interview, he explained that most ordinary Rwandans who became perpetrators, like himself, were motivated by greed and poverty.[1] I pressed him for a more thorough explanation about why he chose to kill.

> KABERA: It's like when the rain falls, and the storm carries everything in its way, and you fail to protect yourself from it. We got confused.

You can imagine seeing authorities telling you, "If you don't do this [kill people], you will be dead [because of the RPF]!" Or, "You will benefit from it!" Those authorities were actually the ones who benefited from it.

Q: Did you consider not getting involved in those actions?

KABERA: Absolutely. We were not even thinking about it [killing].

Q: So, then what?

KABERA: What else is there? When you've never considered doing something?

Q: You never decided to kill?

KABERA: No, we didn't have those intentions. It occurred like a natural disaster.

Q: Why did you kill some and rescue the others?

KABERA: Those ones were kept safe in homes or were kept safe at the mosque, for example. For those who were able to hide in homes, they had people who would stay with them and protect them. Then those people would say, "What would happen if so-and-so is no longer here?"

Q: But then, why did you kill some and save the others?

KABERA: No way. Listen. We were very many together in a group [*pause*]. Imagine the Coaster buses on the tarmac road [*motioning to the highway*]. The bus stops, people get on, and they are carried away. We were many people. We didn't have the same hearts, but we were all carried away. Whenever you tried to speak, they [the authorities] would tell you, "You should be on our side!" [meaning with the government and against the RPF]. So, you didn't know what to do. It's like when the priest talks in the church; you listen to what he says. Even if you didn't do anything, you would stand with the others. But at least they would say that you were there, too. (MUG34)

Kabera's explanation is surprising only in his willingness to speak freely about the genocide and his role in it. Indeed, Kabera confirms several of the common themes in studies of perpetrator motivation and action: obedience, deference to authority, the moral framing of the situation as war, small decisions leading to bigger ones, and the social forces of mob violence. Yet he insists that he never decided to kill: "No, we didn't have those intentions. It occurred like a natural disaster" (MUG34). Kabera's insistence that he never *decided* to kill is easy to dismiss as a retrospective coping mechanism—a way to minimize his legal or moral responsibility. We can effortlessly imagine him as a heartless killer based on his own description of his actions.

Yet Kabera also rescued people, begging the question at the heart of this book: why? During the genocide, he hid and protected three Tutsi neighbors in his home, including a local government official whom the Interahamwe vigorously sought to kill; protected a woman and her children who were hidden elsewhere; and warned a former classmate and friend to hide from an approaching Interahamwe mob. Kabera was what Lee Ann Fujii (2011) called a "killer-rescuer," someone who both killed Tutsi and saved them from genocide. Kabera's case vividly illustrates two significant weaknesses of the standard genocide studies typology of victim, perpetrator, bystander, and rescuer. First, these categories reduce a person, and their often-contradictory beliefs and motivations, to an expected set of behaviors (Fujii 2011, 145). Perpetrators kill. Victims are killed. Bystanders watch. Rescuers help. Second, implicit in the typology is a moral judgment: perpetrators are guilty and evil, victims are innocent and good, bystanders are complicit or corrupt, rescuers are heroic and good. This framework leaves no path for understanding killer-rescuers, like Kabera, or victim-perpetrators, like Idi.

Kabera's retrospective explanation of his actions illuminates very little about why he did what he did more than twenty years earlier. Just as he never *decided* to kill his "brothers," he saved people because "they came to me and told me their problem. I wondered, 'These are my neighbors, what can I do?' So, I put them in my house. We knew each other, they were my friends" (MUG34). In this book, I take seriously Kabera's proposition that he did not *decide* to kill or *decide* to rescue, by applying actor-network theory to illuminate the complexity of agency in genocide. A method of analysis that emerged in science and technology studies, actor-network theory posits that agency is an emergent property of complex networks of relations between heterogeneous components. From the perspective of actor-network theory, Kabera's actions, both killing and saving, emerged from the network of relations between him and other humans (ranging from "brothers" who "shared milk," to neighbors, unknown strangers, Interahamwe militiamen, and local authorities); contextual factors, such as patronage practices, histories of reciprocity and gift giving, expectations for deference to authority, the orders of local authorities, Hutu extremist framing of Tutsi civilians as RPF infiltrators, mob dynamics, the cultural palimpsest of mob justice, and social taboos on killing; and physical factors, such as available farming implements and weapons, roadblocks, and the presence of security patrols.

Actor-network theory removes the moral judgment implied by the standard genocide studies typology of victim, perpetrator, bystander, and rescuer. In genocide, actor-network theory acknowledges that killing and rescue can emerge from the same complex networks of relations between heterogeneous components in an assemblage. This analytical move is necessary because genocide produces what Primo Levi (1989) called a "gray zone" of moral "ambiguity which radiates out from regimes based on terror and obsequiousness" (37). The gray zone "teases out the roles of perpetrator, victim, and bystander in the camps, and suggests that they sometimes do not have well-defined boundaries" (Bernard-Donals 2016, 68), and generates a system of "choiceless choices" (Melson 2005).

Bringing together actor-network theory with the concept of the gray zone illuminates the moral complexity and ambiguity of decision making in genocide. This theoretical framework highlights the ways in which acts of rescue and acts of genocide transpire in the same gray zone and can emerge from similar networks of relations. Conceiving of agency during genocide as an emergent feature of heterogeneous assemblages allows us to see how the same networks produce killing and rescue apart from these actions' morality. Even rescuers who did not participate in the killing often had to lie, bribe, or deny assistance to some to ensure the protection of others. From this perspective, we can understand the ambivalent actions of a killer-rescuer like Kabera and a victim-perpetrator like Idi, as well as the morally dubious decisions of ordinary people who rescued without participating in genocide.

Ordinary Perpetrators in the Rwandan Genocide

How and why ordinary Rwandans participated in the genocide have already been extensively researched.[2] Empirical research on the Rwandan genocide quickly disproved the interpretation that Rwandans killed out of deep-seated "tribal" hatred, an explanation predicated on assumptions about Africa and Africans rooted in white supremacy (Des Forges 1999; Fujii 2009; McDoom 2005; Prunier 1997; Straus 2006). While the most impassioned perpetrators, what Rwandans call *Interahamwe z'interahamwe* (Interahamwe of the Interahamwe), did embark on a murderous rampage against Tutsi and opposition political party members based only on race or political affiliation, ordinary Rwandans participated in violence against Tutsi for a host of other reasons.

Scott Straus (2006) concluded that Hutu men participated in the genocide for two primary reasons. First, they killed "because other men encouraged, intimidated, and coerced them to do so in the name of authority and 'the law'" (122). Second, they participated "because they were scared" of the RPF rebels or "angry about the president's death," which they attributed to the RPF (122). As one confessed perpetrator explained to me, "After Habyarimana's death, this feeling circulated in our blood. We understood he had been killed by Tutsi from outside known as Inkotanyi [RPF rebels]. . . . We did not hate [our Tutsi neighbors]. We married them, and we lived together with them. Only when those people attacked our country, and we knew their accomplices (*ibyitso*) were among us.

Then, at that moment, we began to hate Tutsi" (NKO10). Ordinary Rwandans who were mobilized by local elites or government officials made calculated decisions about whether or not to participate (Straus 2006, 8). They made these decisions repeatedly, over time. From this perspective, the ongoing civil war between the Rwandan government and the RPF provided the "essential rationale for mass killing: security" (8). Average civilians who participated found it morally tolerable to kill because they believed they were protecting their families, the community, or the nation's security.

While this explanatory model fits the Rwanda case much better than the first, it does not fully capture the importance of social ties in the extremely local logics deployed in the genocide. Fujii (2008, 2009) focused on the lowest-level participants, whom she called "joiners." To Fujii, the joiners are the most puzzling subcategory of perpetrators because they "had the most to lose and the least to gain from participating," and they were the most affected by the genocide's social and physical destruction (2009, 16). Fujii concludes that local ties—defined as kinship, economic exchange, shared workplace, political affiliation, and education—and group dynamics mediated individual choices and actions at any given moment during the genocide. This understanding makes it possible to explain why the same individuals who killed Tutsi at a roadblock could hide Tutsi in their home.

Furthermore, Fujii's social dynamic model captures the reality that individual perpetrator motivations do not remain constant over time. The rapidly changing context of mass violence, state policy, and local configurations of power incentivize different kinds of behavior at different points in time and pressure certain people more (or less) than others. When conditions changed, for example when local authorities began to comply with directives from the central government, people made new decisions based on the new context. A perpetrator who first participated because of extreme structural constraints may have later become desensitized to the "psychosocial dissonance" resulting from breaking moral prohibitions against harming other humans (Hinton 2005, 288). They may have moved from reluctant participant to avid perpetrator. The absolutist logic of the genocide—you are either with us (the government / the Hutu Power movement) or against us (and with the RPF rebels / Tutsi)—worked to destroy the social cohesion so vital to daily life in Rwanda. In other words, ordinary Rwandans drew on social scripts, prior experiences of communal or ethnic violence, and social connections to choose a course of action at any given moment. In short, they improvised.

Kabera's testimony confirms both Straus's and Fujii's interpretations, but he also highlights the importance of deeply embedded social scripts, culturally shaped emotions, and prior experiences that shaped people's actions. First,

Kabera evokes deference to authority and the persuasiveness of local authorities. Twice, he mobilized the classic perpetrator explanation, "I was obeying orders." Participants in communal violence and genocide almost universally explain their actions in terms of obeying orders (Hinton 2005, 276–77). Psychologists and philosophers have recognized the weight of authority in shaping people's behaviors and responses to events. In studies conducted in 1961, Stanley Milgram (1974) demonstrated the willingness of ordinary people to obey the instructions of research study personnel, even when those instructions inflicted pain on strangers. While a large body of scholarship has called into question many of Milgram's conclusions, his research continues to shape understandings of the impact of authority and obedience on behavior.[3] Hannah Arendt (1963) argued that evil could be perpetrated in a "banal" manner if situational constraints were strong enough. In the Rwandan genocide, orders from authorities and their framing of the situation as war constituted situational constraints.

While it is true that "in some situations . . . perpetrators are heavily pressured . . . to obey orders" (Hinton 2005, 279), this pressure is not constant, and it does not provide a complete explanation of why ordinary people become killers or participate in mass violence. Unlike Idi in chapter 1, who was tortured for hours and subjected to extreme pressure to kill, Kabera participated willingly, even passionately, in killing. Most perpetrators do have a choice, as historian Christopher Browning (1992) demonstrated in his study of a German reserve police battalion. The battalion Browning studied was made up of working-class German men who had been drafted into the police because they were deemed too old for regular military service (1992, 3–8). On July 13, 1942, the battalion entered a Polish village, rounded up Jewish men for deportation to work camps, and then massacred thousands of women, children, and elders. The battalion, made up of draftees, not volunteers, took this action under orders. Yet Browning found that the battalion members elected to participate in these heinous acts. The battalion's commanding officer had given his men the option not to participate, but very few chose to stand down (1992, 2)—only a "dozen men out of nearly 500" excused "themselves from the impending mass murder" (71). Browning argues that the soldiers' compliance was a result of social-psychological factors shaping group dynamics and deference to authority, combined with the need to make a decision in the spur of the moment (71). The dozen men who stepped out turned in their rifles, and they were relieved of duty that day (61). Those who did not embarked on a long, gruesome campaign of deportations and mass killings across Poland.

Like the men of the reserve police battalion, Kabera had a choice, even if he did not know he was making a choice at the time. Kabera arrived voluntarily at meetings, night patrols, roadblocks, and massacre sites. Many other Hutu men in his neighborhood initially shirked these duties in the face of orders from local authorities. As the perceived threats increased, some Hutu men complied with orders to appear at security meetings, night patrols, or roadblocks but still did not participate in killing. As Kabera said, "Even if you didn't do anything, you would stand with the others," evoking the roles of bystanders in mass violence (MUG34). These small decisions to comply with directives from local authorities made it more likely over time that a person would participate in killing (Straus 2006; Fujii 2009).

In this scenario, deference to local authorities—exhibited in decisions to appear at meetings—and those authorities' framing of genocidal violence as morally justifiable acts of war gradually overcame some citizens' reluctance to join. Central government authorities and Hutu extremist media continued this framing of anti-Tutsi violence as war throughout the genocide. In this context, obedience to authority, supported by the moral justification provided by this framing, pushed some people, like Kabera, to break the taboo on murder. As Kabera said, "You can imagine seeing authorities telling you, 'If you don't do this, you will be dead!'" He implies that the local authorities not only ordered the killing, but they also framed it in terms of self-defense, thus implying it was morally justified. Later, he reiterated the same idea: "Whenever you tried to speak, they [the authorities] would tell you, 'You should be on our side!'"

While Kabera's insistence that he never *decided* to kill may be a retrospective coping mechanism, his explanation highlights the reality that not all action results from a conscious decision. Emotions, states of mind, or bodily sensations also play roles in initiating action. In particular, the effects of crowds propel some people to break social norms and behave in unexpected ways. Crowds can quickly evolve into mobs that engage in scapegoating and jubilant destruction (Tambiah 1996, 266–96). Once the mob is mobilized in this way, the collective violence "takes on a force and agency that has attained its own autonomy" and becomes "efficacious in the construction, production, maintenance, and reproduction of ethnic identity and solidarity itself" (223). Kabera evoked the mob aspects of the violence in the genocide: "We were many together in a group. . . . We were many people."

Mob justice has deep cultural roots in Rwanda, providing what Alexander Hinton (2005) called a "cultural palimpsest" that helps explain the "patterns of violence" that emerged in the genocide (279). In the Rwandan worldview, the power of the group is key to the punishment and, more importantly, the public humiliation of community members who violate social norms. For example, livestock thieves caught in the act of butchering their booty are first severely beaten. Then they are dressed in the entrails, head, and carcass of the stolen animal and marched through the throng to the local government jail, where they face official punishment.[4] This cultural model, combined with the productive nature of crowds and the collective violence they generate, shapes individual action and contributes to the power of the mob. As an Italian priest described it, "The genocide was like a machine. Once it was turned on, it roamed everywhere" (NYA38).

Human Agency: An Emergent Property of Actor-Networks

Questions about perpetrators, rescuers, bystanders, and victims are fundamentally questions about human agency. Why did X choose to do Y to Z? This question evokes the age-old debate over structure and agency at the heart of the social sciences. In political science and economics, scholars tend to assume that humans or institutions behave as rational actors who have free will and exercise agency. While they recognize that humans often do not behave rationally, they justify this assumption as reasonable because it is useful for developing universal theoretical frameworks that explain social and political phenomena. Or they explain nonrational behavior by attributing it to "social forces," which include things like deference to authority, coercion, social ties, cultural scripts, political ideologies, and racist hatred. In these depictions, "social forces play the complicated role of being simultaneously what has to be postulated to explain everything and what, for many reasons, has to remain invisible," and intangible (Latour 2005, 102). Social scientists often "black box" social forces, meaning they place them in containers and label them things like "social influence," "religious belief," or "ethnic hatred," without explaining precisely what these social forces are or how they operate. Other approaches tend to conceptualize structure's relation to agency in one of three ways: as constraining the choices of agents, as generating (or producing) the agents, or as constraining and producing agents through a dialectical process. Because these kinds of theoretical frameworks tend to predict a person will behave consistently in a given set of circumstances, they cannot explain or predict the behaviors of those who reacted differently at various points in the genocide.

In essence, actor-network theory poses a novel solution to the structure-agency question, by describing agency as an emergent property of complex networks (referred to alternately as actor-networks, assemblages, collectives, or hybrid collectives) of relations; the elements in the network are referred to as *components*, *actants*, *nodes*, or *actors*. These components can be human or nonhuman, sentient or nonsentient, living or nonliving, artificial or natural, and material or semiotic. Thus, an assemblage may include humans, animals, inanimate objects, physical features of the landscape, geopolitical impositions (such as borders), symbols, ideas, or abstractions, such as government policy (Callon and Law 1995). The term "actor" has a special meaning in this context: the actor "is not the source of an action but the moving target of a vast array of entities swarming toward it. . . . To use the word 'actor' means that it's never clear who and what is acting when we act since an actor on stage is never alone in acting" (Latour 2005, 46). In other words, from an actor-network theory perspective, human agency is not sited in human actors; rather, it is an emergent property of an assemblage—the set of components (and the relationships between those components) in which human actors are embedded.

Emphasizing the centrality of relations between the heterogeneous components of an assemblage to agency, actor-network theory decenters the rational human subject (assumed by many theories of agency) and instead locates agency in the "complex relationships" between humans and nonhumans "at different moments across time and space" (De León 2015, 39). This analytical move is useful for three reasons. First, it rejects the notion of the liberal human subject, a concept seated in Western understandings of the person, and instead embraces the ways in which individual human beings are constituted by the relations—to other humans, social structures, things, and ideas—in which they are embedded. Put simply, under actor-network theory, a person is only a person in relation to other humans, to society, and to the things and ideas in their environment. Second, actor-network theory does not conceive of external constraints (that is, structure) as determining human action (that is, agency). Rather, it posits that the dialectical interactions between heterogeneous actors produce effects that appear to be human agency. Third, actor-network theory places the constituent entities of an assemblage on "equal ontological footing," whether they are sentient beings, nonsentient things, large material abstractions (such as governments), or small material objects (such as atoms) (Müller 2015, 30). From this perspective, all nodes within an actor network have equal weight in generating effects that appear to be human agency. This analytical move elucidates the significance of nonhuman actors, whether they be government policies, media messages, weapons, perceived threats of invading rebels, patronage, reciprocity or gift giving, or cultural palimpsests like mob justice.

Actor-network theory has been applied to a wide variety of topics in anthropology. Over the past fifteen years, anthropologists have used actor-network theory to explore questions about the environmental impact of climate change on rain forest ecologies (Raffles 2002), disease and the human body (Mol 2003), commodity chains and capitalism (Tsing 2015), human migration (De León 2015), and many other topics. To date, actor-network theory has not been applied to understanding agency in genocide or mass violence. Within political science and international relations, very few scholars have applied actor-network theory (see, for example, Bueger 2013; Kleinschmidt 2015).

The majority of the theory's applications (including those by the anthropologists cited above) have highlighted the significance of nonhuman actors in producing agency. However, one of the theory's earliest articulations focused on the how nonhuman actors create the mirage of human-centered agency. Michel Callon and John Law (1995) asked their readers to imagine "Andrew . . . the managing director of a very large laboratory. He's able, he's personable, and he's fierce. He's an actor. An agent." As part of his job,

> He talks to subordinates, . . . gathers intelligence from outside, visits [the] "head office," where they make decisions about the future of the laboratory. . . . He lobbies. . . . Half the time he's not sitting at his desk. Indeed, he's not in the laboratory at all. He's at head office. He's negotiating. He's collaring people in the pub to bend their ears and catch the latest . . . gossip. Or, he's in London, attending meetings in smoke-filled rooms. Comparing brands of malt whiskey with the powerful in the land. (483–84)

Callon and Law then ask the reader to imagine whether Andrew would still be Andrew without his fax machine, personal computer, email, executive secretary, nice clothes, expensive watch, a train line to London, or the deference and respect of his colleagues. In short, "Is Andrew still Andrew if we reduce him to the status of a tramp?" (484). The obvious answer is "No, not at all." Thus, Andrew's agency is determined not merely by his status as a human occupying his role as a laboratory manager, but it is also determined by all the inanimate objects and relationships to other humans and things that facilitate his ability to act in the world. From this perspective, Andrew's agency is an emergent effect of the assemblage in which he is entangled. As Callon and Law put it, both agency and the hybrid collective itself are "an emergent effect created by the interaction of the heterogeneous parts that make it up" (485).

In this way, actor-network theory understands agency and structure as mutually constitutive. More importantly, the approach accommodates the amorphous, the fleeting, and the rapidly changing in its conceptualization of structure. For example, political scientists frequently think of political parties as structure and the behavior of political party members as agency. Actor-network theory, in contrast, conceives of political parties as heterogeneous alliances (or assemblages) that bring together people, ideologies, organizational forms (such as bylaws and operating procedures), technologies (such as social media platforms), ideological agendas, slogans, and symbols (such as party flags, colors, uniforms, and seals) to achieve an end (winning seats in parliament, gaining cabinet positions, motivating policy changes, shifting the dominant ideology of citizens). In some political systems, such as the United States, political parties appear to be durable structures. In others, political parties appear to change rapidly: forming, going defunct, transforming, or merging with other parties. Conceiving of political parties as heterogeneous alliances allows for a single theoretical framework to understand how they operate in both contexts.

Applying this perspective to Idi's act of genocide, described in chapter 1, illuminates the ways his agency was not his alone. At the roadblock, Idi was accompanied not only by all the other humans present (the Tutsi man, the soldiers, the Interahamwe, his friend who dropped the spear, the older man who said, "But all of these people are Hutu," the local residents manning the roadblock, and the onlookers) but also by those who were absent (his Tutsi mother, his mixed siblings, and his absent Hutu father). In addition, he was entangled in the polarized social categories permeating the atmosphere—Hutu/Tutsi, government soldier/Inyenzi, loyal citizen/accomplice—and the government policy and administrative chain of command that produced the roadblock. Idi was also enmeshed with the roadblock, the spear, the man's papers that marked him as Tutsi, the blood seeping from Idi's bayonet wounds, the physical pain from the wounds, his fear, and so on. This heterogeneous assemblage produced Idi's action. Absent the spear, he could not have performed it. Without the psychological weight of his mixed ethnic background and the polarized atmosphere, he might have succumbed sooner to the soldiers' demands or resisted longer. Actor-network theory demystifies the source of Idi's decisionless action by tracing the assemblage and the components that produced it.

In actor-network theory, social relations, which are like any other relations within an assemblage, are performative, meaning social relations exist because they are performed (or enacted), their performance does something (such as evoke an alliance), and their performance reproduces their existence. Understanding social relations in this way helps illuminate the factors at play in any given act of genocide or act of rescue. Each act of genocide or act of rescue performed (or enacted) a specific set of social relations. For example, Fujii (2008) and Omar McDoom (2014) have shown that ordinary Rwandans were more likely to participate in the genocide if they had social relations or social network connections to other perpetrators. Actor-network theory illuminates why this would be true: acts of genocide enacted these extant social relations, materialized these relations into action, and reproduced their value.

Another innovation of actor-network theory is that it looks for the material manifestations of power sited in specific social relations, in specific practices, and in actual offices, buildings, or physical spaces. An analysis of a complex assemblage, such as "the state," encompasses the manifestation of state power in specific social encounters. "The global, the national and the local are all effects of more or less dense connections" (Müller 2015, 35). As Latour (2005, 184–85) recounts, an actor may simultaneously evoke multiple scales of social organization (the whole of humanity, the nation, capitalism, ethnic affinity, and specific social relations) to justify behavior. Even the largest global organizations "are just made up of local interactions in the sense that they connect one entity with another" (Müller 2015, 35). Thus, actor-network theory highlights the ways micro-level acts of genocide articulate with and become a national policy of genocide.

Actor-network theory thus allows for multiscalar analyses of social phenomena. Each constituent element of an assemblage can itself be understood as an assemblage. This radical deconstructivist stance allows for precise analyses of complex systems. Each component of a complex system can be deconstructed and analyzed to reveal its effects on the actor-network in which it is embedded. These systems, institutions, and abstractions become empirical objects sited in space and time whose properties can be studied and embedded in multiscalar analyses. An actor-network theory analysis of Rwandans' decision making and actions during the genocide renders intelligible the variation in the local effects of national policies by capturing the varied articulation of national policies with regional government entities and local concerns across space and time.

The Moral Gray Zone of Genocide

The stories of Idi in chapter 1 and Kabera at the beginning of this chapter illustrate the fractures in the classic typology of genocide participants—victim, perpetrator, bystander, rescuer—and demonstrate that the categories are not clear-cut. As Michael Bernard-Donals (2016) wrote, "even the categories that seem so useful to us in describing the primary actors during the Holocaust, at least in philosophical terms (and perhaps in historical ones as well), may well break down under their own weight, requiring us to find better terms to describe the complexity and the extremity of the circumstances individuals faced" (67). Furthermore, these categories "can obscure as much as they reveal" (Fujii 2011, 145) by reducing a person, and the often-contradictory beliefs and actions that motivate that person, to an expected set of behaviors. In Rwanda, during the swift evolution of the genocide, as the civilian population was mobilized and enlisted in the state's killing machine, people acting to minimize potential negative outcomes for themselves or their kin sometimes moved from altruistic behaviors (helping their neighbors, coworkers, or kin) to bystander behaviors (actively doing nothing) to perpetrator behaviors (participating in the genocide). They often moved back and forth between these different types of behaviors.

This complexity extends to rescuers as well as perpetrators. Previous studies of rescuers tended to give partial answers regarding how and why they risked their lives, not considering the full complexity of human agency. Rescuers, like perpetrators and bystanders, operated within, sometimes deeply within, the gray zone. Many rescuers—like Kabera—were complicit in the genocidal project or at least profited from it in some way (like Oskar Schindler in the Holocaust). Even those rescuers who were motivated by deeply held moral convictions—whether of common humanity, renunciation of sin, or obeisance to God's commandments—had to make decisions from morally ambiguous positions. As related in detail in the next chapter, an orphanage director who protected hundreds of Tutsi children refused shelter to Tutsi adults trying to escape the slaughter, denying help to some Tutsi to save the lives of those already hiding in the orphanage.

In developing his concept of the gray zone, Levi explores the moral universe of the Nazi concentration camps in Europe. First, he condemns the camp system: "Certainly, the greatest responsibility lies with the system, the very structure of the totalitarian state" (Levi 1989, 44). Even as he blames the system, however, he acknowledges that prisoners (as well as SS commanders, average soldiers, and German citizens) still exercised agency in the face of the Nazi project, no matter how circumscribed: "The concurrent guilt on the part of individual big and small collaborators (never likable, never transparent!) is always difficult to evaluate" (44). Levi considers the moral responsibility of the primarily Jewish prisoner collaborators in the camps and characterizes the culpability of the various prisoners and prisoner-functionaries as constituting a vast gray zone of moral ambiguity: "Terror, ideological seduction, servile imitation of the victor, myopic desire for any power whatsoever, even though ridiculously circumscribed in space and time, cowardice, and finally, lucid calculation aimed at eluding the imposed orders and order. All these motives, singly or combined, have come into play in the creation of this gray zone, whose components are bonded together by the wish to preserve and consolidate established privilege vis-à-vis those without privilege" (43). Prisoner-collaborators included a wide variety of people in between the SS commanders who organized and controlled the camps and the Jewish prisoners arriving on trains from European ghettos, ultimately to die in the gas chambers. They ranged from low-ranking workers, who earned "an extra half-liter of soup" by sweeping, washing kettles, checking for lice, smoothing beds, or serving as night watchmen; to the chiefs (*kapos*) who earned additional privileges by organizing the barracks, leading labor squads, or performing diverse "'delicate duties' in the camps' administrative offices, the Political Section (actually a section of the Gestapo), the Labor Service, and the punishment cells" (44–45). At the pinnacle of the prisoners' hierarchy were the Special Squads (*Sonderkommandos*), which led arriving trainloads of Jews to their deaths in the gas chambers and then "processed" their bodies for disposal in the crematoria.

Prisoner-collaborators helped ensure the camps functioned efficiently, but they did so, Levi is careful to make clear, to procure tiny benefits that prolonged their survival. Levi does not absolve any of the prisoner-collaborators of the moral weight of their complicity, collaboration, or direct participation in the Nazi enterprise. Yet he acknowledges that they faced innumerable, impossible decisions in pursuit of survival in a situation that would almost certainly end in their death. The weeks or months of starvation in the camps (usually coming on the heels of years of deprivation in the ghettos) created a situation where "the room for choices (especially moral ones) was reduced to zero" (50). Levi concludes that the moral ambiguity of this space must be explored and recognized, even if the prisoners do not bear the same moral culpability as the SS soldiers running the camps or the "very structure of the totalitarian state" that produced the evil system (42–43).

Levi reserved the term "gray zone" for Jewish prisoners who collaborated with the Nazi guards and SS officers running the camps, describing it as "a gray zone, poorly defined, where the two camps of masters and servants both diverge and converge" (42). Crucial to the concept is the moral ambiguity of decision making in the gray zone. "The concept of the gray zone applies to the morally charged conduct in a middle ground between good and evil, right and wrong, where neither side of these pairs covers the situation and where imposing one side or the other becomes itself for Levi a moral wrong" (Lang 2013, 127). As Levi describes it, this moral ambiguity is produced through the systemic abjection enforced by the camp system, its harsh coercion, and the dehumanization it inflicted by burdening prisoners with the guilt of their complicity in the persecution of their brethren (Levi 1989, 43). "This institution represented an attempt to shift onto others—specifically, the victims—the burden of guilt, so that they were deprived of even the solace of innocence" (53).

Genocide scholars have applied Levi's concept of the gray zone in many insightful ways (Browning 2005; Horowitz 2005; Melson 2005). Yet some have expanded it beyond Levi's original intent and in so doing have distorted it by placing all perpetrators in the moral gray zone (Lee 2016). Levi reserved the gray zone to prisoners who collaborated with the Nazi guards and with the SS commanders running the camp, but he implied that the concept could be extended to others. For example, he suggested that Nazi guards who assisted prisoners by trading food for gold or valuables might be encompassed in the gray zone. Levi was clear, however, that the camp commander would be excluded, as would SS soldiers who carried out their duties without reticence or who did not recognize prisoners as human beings deserving of respect, mercy, or assistance. Levi's gray zone is not "a place to which *all* human beings—by the fact of human frailty—are granted access, since that would then enable them conveniently to respond to any moral charge with the indisputable claim that 'I am only human'" (Lang 2013, 125).

I apply the concept of the gray zone to the Rwandan genocide to elucidate the moral ambiguity in the choices demanded of ordinary Rwandans facing extraordinary situations. I expand the concept beyond genocide victims complicit in the genocidal project to others—perpetrators, bystanders, rescuers, killer-rescuers—faced with morally ambiguous decisions during the genocide. This expansion of Levi's concept is justified by the circumstances of the Rwandan genocide, which differed in significant ways from the Nazi implementation of the state's "Final Solution," especially in the variety of ways ordinary citizens were mobilized to participate in genocidal violence. This application of the gray zone illuminates the ways that people navigated complex and morally ambiguous decisions on a daily, sometimes even a minute-by-minute, basis.

Idi's story illustrates how the moral gray zone into which ordinary Rwandans were thrust figures into the assemblages that produced individuals' agency. After hours of torture at the roadblock, Idi, a genocide victim in the moment, grabbed the spear thrust in his face and plunged it into the Tutsi man before him. Idi acted to save his own life in an impossible situation, a space where "the room for choices (especially moral ones) was reduced to zero" (Levi 1989, 50). This act produced numerous material and social effects. Most importantly, the Tutsi man died because of it. Yet, it also was a socially productive act for Idi, who had been detained at the roadblock because he was suspected of being an RPF infiltrator, suspicion fueled by his Tutsi physiognomy and his Muslim faith. Through his action, Idi demonstrated his loyalty to the genocidal state, as well as his allegiance to the security forces and Interahamwe at the roadblock. Thus, he removed himself, at least temporarily, from the victim category. Yet, through the same act, he became complicit in his own abjection. He magnified the threat to his mother, to Tutsi generally, and to others of mixed ethnic parentage, like himself.

Idi is in the same position as the Jews assigned to the Special Squads that Levi describes. The Special Squads were made up of prisoners assigned to run the crematoria. They maintained order among newly arriving prisoners and escorted the new arrivals as they removed their clothing and entered the faux shower rooms where they were gassed. After the killing, squad members removed the bodies from the gas chambers, processed them by extracting gold teeth and cutting women's hair, and moved the bodies to the crematoria. After serving in this capacity for a few months, Special Squad members met the same fate as the other Jews in the concentration camps—they were gassed. Levi places Special Squad members outside of moral judgment because the camps, as an institution, attempted to shift the burden of guilt for millions of murders onto Jewish victims via the Special Squads. In the same way, Idi was "deprived of even the solace of innocence" (Levi 1989, 53) by being forced to participate in killing. Thus, Levi's concept of the gray zone demands that we suspend moral judgment of Idi's actions because he was simply trying to survive in a situation where all options were morally dubious.

Kabera had a clear moral choice, but the existence of that choice does not place him outside the gray zone. Kabera is like the SS commander Muhsfeld who Levi describes (1989, 57–58). Muhsfeld showed pity for a young Jewish girl discovered alive in the gas chambers by some tragic miracle. After the Special Squads wrapped her in blankets and warmed her with soup, Muhsfeld considered her case. At first he hesitated, but finally he ordered an underling to kill her with a blow to the neck (57). "That single, immediately erased instant of pity is certainly not enough to absolve Muhsfeld. It is enough, however, to place him too, although at its extreme boundary, within the gray band, that zone of ambiguity which radiates out from regimes based on terror and obsequiousness" (58). Levi judges Muhsfeld as morally culpable yet acknowledges that he was influenced by the gray zone.

Like Muhsfeld, Kabera could have acted on his pity. He could have refused to go when summoned. He could have stood by and watched instead of lifting his weapon to kill. Yet Kabera insists he did not *decide* to kill: "We were not even thinking about it [killing]. . . . The bus stops, people get on, and they are carried away." In Kabera's formulation, the killing happened without him deciding anything. We can doubt Kabera's candor, but we must acknowledge that some acts are decisionless. Much of what we do in the world, even under ordinary circumstances, is structured by things, habits, or forces far beyond ourselves. All of the smaller decisions that preceded the first time Kabera raised his weapon and lowered it on the body of a Tutsi man, woman, or child—the decision to report for security patrol, the decision to carry a weapon, the decision to follow the Interahamwe, the decision to comply with orders to "clear the brush"—made it more likely he would become a perpetrator. When the final decision was made, he did not even notice it. Carried along by "the storm," as he put it, he became an avid killer.

Agency and Morality in the Gray Zone

As a machine, genocide compels killing through psychological, social, or physical obligation. Levi's concept of the moral gray zone created by genocide illuminates the ways that individuals made complex and morally ambiguous decisions within rapidly changing assemblages of heterogeneous components. As these assemblages evolved, those entangled in them made different decisions, sometimes decisions that moved them from one category to another, from rescuer to bystander, for instance, or from bystander to perpetrator. Each decision, made in the depths of the gray zone, was founded on moral impossibility.

In some cases, rescue was only possible within the gray zone. Rwandans who hewed a morally correct path and renounced complicity in the genocide often became martyrs, dying alongside those they tried to save. Moral compulsion was the starting point of rescue, but successful rescue required people to make impossible decisions in deeply ambiguous situations. People who succeeded in rescuing others and did not participate directly or indirectly in the genocide also had the courage and determination to continue to make the same choice, over a long period of time, sometimes in the face of direct threat to their own lives, without wavering from their initial decision. Rescuer behavior and acts of rescue that fall in the gray zone are important to understand because they suggest interventions that could stop mass atrocities quickly. To date, UN-led conflict prevention and peacekeeping efforts operate almost solely bilaterally with states and fail to consider civilians as constituencies to be included in early warning systems, at the negotiating table in peace accords, or in peacekeeping interventions. The devastating outcomes of actions by ordinary civilians, like Idi and Kabera, vividly demonstrate the need to include them in policy analyses.

To be clear, I am not asserting that people who participated in the genocide, who were complicit in its production or implementation or who stood by and passively endorsed it, bear no moral responsibility for their actions. My analysis of the assemblages that produced acts of genocide stands apart from, and is in no way meant to contradict, legal or juridical investigations into genocide crimes or assessments of guilt. Critics of actor-network theory accuse it of being amoral because of its premise of ontological equality between all entities in an actor-network (Amsterdamska 1990; Schaffer 1991). This critique is valid for at least two reasons. First, actor-network theory sets aside questions related to intentionality, autonomy, and responsibility (Latour 2005, 247). It acknowledges that human actors may possess these things, but it does not concern itself with them, because "moral choice and the political sphere are not subject solely to the rational restraints of logic, the disciplinary logic of norms, or potential legal sanction" (Sayes 2014, 139). Second, actor-network theory ignores "the question of responsibility—of which individuals and groups should be held accountable for our moral and political associations" (140). My use of actor-network theory here is not meant to absolve human actors of their moral, political, or legal responsibility. Instead, I intend to illuminate the many ways that human actors and their actions escape rationality, logical norms, and legal sanction, particularly in the exceptional circumstances created by the gray zone of genocide.

3

MUSLIM EXCEPTIONALISM AND GENOCIDE

> **Nta muryango utagira ikigoryi.**
> **(Every family has its idiot.)**
>
> —Rwandan proverb, stated by Ibrahim, a Muslim rescuer (BIR22)

In Biryogo, a tightly packed neighborhood near the downtown business district of Rwanda's capital city, Kigali, Interahamwe militiamen took to the streets shortly after sunrise on April 7, 1994. They initially targeted opposition party leaders and Tutsi families whose sons had fled the country to join the RPF, looting businesses owned by Tutsi or opposition party members and harassing anyone who dared circulate in the streets (Des Forges 1999, 209–10). They quickly moved on to killing any Tutsi they encountered (BIR01, BIR02, BIR04, BIR07, BIR11, BIR12, BIR20, BIR24, BIR25).

In a 2013 interview, Imam Abdul Karim described what happened that day.[1] In 1994, he was twenty-three years old and home for the Ramadan break from his studies at a university in Egypt. He recounted:

> On April 7, we awoke in the early morning hours not knowing what had happened the night before [referring to the downing of the presidential plane]. As we were getting ready to go to Al Ahli Mosque, we heard gunshots coming from all over Kigali. We heard on the radio that President Habyarimana had died. We were used to hearing gunfire in Kigali, but that night it was more intense. We suspected it was a battle between the government forces and RPF troops who were garrisoned in the CND [Conseil National du Développement, the parliament building]. We went to the mosque and prayed. After prayers, some people were afraid to return to their homes and instead came to our house. . . .

> That first day, we hoped that the gunshots and killing would stop after a short period. The RTLM radio [controlled by Hutu extremists] announced that every male adult who remained inside a house would be assumed to be an Inyenzi [RPF rebel]. All adult males had to report [for duty] on the road. We immediately understood that it was a strategy to find their targets. My brother volunteered to go to the road first and came back almost an hour later with alarming news about the killing of our neighbor, a man named Gahima. (BIR01)

This first killing had taken place at the home of Fungaroho, a Muslim Tutsi. About ten Interahamwe militiamen had arrived at Fungaroho's house around 9 a.m. Fungaroho recounted:

> They were a mob. They were shouting and were armed with guns. The children were scared. The compound's steel security gate was locked. We barricaded ourselves in the house. They forced open the steel gate with the help of my friend, a Muslim, who knew the house well—how I eat and where I sleep [he advised the attackers how to break in]. Once inside the compound, they broke all the windows [of the home]. Then they threatened to burn down the house with diesel fuel [with us inside]. I said I would come out so that they would not burn my children alive. I was certain they would kill me. They shot my brother-in-law, and they were about to shoot at me. Then my neighbor [Haruna], who had a rifle, came in through a breech in the rear fence and intervened. He told the guy who was aiming his gun at me, "You kill him, I will kill you." He saved me. The attackers left my house and went next door.
>
> Haruna, who was an older brother of Hassan Ngeze, followed them and protected my house. [Haruna] is a truck driver and currently lives in Tanzania. Here, you see the difference between a real Muslim and the Muslim only in name. Haruna performed many good acts and saved many people. At some point [during the genocide], they wanted to kill him, and he fled to his hometown, Gisenyi. . . . He did not like people to be involved in killing. He hid many people in his house, men and women. (BIR04)

In explaining the heroism of his neighbor Haruna, what Fungaroho left unsaid is just as important as what he said. In saying "you see the difference between a real Muslim and the Muslim only in name," Fungaroho compared Haruna to his younger brother, Hassan Ngeze, a founder of the Hutu extremist political party Coalition for the Defense of the Republic (CDR) and a journalist and editor whose magazine, *Kangura*, spewed anti-Tutsi hatred for years before the genocide. While Haruna rescued his neighbors in Biryogo, Ngeze participated directly in killing Tutsi in Gisenyi.[2] Yet even Ngeze, a virulent trumpet of Hutu ethno-nationalism, helped smuggle dozens of mostly Muslim Tutsi across the border to Congo (GIS01, GIS03). Ngeze's connections to genocidal power gave him greater authority during the genocide and increased his ability to save people.

Fungaroho, a Muslim himself, pinpointed faith as the explanation for these brothers' very different behavior. But as Fidèle, a Tutsi man hidden by his Muslim neighbor, put it, "It's not true to say Muslims didn't kill" (BIR07). In fact, the mob that attacked Fungaroho and killed his brother-in-law Gahima included many Muslim youth from the neighborhood who had joined the CDR militia, the Impuzamugambi.

Fungaroho is not alone in his assertion that depth of religious faith, belief, or practice can explain different behaviors; Pearl Oliner (2004) came to a similar conclusion. Several other researchers have suggested that Rwandan Muslims behaved differently from Rwandans of other religions during the genocide.[3] My research demonstrates that Muslims reacted to genocide much like Rwandans of other faiths. The distinct patterns identified by other researchers are not attributable to religion alone, whether defined as doctrine, shared beliefs, religious leadership, communities of practice, or social ties created through belief and practice. Rather, the actor-networks in which Muslims were enmeshed—including faith, religious doctrine, and religious communities, as well as kin, neighbors, local government officials, political parties, the government, patronage structures, geographical features, and more—molded their agency, sometimes producing resistance and rescue and other times genocidal violence.

The cases of the Muslim neighborhoods in the cities of Gisenyi and Kigali belie the oft-repeated trope that Muslims did not participate in the genocide. Although Muslims in certain rural communities, including Kibagabaga on the outskirts of Kigali, Mugandamure hamlet in southern Rwanda, Nkora in Kayove commune on the shores of Lake Kivu in western Rwanda, and Mabare in eastern Rwanda, organized to help Tutsi or acted collectively to resist the genocide,[4] Muslims in Nyamirambo sector in Kigali and in the Muslim neighborhoods of Gisenyi town reacted differently. In these neighborhoods, widespread violence against Tutsi and anyone else suspected of supporting the RPF began on the morning of April 7, 1994 (Des Forges 1999).[5] Many Muslims in Nyamirambo and Gisenyi sectors organized, led, avidly joined, or reluctantly became ensnared in the genocide.

This chapter discusses the cases of Kigali's well-known Muslim quarter, Nyamirambo sector, and the central business district of Gisenyi town, known as Gisenyi sector. Within Nyamirambo, I focus on Biryogo cell, which was a so-called Swahili camp or segregated Muslim neighborhood during the colonial period. In Gisenyi town, the analysis focuses on the central business district around the main mosque, since the town's Swahili camp was razed when the central business district was laid out, and Muslims moved into neighborhoods throughout the city center.

Muslims in Nyamirambo and Gisenyi town reacted differently from Muslims elsewhere in Rwanda because the residents of these neighborhoods—regardless of religious faith—were enmeshed in actor-networks that primed them for genocide. Actor-network components specific to Muslims and Muslim communities predisposed many Muslims across the country to resist the genocide, but the Muslim neighborhoods of Kigali and Gisenyi were also entangled in economic, social, political, and patronage ties to Hutu extremist politicians and political parties. These actor-networks corresponded to the assemblages that harnessed young Hutu men of all religions to the genocide machine. Combined with deep historical ties between the cities of Kigali and Gisenyi and their Muslim inhabitants, these assemblage components produced genocidal agency in these communities.

The cases of Nyamirambo and Gisenyi illustrate that Rwandan Muslims did not necessarily act exceptionally during the genocide. Rather, Muslims reacted much like Rwandans of other faiths: sometimes resisting, sometimes trying to save people, and sometimes joining. Muslims, just like other Rwandans, were entangled in actor-networks that reached beyond religious beliefs and communities to encompass many other factors. Commerce, Islam, and urbanization, which were inextricably linked throughout the country's history, produced components in the actor-networks that shaped the genocide's geography. In Nyamirambo and Gisenyi, particular local histories of settlement, colonial apartheid policies, urbanization, postindependence politics, and network relations tied to business, trade, and politics enmeshed Muslims more densely in the assemblages that produced acts of genocide than was the case for Muslims in many other communities.

Exploring the differences between Muslim communities in Nyamirambo and Gisenyi and those in other parts of Rwanda allows us to revisit several theories about religious minorities and rescue in genocide. In Holocaust and comparative genocide studies, the general consensus is that "local religious minorities are more likely than their majority counterparts to protect victims of mass persecution" (Braun 2019, 6). In addition, individual members of religious minorities are understood to be more likely to engage in rescue than others. For example, Protestant minorities affiliated with the Calvinist Reform Church rescued thousands of Jews in occupied France and the Netherlands during the Holocaust (Cabanel 2011). During the Armenian genocide under the Ottoman Empire, the tiny Sinjar Yezidi minority in Kurdistan rescued several thousand Armenian

Christians (Ternon 2011). Recently, Robert Braun (2019) sought to isolate the specific factors that encourage rescuer behavior in religious minority communities. Based on studies of minority Catholic communities in Belgium and the Netherlands during the Holocaust, Braun concluded that "leaders of religious minorities . . . [are] more likely to empathize with those targeted by violent purification campaigns" (2019, 6).

However, this empirical rule only partially fits the case of Muslims during the Rwandan genocide, because many other confounding factors produced genocidal violence, resistance, or rescuer behavior. In 1994, Muslims constituted a tiny religious minority in Rwanda, accounting for only 1.2 percent of the population nationwide, while Catholics made up 62.6 percent and other Christians 27.2 percent (Republic of Rwanda 1994, 127). Even in the cities of Kigali and Gisenyi, Muslims were a small religious minority, making up less than 10 percent of the population. But, as the evidence from Nyamirambo and Gisenyi demonstrates, other factors can outweigh the influence of religious minority status. Indeed, elsewhere in Rwanda, majority Muslim communities surrounded by majority Catholic and Christian communities resisted the genocide, protected Tutsi, and engaged in collective rescue.[6] In short, religion may matter but not necessarily in the ways prior social theory suggests.

Muslim Exceptionalism and the Genocide

This book, and the broader research project on which it is based, emerged out of my own curiosity about a trope often heard in Rwanda about the 1994 genocide: Muslims in Rwanda participated in killing less frequently than members of other communities of faith, especially Catholics. French scholar Gérard Prunier summarized the narrative underlying this theme: "Being Muslim is not simply a choice dictated by religion; it is a global identity choice. [Rwandan] Muslims are often socially marginal people, and this reinforces a strong sense of community identification that supersedes ethnic tags, something the majority Christians have not been able to achieve" (1997, 253). Prunier suggests that the social, political, and economic marginalization of Muslims in Rwandan society reinforced the fundamental concept of a unified, global Muslim community (*ummah*) and thus overrode the alliances and divisions that produced racial violence in Rwanda. My research reveals a much more complicated picture, one in which Islam and the historical marginalization of Rwandan Muslims inclined some Muslims and Muslim communities to resist and engage in collective rescue efforts, while others were drawn into genocide by their integration into patronage networks that connected politicians, businessmen, and military officers.

The mythico-historical fact of Muslim resistance to the genocide is prevalent in both Rwandan and international narratives about the 1994 genocide.[7] During fieldwork I conducted in the late 1990s, Rwandans frequently stated that Muslims resisted genocide and offered protection to Tutsi. Leaders in the post-genocide government reinforced these ideas by appointing Muslims to the cabinet and making Eid al-Fitr and Eid al-Adha national holidays, to "thank" the Muslim community, as many Rwandans explained to me at that time. Many Rwandans recounted the story of Sula (Zula) Karuhimbi, a poor Muslim woman and traditional healer who sheltered dozens of Tutsi of all ages in her tiny compound.[8] At the Gisozi Genocide Memorial Centre in Kigali, several Muslim names appeared among the "heroes" recognized in an exhibit about people who helped save Tutsi.[9] International media also took up this message. The US media often portrayed Rwandan Catholics and Christians as particularly murderous and Muslims as not.[10] These positive portrayals have tended to "ascribe a degree of exceptionalism" to Rwandan Muslims, echoing Benjamin Soares and Filippo Osella's (2009) characterization of anthropological studies of Islam.

Muslims were different in one critical way. Muslim religious leaders, unlike their counterparts in other faiths, spoke out publicly against political polarization, racism, and violence in the early 1990s and against genocidal violence in 1994. In March 1992, the Association des Musulmans du Rwanda (AMUR) and its elected leader, the mufti of Rwanda Sheikh Ahmad Mugwiza, issued an official statement on political parties.[11] The message stated that AMUR was apolitical and forbade its representatives at the commune level or higher from holding leadership positions in political parties. It clarified that Muslims could "join the party of their choice, as long as their partisanship [did] not interfere with their faith." Furthermore, it expressed support for the ongoing peace negotiations between the Rwandan government and the RPF and asked everyone involved in the negotiations "to be willing to sacrifice some of their parties' demands so that they can quickly establish a transitional government that suits everybody's needs because that will strengthen the unity of all Rwandans." The statement ended with a clear directive to Muslims and a plea to all Rwandans:

> AMUR takes this opportunity to remind everyone that each and every Rwandan has a right to life. That no one must be a victim of their race [*ubwoko*] or because they come from a certain region. No race is above the other, as the God Lord says in the Qur'an, chapter 49, verse 13, "O mankind, We have created you from a male and a female, and made you into races and tribes, so that you may identify one another. Surely the noblest of you, in Allah's sight, is the one who is most pious of you. Surely Allah is All-Knowing, All-Aware."[12]

By invoking the Qur'an, the statement reminded Muslims that their faith prohibited them from discriminating against their fellow Rwandans, whether they were Muslim or not. In the months and years following this official statement, imams frequently repeated this verse and preached about the issues addressed in the official statement. During interviews I conducted in 2011, 2013, and 2014, many Muslims recited this Qur'anic verse to explain why they helped people during the genocide.

This official statement constitutes a significant factor that distinguished Muslims from Rwandans of other religious faiths: Muslims who regularly prayed at the mosques had a clear statement of Islam's teachings on the matter when genocidal violence began in April 1994. Many Christians, in contrast, were left to divine the morality of the situation on their own. Catholic priests and pastors in other Christian churches failed to speak out clearly and with unity on these issues.

In the early 1990s, most Christian clergy did not preach on topics related to politics, deeming them outside their purview. In the days after the downing of President Habyarimana's plane, the Catholic bishops issued several statements promising "support to the new government" while denouncing "troublemakers" and asking the security forces "to protect everyone, regardless of ethnic group, party, or region" (Des Forges 1999, 245). The Catholic bishops' endorsement of the new government "left the way clear for officials, politicians, and propagandists to assert that the slaughter actually met with God's favor" (246). The Anglican archbishop and national leaders of other Protestant churches issued statements "urging an end to the war, massacres and assassinations," but they did not take a clear stand against genocide (245). In the absence of direct guidance from religious leaders, many Christians accepted government officials' assertions that they were participating in a morally justified war, not a genocide (Straus 2015, 307–9). By contrast, the country's Muslims—at least those who prayed regularly in the mosques—had received two years of direct, clear messaging condemning political extremism, racism, and violence targeting people because of their race or political party.

In the terms of actor-network theory, this difference in religious ideology and teaching constituted distinct components in the actor-networks of Muslims and Christians; those different components interacted in complex and often unexpected ways with other components. Some Muslims were motivated by the messages they received at the mosque; others participated avidly in the genocide or eventually became involved despite the teachings of the imams, activated by social and patronage ties to influential people who became enmeshed in the Hutu Power movement. Whether perpetrators were somehow less devout than those who resisted or rescued, or whether the tug of other elements in individual actor-networks was simply stronger than the pull of faith, the influence of Muslim teachings in the choices of any individual or group must be considered in the context of the complete set of actor-networks in play.

Muslim Social Identities in Rwanda

Muslim social identity was an important component of the actor-networks present during the genocide. Muslims' distinct social identities in Rwanda arose from a deep historical trajectory linked directly to European colonialism, even though the colonial state marginalized Muslims physically, socially, and politically. European colonialism, its administrative policies, and its attitudes toward Islam constructed Rwandan Muslims as an internal, non-Rwandan Other. In fact, for much of the twentieth century, Rwandan Muslims were referred to as "Swahili" (*abaswahili*, literally "Swahili people"). Swahili generally refers to a distinct ethnic group on the east coast in Kenya and Tanzania whose members speak the Swahili language and practice Islam; while many people in East Africa speak Swahili, they are not ethnically Swahili. In Rwanda, however, "Swahili" referred to African Muslims from various ethnic groups, including Rwandans, and distinguished them from Muslims of Omani, Arab, or Indian origin. In Rwandan social discourse, the term was often charged with negative connotations. As José Kagabo (1988) described it, "In the Rwandan context, . . . being Swahili is an existential fact that refers to both a culture and a social status, that is to say belonging to a sociocultural and religious minority in a country where the influence of the Christian church is very great and the majority of the population is Catholic" (12).

The origins of this social construction of Muslims as an internal Other date to the arrival of Islam in the country in the late nineteenth century. The ancient kingdom of Rwanda vigorously resisted penetration by outsiders; as a result, Islam and Christianity both arrived in the country in the late nineteenth century, around the same time as European colonialism.[13] Although the European colonizers sought to limit the influence of Islam, their colonial projects relied on the labor and trade routes that had been established by Arab, Swahili, and other African Muslim merchants. Throughout the nineteenth century, long before the arrival of Europeans, these merchants had created trade routes dotted with outposts from the East African coast inland all the way to Lake Tanganyika (Sirven 1984, 262–67). These outposts grew into economic centers and became sites of Islamic conversion, thanks to the ties forged between traders and the local population (Kagabo 1988, 60–84). At the time, the mwami Mutara III Rwogera of Rwanda exercised sovereignty over a much smaller region than the modern nation-state of Rwanda. Arab and Swahili merchants established a network of markets on the periphery of the kingdom, into what is today southwestern Rwanda, from the shores of Lake Tanganyika (Sirven 1984, 267–69). Their goods, including woven silk and cotton fabrics, beads, and other items, reached into Rwanda via trade conducted through intermediaries in exchange for animal skins and ivory.

When German colonizers arrived in 1895, Swahili and Arab merchants and the culture and goods they brought with them had already influenced people in the region. Perhaps more importantly, those merchants stood ready to launch new trading outposts, which could be provisioned through well-established trade routes to the coast, wherever the Germans established military or administrative posts. Under the influence of the strongly anti-Islamic stance of the White Fathers Catholic missionary society, the Germans were generally hostile to Islam (Kagabo 1988, 18). However, because of Rwanda's relative remoteness, German settlers did not flock to the region as they had to Germany's other African colonies, such as German Southwest Africa (today Namibia). The Germans thus relied heavily on Arab, Omani, and East African traders, almost all of whom were Muslim, to supply German colonial administrators and their staff with imported goods and to export ivory, rubber, and animal skins to the coast (Nigmann [1911] 2005, 2–28). Islam arrived in central Rwanda in 1908, along with the soldiers, porters, and merchants accompanying Dr. Richard Kandt, the newly appointed German Resident of Rwanda, as he picked an uninhabited hill for the site of the new colonial capital, Kigali. Prior to the arrival of the German colonizers, no direct Swahili or Arab influence had reached this region of central Rwanda (Sirven 1984, 288). Mwami Rutarindwa had fought vigorously against allowing foreigners of any origin into his sovereign territories (Des Forges 2011, 15–17). The Nyiginya dynasty's resistance to outsiders crumbled in the face of German colonizers and their superior weapons.

German, and then Belgian, colonial policy in Rwanda sought to preserve the country's indigenous political system as a way of reducing the costs of establishing "effective occupation" over the territory, as required in the Berlin Conference agreements of 1884–1885 (Des Forges 1999, 34; Herbst 2014, 71–72). The colonizers left the mwami and chiefs sovereign over the indigenous population and created a parallel system of governance for colonial subjects and foreigners. As part of these dual systems of sovereignty, European colonizers pursued a policy of apartheid in urban spaces. Europeans and "people of other races" resided in different neighborhoods, first by edict and later by law (Sirven 1984, 155). The colonial authorities restricted the movement of non-European people. Africans who worked in European neighborhoods, including household workers, were required to leave those neighborhoods before curfew each night (157).

Rwandans were prohibited from spending more than three days in a town or village if they did not have a residential permit issued by the Belgian Resident (160–61). Although their mobility was limited in urban spaces, many Rwandans enjoyed greater freedom of movement in rural spaces, where the mwami's customary authority remained sovereign.

The nonindigenous African population, including Muslim Africans from East Africa and others who ran businesses or worked for Europeans, faced restrictions on both their residences and their movements. They were required to live in so-called Swahili camps from very early in the colonial period. Unlike indigenous Rwandans, who could move freely in rural spaces, Muslims faced restrictions on their movements anywhere outside the Swahili camps because they were not considered subjects of the mwami or of customary law.

These colonial projects of separation and differentiation had long-term effects on postcolonial and contemporary social relations in Rwanda. Aboubakar, a Rwandan scholar and lifelong Muslim resident of Nyamirambo, described the Swahili camps and their lingering effect on Rwanda's urban landscapes:

> From 1913 to 1960, Islam was a scorned religion without any legal status in the country. Even administratively speaking, Muslims were kept separate. They were placed in what used to be called "Swahili camps." . . . These settlements were difficult to enter or to leave. That's why you find a heavy concentration of Muslims in Biryogo. It was a camp, which was separately administered under the colonial administration, not under customary administration. Muslims had their own chief who dealt directly with the colonists, while other Rwandans had their customary administration: the mwami, the chief, the deputy chief, and their agents. It was the mwami who dealt with the colonial administration. . . . Muslims, on the other hand, belonged to the whites. They were the colonizers' people. They had their own administration, their own court, . . . which was under the Belgian administration [not the customary administration]. (NAT01)

Muslims remained separately administered and physically separated until independence.

Colonial apartheid and the durable impact of Swahili camps on the topography of certain towns and settlements contributed to the actor-networks that produced particular actions and behaviors during the genocide. This administrative and physical separation reinforced the notion of Rwandan Muslims as non-Rwandan and Other. As Aboubakar explained, Muslims "could practice their religion inside the camp, but they were not allowed to preach Islam outside it. With that marginalization, Muslims had no contact with the Rwandan people.

Anyone who converted to Islam was run out of their family and their home. They would go live with the 'Swahili'" (NAT01).

Colonial policies regarding education further contributed to the social and economic marginalization of Muslims. German and then Belgian colonizers left education in the hands of Christian missionaries, especially the Catholics. The first schools built by Catholic missionaries in Rwanda under the German colonizers were intended to educate "the sons of noblemen, especially chiefs"—thus, primarily Tutsi noblemen—for service in the colonial administration (Sirven 1984, 286). Muslims were formally excluded from these schools because of their religion and social status, as merchants, tradesmen, and workers. The exclusion of Muslims from the education system continued in the postindependence period. After independence, the Catholic Church remained influential in Rwanda, and its many missionary orders continued to run the majority of schools, especially secondary schools, up until the twenty-first century (Carney 2016). The Anglican and Seventh-day Adventist churches founded schools, as well. When the Muslim community sought to create educational establishments, Christian churches often lobbied the government to thwart such efforts (KIG05).[14]

Under the Second Republic (1972–1994), the government mandated universal primary education and created national testing for admission to secondary schools. As a result, large numbers of Muslim children attended school for the first time. However, almost all state-supported secondary schools were run by Christian institutions, and some Muslim parents feared their children would convert to Christianity if they studied in Christian schools. As a result, they discouraged their children from continuing their studies beyond primary school. Furthermore, students with Muslim names often found their names mysteriously removed from secondary school rosters at some point between the Ministry of Education's publication of the lists of test scores and school placements and the final enrollment rosters at Christian schools. Some Muslims changed their names to Christian ones so they could continue studying (BIR15).

In a 2011 interview, Imam Hussein, a regional representative of AMUR, summed up this history: "Muslims never had a chance to go to school because of politics. . . . From that time of colonists, up to the First Republic, the only Muslims who were able to study are the ones who had the means to change their names to a non-Muslim one. It continued in the same way during the Second Republic, but it wasn't as obvious. Muslims were still treated poorly during Habyarimana's time" (GIS01). As a result, few Muslims achieved much formal education beyond primary school, unless they found the means to continue their studies abroad (Kagabo 1988, 218; Kasule 1982, 41).[15] This history and social identity were components of the complex networks of relations that shaped the variety of behaviors and actions Muslims performed during the genocide.

Another significant component in the assemblages of many Muslims was the distinctive pattern of conversion and intermarriage among Muslims that emerged throughout Islam's history in Rwanda. Because the first Muslims in Rwanda came to do business, not to proselytize (Trimingham 1964, 12), the first conversions to Islam occurred within homes or businesses as a result of interaction between Muslim employers and local employees, who were most often male (GIS01). Rwandans who sought work with Arab and Swahili merchants were often of low socioeconomic status and thus more likely to be Hutu or Twa than Tutsi (Kagabo 1988, 60–84). Over time, these employees often adopted their employers' language, culture and, ultimately, their religion. Thus, Islam was almost exclusively a religion practiced in cities, towns, and commercial centers and not in rural areas.[16]

Marriage became another engine of conversion in the early colonial period. Noblemen and chiefs, most of whom were Tutsi, sought to build alliances with Arab and Swahili merchants through marriage. The nobles saw strategic opportunity in these relationships because these merchants appeared to understand the European colonizers' ways. Thus, noblemen sought to marry their daughters to Muslim merchants to gain privileged access to Europeans. These wives converted to the religion of their new husbands: Islam. According to Rwandan social logic, non-Rwandan Muslim Africans had lower social status than nobles, and thus Rwandans assigned them to the category Hutu.[17] Thus, these early marital arrangements established a pattern of (Hutu) Muslim men marrying Tutsi wives that continued throughout the twentieth century. As a result, by 1994, the family histories of many Rwandan Muslims included generations of intermarriage between foreigners, Hutu men, and Tutsi women. These multiracial families encountered unique pressures during the genocide, which simultaneously pushed them to rescue people and to become entangled in genocide crimes, ranging from participating in security patrols to killing.

The colonial apartheid system, Muslims' residence in cities and towns and exclusion from agricultural production, and Catholic hostility to Islam all contributed to the social, economic, and political marginalization of Muslims. The anti-Muslim teachings of the Catholic Church and Catholic schools caused Rwandan Muslims to be poorly perceived by their compatriots. Common epithets for Rwandan Muslims included "liar, trickster, thief, dirty, bawdy, crude, indiscreet, [and] ignorant" (Kagabo 1988, 225). In the popular imagination, Muslims came to be perceived in much the same way as the marginalized Twa, equally reviled by Hutu and Tutsi (Kagabo 1988, 45). Non-Muslim Rwandans tolerated Muslims and traded with them, but they rarely established deep social ties marked by gift giving and reciprocity, hallmarks of durable social relationships in the Rwandan worldview, as documented by Danielle de Lame (2004, 2005).[18]

Negative perceptions of Rwandan Muslims continued in the postcolonial period, under both the First (1961–1973) and Second (1973–1994) Republics. Rwandan Muslims continued to be perceived by their fellow Rwandans as foreigners, live separate social lives from the non-Muslim majority, and suffer economic and political marginalization. This long history of marginalization, along with the distinct language and cultural habits of Rwandan Muslims and the Islamic teaching that believers are unified in their faith (Qur'an 49:13), meant that Rwandan Muslims not only constituted a religious minority everywhere in Rwanda; Muslims also inhabited a racial gray zone, existing outside or across the racial categories of Hutu, Tutsi, and Twa. Their dual status, as simultaneously an internal Other and racially ambiguous, made them vulnerable to particular kinds of conflicting pressures during the genocide, which simultaneously presented opportunities for Muslims to engage in acts of rescue and pressured them to engage in acts of genocide—just like other Rwandans.

Primed for Genocide: Kigali and Gisenyi

Many factors fed into the actor-networks that primed residents of Kigali and Gisenyi for genocide. These two cities—the largest in Rwanda in 1994—had been central hubs for business and commerce since their founding in the early colonial period. Under the Second Republic, the cities grew in importance because President Habyarimana hailed from Gisenyi prefecture and governed from Kigali. Habyarimana's extensive use of patronage to ensure loyalty tied people in both cities to the MRND political party, the government, and the military.

Patronage ties to Habyarimana, key members of his inner circle, and the MRND were indispensable in many facets of political, social, and economic life. For the vast majority of ordinary Rwandans, who became members of the MRND party at birth, MRND membership meant nothing beyond citizenship. Active engagement with the party apparatus was necessary, however, for anyone who had political ambitions, worked as a civil servant, or served in local government. In urban areas, state and party patronage played a larger role in daily life: "A person who was in MRND would get things; the one who wanted a driving license would get [it] easily" (BIR20). As a result, more people in the cities, especially men, were involved in the party. MRND (or later CDR) patronage was particularly important for businessmen. As Robert, a government employee who lived in Gisenyi, described, "Let's just say that back then, in order to get a loan, security—the MRND, which was Habyarimana's party and this area [Gisenyi] was his birthplace—let's say that to get all that, you needed to belong to that party" (GIS44). Not only Habyarimana, but also his wife and her brothers, and a web of people linked by bloodlines and intermarriage, originated from Gisenyi prefecture. In the years leading up to the genocide, this web of people around the president and first lady became "a parallel network of power within the army, the party, and the administration" (Guichaoua 2015b, 49). This network laid the groundwork of Hutu ethnonationalism that arose in the early 1990s and then fueled the genocide.

In the wake of political liberalization in 1990, Gisenyi and Kigali became strongholds for the MRND and the CDR parties. Gisenyi town became the center of Hutu extremist politics when Joseph Nzirorera, who came from Gisenyi, founded the CDR party. The CDR also had strong ties to Biryogo The national president of the CDR's Impuzamugambi youth wing cum militia lived there and recruited members from among the domestic workers, day laborers, and renters who lived in Biryogo and the larger neighborhood of Nyamirambo. Hassan Ngeze also recruited CDR and Impuzamugambi members in Biryogo, Nyamirambo, and Gisenyi. Local chapters of the Interahamwe and Impuzamugambi in Kigali and Gisenyi recruited large numbers of young men from these neighborhoods into their ranks between 1992 and 1994. This web of influential people at the highest levels of official and unofficial power in the country, as well as their economic, social, and kinship ties to these neighborhoods, comprised assemblage components that predisposed Hutu men in them to genocidal action in the wake of President Habyarimana's assassination.

The compulsion to express party allegiance was another actor-network component that set the stage for genocide, particularly in Gisenyi and Biryogo. Rwandans were, in theory, free to join whatever party they wished. However, that choice was largely illusory: "Everyone needed to register with a political party. You had to show your political party membership. You know, they even introduced [membership] cards. It started at low levels [of government administration], in the cell. Even if you asked me which membership card I owned, I would tell you! It said MRND. MRND was the party with the most members. . . . You needed a membership card and a party where you paid membership dues whether you agreed with it or not. It was a requirement" (GIS61). The MRND and CDR both used coercion to recruit members. Furthermore, party membership conferred significant patronage benefits at the local, regional, and national levels; resisting membership, for many, was economically untenable.

Another factor in the assemblages in Biryogo and Gisenyi that primed these cities for genocide was the heavy presence of the Interahamwe and Impuzamugambi. These youth wings engaged in violent attacks against Tutsi civilians and political opposition members in the years leading up to, and continuing after, the Arusha Peace Accords in August 1993. "Between 1992 and 1994 . . . the Interahamwe started killing people in different places. They said that there were enemies who needed to be chased. There were three ethnic groups: Hutu, Tutsi and Twa. That's how we faced problems. They would put Tutsi and the people called 'accomplices' in prison" (BIR18). These killings were organized around the allegation that the RPF had embedded soldiers hiding in the local population, and especially in the leadership structures of other parties. Hutu Power leaders mobilized the militias to defend the nation by finding these "infiltrators" and killing them: "Most of the people who were attacked worked with the MDR, RPF, PSD, PL, and other parties I don't recall. The MRND and the CDR . . . said that RPF accomplices [*ibyitso*] were hiding in other political parties and wanted to overthrow the established Hutu government" (GIS66). "They killed many Tutsi and Hutu who were against MRND" (BIR02). "They killed my paternal cousin, accusing her of supporting RPF because she was a PL party member" (BIR17). As one interviewee said, "Interahamwe and CDR would find reason to kill people" (BIR03). The perpetrators of these attacks were rarely pursued or punished by police or government officials, creating a culture of impunity.

The historic links between Kigali and Gisenyi, the importance of patronage to commerce and politics in both cities, and the influence of the MRND and CDR and their youth wings all prepared these cities for immediate participation in genocidal violence. Those same network components powered the persistent violence of the genocide machine once it was unleashed. Many young, male Muslims in these neighborhoods were predisposed to engage in acts of genocide by their ties to the Hutu Power movement. The deep historical ties between Muslims, commerce, and urban spaces in Gisenyi and Kigali intersected with these patronage ties in insidious ways to incline these communities toward genocidal violence. Finally, the kinship and social ties among Muslims within and between these communities produced countervailing forces during the genocide, pushing some to participate in genocidal violence and others to resist it.

Before colonialism, Rwandans lived in homesteads (*ingo*) scattered over the country's hills. Even the central court was itinerant until the reign of mwami Musinga in the late nineteenth century; it became fixed at Nyanza only in 1899 (Des Forges 2011, n27; Sirven 1984, 44–46, 259). That same year, the German East African Protectorate Force established a military post in Gisenyi, on the edge of the mwami Musinga's formal sovereignty (Nigmann [1911] 2005, 225; Sirven 1984, 271). The Protectorate Force was made up mostly of Muslim Africans from regions already subjugated to German colonialism.

A second colonial outpost followed in 1908, when Richard Kandt established a new city, Kigali, as the capital of the new colonial province. Kandt selected an uninhabited hill, Nyarugenge, situated at the approximate geographic center of the new colonial province (Sirven 1984, 285). He chose the hill because it was far from the mwami and his central court in Nyanza. The site was also well positioned to serve the commercial purposes of exporting goods from the interior of central Africa to ports on the Indian Ocean coast of German East Africa.

These two colonial outposts at Gisenyi and Kigali grew into Rwanda's first towns. By 1910, Gisenyi was the largest town in Rwanda, home to twelve Europeans and more than seven hundred Africans, most of whom were not Rwandan (Sirven 1984, 296). In 1911, Kigali's population was half this size (287). In both towns, most African residents were Muslim, and the majority of businesses were owned by Muslims, including Arabs, "Asians," and Africans (287).

The commercial trade linking Gisenyi to the eastern Democratic Republic of Congo, Gisenyi to Kigali, and Kigali to East Africa flowed through the Swahili camps of these German colonial outposts (see map 4). After the towns were founded, Arab, Indian, and African traders quickly established trading posts (266, 271). By 1912, the flow of trade between Gisenyi and Kigali was the largest in the German colony of Ruanda-Urundi, having exceeded that between Bujumburu and Ujiji, which had been established nearly thirty years earlier (300). Rwanda's trade continued to flow along the same routes between Gisenyi and Kigali through the First and Second Republics, even as the country's towns remained small. As urbanization began to intensify in the late 1970s, when Rwanda was among the most underurbanized countries in the world, Kigali and Gisenyi were its largest cities (6).

Increasing urbanization and the end of colonial apartheid brought greater diversity—including religious diversity—to the cities. However, the dense commercial, social, and kin ties between Muslims in Biryogo and Gisenyi town persisted. Many Muslim businessmen maintained households and families in both cities. Most Muslims in these cities had relatives in the other city, where they could expect to be lodged if they visited. For example, Hassan Ngeze regularly moved back and forth between Biryogo and Gisenyi to conduct business and attend meetings in Kigali. Although his primary residence was in Gisenyi, Ngeze had kin connections to Biryogo, and his ally and political collaborator Stanislas Simbizi, the national president of the Impuzamugambi, lived in Biryogo. For most Muslims, these connections went beyond affinities based in Islam or connections through the religious teachings of mosques organized under AMUR. Rather, these ties were supported and reinforced by a number of factors. Islamic rules about lending and finances reinforced economic ties within Muslim social networks and between these two cities. Rwandan cultural practices around kinship obligations within lineages further reinforced social and economic ties.

The pressures created by this proliferation of social, economic, kinship, and political ties often conflicted with religious imperatives. Muslims in Biryogo and Gisenyi often asserted that devout Muslims refused to join political parties in the 1990s because the mufti and AMUR, as well as the imams in the mosques, advised them not to. Omar Rugagi (BIR08) recounted that imams in Biryogo preached against getting involved in politics: "In the mosques, they banned people from joining political parties" (BIR08). But many Muslims did join the parties, whether for patronage benefits, out of fear, or for other reasons.

Patronage was vital for urban Muslims. The vast majority of Rwandan Muslims earned a living through trade, commerce, transportation, or urban occupations such as tanner, cobbler, worker, driver, mechanic, or shop owner. The deep roots of Muslim trade, and Muslims' historical exclusion from formal education, predisposed them to these occupations. The need for patronage to succeed in business made Muslims vulnerable to the intense pressure to engage with the MRND party.

Further, most government officials in the cities' Muslim neighborhoods were Muslim, and their positions required them to be active MRND—or, later, CDR—members. As a Muslim Gisenyi resident explained, "At that time, there was MRND, there was PL, there was PDI. These were the most notable parties here. I was in MRND. It was the strongest party. Everyone was a member" (GIS23). Most Muslims we interviewed in Gisenyi—whether genocide survivor, confessed perpetrator, community member, or rescuer—reported having membership in the MRND in 1994 (GIS23, GIS24, GIS27, GIS37, GIS46, GIS61). They joined because "only the MRND was powerful," as Nasser (GIS27), a Hutu Muslim man who saved many people during the genocide, put it. MRND membership made life easier. It opened access to patronage and offered suspected RPF sympathizers—especially Tutsi—protection from harassment. "Everybody had to be MRND. Even me, because I had to save myself even if it was not in my heart. We all did that," one Tutsi genocide survivor explained (GIS37). "A few people, like Tutsi, for example, joined PL. Other people joined PSD, PDI . . . but if you expressed ideas that went against that powerful party [the MRND], you would have problems" (GIS01).

Local officials in Biryogo and Gisenyi remained in the MRND party or switched to the CDR, depending on their patronage ties and their perception of the benefits of membership in one party or the other. The ties created by party membership and its associated patronage networks had real effects on the course of the genocide. As Lee Ann Fujii (2008, 2011) and Omar McDoom (2013, 2014) demonstrated, social ties to Hutu Power political party members increased the likelihood that an ordinary Rwandan would join in the genocide. Ordinary Rwandans were primed for anti-Tutsi violence and compliance with state directives in the years leading up to the genocide (Thomson 2019).

Patronage ties to and membership in the MRND and CDR had significant consequences for Muslim youth in Biryogo and Gisenyi, who became prime targets for recruitment to the Interahamwe and Impuzamugambi. In other Muslim enclaves, Muslim youth largely avoided party membership, supported PL or the moderate wings of the PSD or MDR, or secretly supported the RPF. In Biryogo and Gisenyi, however, Muslim youth joined the Interahamwe and Impuzamugambi because their fathers, uncles, and brothers were party members or to access patronage networks.

Recruitment for the militias was persistent and ever present. A genocide survivor, Fidèle, who was protected by a Muslim neighbor in Biryogo, explained, "A man called Mugenzi who worked at PetroRwanda recruited heavily for the Interahamwe [here in Biryogyo]. He wanted everyone to join. The strength of the Interahamwe here was a factor that pushed Muslims to participate here. The CDR was as virulent as MRND [in Biryogo]" (BIR07). Militia members rapidly became militarized, as described by a genocide survivor from Gisenyi, Eugénie (GIS56): "The MRND party had a militia called Interahamwe. Mostly young people who worked hard to earn their living—day laborers [*abakarani ngufu*], who carried luggage or loaded and unloaded trucks. Interahamwe recruitment occurred between 1990 and 1993. Then they went for training. When they returned, they had military boots and uniforms with ranks. After their return, they had a much more elevated status than before and started creating trouble, such as closing roads with barriers. They [the Interahamwe and CDR] were powerful [*Bari bafite imbaraga*]. It was terrifying" (GIS56).

Both parties used the threat of physical violence to reinforce their political power; the youth militias were tools to proliferate that violence. "Those parties taught their partisans killing" (GIS29). "Especially the CDR people were very wicked. Young Muslims mixed in the CDRs and other parties" (GIS59). Khalid, a Muslim genocide perpetrator from Biryogo, explained, "It's the CDR which caused many problems. I was a member of MRND, but I was not an Interahamwe. There was a card like this one which you could buy at five thousand francs. The one who had that card was an important Interahamwe. The others were simple members. I didn't have time to go and train with them" (BIR27). Although Khalid claimed to not be in the Interahamwe, he confessed to killing and looting during the genocide and served time in prison for his crimes.

Thus, young Muslims' participation in the militias primed Biryogo and Gisenyi for genocide, by perpetuating early violence that desensitized people and by creating ties that pulled people toward participating. Once the genocide began, Muslim militia members participated; their presence increased the likelihood that other young Muslims would be conscripted into the killing squads. The dominance of the MRND and CDR meant that Muslim local officials faced extreme pressure to comply with genocidal orders issued by party leaders or government officials above them in the hierarchy. The historic links between Muslim communities in Gisenyi and Biryogo produced dynamic, dialectical ideology and material relationships between genocide leaders, such as Stanislas Simbizi and Hassan Ngeze, which further reinforced the priming for violence. The history of commerce and the importance of patronage links to state power laid the foundation for the assemblages that produced genocidal agency in these neighbors among Muslims and non-Muslims alike. All these factors prepared Muslim men in Biryogo and Gisenyi, especially young men, for genocide.

The Genocide Timeline in Nyamirambo and Gisenyi

The start date and duration of genocidal violence in a given locality were other components in the actor-networks that produced acts of genocide and rescue. The growing body of comparative genocide studies research on rescue has demonstrated the impact of genocide policies and time frames on rescue (Sémelin, Andrieu, and Gensburger 2008, 2011). In particular, the contours of genocide policy, the resistance of government officials, and the varied time frames—of days, weeks, or months—during which officials succeed in delaying the onslaught interact in complex ways to make rescue more or less likely to succeed (Andrieu 2011, 499). "Each genocide takes place in a particular time frame. . . . Each of these situations spawned a different type of rescue," as Claire Andrieu puts it (2011, 503). In Rwanda, "due to the swiftness with which it was performed, killing onsite or in roundup points close to the victims' homes left little leeway for rescuers to act" (503). My research confirms this finding and also demonstrates that the duration of widespread genocidal violence in a locality significantly impacted rescue. Where anti-Tutsi violence was delayed and continued for the shortest time, Rwandans' initial offering of help to their Tutsi kin, neighbors, friends, and coworkers was more likely to end in successful rescue. Where the violence began immediately and continued the longest, rescuers who persisted were more likely to be caught and face serious consequences, even death. Thus, many people abandoned their rescue efforts in the face of increasing risk. In these places, rescue efforts often failed.

Genocidal violence broke out in Biryogo and Gisenyi a few hours after daybreak on April 7 and continued for months—at least 88 days in Biryogo and 101 days in Gisenyi, until the cities were finally liberated by the RPF. In Gisenyi town, widespread genocidal violence began in the early morning hours of April 7, 1994. A network of military, police, government leaders, and MRND and CDR party leaders organized and initiated it. On the night of April 6, within hours of the presidential plane's downing, Colonel Anatole Nsengiyumva, a Rwandan military officer; the chief of police in Gisenyi town; and the *conseiller* of Gisenyi sector, which covered the central business district and residential areas along the lakeshore and near the center of Gisenyi town, called a meeting with local leaders of the Interahamwe and Impuzamugambi.[19] They ordered them to mobilize their members, who had been sent for paramilitary training in 1993, and to mount a counteroffensive against the RPF. Colonel Nsengiyumva told them "the enemy is none other than Tutsi."[20] He instructed them to set up a roadblock in front of La Corniche, a hotel and bar located two blocks from the Grand Barrière on the main road, to stop any Tutsi trying to cross the border. Interahamwe and Impuzamugambi followed through on these directives. Roving bands of militiamen began attacking people around the city shortly after daylight on April 7. Mohamad (GIS28), a Hutu Muslim who saved dozens of people during the genocide and who has been formally recognized as an *indakemwa* (morally beyond reproach) by Ibuka, described what happened:

> The seventh [April 1994], that's when we heard that the plane of Habyarimana had been shot down. After that, everyone got scared. It was shot down the night before, I think, but most people heard about it around 7 or 8 a.m. [on April 7]. By 10 a.m., some of us could still move around, but we did so in fear. We started hearing, "This person, a Tutsi, is dead." When you listened to the radio, you would only hear about the killings. There was a unit of Interahamwe here [in Gisenyi] that seized the town immediately. It didn't look like there was any [government] authority. They took guns, machetes, clubs . . . and started hunting for everyone called "Tutsi." (GIS28)

Likewise in Biryogo cell and Nyamirambo sector in Kigali, the Interahamwe and Impuzamugambi militias immediately took control of the streets and began killing Tutsi civilians and opposition party members. The genocide in Nyamirambo continued until RPF troops liberated Kigali on July 4, 1994. On April 12, the RPF's Third Battalion took Mount Rebero, on the western outskirts of Kigali (Nsengiyumva 2020). Although the RPF position was only two and a half miles from Biryogo, navigating through endless roadblocks inside the city limits and then crossing the battle lines between the government troops and the RPF rebels was nearly impossible. Biryogo was among the last parts of the city to be liberated, despite its proximity to this key RPF position (Rutayisire 2014).

The genocide continued in Gisenyi until July 17, 1994, when the advancing RPF troops liberated the city, driving the remnants of the Rwandan army and the interim government into exile. In mid-June, the interim government relocated to Gisenyi, where it continued to pursue war against the RPF rebels and genocide against Tutsi civilians (Des Forges 1999, 302). French soldiers with the peacekeeping operation known as Opération Turquoise arrived in Gisenyi on

June 24. Despite their orders to establish safe zones and protect civilians, the French troops "did not interfere with the militias" or their roadblocks in Gisenyi, and they failed to stop the killings of Tutsi civilians (675). The genocide in Gisenyi continued until RPF troops routed the remaining government soldiers from the city.

In both Gisenyi and Nyamirambo, the immediate start of killings and the long duration of anti-Tutsi violence significantly increased the pressures on all residents, including Muslims, to join in the violence, stop resisting the genocide, or stop assisting or protecting Tutsi. In both cities, Interahamwe and Impuzamugambi members responded immediately to Hutu extremist media calls for revenge against RPF supporters and the RPF, whom the Hutu extremists blamed for the president's assassination. In several communities across the country—including Biryogo and Gisenyi—they began attacking and killing Tutsi and opposition party members in the early morning hours of April 7, just hours after the president's plane went down.

In Biryogo cell, Stanislas Simbizi mobilized Impuzamugambi militiamen at his home on the morning of April 7 (BIR05). He riled up the assembled members with speeches condemning the RPF for the assassination of President Habyarimana, and he told them that RPF infiltrators were hiding in Biryogo, an idea repeated by the Hutu extremist media in the weeks leading up to the genocide.[21] The militiamen then poured out of Simbizi's home and went looking for people to kill (BIR05). Among the first households they attacked was Fungaroho's (BIR04), where they killed his brother-in-law Gahima and pillaged Fungaroho's house before Haruna intervened. The Impuzamugambi from Biryogo attacked and killed many Tutsi and political opposition members that day. At the west end of Biryogo, on Nyamirambo's main road, government soldiers erected roadblocks next to the El Fath mosque, commonly referred to as the ONATRACOM mosque because of its location across the street from the National Office of Public Transportation (Office Nationale de Transport en Commun) headquarters. Militia members assisted the soldiers in manning the roadblock throughout the genocide. Basir (BIR05) was head of the cell council in Biryogo in 1994 and an MRND member:

> On April 8, 1994, Stanley Simbizi and his men put the roadblocks in front of a cabaret owned by a CDR member named Wellars Gakeri close to the [Biryogo] mosque. Gakeri was not a Muslim. [Simbizi] placed the roadblock at that place because he was collaborating with the cabaret owner. . . . They stopped everyone and asked them for the ID. . . . [The militiamen] were well organized. They manned the roadblocks with twenty people at a time, armed with Kalashnikov rifles and other

> firearms. There were four roadblocks in the [Biryogo] mosque area: one at the curve in the entry [road], one at the market, one near the mosque, and one at the [dirt] road that leads to the asphalt [road]. (BIR05)

As a result of the roadblocks and heavy presence of military and militias, the imams closed these mosques throughout the genocide.

Very few mosques in Rwanda became massacre sites during the genocide, unlike the multitudes of churches in which massacres took place. Although this fact has often been cited as evidence of Muslim resistance to genocide, my research discovered a quite different explanation. AMUR and its imams closed most mosques and told Muslims to pray in their homes. Catholic clergy and other Christian pastors, for their part, allowed people to seek shelter in churches. Very few mosques became massacre sites because people were not allowed to congregate there during the genocide.

A notable exception was the Islamic Cultural Center at the western end of Nyamirambo, which was commonly known as the Qaddafi mosque because it had been built with financing from the Libyan government. The Islamic Cultural Center's large compound housed the largest mosque in Rwanda and several other multistory buildings with offices and classrooms. Hundreds of Tutsi and political opposition members, both Muslim and non-Muslim, sought refuge there, and during the genocide's first week, Rwandan soldiers and militiamen killed dozens of them (Des Forges 1999, 210). In the following months, militiamen repeatedly tried to enter the mosque grounds, and they killed several people who had sought refuge there. Yet they never succeeded in launching a large enough attack to overrun the security patrols organized by those inside the Islamic Cultural Center grounds.

An important actor-network component that shaped the reactions of ordinary people was the stance of local government officials, especially at the commune, sector, and cell levels, as well as other influential elites. In Nyamirambo and Gisenyi sectors, these officials were often Muslim, but they also were members of the MRND or CDR and had patronage ties to Hutu extremists. As a result, many Muslim local government officials organized, facilitated, or participated in the killing in these places. On April 13, once genocide became a nationwide policy, these local officials organized systematic searches for and killings of Tutsi and opposition members.

One of the most prominent local officials who organized killings in Nyamirambo and Biryogo was Amri Karekezi, who was the *conseiller* of Nyamirambo sector.[22] "Amri Karekezi, a Muslim, had real power. He was a big boss. He also controlled Majengo mosque," which was in Nyamirambo across the main road from Biryogo cell, as Fungaroho explained (BIR04). Fungaroho emphasized that Karekezi was not only a government leader but also a leader in the Muslim community, given stature by his unofficial influence in the Majengo mosque. Many interviewees stated explicitly that "Amri Karekezi . . . organized the killing" (BIR07).[23]

Karekezi's attitudes and actions contributed to the genocide's moral gray zone in Nyamirambo, especially for the Muslim government officials below him in the chain of command. As government officials, their duty was to implement policy and orders from above. But obeying those orders during the genocide risked committing grave sins, engaging in activities AMUR and the mufti had explicitly warned them not to. While their positions as party members and government officials created pressure for them to participate in the genocide, their political power and influence also made it possible for them to engage in rescue.

Basir was one such official; he was head of the cell council in Biryogo and an MRND member in 1994. He reported directly to Amri Karekezi. Basir was a Hutu Muslim who had a Tutsi wife. Basir protected several Tutsi neighbors, friends, and affinal kin for two and a half months, from April 8 until he fled with his family to Goma on June 22. Although Basir served ten years in prison for genocide crimes, in our interview he carefully sidestepped questions related to his participation in the genocide. When asked whether he had received administrative orders from Karekezi or others to organize killings, he responded, "I did not receive any orders that led to killings." Given others' testimony about Karekezi and his prosecution for genocide crimes, Basir's statement is difficult to believe.

Regardless of his complicity, Basir's ability to please his immediate superior, his own authority as a local official, and his social ties to CDR and MRND leaders increased his ability to protect his Tutsi wife and kin, neighbors, and friends. Fidèle (BIR07), one of the people Basir protected, could not say whether Basir had participated in the genocide because he himself was in hiding, but he could explain the complex relationship between perpetration and rescue generated by actor-networks during the genocide: "Not everyone in MRND was absolutely involved in killing because those who rescued more people were mostly MRND members. They had the power to do it. In my opinion, the roots of genocide lie in the large preceding campaign of hate against Tutsi. Yet not all Hutu were killers" (BIR07). And not all MRND leaders or government officials joined in the genocide. For example, Hashimu (GIS42), a Muslim and genocide survivor, was a sector-level official in Gisenyi and MRND party member in 1994. He did not participate in the genocide. He and his family were protected by other Muslims in his neighborhood.

Many Muslims in Nyamirambo did kill and became notorious killers during the genocide. Fidéle listed some of them: "Karim was a mechanic, and an MRND member. He liked to fight. He was an infamous killer of Biryogo. They called him Karim-the-Machine. He fled the country. Karim's boss was Amri Karekezi, who was also the *conseiller* of the sector. . . . In all villages [*imidugudu*, the lowest administrative unit in Rwanda in the 2000s] where killings occurred, there were leaders who organized the killings. Ndagije slaughtered people, Majariwa, Karim. Amri, Kitonsa, and Majariwa were among the organizers" (BIR07). All the genocide organizers Fidèle mentioned are Muslim, at least in name. We did not gather data on whether they prayed regularly or observed Islam's other obligations. In particular, Fidèle's denunciation of a prominent AMUR leader captures the interlaced assemblages that generated ambivalent agency: "Sheikh Tembo was an AMUR representative at the time of the genocide. He was involved in looting property; he had an MRND flag on his property" (BIR07). In identifying Sheikh Tembo as complicit, Fidèle mobilizes the sheikh's MRND flag as evidence of the sheikh's problematic position in the interwoven assemblages within which many Muslims existed: fidelity to AMUR's official statement against political partisanship and loyalty to the MRND party and its patronage.

As in Biryogo, the majority of local government officials in Gisenyi's Muslim neighborhoods were both Muslim and members of either the MRND or the CDR. They faced similar moral conundrums as officials in Biryogo, and many of them organized, facilitated, or participated in the genocide. Their decisions and actions often determined the hyperlocal shape of violence during the genocide. In some places, they organized to protect the small geographic areas under their jurisdiction while encouraging young men from their neighborhoods to join the militias in committing acts of genocidal violence elsewhere.

Many Muslim youth in both Biryogo and Gisenyi participated in the genocide, as members of the militia or in other ways. All over Rwanda, young Hutu men who had not joined the Interahamwe or Impuzamugambi before the genocide faced pressure to join in "security efforts," as local officials referred to the roadblocks, search parties, and killing squads (Fujii 2008, 2009, 2011). Antoine, a Hutu and Seventh-day Adventist from Gisenyi who was a nineteen-year-old student in 1994, explained, "Some [Interahamwe] were trying to force me to join them, saying that I was a traitor [*icyitso*, meaning RPF supporter]. They came every day yelling for me. Sometimes they knocked at our door. Family members would ask them to leave, telling them that I was still a child who would not know what to do [if I went with them]" (GIS11). Ali, a Muslim who was twenty years old at the time of the genocide, was subjected to intense pressure to participate in the killings. Militia members and Hutu Power supporters harassed him because he had a Hutu father and a Tutsi mother. His "mixed" parentage made them suspicious that he supported the RPF. As Ali explained,

> During that period of the genocide, there were people who were called *ibyimanyi* [half-breeds], people who were born from a Hutu and a Tutsi.

> At that time ibyimanyi [were] harassed. When they [security patrols] went on their rounds through the neighborhoods, they would look for people who didn't share their ideologies, and they would say that ibyimanyi could not be completely trusted.
>
> They would wake me up at night and say that there was no way they would spend the night keeping watch while a Tutsi slept. They would say that I was my mother's—and not my father's—son. They would say, "Look how tall he is! Look at his nose." And examine all the physical characteristics they used to check, and see me as . . . I don't know. They viewed me as someone who didn't share their ideologies. They would then make me get up and make rounds, saying that there was no way they were going to watch over me as I was sleeping. (GIS66)

Resisting this mobilization required savvy tactics of passive resistance or patronage ties to powerful people with influence over the Interahamwe. Sometimes parents' statements could save a young man from security duty, as in the case of Antoine, whose parents were both well-respected Hutu professionals. In other cases, patronage ties could facilitate the intervention of a government official or an MRND or CDR party leader to excuse someone from security duty. The assemblages in which individuals and families were embedded made these options more or less possible.

As a Muslim, an ibyimanyi, and son of an ordinary merchant, Ali did not have the social capital or patronage ties to refuse for long. Ali's father eventually advised him to go on security patrols as a way to protect himself and the family. Ali clarified:

> [My father] told me, "Get up and be with them, do not kill if they do. Just go with them and sit where they sit, to show them that you're with them. If they keep on saying that you are an accomplice, they will kill you as well." So . . . I would go with them. . . . Sometimes, when they came to wake me up, [my father] would give them money they called "flashlight fees" to buy batteries for the flashlights they would use at night. That was money they bought alcohol with. . . . He would give them like five thousand francs to buy me a night off. (GIS66)

His father's advice and his own decision to participate plunged Ali into the genocide's moral gray zone. Ali and his family understood his actions at the time as a way to protect himself and his Tutsi kin by giving the appearance of compliance with orders from local officials. By joining the militiamen, Ali stopped their threats against his family. After the genocide, however, Ali was imprisoned and prosecuted for genocide crimes. He was found guilty and served over ten years in prison. During an interview in 2011, Ali insisted he had not participated in the genocide. Instead, he claimed he had confessed to reduce his sentence and leave prison (GIS02). At a second interview in 2013, he acknowledged his complicity in the genocide. He explained that his presence at the roadblocks had given the Interahamwe the strength to kill people, even if he did not kill anyone himself (GIS66). Although Ali did not kill, many other Hutu men who reported for duty on the roadblocks without imagining they might kill someone did in fact kill; participating in the roadblocks certainly increased the odds a person would eventually kill.

The immediate start of genocidal violence in Biryogo and Gisenyi on the morning of April 7, 1994, generated increased pressure on ordinary people—both Christian and Muslim—to join in the genocidal project. Local government officials who were Muslim and members of the MRND and had Tutsi kin found themselves engulfed by the gray zone of genocide and its choiceless choices. Muslims who joined in acts of genocide—even minimal ones like standing at a roadblock—helped propel the genocide machine and entangled more Muslims in genocidal violence.

Community Cohesion, Muslim Solidarity, and Rescue

The events in Nyamirambo and Gisenyi demonstrate that Muslim exceptionalism during the 1994 genocide of Tutsi is a myth. The actor-networks that tied these Muslim communities into Hutu extremist political parties, their militias, and related political and commercial patronage networks produced genocidal agency. The density of social network ties to perpetrators increased the probability that ordinary Rwandans joined in genocide crimes (Fujii 2008, 2011; McDoom 2013, 2014); this same principle holds for Rwandan Muslims. Yet religion did make a difference in at least two significant ways. First, Muslim genocide perpetrators generally avoided killing other Muslims. Second, some Muslims in these neighborhoods, especially those descended directly from inhabitants of the Swahili camps during colonialism, organized efforts to resist the genocide and protect Tutsi. These efforts were shaped by the unique history of Islam in the region, social cohesion among Muslims, and Muslim reactions during earlier episodes of anti-Tutsi violence. In Gisenyi, rescue efforts often entailed smuggling people across the border to safety in the Congo, as discussed in chapter 5. In Nyamirambo, these efforts emerged around the geographic heart of the former Swahili camp in Biryogo cell and involved hiding and protecting Tutsi kin, neighbors, and even strangers who fled from other neighborhoods and sought safety.

In Nyamirambo and Gisenyi, Muslims with membership in the MRND, CDR, the Hutu Power movement, or their militias joined in the genocidal project quickly and with little or no coercion. In this regard, they reacted in the same way as Catholics, other Christians, and Rwandans of other faiths who had joined the Hutu Power movement in the months before the genocide. Yet their religious background still affected Muslims' actions. Eugénie (GIS56),[24] a Catholic woman from Gisenyi, explained,

> During this period between 1990 and 1994, not a single Muslim youth dared kill another Muslim. What they did instead was point out people to be killed so that others who were not Muslim could kill them. Young Muslims did, however, kill other people who were not Muslim.
>
> I can give an example of a Muslim I know. He was my neighbor, and the head of the Interahamwe [in the area]. I asked him, "Why are you killing people?" He replied, "I have done what I can do. I am the leader of this youth. I told them that we should not kill others, but there are some who listened and others who did not listen. I enrolled in the Interahamwe to protect my family, not to kill people." (GIS56)

Claims similar to those of Eugénie's neighbor—that he joined the Interahamwe to protect his family—are frequently mobilized by genocide perpetrators in Rwanda. They cast their participation in the violence as an act of self-defense to protect themselves, their kin, their communities, or the nation. It is difficult to assess the degree to which these statements reflect perpetrators' encounters with active threats at the time (as recounted by Ali); their general perception of the situation at the time and their acceptance of government, media, and leaders' portrayals of the RPF and their danger; or retroactive explanations that ease their conscience by minimizing their guilt. Given that Eugénie's neighbor was not only a member but also an Interahamwe leader, it is doubtful that self-protection was his only motive in joining and rising to a leadership position.

As Eugénie points out, Muslim militiamen avoided participating directly in the murder of other Muslims, for example by giving information to other militiamen so they could kill Tutsi Muslims. These actions may have resulted from the Islamic directive against murdering innocent believers, social cohesion within the Muslim community, or a general reluctance to murder kin, friends, or neighbors. Which motivations prevailed is impossible to determine; the Muslim perpetrators we interviewed avoided speaking directly about their genocide crimes. Likely, all three factors—and possibly others—influenced their actions. Social cohesion was almost certainly a factor, perhaps one with a stronger influence than religious belief or Islamic teachings. As in many minority communities, social cohesion among Rwanda's Muslims was strong, a result of the program of segregation that began in the colonial era. Segregation marginalized Muslims from the rest of Rwandan society, but it also generated a great deal of social cohesion among Muslims living in Swahili camps, as Aboubakar described: "During Ramadan, no one would take the evening meal alone, we took it in the community. The neighborhood was divided in many zones. The people from each zone would meet at a certain place to break the fast. All the food was taken there, and they would eat together" (NAT01B). This history of social cohesion laid the groundwork for acts of rescue in the neighborhood during the genocide. In many communities in Rwanda, social cohesion prevented local people from killing their neighbors, friends, or coworkers; genocidal violence in these places was initiated by outsiders (as related in detail in the next chapter). Indeed, this was the case in Biryogo: the most prominent Muslim genocide perpetrators there—including Ninja, Karim-the-Machine, and others—grew up elsewhere.

While some Muslim militiamen participated indirectly in killing Muslims, others tried to protect some people. Eugénie explained how Muslim Impuzamugambi members protected her mother throughout the genocide. Eugénie was born to a Hutu father and a Tutsi mother. She was raised in a Muslim household because her mother was Muslim, but her father, whom she never knew, was Catholic. Eugénie had gravitated to the Catholic Church as an adolescent. During the genocide, Muslim militiamen protected her mother:

> Many Muslims live in this neighborhood. Since my mother was Muslim, and those Muslim youths were CDR members, which was the main party [responsible for the genocide], they protected my mother. . . . A special characteristic of this Muslim youth is that the majority were born of Tutsi Muslim mothers. That is to say, their uncles were Tutsi. Because of these reasons, most of these youth hid or protected a lot of people. Because they had a lot of family members [who needed protection], and they really had the strength to do it. Generally speaking, authorities representing CDR in the government were not Muslims, but this did not impede these young people's ability to protect their families. My mother, being Tutsi Muslim, she remained here at home all day, weaving grass mats. (GIS56)

Eugénie explicitly identified the kin relations among Muslims and the historic pattern of intermarriage as key to shaping young Muslim men's actions during the genocide. These youth found themselves embedded in actor-networks in which kin relations pulled them to engage in rescuer behavior while their party membership, social ties to age mates engaged in genocide, and patronage ties to CDR politicians simultaneously pushed them to engage in perpetrator behavior and amplified their ability to rescue.

Biryogo's history as a Swahili camp under European colonialism produced unique opportunities for rescue. Biryogo had remained legally segregated until independence. Islamic customs and practices dominated in the neighborhood: no alcohol or pigs were allowed inside (NAT01B). After independence, Biryogo quickly diversified. The neighborhood's close access to Kigali's central business district made it highly desirable to civil servants, businessmen, and workers. By 1988, Muslims were "no longer the majority in Biryogo" (Kagabo 1988, 213).[25] Aboubakar explained that Muslims began to lose their solidarity and social cohesion "when they started meeting non-Muslims" and adopted more individualized lifestyles (NAT01B):

> It was after independence. I think that it was in the year 1960 [that the changes began to happen and continued] up until 1990. After 1990, it was completely finished. Everyone by himself. Before it was people together: poor, rich, all at the same table. On the day of Eid [al-Fitr], all the doors were open. From the mosque, you would stop at each house. Everyone would tell you, "Come in, come in." For now, all the doors are closed. . . .
>
> Up until 1959, 1960, only Muslims lived in Biryogo. You could not live in that neighborhood if you were not Muslim. In the end, after the independence, non-Muslims came to live in the neighborhood, and Muslims began to leave. Look at myself, I came from [Biryogo], but now I live here [another neighborhood in Nyamirambo]. The contact with my world, my community is less frequent.

Although the social cohesion among Muslims in Biryogo began to disintegrate during the postcolonial period, the neighborhood's historic core near the Biryogo market and Biryogo mosque still housed numerous families directly descended from the Swahili camp's original inhabitants. In addition, the area still retained many of the topographical features of the Swahili camp, such as hidden passageways between compounds and limited entry roads into the neighborhood. During the genocide, these original families organized to protect people targeted by the militias. Their actions were shaped by the particular discursive traditions of Islam in Rwanda, by the long history of Muslim and, more recently, Tutsi exclusion, and by the distinct spatial arrangement of the neighborhood resulting from the colonial apartheid system.

The unique history of the neighborhood had created special bonds among residents that ensured no one from those few blocks of homes near the market was killed until June 24, when the battle lines between government troops and the RPF rebels drew near, reaching Nyamirambo. Ibrahim (BIR22), a Muslim man in his fifties, organized resistance to the genocide with his neighbors. Ibrahim explained their efforts: "We got together and decided that they [the Interahamwe] would not get anyone from us. . . . We shared the same convictions. We felt that if anyone attacked one of us, it was like we were all attacked. We had to be unified so that if anyone came in [to the neighborhood], they would find us all together. We said, "If they try to kill us, they will have to kill us all." When asked how they organized to defend themselves, Ibraham said, "We didn't do anything in particular; we only had that mind-set, and it guided us, that's all. For us, if anything should happen to you, it's like it happens to me, too. If someone comes to your home, I feel like he will come to mine as well. We felt like we were one person. They can come to attack with a gun, let's say, and if they shot someone, we could catch them too. We didn't even have any weapons. They were just words, to make an effort and to be brave" (BIR22). Social cohesion and unity of intention, built up over generations, provided resolve against the genocide. Ibrahim's Muslim neighbors occupied the same plots their grandparents or great-grandparents had occupied when Biryogo was a Swahili camp. Muslim residents had kinship ties and friendships based on generations of reciprocity, gift exchange, and marriage. They remained close-knit even as Catholic and Christian families moved into the neighborhood. As Ibrahim explained it, no one made a formal decision to take defensive actions; those actions simply happened organically, emerging from their resolution to resist.

Working from that resolve, Ibrahim and his neighbors organized roadblocks to keep Interahamwe and Impuzamugambi militiamen out of the streets near the market. Unlike the roadblock next to the ONATRACOM mosque, which was organized by Stanislas Simbizi and manned by the Impuzamugambi, the roadblocks near the historic Swahili camp were used to protect people. Khassim explained the residents' efforts: "It was a general obligation to establish roadblocks, and Muslims complied with the rule. As Muslims, we knew each other at our local roadblocks. We discussed it together, and we decided not to participate in the killing" (BIR03).

Biryogo residents not only protected people from the neighborhood; they also saved Tutsi who fled from other parts of the city to the neighborhood. People sought refuge in Biryogo because Muslims there had offered protection during earlier episodes of anti-Tutsi violence. In 1959, for example, the Swahili camp in Biryogo had sheltered Tutsi and supporters of the Union nationale rwandaise (UNAR, Rwandan National Union) monarchist party (NAT01). Aboubakar described this earlier violence: "What some call the Hutu Revolution came in 1959—the Hutu revolution against Tutsi. Hutu started hunting and killing Tutsi. Tutsi fled. Some emigrated. Others sought refuge in the Swahili camps. All Tutsi who were targeted were supposed to be relocated in [internally displaced person] camps in Nyamata and in Rukumbeli. . . . Tutsi concentration camps.

Those people who didn't want to go [to these camps] sought refuge with the Muslims . . . in the Swahili camps. Hutu chased Tutsi from their homes, and then they were received by Muslims" (NAT01). Many Tutsi and political opposition members remembered the Swahili camps—as well as churches and schools—as places of refuge that had not been violated during earlier episodes of violence. Although some Christians feared Muslims, those with family memories of the safety they had found among them fled toward Biryogo and other historically Muslim neighborhoods, like Mugandamure near Nyanza (see next chapter).

The historic pattern of intermarriage between Hutu Muslim men and Tutsi women further contributed to social cohesion and resistance to genocide in Biryogo. Khassim explained, "Many of us had Tutsi wives. For those of us with a Tutsi wife, killing a neighbor's wife or children would be like killing our own family. We did not have any formal discussions to keep us away from the killing. Everyone was guided by faith and our commitment not to kill" (BIR03). Because Muslims who did join in the genocide avoided attacking Muslim households, Hutu Muslim men in Biryogo were generally able to protect their wives and children as well as other family members. As a result, Tutsi family members from other neighborhoods in Kigali or parts of the country fled to them for protection. Omar protected his wife's nephews and a niece, a journalist whom the Hutu Power extremists vigorously sought to kill.

> OMAR: Each one of them came [here] when they were able to, because they thought, "It's our aunt's place, I will go there!" . . .
>
> Q: How did they manage to reach your house?
>
> OMAR: It was like committing suicide! There was luck involved, you could pass one roadblock, then avoid another. It was really just luck.
>
> Q: Weren't you afraid of being killed by the Interahamwe because you were hiding them at your house?
>
> OMAR: Of course, we were afraid. But we all knew we could die at any moment. The streets were full of dead bodies. . . .
>
> Q: Did you ever consider asking them to leave your house so that you could save your wife?
>
> OMAR: That would have been impossible. When the first two arrive[d], I asked my wife incredulously, "How were they able to come?" And she replied, "They've come. We shall die together, if necessary." (BIR23)

Even though Omar discounts the courage of their decision and portrays it as the only possible avenue, the choice was still a risky one. Although many Muslim residents of Biryogo testified that the killings in the neighborhood were less fierce than elsewhere in the city, the cooperation of the *conseiller* Amri Karekezi with the Hutu Power extremists made it hard to protect people. In June, militiamen came with direct orders from the *conseiller* to arrest a Tutsi family. "We were not strong enough to resist them," Ibrahim remembered (BIR22). The militiamen took the husband, wife, and child away and killed them. They were the only people from Ibrahim's cell who died in the genocide.

Even though Amri Karekezi allowed Muslim families to protect other Muslims—perhaps recognizing religion's influence on his actions—the *conseiller* actively withheld protection from Christian Tutsi. Sylvestre, who was Catholic and Tutsi, fled with his mother, Scholastique, and siblings, who were also Tutsi and Catholic, to hide at his Muslim uncle's home. On April 7, 1994, an Interahamwe attack squad arrived at their house, and the militiamen "ordered" the family "to come out" (BIR18). Scholastique, Sylvestre, and the other children stood in front of their home as the Interahamwe deliberated among themselves.

> SYLVESTRE: They told us they would return at 2 p.m. Then they left. Our neighbor, a woman, came and said, "Be careful. They are coming back to kill you." At 2 p.m., the attack squad returned. We ran away without the slightest idea where we were going. We thought of Khassim [their Muslim uncle]. . . .
>
> Q: What happened when you reached Khassim's house?
>
> SYLVESTRE: He welcomed us and invited us to stay. We told him what had happened to us. The problem was that the people manning the nearby roadblock had seen us entering Khassim's compound. They called a security meeting and interrogated Khassim about who we were and where we were coming from. (BIR18)

The local security council, which included several Muslim men, insisted that Khassim's guests needed authorization from the *conseiller*, Amri Karekezi, to remain at Khassim's home. Karekezi refused to give it, forcing Khassim to find another hiding place for Sylvestre and his family: "We stayed at Khassim's for three days, then we left. Khassim escorted us to an old man and asked him to keep us. That old man hid us until the end of the war" (BIR18). Sylvestre's mother, Scholastique, later returned to Khassim's home and remained there until the RPF liberated Biryogo. During the day, Khassim helped Scholastique hide in the nearby woods in pits in the ground, which he covered with underbrush. At night she "would go back inside his house. Sometimes Habyarimana's soldiers would come and search the house, but they never found [her] there" (BIR19).

Khassim's actions to protect his Tutsi Catholic sister-in-law and other Tutsi kin—both Muslim and Christian—illustrate that rescue was possible under some conditions. Khassim was an ordinary Muslim man who earned a living as a driver. He was neither wealthy nor powerful. He had never sought political positions nor patronage ties to people who joined the Hutu Power movement. His lack of social ties and reciprocity obligations to powerful patrons gave him more autonomy and the ability to avoid participating in the genocide even in minor ways. For example, he refused to report for security patrols: "Interahamwe members were usually the leaders of the roadblocks. And we were required to participate in security patrols. But I did not go. Many local residents did not go since we were afraid of soldiers passing through the roadblocks. Interahamwe from the neighborhood manned those roadblocks" (BIR03). By refusing to go on security patrols, Khassim further insulated himself from both the pressure and opportunity to participate in the genocide. This choice helped ensure that he did not become ensnared in genocide crimes. At the same time, he was able to protect his sister-in-law and helped save his nieces and nephews, thanks to his solidarity with his Muslim neighbors who were opposed to the killing.

While Khassim rescued Tutsi kin, other Muslims in Biryogo saved neighbors or even strangers. Natalie, a Tutsi Catholic, was in her late forties in 1994. She survived along with her children, thanks to a Muslim family who also saved dozens of others. Early on the morning of April 7, Impuzamugambi militiamen killed Natalie's sisters and their husbands. Natalie's neighbor, who was a militia member, informed her of her sisters' deaths and warned her that she and her children were in danger.

> NATALIE: The Interahamwe who told me about my sisters' death was not a killer. He was just a young man. His father [Karaha] hid us. . . . After [the young man] warned us, I left my house early in the morning. I remember stepping over bodies on the road. I entered Karaha's house from the back courtyard. He let me inside. There were already many other Tutsi hiding in the house. . . . [During the genocide,] Karaha would stand in front of his house and announce, "Nobody shall come here. The people that you are looking for are not here. They fled to other places and might have been killed there."
>
> Q: How did he have this courage in front of Ninja [nickname of a notorious killer and Rwandan Armed Forces soldier who killed scores of people in Biryogo]? Did he have a gun?
>
> NATALIE: Karaha had a son who was in the Presidential Guard. The son told everyone, "If anybody dies here, you will answer to me." . . . Karaha had a sword that he wore [motioning to her waist] all the time. He would tell the Interahamwe, "If you come here, you will see [the consequences]." Even Hassan Ngeze and Ninja, who organized

the attacks, did not dare confront him. That is why the Interahamwe could not go into his house. Even before the genocide, he helped people that the Interahamwe were going to kill.

Q: How many people were hiding, and how did he hide them?

NATALIE: Karaha had two wives and owned two houses. Twenty-five people hid in those two houses, especially under the beds in the bedrooms.

Q: Where did you hide?

NATALIE: I hid in a storage room where they put food and other things for the house.

Q: How long did you stay?

NATALIE: I stayed a month in Karaha's storage room . . . until the end of May. (BIR11)

Although Natalie and her children survived, she never learned the precise fate or burial place of her Tutsi husband, who was working at the airport on the night the president's plane was shot down.

Karaha, his wives, his Interahamwe son, his Presidential Guard son, and other children saved over two dozen people during the genocide. As Natalie explained, Karaha had this power because one of his sons was a Presidential Guard soldier. In addition, another son's membership in the Interahamwe and complicity in the genocide allowed him to warn Natalie, saving her life, and enabled his family to save people. During the genocide, Interahamwe and Impuzamugambi members often had access to the most useful information, and they sometimes used it to help people they knew. Social ties are a key element of the actor-network that shapes agency; in this case, the family's social ties to powerful people in the MRND or CDR political parties, the government, the military, or the police strengthened their ability to save people.

The Difference Religion Can Make

So why did Muslims like Khassim, Ibrahim, and their neighbors resist the genocide and work to save people, while other Muslim men led the death squads or collaborated in the killing? When asked how he and his neighbors had maintained such unity of conviction, Ibrahim explained that their shared faith helped, since the majority of them were Muslim, but he added that the neighborhood Christians also joined them. As he described it, "We were always together. We always talked with each other. We were never divided. When we saw something wrong happening, we asked ourselves, 'What can we do?'" At the core of the action Ibrahim was involved in seems to have been a deep social cohesion, even stronger than religious teaching. Khassim, for his part, explained his family's actions in religious terms: "Our conduct was based on our faith and its teachings of respect for human life. We did not counsel each other. We simply acted from our faith. . . . We did not have any formal discussions to keep us away from the killing. Everyone was guided by faith and our commitment not to kill" (BIR03). That simple conviction, combined with protective social connections, empowered Khassim and his family to rescue, as Sylvestre recognized.

> SYLVESTRE: [Khassim] was not among the people who could have been killed [meaning he was Hutu]. Besides, he was family. Neighbors were afraid of hiding people. In case you hid people and were found, the Interahamwe could kill those people and kill you along with them.
>
> Q: You were not afraid that Khassim might betray you?
>
> SYLVESTRE: No.
>
> Q: Why not?
>
> SYLVESTRE: You cannot know what people think. He was family. We could not have known what he was really thinking; but if he had any thoughts, he would have told us to get out of his house. Given that he did not act in this way, we trusted him. (BIR18)

Scholastique responded similarly. "There was no one else who could have saved us. . . . He held his breath [*Yafunze umwuka*]. Maybe he took it upon himself because I was his mother-in-law. He might have thought, 'If I die, so be it.' In any case, he endured it. He protected me" (BIR19).

Clearly religion, including moral teachings, shared convictions, and social bonds forged through religious practices and shared festival meals, inclined Khassim and Ibrahim to resist the genocide and save Tutsi kin, neighbors, and friends, even in the face of increasing threats. Perhaps more importantly, however, the assemblages of social ties imbricated with their Muslim identities and historically embedded in the geographic space of Biryogo created opportunity and enabled them to enlist others in their efforts.

Elders within Biryogo's Muslim community had lived under colonial apartheid in a legally segregated neighborhood, and many more still lived in the spatially distinct Muslim neighborhoods that continued to exist after the colonial apartheid system was abolished. Thus they understood themselves to be part of a distinct community within Rwanda, set apart from the mainstream. They also understood themselves to be part of the global, imagined Muslim community (*umma*). Both of these understandings governed the actions of individual Muslims in the genocide. As Talal Asad (1986) argued, Islam is best understood as a discursive tradition that connects in different ways "with the formation of moral selves, the manipulation of populations (or resistance to it), and the production of appropriate knowledges" (7). Islam as a discursive tradition has a particular history situated in a political economic context; it has a past, a present, and a future.

In essence, Khassim lived his faith. While all retrospective explanations of action are colored as much by the present as by the past, Khassim's statements about his motivation reflect Asad's explanation of Islamic orthodoxy as residing in the hands of Muslim practitioners. Although many Muslims in Biryogo justified their actions by mobilizing Islamic teachings or verses from the Qur'an, we should heed Asad's locating of Islamic orthodoxy in the hands of Muslim practitioners rather than in the realm of received or proscribed doctrine: "Whenever Muslims have the power to regulate, uphold, require, or adjust correct practices, and to condemn, exclude, undermine, or replace incorrect ones, there is the domain of orthodoxy" (1986, 15–16).

Even among Muslim perpetrators, religion made a difference. While Muslims who joined the Hutu Power movement in the early 1990s attacked anyone they suspected of being Tutsi or RPF supporters, they avoided killing or attacking other Muslims. Either they attempted to protect Muslims, or they participated in attacks on Muslims indirectly. Whether the aversion to attacking Muslims was due to religious beliefs, social proximity within the close-knit Muslim community, or other reasons was not possible for me to determine, because the Muslim perpetrators we interviewed avoided speaking directly about their genocide crimes.

Biryogo and the larger neighborhood of Nyamirambo illustrate the ways in which Rwandan Muslims were similar to other Rwandans in their reactions to the onset of the genocide. Many Muslims in these communities were enmeshed in patronage networks in much the same way many Catholics were. When patrons in these social networks joined the Hutu Power movement in the early 1990s, their clients became more likely to join in the genocidal violence. Thus, Muslims in Biryogo and Gisenyi, who were more likely to have developed patronage connections to the MRND, CDR, or government members, were more likely to participate in the genocide than Muslims in other communities whose members had fewer such ties.

Thus, like predominantly Christian communities, Muslim communities responded in different ways and on different timelines. The components of local assemblages were grounded in different local histories and topographies that emerged during European colonialism and shaped Muslim communities, social identities, and urban space. The evolution of Biryogo and Muslim neighborhoods in Gisenyi during the postindependence period produced dense kin, social, business, and political ties with the Hutu extremists who took control of the government. In the theoretical language of actor-network theory, the assemblages that encompassed Muslims in Gisenyi and Biryogo greatly resembled the assemblages encompassing Catholics, Christians, and Rwandans of other faiths. Muslims in these communities were deeply embedded in the same patronage networks as other Rwandans. The majority of these patronage networks joined the Hutu Power movement in the early 1990s. These social ties made it more likely that Muslims in these neighborhoods would become involved in the genocide. As a result, the reactions of these communities to the onset of racial violence contrast with the reactions of the Muslim communities of Kibagabaga, Mugandamure, and Nkora, which were embedded in distinct assemblages that inclined these communities to resist the genocide, to protect Tutsi, and even to sacrifice their own lives to save others.

In communities where Muslims had fewer patronage and social ties to the Hutu Power movement, religion had a greater impact on Muslims' behavior. The next chapter examines community-level rescue efforts in the Muslim neighborhood in Mugandamure, a hamlet in south-central Rwanda, as well as at two nearby sites where Christians engaged in rescue. The chapter demonstrates that participating in a faith community, whether at a mosque, church, or prayer group, that emphasized prayer and social interaction across racial lines and explicitly addressed the political context leading up to the genocide or described racial discrimination as sinful greatly increased the likelihood that people would oppose the genocide, attempt to rescue people from death, and persist in those choices even when faced with growing danger.

4

RESISTANCE, RESCUE, AND RELIGION

Abel Gihanga and Ezekiel Kambanda saved the Tutsi on Rubona hill. . . . It's the truth from God in heaven. If it hadn't been for them, we would all have perished.

—Faustin (NYA32), a Tutsi genocide survivor

On Rubona hill on the outskirts of Nyanza town in Nyabisindu commune, two men banded together to keep the genocide at bay: Abel Gihanga, a local administrator (*responsable*), and Ezekiel Kambanda, the president of the local government council (*cellule*).[1] Both were Seventh-day Adventists and recognized leaders in their church and in Rubona, where they had grown up. They were Hutu men who had married sisters, Tutsi women from another district in southern Rwanda. Their mutual kinship relations reinforced the ties of friendship and neighborliness among their families and with other people in Rubona.

Abel described the effect of President Habyarimana's assassination on their small community: "The night of Tuesday, April 6, 1994, and the following day hit us like a lightning bolt. It was such a shock. On the morning of April 7, 1994, Tutsi began to come to me seeking refuge. Twelve people came to me in my capacity as the *responsable*" (NYA29). Despite the community's rising fear, its governor and mayor, who opposed the genocide, succeeded in containing anti-Tutsi violence and keeping the genocide at bay for two weeks. Then, on April 21, Nyanza town was suddenly engulfed by the genocide. Ezekiel explained: "We saw the national police going into the neighborhoods and ordering local leaders to erect roadblocks. . . . They told the local leaders that they should use the roadblocks to find their cockroaches and traitors [*inyenzi n'ibyitso byazo*]. They did not explicitly say that they were searching for Tutsi [but everyone understood what they meant]. People started looking for a safe place to hide. Some came to Rubona, but others went to Mugandamure, which was safer" (NYA28). Pauline, a Tutsi resident of Rubona, described what happened next:

> In Rubona, people were good; they helped each other. They even helped people fleeing from other places who were looking for refuge. They showed empathy to those people who needed help. The young men defended the victims. Two elders, named Ezekiel and Abel, played a significant role in unifying young people. These two wise elders counseled the youth not to join in the killing and asked them to protect others. These men were respected in the village because they were our leaders. . . . Both men were Hutu Adventists married to Tutsi women. . . . It was not easy for us to survive, even though we were protected and united, because there was no food, no water. Our life was not easy. But thanks to our two good leaders, we survived. (NYA27)

Faustin, who was in his forties and a member of the Nyanza cell committee, also attributed his survival and the survival of Tutsi in Rubona to Ezekiel and Abel. "Abel refused to give orders to kill people. If he hadn't been there, we would have all been killed, myself included. He was a Christian . . . an Adventist. Nothing [bad] happened where he lives; nothing happened to us, yet we're neighbors. There are no ruins; the attackers only managed to kill one person whom they snatched away. We don't even know where or how he was taken" (NYA32). Ultimately, Ezekiel and Abel mobilized Rubona residents to save the community's Tutsi residents, as well as dozens of others who fled to Rubona seeking refuge.

Pauline did not identify the source of Ezekiel's and Abel's courageous actions. She mentioned the men's marriage ties to Tutsi women as relevant but not as the primary cause of their actions. Faustin mentioned Abel's religious character and later credited Ezekiel's actions to his faith. Yet religion alone cannot explain their courage; many other members of the same Adventist congregation joined in the killing. Furthermore, although Pauline and Faustin attribute the miracle of their survival to Ezekiel and Abel, other factors were also important. As Pauline emphasized, Ezekiel and Abel's leadership was important, but so was the community's social cohesion and unity. Pauline implicitly compared the young men of Rubona "who defended the victims" with those of surrounding neighborhoods who joined the Interahamwe in killing people, destroying property, and looting. She underscored the fact that Ezekiel and Abel's authority derived not only from their official positions in the local government but from their relationship to the community: they "were respected in the village." They were also leaders in their church who could draw on the moral authority of their Adventist religion to guide their actions and unify people of many different faiths in their home community.

The people of Rubona hill were not alone in their efforts. People organized collective rescue efforts and saved hundreds, perhaps more than a thousand, in or near Nyanza town at Rubona hill, the Centre Saint Antoine orphanage, and the hamlet of Mugandamure. The different trajectories of violence and rescue in these three communities reveal the varied nature of genocidal violence at the micro level and the significant consequences of local social histories, relationships, leadership, social cohesion, and decision making in the genocide's gray zone. Widespread killing in the region around Nyanza town did not begin until April 21, 1994, two weeks after anti-Tutsi violence erupted in Kigali, Gisenyi, or Gikongoro prefecture (see maps 1 and 2). This delayed start to the genocide in south-central Rwanda emerged from regional divisions, politics, government leadership decisions, distinct local histories, and multigenerational intermarriage between Hutu and Tutsi in the region (Longman 2009; Wagner 1998). These characteristics predisposed the region around Nyanza to resist the genocide. In other words, distinct actor-networks in south-central Rwanda produced dynamics supporting rescue and resistance more than in other places.

A few pivotal events between April 19 and 21 reconfigured those actor-networks to generate genocidal violence. As a result, massacres engulfed Nyanza. But these regional actor-networks intersected with more local ones to produce unique assemblages. These hyperlocal assemblages produced different outcomes at Mugandamure, Rubona, and the Centre Saint Antoine, which became sites of collective rescue and safe havens for fleeing Tutsi.

These cases illustrate the significance of particular local factors, including leadership, social cohesion around local identities that transcended Hutu-Tutsi distinctions, and topography, in generating genocide resistance, individual acts of rescue, and collective rescue efforts. At each site, rescue efforts were organized by people of different religious faiths: Seventh-day Adventists, Catholics, and Muslims. These cases demonstrate that although religion was not a determining factor in rescue, it still influenced the options available to people and the choices they made. Finally, the events at these sites illuminate the organic nature of decision making in the moral gray zone of genocide, the moral ambiguity of rescue, and the importance of persistence in the face of increasing threats.

First Resistance, then Genocide in Nyanza Town

The delayed start to the genocide in the region around Nyanza both arose from and induced actor-networks distinct from those in other regions, such as Kigali and Gisenyi, where anti-Tutsi violence began on April 7, 1994. Nyanza's history as the seat of the Nyiginya kingdom from the end of the nineteenth century through the colonial period, regional divisions between south-central and northern Rwanda, and the impact of previous waves of anti-Tutsi violence inclined residents native to Nyanza and the region against genocidal violence in 1994. Regional and local leadership fortified this resistance for two weeks.

In the days immediately after President Habyarimana's assassination on April 6, 1994, Butare and Gitarama prefectures remained calm and relatively free of genocidal violence. In Nyanza, the population respected the curfew announced on the national radio. An Italian priest who lived in Nyanza explained the situation:

> When it started in Kigali on the sixth and seventh [of April], here in Nyanza, we didn't feel it. . . . When I talked to the missionaries who had lived in Burundi [during that country's civil war], they were very worried. They said that Rwanda was very dangerous. In February 1992, there had been killings of Tutsi around the country. The extremist propaganda was spreading lies. It was all the work of demons. But I didn't see that among the people of Nyanza. . . .
>
> In the end, no, I didn't feel the imminent catastrophe. I could see that people were very scared after the shooting down of the plane, but here in Nyanza I still did not see genocide. . . . If I can say it, the genocide in Nyanza was imported. It was not internal. The genocide came to Nyanza from elsewhere. (NYA38)[2]

Several factors primed Nyanza to react differently to genocide, forcing the central government to import genocide to south-central Rwanda. Regionalism predisposed many southern Rwandans and native Nyanzans to oppose the genocide in 1994. Opposition to the genocide by provincial, district, and local government officials delayed the onset of genocidal violence and persisted long enough in some places, like Rubona and Mugandamure, to result in successful rescue of thousands of Tutsi lives.

The region's unity and resistance to genocide emerged, in part, from historical divisions between Banyanduga (Nduga people) in south-central Rwanda and Bakiga (Kiga people) in the highlands of northern Rwanda. These distinctions dated to the precolonial period, when Nyanza lay at the heart of the Nyiginya kingdom, and the northern highlands were governed by largely autonomous Hutu chieftancies. These regional distinctions remained significant through the colonial period and increased in importance during the postcolonial period. Rwanda's first president, Grégoire Kayibanda, was from south-central Rwanda. Under his administration, Hutu Banyanduga benefited more from patronage than did Hutu from northern and western Rwanda. This disparity produced grievances among Hutu Bakiga, who backed a coup d'état in 1974 by army general Juvénal Habyarimana, a Hutu from northwestern Rwanda. Hutu from the northern highlands rose to prominence in Habyarimana's administration, while former president Kayibanda and many prominent Banyanduga from his administration died in prison. Throughout Habyarimana's presidency, patronage benefited Hutu Bakiga more than people from other regions, breeding frustration and discontent among Hutu from other regions and Tutsi in general.

This political history underlay many of the political divisions that emerged during the rise of multiparty politics in the early 1990s (Burnet 2012; C. Newbury 1998; Thomson 2018). The MRND and CDR parties, which eventually coalesced into the Hutu Power movement, secured the most ardent support from northerners, especially Hutu, while Rwandans of all races in central and southern Rwanda supported the opposition parties—the MDR, PSD, and PL. In Nyanza, most native residents joined one of these opposition parties. In response to the rise of Hutu ethnonationalism, the MDR and PSD eventually split in 1993 between moderate and Hutu Power factions. Hutu extremist propaganda created a perception of the PL as the internal wing of the RPF, though the PL operated independently. In April 1994, most Nyanza residents remained loyal to the moderate wings of the MDR and PSD and thus resisted calls to anti-Tutsi violence.

The eruption and aftermath of anti-Tutsi violence around Nyanza in 1959 and the early 1960s reduced the importance of Nyanza in the country's structure and created a foundation for patterns of flight and refuge in 1994. Because Nyanza had been the seat of the Nyiginya dynasty throughout the colonial period, its population included many nobles, chiefs, and their extended lineages. The violence in 1959 and the early 1960s targeted members of UNAR, the monarchist party, as well as (Tutsi) nobles and chiefs. Hundreds of Tutsi from Nyanza fled the country, dramatically reducing the town's population. Partly as a result, the new administrative structure imposed on the country after independence relocated most regional government offices from Nyanza to Kigali or Butare. Still, despite the town's decline in population and importance, the many Catholic schools, monasteries, and convents founded in Nyanza during the colonial period continued to thrive and draw new people to the town. Ties between President Habyarimana and the Catholic Church bolstered Nyanza's significance as a town, even though it no longer served a prominent administrative function (Carney 2016). The Habyarimana government filled the parastatal companies based in Nyanza with Hutu functionaries and workers from northern Rwanda, who were loyal members of the MRND or CDR parties. Their presence reduced any lingering influence of monarchists in Nyanza. These outsiders, loyal to the patrons who had secured them work, played a key role in initiating the genocide in Nyanza.

Regional and local government administrators also played a decisive role in delaying the start of the genocide in south-central Rwanda. The governor of Butare prefecture and the mayor of Nyabisindu had opposed the rise of Hutu extremism in the early 1990s, favored centrist politics, and joined opposition parties after political liberalization in 1991. The governor of Butare prefecture, Jean-Baptiste Habyalimana, a Tutsi, was a member of the PL. Jean-Marie Vianney Gisagara, the mayor of Nyabisindu commune, was a Hutu and member of the PSD, but he refused to join the Hutu Power wing of the PSD when it split in 1993 (Des Forges 1999, 496). Mayor Gisagara had grown up on Rubona hill, as a neighbor of Abel and Ezekiel. He was Hutu, but "his mother and uncles were Tutsi" (NYA29). As Abel explained, Gisagara refused racist politics because he "was on both sides, and he got along well with all people" (NYA29).

In the aftermath of the president's assassination, Habyalimana and Gisagara sought to maintain law and order and contain anti-Tutsi violence. On April 7, "orders came from the national police. Mayor Jean-Marie Gisagara, who had a clear perspective of things, called the local leaders to a meeting. He said we should not let our people get involved in the violence that was going on" (NYA29). Mayor Gisagara used the police forces under his command to resist attacks from neighboring Gikongoro prefecture, where the genocide began on April 7 (Des Forges 1999, 467).

Habyalimana and Gisagara continued to oppose the genocide after it became national policy on April 12. At first, the local commander of the national police and most mayors in Butare prefecture worked with Governor Habyalimana to counter violence (Des Forges 1999, 354, 432). In Nyabisindu, the mayor faced many vocal and dangerous opponents—several of the senior military officers stationed in Nyanza were Bakiga from northwestern Rwanda and loyal to General Bagosora, the key military officer behind the genocide—but Gisagara remained steadfast in his opposition (439, 441; NYA29). He arrested former soldiers and other civilians who attacked residents (469).

Then, on April 17, Governor Habyalimana was dismissed from his post, presumably because he had refused to execute the central government's genocidal plan (448). A new governor was sworn in on April 19, marking a dramatic turning point for the region. The interim government turned the ceremony, which was held in Butare town, into a rally to mobilize the region's local officials to carry out genocide in their communities. The country's interim president, interim prime minister, and numerous ministers were all in attendance, which was unusual for the swearing-in of a local government official. The president, prime minister, and minister of family and women's affairs were all from Butare prefecture and had dense social and patronage ties in the region. All the mayors from Butare prefecture also came. The prime minister gave a fiery speech calling for a "final war" and denouncing "those who sympathized with the enemy," meaning those who refused to seek out and kill Tutsi and anyone else who supported the RPF (457–58). The ceremony converted most mayors from protectors into perpetrators. Most returned to their communes and began to order killings, looting, and destruction of property, but not Mayor Gisagara. In fact, during the ceremony, Gisagara attempted to enlist the support of other government officials in his efforts to maintain security in the region, but they all refused (496–97). Mayor Gisagara returned to Nyanza to continue to try to stop anti-Tutsi violence.[3]

The situation in Nyanza town and Nyabisindu commune changed dramatically on the morning of April 21. That morning, a convoy of trucks carrying government soldiers and national police arrived in Nyanza to take control (Des Forges 1999, 497; NYA31, NYA33, NYA29). They started by firing Mayor Gisagara: "Army commander Barahira called a meeting of [local government officials] to provide instructions for killing Tutsi. Since the mayor [Gisagara] was against killing he was replaced by a *conseiller* [sector-level leader], nicknamed Masango (NYA29, government official in 1994). The police and soldiers then fanned out into all sectors of Nyabisindu commune (497). Pauline recounted:

> Workers from the government forge, the dairy, and Electrogaz came to my village with RAF [Rwandan Armed Forces] soldiers. They said that my village was a cockroaches' nest [*indiri y'inyenzi*]. They searched everywhere and brought us together in one place. They asked for our identity cards. Then they started talking about some of us, saying that we weren't Hutu or that we had changed our race from Tutsi to Hutu [*kwihutura*]. They killed a woman and her three children. She wasn't from Rubona. She had come seeking refuge because all her in-laws and her own family had already been killed elsewhere. (NYA27)

Once outside forces initiated the genocide, Nyanza residents who hailed from northern Rwanda—Gisenyi, Ruhengeri, and Byumba—or from Kigali immediately joined in the killing. These outsiders worked in the Nyabisindu Dairy, the public utilities, and other parastatal enterprises in Nyanza and had secured their positions through patronage networks tied to the MRND, CDR, and Hutu Power movement. Thus the cultural logics of patronage fueled the initial genocidal violence in Nyanza.

The "armed soldiers . . . started killing to set an example to others to kill" (NYA33). "They had lists they had prepared; it was prepared work" (NYA38).[4] The new authorities "told Hutu they needed to exterminate all Tutsi and seize their property" (NYA31). Most sector- and cell-level officials—people who had been protecting Tutsi in their communities for weeks under Gisagara's leadership—transformed from protectors to killers overnight, aligning themselves with the national policy of genocide.

As the trucks arrived, Mayor Gisagara and communal police officers loyal to him fled to a friend's home in a rural part of Nyabisindu commune (Des Forges 1999, 497). Security forces searched systematically to locate them. "At some point the Presidential Guard soldiers and Interahamwe came together" (NYA31) and found Gisagara, arrested him, and brought him back to Nyanza town. "They tied him to the back of a Toyota Hilux pickup truck. They dragged [him] behind it and paraded through all of Nyanza town. Then they killed him by amputating parts of his body one by one" (NYA29, government official in 1994). This lynching drew on the symbolic power of Rwandan cultural traditions of mob justice. It vividly demonstrated to Nyanza's residents the interim government's force and illustrated the fate awaiting those who continued to resist the national policy.

Nyanza natives perceived this first day of genocide—the arrival of soldiers and police in trucks on April 21—as an invasion. At first, they remained unified in face of the assault, but their resolve crumbled with the killing of Gisagara. The violent public spectacle crushed local resistance. It inflamed the passions of militiamen already on site and encouraged Nyanza residents who wanted to join in the violence but had been deterred by the mayor's opposition and the threat of arrest. These people responded with immediate and ghastly violence, joining the soldiers and Interahamwe from outside town in killing Tutsi families and opposition political party members who refused to participate in the killing.

Finally, the spectacle terrorized Tutsi and those opposed to the genocide, causing many of them to give up hope or lose the will to try to save themselves or others. Many people who had been hiding Tutsi asked the refugees to find other places to hide. Some turned Tutsi refugees they had sheltered over to Interahamwe mobs. In Nyanza's collective memory of the genocide, Gisagara's lynching marked the start of the onslaught and the end of any kind of concerted or collective rescue attempts. The start of the genocide in Nyanza is typical of much of southern Rwanda, where local people initially resisted and then outsiders initiated widespread anti-Tutsi violence. Across southern Rwanda, especially in Butare prefecture, this shift from resisting to killing led to the swift and near total extermination of Tutsi in the region. In the two weeks before April 21, tens of thousands of Tutsi and others who feared the Hutu Power extremists had sought refuge in churches, schools, and government buildings. Initially, local officials and security forces protected them. Once they adopted the national policy of genocide, their targets were concentrated in locations they could easily surround and attack.

Safe Havens from the Storm

Rural Rwandans, particularly elders, have long used the term *umuyaga* (storm or wind) to refer to "sudden, radical intervention of the authorities in local life" (de

Lame 2005, xv). This allegory of state authority captures ordinary Rwandans' perceptions of the state as a potentially destructive force. When genocidal violence engulfed Nyanza town and the region on April 21, most residents experienced it as a storm or destructive wind that crushed local authority. Yet at Mugandamure, Rubona, and the Centre Saint Antoine orphanage—all located in or near Nyanza town—Hutu and Tutsi residents persisted in their opposition to the genocide and created safe havens.

Mugandamure was on the other side of Nyanza town from Rubona hill. Although it was less than two miles from the center of Nyanza town, Mugandamure sat just outside of Butare prefecture, in Kigoma commune, Gitarama prefecture. Despite this difference in government administration, Mugandamure's residents were historically, economically, and socially much more tied to Nyanza town than to Kigoma commune's largest town, fifteen kilometers away. The Muslim community in Mugandamure saved hundreds of lives during the genocide.

Between April 7 and April 21, 1994, local government officials in Mugandamure, most of whom were Muslim, and informal leaders within the Muslim community organized a collective resistance to the genocide. "Nothing happened here before April 22 because Hutu and Tutsi people were living together [peacefully]. We had installed barriers at all entrances to Mugandamure to prevent any infiltration by outsiders. We held a meeting, Hutu and Tutsi together, to discuss what we should do. We divided into groups to defend strategic places" (MUG55). As discussed in more detail later in this chapter, Mugandamure's topography made it possible for residents to erect roadblocks to limit outsiders' access to the community. With access from the outside limited, Mugandamure remained quiet despite the escalating tension:

> We noticed that things were getting worse and worse. The tense situation was mostly among the elite. We saw Interahamwe passing by here on their way to political meetings. The killing started when [President] Habyarimana died. We heard stories of massive killing happening in Kigali and other areas moving progressively toward here. The Hutu population received instructions and cleaved themselves [from Tutsi]. The danger reached our area after two weeks, around April 22, when the Presidential Guard came here to kill people" (MUG20).

As another interviewee reported, "Before that day [April 22], it was not too bad; we could walk back and forth to Nyanza" (MUG27).

April 22 was a Friday, the most important religious day of the week for Muslims, and many Muslims from Mugandamure had participated in the funeral of a community elder. "On that day, we heard gunshots. One of the things that really helped people was that many Muslims had attended the burial of an elder who lived here. So, we did not read the *jumaa khutba* [Friday sermon]" (MUG21). Because of this, not many people were gathered in the mosque when the soldiers and Interahamwe arrived. As a result, most people had the chance to flee or hide. Nonetheless, the soldiers shot and killed about five people, all of them Tutsi. "The Interahamwe militiamen with them attacked and cut several people with machetes and stole things" (MUG32).

After this initial attack, Mugandamure's residents regrouped and redoubled their efforts to protect their community. As the soldiers withdrew, they ordered local officials to "'organize night rounds, find Tutsi where they are, burn their houses, and take everything they own'" (MUG32). The cell-level officials, the Imam Sheikh Saoudi, and elders in the community—all of whom were Muslim, born and raised in Mugandamure—met to discuss the situation. They decided to ignore the soldiers' orders as well as those from the Kigoma mayor and sector-level officials. The local government officials organized the community to keep Interahamwe mobs out. Instead of succumbing to terror like the residents of Nyanza town, Mugandamure residents collaborated to hide and protect Tutsi refugees who sought shelter there. These collective actions emerged from local assemblages that encompassed long histories of settlement, intermarriage between Muslims and non-Muslims and Hutu and Tutsi, and aspects of religious belief and practice emerging from local manifestations of Islam.

As massacres engulfed Nyanza town and surrounding communities on April 21, two Italian priests of the Rogationist order, Father Eros Borile and Father Vito, saved the lives of more than eight hundred children at the Centre Saint Antoine orphanage, along with two Tutsi priests and the orphanage's Hutu and Tutsi staff members and their families. Located on a small, walled campus in Nyanza town, the orphanage encompassed dormitories, a chapel, and several other buildings that housed offices, storerooms, and an infirmary, dispersed on a hillside among trees and green spaces. Father Eros had managed the orphanage since 1992. On April 6, 1994, the orphanage housed 182 orphans, including 15 children from northern Rwanda who had lost their families in the war there (NYA38). Shortly after President Habyarimana's assassination, Father Eros was ordered to evacuate with other Italian citizens, but he refused because there were not yet massacres in Nyanza and the radio was still broadcasting the news.[5] On April 16, Father Vito, who was head of the Rogationist orphanage in Kigali, arrived at the Centre Saint Antoine with around fifteen adults and over a hundred children. They had evacuated from the orphanage in Kigali because "it was caught in the crossfire between the RPF and the Rwandan army" near the Amahoro National Stadium (NYA38). In Nyanza, things remained tense, but calm.

As Father Eros and Father Vito, along with the children and staff, waited to see how the situation would evolve, Tutsi children began arriving, seeking refuge. Children arrived at the orphanage in different ways. Some Tutsi residents of Nyanza brought their children to the orphanage to hide them. Government officials and soldiers brought children survivors of massacres in places where killings had already started (NYA38). The soldiers "escorted them past the roadblocks and brought them [to us]. Even the Gikongoro governor [who had organized the genocide beginning on April 7] sent us children escorted by soldiers. They were the children of the prefecture employees who had been killed. In this way, the number of children in the orphanage began to grow" (NYA38).

The day after Mayor Gisagara's lynching and the start of widespread killings in Nyanza town, three government soldiers arrived to search the orphanage grounds for "RPF infiltrators." They warned the priests they must not allow anyone to come onto the orphanage grounds. Based on the massacres that had occurred at churches elsewhere, the priests understood the warning as a threat regarding the potential consequences of granting refuge to adults. The priests and their small staff tried to maintain calm and order among the orphans. As massacres engulfed Nyanza town and the surrounding communities, children kept arriving in a steady flow, up until the RPF liberated the region in May 1994. Local Hutu brought orphans whose parents had been killed in the unfolding genocide. Soldiers, national police, and government officials also continued to bring children. Some young people arrived by themselves after sneaking past Interahamwe mobs, roadblocks, and search parties. Théoneste, a Tutsi youth of around eighteen years of age who survived thanks to Fathers Eros and Vito, explained: "My friends and roommates were Hutu. We had gone to school together. They managed to get me into the orphanage; that's where I survived. It was near our home. We avoided the roadblocks by using the footpaths in between. When we reached the barbed-wire fence, they stood there while I was getting in. They called the other young men who were in the orphanage to take me inside. I became a child among others. We used to spend the day splitting wood, cooking food . . . among the other children there" (NYA31). Some children arrived injured: "We received a little girl from outside; she was seven years old. She had been wounded by a machete on the foot, and she was very tired. Later there were more [wounded children], from Gikongoro" (NYA38). To protect everyone inside, Fathers Eros and Vito ordered the staff to falsify the orphanage registries to make it appear as if all the children had been at the orphanage since before April 6. When police, army commanders, government officials, or militiamen tried to enter the campus to search for Tutsi in hiding, the priests insisted they were "only taking care of orphans" and showed them the registries (NYA38).

Although Fathers Eros and Vito struggled to feed the children as their numbers grew, they were lucky the storerooms were full when the president's plane was shot down and the genocide began. Father Eros explained:

> The Sunday which preceded April 6 [1994] was Easter Sunday. We had come [to Kigali] to collect a delivery from WFP [the World Food Program] around March 30. . . . I received five and a half tons of food. . . . Between April and May [1994] we didn't get anything else, so we survived on that support from WFP. When we heard that there were massacres [between April 7 and 20], we tried to buy all the food we could find in the stores of Nyanza. Right before Easter, we had [also] received aid packages from France, five or six packages of medicine. They [the French] had collected things from hospitals, so we had things we had never usually had in our infirmary. The Nyanza hospital was devastated, pillaged. So, those medicines were a blessing because we had those things which had come from France. It's extraordinary, they came right at the right moment. (NYA38)

In what Father Eros described as "a blessing," we can see the results of actor-networks joining human and nonhuman entities to produce specific effects. The priests' efforts to save the children were not theirs alone. Their agency arose in an actor-network uniting the World Food Program's food aid (and the American farmers who grew it; the trains, ships, and trucks that moved it around the world; and the UN workers who coordinated its delivery); the French medical supplies and medicines (and the hospitals that donated it, the doctors and nurses who gathered it, and the trucks and airplanes that brought it from France); the telephones and shortwave radios that transmitted the messages; the soldiers who guarded the orphanage at night; the orphanage staff and their fabrication of the orphanage registries, as well as the registries themselves; and the orphans' own collaboration in cleaning, cooking, caring for younger children, and guarding the orphanage's perimeter.

In Rubona, residents returned home after the initial invasion by security forces on April 21. Ezekiel Gihanga, Abel Kambanda, and Abel's brother Gaspard quickly regrouped, organized roadblocks, and recruited security patrols from among the residents as the police and sector head had demanded. Instead of using the roadblocks and security patrols "to find their cockroaches and traitors [*inyenzi n'ibyitso byazo*]" as ordered, however, Rubona residents used them to protect residents and the people they were hiding (NYA28). As Ezekiel described it, the Hutu residents of Rubona "pretended to be with the attackers" to keep others from coming into the neighborhood to look for Tutsi (NYA28). In addition, they sought information from Interahamwe "who told them ahead of time of planned attacks" so residents could move Tutsi refugees to hiding places (NYA28). Ezekiel explained the increasing danger of the situation: "Things went from bad to worse because the [commune and sector] officials began to help the national police. They organized search parties to look for people. Those people of good conscience [*umutima mwiza*] hid Tutsi in their homes. Then, a warning was issued that whoever hid Tutsi would be forced to kill them with their own hands, and then they would be killed as well" (NYA28). Despite the increasing intensity of the threats, Rubona residents persisted in their efforts. Ezekiel and Abel alone hid dozens of people in their homes and on their farms. They enlisted help from their kin and neighbors, who hid additional people. Working together, residents managed to save the lives of dozens of Tutsi who took refuge in Rubona.

Rubona, Mugandamure, and the Centre Saint Antoine orphanage remained safe havens for Tutsi throughout the genocide, at great risk to these communities' residents. Unlike elsewhere in Nyanza, local leaders on Rubona hill, in Mugandamure, and at the Centre Saint Antoine orphanage continued to oppose the genocide in the wake of Gisagara's lynching. The miraculous outcomes achieved in these places were not predetermined or self-evident on April 21, 1994. Residents' unity and persistence in the face of terror maintained these safe havens, which materialized from existing actor-networks and assemblage components that coalesced and cleaved in the dynamic context of the genocide. The specific histories, social cohesion, and topography of these three communities reinforced collective rescue efforts and helped make them successful.

Social Cohesion in the Face of Terror

Although the initiative and resolve of local leaders—both formal and informal—were common factors in rescue efforts at Mugandamure, Rubona, and the Centre Saint Antoine orphanage, they alone were insufficient. Local leaders at these sites organized rescue efforts, but they would have failed without the support and unity of community residents. Social cohesion within these communities helped them persist in the face of the genocide's terror. This cohesion emerged from heterogeneous local histories of settlement; intermarriage between lineages and races; kinship relations; and sometimes shared religious faith, belief, and practices. In other words, social cohesion is an emergent, agentive effect of actor-networks.

In Rubona, leaders and residents relied on the long history of community relations, friendships, and kin relations to reinforce their bonds. Rubona hill stands out not only for the unity of its residents during the genocide but also for their religious diversity. Abel and Ezekiel were Adventists, but Rubona residents belonged to many different faiths: the neighborhood was also home to Catholics, Anglicans, Pentecostals, and Muslims (NYA28). In many other communities where local leaders and residents organized against the genocide, such as Mugandamure, social cohesion was built in part on bonds of shared religious faith and practice. In Rubona, that cohesion emerged from several heterogeneous factors, including the continuous habitation of the hill by certain lineages, interlaced kinship ties resulting from intermarriage, and the long history of intermarriage between Hutu and Tutsi in the community. Many Rubona residents were descended from lineages that were among the first occupants of the hill, including Abel and his brother and Ezekiel. Many of these lineages had intermarried over several generations. For instance, Abel and Ezekiel had married sisters. Thus, their children were simultaneously *abamuvandimwe* (siblings or parallel cousins) and *ababyara* (cross cousins). These overlapping kinship ties reinforced social cohesion, which was further strengthened by neighborly mutual support in the form of everyday borrowing and lending or shared labor in each other's agricultural fields. Ongoing cycles of gift exchange between families in honor of births, diplomas, weddings, and funerals maintained kinship ties and reinforced bonds among neighbors.

The intermarriage between Hutu and Tutsi lineages in Rubona over several generations further predisposed inhabitants to reject racism. For example, Mayor Gisagara, who was from Rubona, had a Hutu father and Tutsi mother. Likewise, Ezekiel and Abel, both Hutu, had married Tutsi women. Yet neither Ezekiel nor Abel mentioned their interracial marriages as factors in their decision making in the 2013 interviews. Aside from stating that his eldest son was killed during the genocide "because he looked Tutsi," Ezekiel never explicitly mentioned his family's mixed race (NYA28). He did, however, speak more generally about race and the genocide, saying, "Hutu and Tutsi don't hate each other; what happened was just a political issue. *Umutima ntugira urwango*, i.e., a heart has no hatred. It is politics that brings this hatred" (NYA28). Similarly, Abel minimized the impact of his marriage on his actions: "I was married in 1970. At that time, I did not know my wife's race. We were simply in love. I learned it after. So, [in 1994] I had to stand between where I am from and my wife. It was not heroism. By the grace of God, He gave me the strength." Asked if he would have defended Tutsi if his wife was not a Tutsi, he responded, "So many people had Tutsi wives and killed [Tutsi]. But for me, I am Adventist, and God told us not to kill." While Abel and Ezekiel did not attribute their actions to their interracial marriages, other community members saw it as relevant. Both Pauline and Faustin, who were rescued by Abel and Ezekiel, said that Abel and Ezekiel understood the dangers of racism since they had Tutsi wives themselves.

Mugandamure's many Muslim residents explained their community's social cohesion as being born of their shared religion and ritual practices. They explained that their hamlet's way of life was different from that of other places:

> What I can add regarding this township of ours . . . is the brotherhood [*ubumuvandimwe*, state of coming from the same womb; relationship between siblings] we shared. Back then, you wouldn't worry if your child went to a neighbor's house—fear that anyone would hurt him, give him poison, or anything. No! A child could eat anywhere. No one would have feared to say, "Come in, have a little food." That's our particular culture, here in Mugandamure. . . . The genocide showed me that unity we had. Yet it was something very hard, the fact that no one decided to betray anyone—maybe there was like 1 percent [who did], but the remaining 99 percent shared the same purpose. That's all I can say. We had harmony. (MUG37)

Part of this sense of brotherhood was grounded in residents' Muslim identity, strengthened by generations of social, political, and economic marginalization in Rwanda. For Mugandamure residents, this marginalization helped instill a strong sense of both community identity and Muslim identity that superseded the distinctions between Hutu, Tutsi, and Twa. Furthermore, as Banyanduga, Mugandamure's Muslims did not have access to Bakiga patronage networks, as some Muslims in Gisenyi and Kigali did. As a result, most Mugandamure residents saw themselves as outside the political conflicts between Hutu and Tutsi.

In local people's imagination, the site of Mugandamure was deeply and historically connected to Rwandan Muslims and to the mwami (king) and central court. According to local lore, Mugandamure's distinctive name, which is not (quite) Kinyarwanda, was attributed to Mwami Musinga. A community elder, Issa, who was born in 1916, recounted, "I grew up hearing people say there was someone named 'Fundi Amri,' who was a Ugandan. People called him 'Muganda Amri' [the Ugandan Amri]. This might be the origin of the name Mugandamure" (MUG24). Issa continued his story, which underscores the historical links between Islam, the mwami, the community, and its topography:

> When Amri arrived here, he specialized in adding ornaments to clothing, especially making fringes on the edges. Someone who had seen his craftsmanship told Mwami Musinga about Amri's skills. . . . The mwami summoned Amri to Rukari [site of the central court, about four kilometers away]. . . . When Amri was introduced to the mwami, the mwami asked Amri where he was from. Amri responded that he was from Uganda. Then Amri showed the mwami samples of his work and

explained how he made the fringe. The mwami commissioned some pieces.... The mwami liked them when they were finished. (MUG24)

Other elders in Mugandamure interviewed in 2013 and 2014 recounted similar versions of this story and added that Amri and Mwami Musinga became friends.

Around Muganda Amri's home and workshop, Mugandamure sprouted into a commercial settlement near the national highway connecting Nyanza to the colonial administrative capital at the time, Astrida (known as Butare in 1994 and now called Huye), and to Kigali, the commercial capital of Rwanda during the colonial period. In the early 1950s, Mugandamure became a Swahili camp when Belgian colonial administrators forced the Muslims living in Nyanza town to leave. "The [white] Roman Catholic priests claimed that the *adhan* [call to prayer] in the morning made too much noise and woke up people's children" (MUG22; similar statement from MUG24). No doubt the Catholic priests, seeking to contain Islam, also wanted to distance Nyanza's growing Muslim community from the nobles and the central court (MUG01).[6]

When Mwami Rudahigwa learned that the colonial government was forcing Muslims to destroy their homes and move, "[he] purchased Mugandamure for the Muslims.[7] Then, he called the agronomist Dibwa [Dubois].... He told Dibwa to build roads on that hill, horizontally and vertically, from [this first] house, to the other side. Then, he asked Dibwa to take a census of the Muslims and build houses for them all. The mwami authorized Dibwa to request progressive repayment from our income. Dibwa built these houses that you see here [gesturing to the first row of houses] that we call Amajyambere [Development project]" (MUG24). The Amajyambere houses were all identical in design, four small rooms under low, sloping roofs made of ceramic tile. They were constructed of fired bricks held together by mortar. These sturdy building materials lasted for decades. Most of the houses still stood nearly sixty years later in 2013, having needed only minor repairs.

During the genocide, Mugandamure's residents collaborated to defend the community against violence from outside, protected Tutsi living inside the community, and hid, sheltered, and protected people who were fleeing from other places, whether they were Muslim, Christian, Tutsi, or Hutu. "Mugandamure remained relatively safe due to Muslims' solidarity. Interahamwe made attempts to enter and conduct attacks in Mugandamure without success. The Muslim residents collaborated to resist them" (MUG33). Raissa, a Tutsi Muslim woman, explained, "Muslims organized and protected our children by separating them from us and taking care of them in their families with their own children" (MUG20). The social cohesion in Mugandamure reinforced the community's ability to resist the genocide and helped residents maintain unity, unlike Muslims in Gisenyi, Biryogo, or even nearby Nyanza (MUG53).

At the Centre Saint Antoine orphanage, maintaining unity among the children inside was a challenge because the children did not have long-standing histories to rely on, as did the Rubona and Mugandamure communities. The orphanage housed many children who had been living there before the genocide, including orphans whose parents had been killed by the RPF. Many of the adolescent boys had been attending the Christ-Roi Secondary School across town where the headmaster supported the Hutu Power movement. In his homilies, he had railed against the RPF, the civil war, and the risks of a "return to Tutsi colonialism" in the years leading up to the genocide. Once Tutsi children began arriving at the orphanage, these adolescent boys began speaking against their presence in the racist language of Hutu extremism. Father Eros recounted, "The hardest thing during the genocide, the most important thing, was to maintain unity among the children. Among the orphans there, I had several whose parents had been killed by the RPF in the north. They were susceptible to the extremist propaganda that preached hatred of all Tutsi as RPF accomplices. I had to constantly remind them that they were children of God and innocent and needed to remain unified."

Thus, the complex and shifting contingencies of genocidal violence in the region around Nyanza were mirrored inside the walls of the orphanage. Throughout April and May of 1994, Fathers Eros and Vito worked hard to counter this propaganda and reinforce Christian ideologies of compassion, charity, and peace in the children. As discussed in detail below, the priests relied on Catholic theology and ritual to shape the children's understanding of what was happening outside the orphanage walls and to forestall it spilling inside.

While Fathers Eros and Vito worked intensely to reinforce and produce social cohesion among the children in the orphanage, social cohesion in Rubona and Mugandamure emerged organically from the long histories of social interactions, intermarriage, reciprocity, kinship relations, and collaboration over generations. In all communities, social cohesion was key to collective action and persistence in the face of increasing threats. Local leadership, both formal and informal, provided a necessary reinforcement of residents' initial reactions to help their kin, neighbors, coworkers, and eventually strangers seeking protection.

Topography, Authority, and the Social Meanings of Boundaries

At Rubona, Mugandamure, and the Centre Saint Antoine orphanage, the sites' topography and morphological features reinforced the social cohesion that underlay effective resistance and provided significant opportunities for rescue. These geographic actor-network components physically demarcated boundaries and had histories that imbued them with social meanings. These heterogeneous components coalesced into assemblages where local authorities could wield legal and symbolic power that interrupted state sovereignty by opposing the national policy.

As a hill, Rubona's topography allowed residents to close off the community with roadblocks after the initial attack on April 21. A single unpaved road and a few footpaths were the principal connections between Rubona and other neighborhoods on the outskirts of Nyanza town. After the initial attack, Ezekiel and Abel, who exerted formal authority as cell-level officials and informal authority as respected community elders and Adventist leaders, erected roadblocks to close off the road and footpaths into Rubona. Although they appeared to comply with government orders coming from above, they used the roadblocks to disrupt the national policy of genocide and mount a self-defense initiative. They instructed the Hutu men from Rubona who manned the roadblocks to allow Tutsi who were fleeing to enter Rubona and to forbid entry to anyone else. When soldiers, police, or Interahamwe attack squads arrived at their roadblocks, the Hutu residents of Rubona "pretended to be with the attackers" to keep them from coming into the neighborhood to look for Tutsi (NYA28). This appearance of compliance shielded the men at the roadblock from potential attack and protected Rubona from house-to-house searches conducted by outsiders. Although Ezekiel and Abel led these efforts, they would not have succeeded without the cooperation and support of Rubona residents.

In Mugandamure, access to the community was similarly limited. The primary entrance into the neighborhood was via a dirt road that left the highway. A wide footpath, which passed through the marshes, farmland, and wooded areas in a valley, connected the far side of Mugandamure to Nyanza town. A few smaller footpaths connected Mugandamure to surrounding neighborhoods, but the hamlet was still largely self-contained in 1994, as it had been since the colonial era. As in Rubona, Mugandamure's residents took advantage of the neighborhood's contained geographic space and used roadblocks to keep out Interahamwe militiamen and delay security forces so people could hide (MUG06, MUG37 MUG55, MUG20). "Here, we had nine roadblocks around our village. It's our people who guarded them, and nobody died at them. Young men would be at the roadblocks while older men were inside the town" (MUG06). Roadblocks provided an opportunity to identify those entering the community:

> At that roadblock, when we saw that it was only one or two people, we would not let them in without asking them why they came and what they were going to do in the township. You would see whether he was bringing anything which could harm people [i.e., weapons] or whether they were traitors. The older people were the ones who asked them

> questions. As for us, we just stood there, looking like the young men we were. We would wait for the old men to say whether a person was okay [to let in]. (MUG37)

The roadblocks served as a first line of defense against searches, whether by Interahamwe militias, civilian search parties, the police, or the military: "When the Interahamwe arrived at the roadblocks, our people manning the roadblocks would spend time arguing with them to give people [inside the neighborhood] time. That's when we would start escaping through the passages [between houses to hide]. That's how we survived" (MUG06). When security forces accompanied Interahamwe militiamen, Mugandamure residents at the roadblocks did not try to stop them but deferred to their authority as official representatives of the state. These strategies worked well because they limited searches to military or police and prevented Interahamwe and civilian mobs from entering the hamlet.

Beyond these physical boundaries around the hamlet, community residents took advantage of artifacts stemming from the community's history as a Swahili camp. Inside the neighborhood, household components were connected by small passages, gates, and doors. During the colonial era, these passageways had allowed Muslim residents to circulate inside the walls of the Swahili camp. During the genocide, residents used them to protect Tutsi. When security forces entered Mugandamure to conduct searches, people moved secretly between houses to avoid detection. "You could run to a neighbor's house and hide there. Someone would tell you, 'They've left your home.' Then, you would go back there. The passages helped a lot" (MUG06).

At the Centre Saint Antoine, those inside benefited from the orphanage's design. Walls surrounded the compound on three sides, and a fence topped with barbed wire closed the side of the campus next to a small copse. A large, reinforced-steel gate blocked the main driveway into the compound, and steel doors marked the few walkway entrances into the orphanage. On April 7, Father Eros issued orders to the staff and children that no one should be admitted to the compound, including government officials or security forces, without his authorization. The priests then organized the children to protect themselves. "I asked the oldest Hutu children to guard the orphanage: the twelve-, thirteen-, and fourteen-year-olds during the day and the older ones at night. We gathered all the weapons we could find: metallic bars . . . I am not sure what else. That's how we organized ourselves" (NYA38). The walled compound allowed the orphanage to limit access, keeping out mobs and Interahamwe soldiers.

The physical boundaries separating these three sites from other neighborhoods or nearby houses delineated space to be protected and boundaries to be maintained. These physical boundaries were also imbued with social meanings attached to the sites and the people who inhabited them. The physical boundaries served as material manifestations of local authorities' power and residents' unity.

Rubona hill had existed as a cohesive administrative unit since at least the nineteenth century. Before the arrival of the European colonizers, overlapping chieftancies responsible for different duties, such as land chieftancies (*ubutaka*), pasture chieftancies (*umuheto*), and army chieftancies (*intore*), oversaw the same geographic areas (C. Newbury 1988, 42–46). The smallest unit of the land chieftancies was the hill, and Rubona hill was born as such a land chieftancy. In the twentieth century, Rwanda's internal administrative boundaries changed multiple times, but each time, Rubona hill remained a cohesive subunit nestled within changing superior administrative units. The persistence of Rubona hill as an administrative subunit, along with kinship ties among Rubona's farming lineages dating back to at least the nineteenth century, produced a social identity—the "people of Rubona." Rubona residents conceived of themselves as a unified whole (an "us") to be maintained and defended against outsiders (a "them"). The interlacing social and physical boundaries around the Rubona community instilled additional power in the actor-networks unifying residents and empowering them to defend the community against attacks from outside.

In Mugandamure, the community's unique social history as a Swahili camp created by Mwami Rudahigwa himself infused the physical boundaries around the site with social meaning. Mugandamure's history as a Swahili camp and the social cohesion among its residents had generated a clear concept of people "who belonged to Mugandamure." It was a staple of local lore that Mugandamure had sheltered UNAR supporters and Tutsi fleeing violence during prior moments of political turbulence in the 1950s, 1960s, and 1970s. Thus, in 1994, Tutsi fled to Mugandamure, seeking safety with its Muslim residents, because Mugandamure had a history of providing refuge. When these refugees arrived at the community's roadblocks, residents allowed them in and turned anyone else away.

At the Centre Saint Antoine orphanage, the physical boundaries around the compound also signaled the power of the orphanage as a Catholic institution that served orphaned children. Catholic faith did not keep Interahamwe militiamen from killing Tutsi, but the militiamen dared not attack a Catholic institution run by white priests to kill orphaned children. As both priests and white foreigners, Fathers Eros and Vito had high status in the eyes of the Interahamwe, police, and military, making potential attackers think twice about directly threatening or attacking them. Their relatively high status also allowed the priests to use arguments based on the rule of law to oppose search of the orphanage grounds, even though state officials and security forces were implementing a national genocide policy. The priests allowed soldiers or police to enter when they had legal standing to do so, such as a search or arrest warrant, but they categorically refused entry to militiamen or other civilians on the basis that they had no legal standing to enter.

Nonetheless, the priests faced frequent visits from Interahamwe, soldiers, police, and civilians who were looking for Tutsi or opportunities to loot. The priests deflected them by mobilizing the symbolic power of their charges. The deeply embedded cultural notion of children as innocent and as noncombatants discouraged potential attackers. In addition, it was widely known in Nyanza that the orphanage housed Hutu orphans whose parents had been killed by the RPF in northern Rwanda. This knowledge also helped shield the orphanage from attack. Théoneste explained, "When people went [to the orphanage] to search for Tutsi, [Father Eros] told them, 'I am taking care of children [here]. These are my orphans. . . . I have no Tutsi in this center.' Yet he saved many [Tutsi] children who had come from outside" (NYA31).

In Rubona, Mugandamure, and the Centre Saint Antoine orphanage people used the physical demarcation of their space to control access and to shelter Tutsi within it. At each of these sites, interlaced and sometimes competing authorities wielded power over space; where those authorities were in accord, widespread rescue was possible. In Rubona and Mugandamure, cell-level government officials, informal elders in the community, and respected religious leaders remained unified in their opposition to the genocide. Their combined power helped mobilize residents and discouraged potential opponents from challenging their authority. At the Centre Saint Antoine, protecting the children and others inside the orphanage became more difficult as the genocide continued. Fathers Eros and Vito used their precious telephone line—and their status—to lobby government, police, and military officials for protection and assistance. When Interahamwe attack squads threatened to attack the orphanage, the local police commander reinforced the priests' authority and sent police officers to protect the orphanage (NYA38, NYA31). A local military commander deployed soldiers to protect the orphanage at night.

As the genocide continued, however, a fissure appeared in Mugandamure's unified resistance. As Amdun, an elderly Muslim resident explained, there was unity among Mugandamure residents "except for those who entered into politics" (MUG22). When asked specific questions about Muslims who had participated in the genocide, almost everyone named Hadji Djumapili, a wealthy merchant and Hutu Muslim (MUG20).[8] Hadji Djumapili was well connected to high-ranking officials, including the mayor of Kigoma, Célestin Ugirashebuja (MUG27).[9] Ugirashebuja actively supported the genocide by organizing meetings of local officials and then ordering them to set up roadblocks and hunt down inyenzi, monitoring the work of people manning the roadblocks, and allowing communal police under his command to organize and lead killings within

Kigoma commune.[10] Many Mugandamure residents thought it was Djumapili's connections to Ugirashebuja that led him to collaborate in the genocide. Habineza, a Tutsi Muslim man and genocide survivor from Mugandamure, explained, "Djumapili . . . decided to become involved [in the genocide] after a visit to the mayor's house. . . . Djumapili tried to mobilize people around the idea that the government had sentenced all Tutsi to death and that the community must obey government orders to avoid problems with the government in the future" (MUG27). According to Mugandamure residents, Djumapili collaborated by providing intelligence to the security forces before the first attack on April 22 and then continued to inform security forces how Mugandamure residents were protecting Tutsi refugees: "He went around saying that people should become more involved in what the government wanted instead of staying at the mosque, 'blah blah blah' [talking about unimportant things]. He even denounced people. The young Muslim men responded. They told him that if he wanted killing to take place here [in Mugandamure], then we should start with his wives, who were Tutsi" (MUG20). When the RPF arrived at the end of May to liberate Mugandamure, Hadji Djumapili fled with his family and never returned. It was rumored he had died in Congo.

Despite Djumapili's actions, Mugandamure's resistance held, sustained by the community's social cohesion, the unified leadership of its formal and informal leaders, and the social and physical boundaries around the community. In Rubona, topography and social boundaries reinforced the community's internal authority and helped residents deflect Interahamwe assaults. Similarly, the walls around the Centre Saint Antoine physically marked the social boundaries of the priests' authority, as clergy, as foreigners, and as protectors of "Hutu" orphans, reinforced by the religious institution they represented.

Religion as a Polyvalent Assemblage Component

Rescue efforts in Rubona, Mugandamure, and at the Centre Saint Antoine were organized by people of different religious faiths: Seventh-day Adventist, Catholic, and Islam. Studies of the Holocaust and Armenian genocide have confirmed that dominant religious institutions often participate, facilitate, or are complicit in genocide. The theory emerging from these studies predicts the complicity of the Catholic Church in the Rwandan genocide. As an institution, the Rwandan Catholic Church contributed to the genocide by reinforcing state power, failing to condemn rising Hutu extremism, and failing to make explicit statements against genocidal violence in April 1994 (Des Forges 1999, 245–46). While the Catholic Church failed as an institution, its constituent components—various religious orders active in Rwanda, schools, health clinics, orphanages, and individual priests, nuns, monks, lay ministers, and employees—engaged with rising Hutu extremism, anti-Tutsi violence, and ultimately genocide in heterogeneous ways. Catholic priests, monks, nuns, and lay ministers played a variety of roles in the genocide; some worked to protect people and rescue Tutsi, while others led attacks on churches or organized killings. Because people fled to churches and places where Tutsi had been safe in previous instances of racial violence, Catholic churches—like schools, convents, monasteries, and government buildings—often became massacre sites during the genocide.[11]

Studies of the Holocaust (Braun 2019; Cabanel 2011) and the Armenian genocide (Ternon 2011) conclude that religious minorities are more likely to engage in acts of rescue or assistance than people of other religions. Yet members of religious minorities participated in the 1994 genocide of Tutsi in Rwanda, challenging these theories. As discussed in chapter 3, Muslims in Nyamirambo and Gisenyi organized the Interahamwe and Impuzamugambi militias, led attacks on Tutsi households, and directly participated in killing. The Seventh-day Adventist Church in Rwanda was also a tiny minority, yet in some places Adventist pastors organized killing. Elizaphan Ntakirutimana, the former head of the Seventh-day Adventist Church in western Rwanda, was sentenced by the ICTR to ten years in prison for aiding and abetting genocide (Simons 2003). People of all religious faiths, including clergy, became embroiled in the genocide, suggesting religion alone cannot explain their actions.

Much of the research on religion and genocide has investigated potential connections between genocide and religiosity, religious faith, or the moral teachings of religion. These studies conclude that religion contributes to the development of internal dispositions like altruism (Oliner and Oliner 1988; Monroe 1996), compassion (Monroe and Martinez 2009), inclusive notions of identity (Fogelman 1994), and moral orientations against genocide (Longman 2009; Seidler 1992; Viret 2011a). At Mugandamure, the Centre Saint Antoine, and Rubona, religion—comprising moral orientations, faith, practice, and communal ties created through ritual—played a role in rescue, even if it was not a determining factor. The exceptional actions of Abel and Ezekiel in Rubona, Fathers Eros and Vito at the Centre Saint Antoine, and the Muslims of Mugandamure emerged from assemblages that encompassed religious teaching, belief, faith, practice, and many other components.

In Mugandamure, the shared faith of the community's residents, their social marginalization throughout the twentieth century, and the community's history as a Swahili camp predisposed its residents to present a united front. Islamic teachings on human diversity, and especially racial difference, further shaped residents' worldview, priming them to resist genocide. Explicit communication on politics from religious leadership, including the mufti, the Association des Musulmans du Rwanda (AMUR), and individual imams, helped ensure clarity among Muslims on the relevance of their religious teaching to the immediate political situation (see discussion in chapter 3). Mugandamure had a particularly vocal leader in this respect, one who preached against the genocide. Sheikh Saoudi, the imam at Mugandamure, had long preached about unity. "At the mosque, [the religious leaders] used to say, 'We're all the same. We don't recognize this distinction between Hutu and Tutsi'" (MUG37). After the April 22 attack on Mugandamure, Imam Sheikh Saoudi decided, "If I preach to them, they will harm no one. So, I gave *khutba* [sermon] to tell people to protect each other, to take care of each other, and even to use the passages between the houses to save those who were targeted" (MUG21). As Raissa recounted, "Sheikh Saoudi was the imam. He preached that it was a sin for a Muslim to kill another Muslim or any other person. People listened; nobody here got involved in the killing. Prayers at the mosque became our routine as many people took refuge there" (MUG20).

Mugandamure's Muslim community believed their faith superseded distinctions between Hutu, Tutsi, and Twa, in part because of Islamic teachings on the equality of all Muslims before God and the brotherhood of all humanity (Qur'an 49:13), and in part because of their distinctive Muslim identity. These factors largely erased racial distinctions among Muslims and between Muslims and their non-Muslim neighbors. Thus, their ecumenical way of life and tolerance between Muslims and non-Muslims helped Mugandamure's residents remain unified against top-down pressures to commit acts of genocide.

A final key factor setting Mugandamure apart from other Muslim communities was the presence of Ansar Allah, a Muslim movement that emerged in the 1980s in Rwanda and eventually grew into a sect unique to Rwanda that emphasized ecumenical brotherhood as a way of introducing Christians and nonbelievers to Islam.[12] Moussa, an Ansar Allah member from Mugandamure, explained the origins of the association:

> Ansar Allah is a Muslim association; it started in 1982. It started with the teaching of Islam [*da'wah*]. There were many things which were not working. We had realized that there were Muslims who were taking alcohol; there were Muslims who were doing things which are not fit for men. We chose to create an association which would fight against all those things which were not working well within Islam. That's exactly what we can call *da'wah*. We thought that we needed to preach Islam, that we needed to call for Islam. Of course, regarding the call to Islam, we call those who are not Muslims. We also must organize Muslims who are already part of Islam if their behavior is no longer correct. (MUG54)

Ansar Allah began as a movement within AMUR; its members were primarily Rwandan Muslim male youth who admired the teachings of a Libyan imam who worked out of the Islamic Cultural Center in Nyamirambo, Kigali. In the early 1990s, Ansar Allah operated within AMUR and was charged with proselytizing (*da'wah*), but by 1994, Ansar Allah had split from AMUR. A former Ansar Allah member from Mugandamure, when asked if he knew about the movement, explained, "Yes. I was part of it for some time. It started here in the years 1987 or 1988 from Kigali, brought by Bashir and Ahmed, who were from here. They came with a group of youth, as preachers. . . . We thought it was about spreading the Muslim messages, about the da'wah and following the Qur'an and Sunnah [practices of the prophet Mohamed]" (MUG21). In the late 1980s and early 1990s, Ansar Allah's focus was preaching to non-Muslims in rural areas to spread Islam beyond Rwanda's cities and towns (MUG53). By 1994, Ansar Allah had congregations in rural communities throughout central and southern Rwanda, including Mugandamure, Kibagabaga, Nyamata in Bugesera, and Mabare (near Rwamagana), among others (Doughty and Ntambara 2005). At the time, Ansar Allah adherents perceived themselves as stronger, better, and more faithful Muslims than those who prayed in mosques supervised by AMUR because Ansar Allah members renounced practices forbidden by Islam and believed their understanding of Islam was more correct.

Ansar Allah members played a decisive role in organizing Mugandamure against genocide. The Mugandamure leaders who organized the community's resistance to genocide were current or former Ansar Allah members. The older men led the action, while the younger ones provided the muscle to man the roadblocks and present a united front to oppose the Interahamwe. In fact, Ansar Allah had a significant presence at most sites across the country where Muslims engaged in community-level collective action to oppose the genocide. The Ansar Allah members saw their education and training within the association as foundational to their actions during the genocide. Moussa explained:

> During that time, I was an intellectual; I was a teacher. I knew well what evil and good were. Given that I was a Muslim, specially trained by Ansar Allah, I had to fight against genocide. I have come to realize that Muslims refused to join those people who committed genocide crimes because the government didn't like Muslims. . . . The government was in favor of the genocide, but Muslims were not going to follow what the government had instigated. Personally, I had been taught by Ansar Allah for years and years. Wherever they were, Ansar Allah members all fought against the genocide. (MUG54)

Ansar Allah teachings also contributed to resistance on a practical level. Among the founders of Ansar Allah was a medical doctor with an Omani father and a Rwandan mother. He had trained Ansar Allah members not only in religion, Islamic law (sharia), Islamic politeness, and the proper relationship between Islam, Muslims, and politics, but also in first aid. "Those first aid lessons helped us fight against genocide; we patched up those who were wounded" (MUG54).[13]

At the Centre Saint Antoine, religion was important in at least two ways. First, it strengthened the resolve of Fathers Eros and Vito in the face of the ever-increasing threats posed by the Interahamwe, government, and security forces. Having a colleague of the same nationality, from the same religious order, committed to the same mission and immersed in the same religious practices, helped them persist. Father Eros explained how Father Vito's arrival helped him decide to stay in Rwanda instead of evacuate: "Then we were two. Being with someone else comforted me. Talking to him, consulting each other." The presence of two Tutsi priests from their order also reinforced their commitment to protecting the orphanage and its inhabitants.

Father Eros and Father Vito were exceptional in the courage they demonstrated, rooted in their deep Christian faith built over decades of religious training in seminary and ongoing acts of charity ministering to orphans. The majority of foreign Catholic clergy evacuated the country in convoys organized by foreign governments and militaries. Among foreign clergy who remained, not all engaged in acts of rescue or persisted in rescue efforts until the genocide's end. Some even turned people over to the Interahamwe during the genocide (Des Forges 1999, 538). In Nyanza, one of the primary opponents of Fathers Eros and Vito was a Rwandan priest named Hormisdas Nsengimana, the headmaster of the Christ-Roi Secondary School. Father Nsengimana had indoctrinated many Hutu children from the orphanage with anti-RPF and anti-Tutsi ideologies during daily Mass at the school.[14] He attended the meeting held by the military commander Barahira to orchestrate the initial massacres in Nyanza on April 21 (NYA31), and he allegedly "sent Interahamwe to kill three Tutsi hiding in the orphanage" and threatened Father Eros with violence if he did not turn the children over (NYA20).

Father Eros's Catholic faith influenced his perception of the unfolding events in April 1994. In a 2014 interview, Father Eros often mobilized religious interpretations to explain the genocide and its evil, saying things like, "These things are beyond comprehension. It was the work of demons." Later in the same interview, he characterized the Interahamwe militiamen as personifications of the devil:

> Three men came to the gate after nightfall. [*He pauses, shivers, and then shakes his head as if to erase an image from it, then continues.*] They were the personification of the devil. Their eyes were empty. They were

> sweating profusely and covered in blood. Their clothes were hanging from them in tatters. In their hands, they carried machetes, hammers, nail-studded clubs, chains. [*He pauses again, removes his glasses and wipes his eyes, and then continues.*] Their weapons were also covered in blood and had shreds of flesh hanging from them. To see them was to become insane. This image haunts me. (NYA38)

Father Eros contrasted this evil with his and Father Vito's efforts to protect the children and their Tutsi staff members (Burnet 2015). He also explained the role of Catholic practice as a unifying force that the priests intentionally mobilized to maintain unity among the children. The children attended morning Mass upon awakening and vespers before going to sleep at night, as well as mealtime prayers, as part of the orphanage's daily routine. This routine became even more important during the genocide, as a mechanism to maintain unity. As Father Eros explained, "I used to shout during the Mass in Kinyarwanda, 'Do you want to kill someone else? If you are a child who fears God, you cannot do this. We are all children of God.'"

In religiously diverse Rubona, the role of religion was less prominent. Genocide survivors in Rubona—whether Adventist, Catholic, or nonreligious—attributed Abel and Ezekiel's actions to several factors, including their kinship ties to Tutsi, the mutual understanding arising from those ties, and their strong Christian values. Ezekiel explained that his faith clarified the morality of the situation and gave him the courage and will to act, but he acknowledged that nonreligious people could also act as he did:

> Q: Where did the moral strength come from? What makes somebody die before they kill another person, yet another person weakens and kills?
>
> EZEKIEL: It's God's commandment that killing is a sin; it has to stay alive in people's belief.
>
> Q: What about the fear of death?
>
> EZEKIEL: Yes, the fear of death can make someone do what they do not want to do. But if your beliefs are truly in you, if they have entered inside you, they make you strong.
>
> Q: What made you preach to defend and hide people during that time despite the danger?
>
> EZEKIEL: In my opinion, it depends on how you are, how you were made, and how you believe. There are some people who change, but there are others who know that what is right will always be right, not necessarily from a religious belief. Even those who don't pray or have no religion can make a distinction between right and wrong. (NYA28)

At one point in the interview, he cast his actions in terms of a sense of common humanity:

> EZEKIEL: I was not afraid to hide those people because I knew that they had committed no crime. If it was necessary to be killed with them, I was ready to die with them because we were the same. None of us had committed a crime. I knew that they were innocent neighbors. (NYA28)

That sense of a broader unity, reaching across religious or racial lines, was a central theme in interviews. Nearly all the rescuers we interviewed in 2013 and 2014 mobilized the concept of their shared humanity with the people they saved, whether or not they gave additional explanations for their motivations or decision making. Ezekiel attributed his actions, at least in part, to his religious beliefs, but many other members of his Adventist congregation participated actively in the genocide. In fact, Abel and Ezekiel dared not lobby church members to resist the genocide. As Ezekiel explained, "It was not possible to advise people in the church.... It was not easy to tell everyone because you could not know who was good or not. Except for your closest neighbors, relatives, and close friends that you know very well" (NYA28). Thus, the impulse to rescue clearly came from some other source besides religion.

Religion alone cannot fully explain the collective rescue efforts in Rubona, Mugandamure, or at Centre Saint Antoine. Religion did play a role in rescue, but it was a set of polyvalent components in the assemblages that preceded, coalesced, and dissolved over the course of the genocide. Perpetrators, killer-rescuers, bystanders, survivors, and rescuers navigated the same rapidly changing context yet arrived at different decisions or engaged in different actions. Like those who became perpetrators, people who rescued improvised their actions. Their strategies responded directly to the violence and the changing assemblages of power, politics, space, social relations, and artifacts emerging from the genocide and its effects. Rescue was not an accident, nor was it random, but it was also not an obvious choice or a predetermined outcome of a particular religious belief or moral disposition.

Genocide Timelines, Decision Making, and Persistence in the Gray Zone

In Mugandamure, Rubona, and at the Centre Saint Antoine, residents' collective resistance to the genocide culminated in rescue thanks to several interrelated factors. First, the relatively late start of genocidal violence in the region delayed the onset of threats against Tutsi residents and pressure for others to join in the violence. Second, the timely arrival of the RPF saved thousands of Tutsi who successfully hid or had been protected by others for more than four weeks. Third, once genocidal violence began in Nyanza, the risks of helping or hiding Tutsi increased as time went on. Residents were required to make decisions repeatedly over time based on limited information. In the genocide's gray zone, they often faced choiceless choices—situations where all options were equally terrible or morally problematic. The successful, collective rescue efforts at Mugandamure, Rubona, and the Centre Saint Antoine emerged from these entangled assemblage components.

The comparatively short genocide timeline in the Nyanza region helped make rescue efforts successful. In Nyanza, the genocide lasted only thirty-seven days, whereas elsewhere it continued for more than a hundred days. Widespread killings around Nyanza began on April 21, 1994, two full weeks after anti-Tutsi violence erupted in Kigali immediately after the downing of the president's plane. The genocide in Kigali continued for at least eighty-eight days, lasting until the RPF liberated the city on July 4. In Gisenyi, killings continued for at least 101 days, from April 7 until July 17, when the Rwandan army, interim government, and hundreds of thousands of civilians fled the advancing RPF troops.

The delayed start date in Nyanza meant most of the population's initial reactions—to help their Tutsi kin, neighbors, classmates, and coworkers—persisted longer than in other places because it was not tested. For the first two weeks, the impulse to help was supported by local government officials at the cell, sector, commune, and province levels. This support reinforced residents' decisions to assist Tutsi and minimized threats against rescuers and potential victims, encouraging rescuers to continue in their work. However, once local leaders adopted Hutu extremists' stance and began to implement the genocide on April 21, many of those who initially opposed the killing joined in the violence.[15] In Nyanza, the lynching of Mayor Gisagara and public killings of Tutsi terrorized residents and discouraged them from persisting in their assistance to Tutsi. As the genocide intensified in Nyanza, the probability of being caught hiding Tutsi also escalated. Local officials organized security patrols to search house by house. Local officials instructed everyone to be vigilant, watch for signs of Inyenzi-Inkotanyi in hiding, and denounce infiltrators and "accomplices" of the enemy (Des Forges 1999, 251). Neighbors began to spy on each other and take note of changes to neighboring families' routines. The increasingly tense climate led to denunciations of people suspected of harboring Tutsi. People caught up in the genocide machine could not predict what might come next. Faced with these mounting threats, some people who had been protecting Tutsi continued, and others who had been hiding Tutsi asked them to leave.

Perhaps one of the most powerful mechanisms used to dissuade people from continuing to hide or help those targeted was the potential consequences for being discovered in these acts. Tragic stories of rescuers who were punished for their actions, though relatively rare, had amplified effects. Évariste explained how his own sons were killed because he had refused to report for duty at a roadblock and participate in killing Tutsi:

> ÉVARISTE: Two of my sons were killed when we fled. Someone informed on them. They had called me to stand on a roadblock, and I didn't want [to]. Then, when my wife and sons tried to run away, someone killed my sons.
>
> Q: But you are a Hutu? Why did they kill them?
>
> ÉVARISTE: They killed them because I did not want to be on the roadblock, and I did not want to participate in the killings. Also, their mother was a Tutsi. But the main reason was that I didn't want to participate.
>
> Q: Why didn't you want to kill?
>
> ÉVARISTE: They were targeting Tutsis, and my wife was Tutsi. How could I kill her brethren? Also, I had told myself that I would never kill anybody. . . .
>
> Q: How old were your sons who were killed?
>
> ÉVARISTE: One was married and left a baby, and another was an eighteen-year-old young man. People promoted evil deeds, and even the man who informed on them was their godfather. He is the one who sent them for death. (NYA21)

Évariste paid a high price for resisting. Many others who faced similar situations caved to the pressures and became perpetrators. Only a few cases like this had an amplified effect in the context of the genocide.

Stories about people killed for hiding Tutsi spread quickly via the rumor mill, known in francophone Africa as the *radio trottoir*, "sidewalk radio." Rwandans often relied on the *radio trottoir* because it was more truthful and informative than the official news broadcast on the national radio. The informal circulation of these stories alongside the ongoing threats and misinformation broadcast by the national radio and infamous Radio-Télévision Libre des Mille Collines (RTLM)—with its slogan, "If you are caught hiding Tutsi, they will kill you" (GIS35)—terrorized everyone. As a result, many people who had been hiding Tutsi became too afraid to continue and asked them to leave or to pursue new strategies. These stories also dissuaded people from offering assistance to those who came seeking it. Yet, in a few safe havens like Mugandamure, Rubona, and the Centre Saint Antoine orphanage, some courageous people persisted and continued to help Tutsi despite the increasing danger.

Father Eros and Father Vito remained at Centre Saint Antoine until May 23, when they were evacuated to Burundi by the Italian consul, who arrived at the orphanage with an Italian priest and a medical doctor to relieve the exhausted priests (NYA38). The priest and doctor brought by the consul stayed to take care of the children and protect the local staff. They remained until RPF soldiers established control over the area, effectively ending the genocide in the region by May 30 (Des Forges 1999, 302). The relatively swift arrival of RPF troops ensured the safety of at least 821 children at the Centre Saint Antoine orphanage.[16] In mid-July 1994, after recuperating in Burundi and Kenya, Father Eros returned to Rwanda and joined the children in Nyamata, in the neighboring Bugesera region, where the RPF had evacuated them in cooperation with the Red Cross. Unfortunately, twenty-four children died because of the rough conditions (NYA38). Father Eros accompanied the surviving children back to the orphanage in Nyanza.

The relatively short length of the genocide in Rwanda and swift arrival of RPF troops in Nyanza ensured the safety of the thousands of Tutsi, as well as the courageous Muslims of Mugandamure, Hutu residents of Rubona, and the Hutu and Tutsi staff of the Centre Saint Antoine orphanage who had risked their lives to protect them. Nonetheless, tens of thousands of Tutsi and opposition political party supporters died in the Nyanza region during the genocide, including hundreds of people who had sought protection at the regional football stadium.

Another important assemblage component in successful rescue was people's dynamic decision making in the context of the genocide. As events unfolded in April 1994, Rwandans could not imagine what horrors would ensue in the coming weeks and months. Each day, individual Rwandans had to make decisions based on very limited information from the national radio, the RTLM, or the RPF's Radio Muhabura—if they had a radio and could capture their broadcasts—or from the *radio trottoir*. The ultimate outcome of any person's efforts was the product of a series of small decisions and events that unfolded over time. The people making these decisions were entangled in dynamic, interlaced actor-networks that preceded and then coalesced or dissolved during the genocide. Their decisions—sometimes strategic and calculated, sometimes intuitive and spontaneous—were emergent effects of these actor-networks.

For instance, Father Eros's decision to stay in Rwanda in early April was not a foregone conclusion as the violence began. Rather, the decision to stay emerged from a series of smaller decisions and events:

> On the seventh or eighth [of April], I got a call from the Italian consulate in Kigali and from the [Italian] Embassy in Kampala. They advised me—well, more like ordered me—to evacuate. I did not decide right away that I was staying. I said, "Let's see how the situation evolves." There were no massacres in Nyanza and in Butare. The radio was broadcasting news; there were massacres in Kigali, in the north, and in Gikongoro [to the south].
>
> So, I started to think about [whether to leave], but then an event changed the situation. There was a priest I had lived with at the seminary in Rome, [Father Vito]. He had a small orphanage here in Kigali. It was caught in the crossfire between the RPF and the Rwandan army for ten days. On the sixteenth, they left Kigali with the children and ten to fifteen adults. They reached Nyanza on the seventeenth or sixteenth.... So, then we were two. Being with someone else comforted me. Talking to him, consulting each other....
>
> They started killing on the twentieth. The priests of Mugombwa left the parish church where people were killed [on April 20]. They called us from Butare, where the phones were working. Again, we decided to stay. Why? We were not sure of saving the children by staying, but if we left, how were we going to justify ourselves? We decided to do what we could do. (NYA38)

Throughout his account of events, Father Eros emphasized the small decisions that he made in changing circumstances—staying in Rwanda instead of evacuating, protecting Tutsi staff members and their families, continuing to stay, accepting Tutsi refugee children into the orphanage, refusing entry to Tutsi adults seeking refuge, falsifying the registry of orphans to disguise Tutsi children, organizing the orphans to defend the center's perimeter, enlisting the help of the police and military commanders, and using Catholic rituals to unify the orphans. These decisions culminated in the miracle of more than eight hundred children's lives saved. Likewise, Rubona's and Mugandamure's residents repeatedly decided to protect Tutsi residents in their communities from outside attackers, accept Tutsi fleeing from other places, and hide and defend refugees. In short, successful rescue was the product of repeated decision making over time and persistence in the face of increasing threats.

This gradual decision making unfolded in the genocide's gray zone, where people often had choiceless choices. Sometimes, attempts to save people resulted in a rescuer becoming a perpetrator. Pauline described one such case in Rubona where "a man got involved in the killings unintentionally" (NYA27). A Tutsi woman had hidden in her Hutu father-in-law's house in Rubona. On the day the Interahamwe overran the community, they found her. They ordered her husband "to kill her. He refused" (NYA28). The mob detained the couple and took them to Bunyeshywa, a place where the Interahamwe were killing people and dumping their bodies in mass graves; the husband's "elder brother followed them trying to rescue her and to get his brother out of trouble" (NYA28). "He followed them all the way to Bunyeshywa. He tried to protect her all along the way" (NYA27).

At Bunyeshywa, the brother pleaded for his brother and sister-in-law's lives for hours; finally, the Interahamwe "ordered him [the elder brother] to beat her to death. They threatened to kill him [and his brother] instead of her if he did not do it" (NYA27). The elder brother eventually complied with their orders, perhaps to save his brother and his own life, perhaps to end the emotional turmoil and torture at the massacre site, like Idi at the roadblock (chapter 1). "He hit her once, and then others killed her" (NYA27). In Gacaca court, the man confessed. Pauline, a genocide survivor and Gacaca judge, testified on his behalf, "His primary intention was to protect her, not to kill her" (NYA27). The judges considered his intentions, the duress of the situation, and his confession and sentenced him "to seven years in prison and four years of community service" in lieu of a life sentence (NYA27). In the gray zone, good intentions often led to terrible outcomes.

The gray zone also necessitated many smaller and less arduous decisions that still were morally ambiguous. Sometimes, the gray zone required deft decision making amid the chaos. Raissa recounted such an incident in Mugandamure: "The second [large] attack came in early June. [An Interahamwe mob came] to Twaha's house, a Hutu Muslim, to steal his wife's jewelry. She was Tutsi. Young Muslim men [from the neighborhood] intervened. They caught the Interahamwe and escorted them out of the neighborhood. A Hutu Muslim man, Habibu, who had come with his Tutsi wives from Biryogo [in Kigali] to hide here, advised the young Muslim men to let the Interahamwe go unharmed" (MUG 20). The neighborhood men wanted to exact punishment according to the logics of community justice and demonstrate their authority over Mugandamure, by beating the militiamen. Habibu interceded, intuitively recognizing that beating the men would likely cause the militia to return to Mugandamure with the backing of government officials, police, or military, who could order a systematic search of the neighborhood—an eventuality that would endanger the lives not only of the hundreds of Tutsi hiding there but also of the Muslim Hutu protecting them. Habibu's spontaneous intervention seeking mercy for the attackers served the greater moral good of protecting innocent people's lives.

The decisions of government authorities and military or police commanders often created morally ambivalent situations for people under them in the chain of comment. For example, the soldiers who guarded the Centre Saint Antoine orphanage at night had spent the day killing people. As Father Eros explained, "The soldiers who would come to protect us at night would recount stories of what they had done during the day to the children. How many people they had killed." Entangled in the genocide's moral gray zone, the soldiers killed "RPF infiltrators," "traitors," and "enemies of Rwanda" during the daytime when they were ordered to. At night, their same officer sent those soldiers to protect the children at Centre Saint Antoine, where they helped save the children.

The gray zone also required smaller moral compromises; people engaged in rescue had to lie constantly. At times they even had to pretend to be killers themselves. One night in May 1994, Djumapili recruited men from outside Mugandamure to search for a university student rumored to be hiding at someone's house in Amajyambere. The Muslim men at the neighborhood roadblock were unable to stop Djumapili and his mob from entering Mugandamure that night. The mob forced residents to sit outside while they searched each house for the student. When they found him hiding in Raissa's house, Djumapili accused Raissa of hiding RPF spies. Habineza, who was among the residents forced to sit outside, described what happened next:

> They wanted to take [the student] to the police roadblock on the highway. But the Muslims said no, that they would take care of him themselves. Yusuf, who was a much-respected, wealthy man who lived down by the mosque and who traveled regularly to Dubai for business, intervened. . . . Yusuf proposed to take [the student] to his house for the night, saying that he would sort out the situation in the morning. In the morning, Mama Jolie took [the refugee] and asked her renter to bring him to Gasoro, near where the RPF lines were. (MUG27)

By asserting "they would take care of him themselves," the Muslims of Mugandamure used the absolutist logic of the genocide to position themselves on the side of the genocidal state. The collective unity of their move undermined Djumapili's authority, which was backed only by the force of community outsiders. Yusuf then leveraged his superior social capital to take charge of the situation and negotiate an alternative ending. The community's collective lies saved the man's life.

At the Centre Saint Antoine orphanage, the gray zone of genocide similarly forced the Italian priests to make morally dubious decisions to save the children and staff in their protection. For instance, Father Eros was forced to deny shelter to others. On April 22, the day after the killings started in Nyanza, three soldiers "entered the center to search," and warned Father Eros, "Absolutely, no one must come into the center!" (NYA38). Later the same day, "some civilians managed to sneak into the center. I found them, and I forced them to leave because I feared that there would be a massacre like those that had occurred in churches. When the Interahamwe heard that there was a group of Tutsi somewhere, then right away they would come to kill them" (NYA38). As he recounted his decision, Father Eros's body language made clear the moral burden of his choice: his shoulders slumped, he bowed his head, and he rubbed his forehead. Fathers Eros and Vito succeeded in saving these children by refusing to help others. Had Father Eros given refuge to these others, his efforts would have likely resulted in a massacre.

To further illustrate the impossible life-or-death decisions they faced, Father Eros recounted their inability to protect the three Tutsi priests from the Nyanza parish who came to the orphanage seeking shelter:

> We received three Tutsi priests at our orphanage from Nyanza. We tried to hide them, but they had come during the day, so neighbors knew they were there. We tried to hide them, but there were people spying on us clandestinely, so we weren't able to hide them. We were seriously in danger. We suggested to the priests that for the sake of everyone, we needed to move them somewhere else and find them a new place to hide. We contacted Gahamanyi [the bishop], then Gahamanyi contacted a military commander. Then, the commander [of the local police] told us that we were in danger, that it was absolutely necessary to move the priests somewhere else.
>
> On May 3, six soldiers came to search the center. They were only looking for those priests. They didn't touch any other Tutsi. . . . It's only the three priests who were taken by the soldiers. They said they were taking them to protect them, but about ten kilometers [6.2 miles] from Nyanza they gave them to militias at the roadblock, and they killed them. It was on May 4, I think. (NYA38)

As Father Eros recounted these events, his face was pained. The burden of the three priests' deaths clearly weighed on his conscience, even if he recognized they had done what they could to try to save them.

Although Rubona, Mugandamure, and the Centre Saint Antoine orphanage faced the same terrible storm as the region around Nyanza, their unique histories, the social cohesion of residents, and the local genocide timeline helped make residents' rescue efforts both possible and successful. Father Eros explained it in religious terms, stating that these "small miracles" amid the "overwhelming evil" of the genocide were "signs of God's presence."

Actor-Networks in the Space of Death

Collective, community-level action to hide and protect people in the genocide was rarely successful for long, but residents of Rubona, Mugandamure, and the Centre Saint Antoine succeeded in saving more than a thousand lives over six weeks. Their efforts ultimately succeeded thanks to the relatively late start of mass violence and the timely arrival of the RPF in the area. In Mugandamure, the community's heroic efforts cannot be attributed solely to exceptionally good character or profound Muslim faith. The community's collective action to hide and protect people arose from deeply woven interactions of actor-networks involving the built and natural environment, local social history, politics, identity, and faith. This collective action of rescue was not an accident, nor was it a predetermined outcome; rather, it arose from contingencies and interactions of people improvising reactions to extraordinary circumstances.

In these three communities, residents responded to the same genocide policy enacted in Nyanza in a very different way. The trajectories of these communities illustrate the local nature of genocidal violence in Rwanda and the importance of local social histories, relationships, and unity to foster community-level action for rescue. The 1994 genocide of Tutsi entailed the articulation of national-level policies implemented by national-level actors that required the participation and support of local actors who had their own power relations, local histories, social networks, and understandings of the situation. Once prefecture, commune, and sector authorities in Nyanza capitulated to the demands of the genocidal state, a new actor-network coalesced, and the remaining local authorities switched from resisters to implementers and perpetrators. The rapid onset of widespread violence in Nyanza following the lynching of Mayor Gisagara typifies the most common pattern of genocide in communities that initially resisted. The region also reflects the general pattern of genocidal violence in southern Rwanda, where widespread killing was often imported (or imposed) from outside. The case demonstrates that some elites outright refused genocide as a policy, while many others were slow to adopt it. The events in Nyanza substantiate the argument that early intervention by the international community could have quelled the spread of violence and prevented hundreds of thousands of deaths.

The shift from resistance to genocide enacted what Michael Taussig (1984) called "the space of death"—a liminal space dominated by irrational and eschatological thinking (468–69). This space of death substantiates a "culture of terror" that renders the potential objects of torture as "hated and feared, objects to be despised, yet also of awe, the reified essence of evil in the very being of their bodies" (470). Thus, the space of death mobilizes the productive power of torture and violence to perpetuate itself, entangling more people—whether as perpetrator or victims—in itself. As power shifted from resisters to perpetrators, ordinary Rwandans in Nyanza faced new pressures from local officials to participate in security patrols, transform defensive security barriers into killing sites, destroy their Tutsi neighbors' homes, and hand over their kin, friends, neighbors, and acquaintances to Interahamwe or security forces. In Mugandamure and Rubona, however, sector- and cell-level officials refused to comply. The power shift never occurred, so the space of death never intruded to entangle residents in these communities. Instead, these communities maintained their unity and worked together to keep genocidal violence from penetrating the neighborhood, even as the context of the genocide shifted and changed.

The sense of unity shown at Mugandamure, Rubona, and the Centre Saint Antoine orphanage in the face of genocide and their collaboration to protect Tutsi kin, friends, and neighbors as well as strangers who sought refuge from elsewhere were rare in 1994. Their stories illustrate the complex interplay of physical infrastructure, topography, social relationships, local leadership, assistance from government officials or military and police officers, luck, the power of religious belief to reinforce courage in the face of terror, and incremental decision making in the production of any specific outcome. Although local leaders were key to successful rescue at these sites, they could not have saved people on their own. While their will to help was their own and guided their decisions, their agency and the success of their actions emerged from the local actor-networks that coalesced during the genocide.

The next chapter contrasts these collective community-level efforts with the special opportunities for rescue offered by Rwanda's national borders. Tutsi men, women, and children could find safety in the neighboring countries of Zaire (now the Democratic Republic of the Congo), Uganda, Tanzania, or Burundi, if they were able to evade Rwandan border officers and those mobilized to participate in the genocide. The chapter explores the strategies people used to cross the border in the town of Gisenyi, where many courageous people smuggled Tutsi across the border.

5

THE BORDER AS SALVATION AND SNARE

> **When I reached Goma, I . . . turned to look at Rwanda. In my heart, I felt anguish, believing I could never return because of everything I had seen there.**
>
> —Pacifique, genocide survivor (GIS20)

In 1994, Jeanne d'Arc was a widow in her late sixties with several grown children and more than a dozen grandchildren, ranging in age from a few months old to their early twenties. She lived in Majengo, a densely populated neighborhood in Gisenyi town not far from the border with Goma, Congo. Her daughter and several of her grandchildren lived with her in the family compound. On the morning of April 7, the national radio instructed Rwandans, like Jeanne d'Arc, to stay home. Around 10 a.m., a mob of Interahamwe militiamen, including many young men from the neighborhood, arrived at her neighbor's house. First they seized a neighbor's truck, saying they needed it to round up *ibyitso* (accomplices, meaning RPF spies or sympathizers). Then a neighbor told the militiamen she had seen their neighbor, Étienne, a Tutsi and father of five, go hide in a small building behind the main house in Étienne's compound. The Interahamwe entered the building and apprehended Étienne, along with his eldest son, who was hiding with him. The militiamen told Étienne they were taking him and his son to the commune office for questioning. As they loaded Étienne and his son into a red Hilux pickup truck, he told his family, "Don't worry. I have my ID card with me. I know the mayor will let us go because we've always been friends" (reported by GIS20).

Little did Étienne know that when the militiamen said they were taking them to the "commune," they meant "the Red Commune," or municipal cemetery, which had become the principal killing field in Gisenyi town. When the Interahamwe abducted people, they said they were going to the commune office to keep them calm. Thus, they nicknamed the site the Red Commune (*la Commune Rouge*), because of the bloodstained ground. Étienne and his son never returned. A few days later, Jeanne d'Arc heard an Interahamwe militiaman threaten Étienne's family, "Do not wait for them to come back! We did not take them to the commune office. We took them to the cemetery."

In the days that followed, Jeanne d'Arc and her family resumed their daily routines. They often stayed inside the compound to avoid the roaming bands of Interahamwe. Her sons, sons-in-law, and grandsons reported for "security duty" at the roadblocks and night rounds as demanded by local officials.

Groups of Interahamwe returned to Étienne's home frequently. Sometimes, Jeanne d'Arc heard yelling coming from inside. She occasionally saw Étienne's wife, Verdiane, sneaking in or out of the compound before sunrise or after nightfall, presumably returning from a hiding place. Verdiane appeared to have been beaten; she had wounds on her face, shoulders, and arms.

One night in June, the police came to Étienne's house. They demanded someone open the door, but it remained closed. No sound came from inside. The police tried to break down the door, but they failed. They then went from window to window, shooting blindly into the house. Still, no sound came from inside. None of the neighbors dared ask the police what was wrong. The police eventually left.

In the morning, the neighbors went to Étienne's house. They discovered that his second-eldest child, a daughter, had been shot in the head and died during the night. Étienne's fourteen-year-old son, Pacifique (GIS20), was covered head to toe in her blood. The neighbors helped Étienne's family bury the girl in their garden.

That evening, the Interahamwe again returned to Étienne's home. This time they managed to get inside. They raped and severely beat Verdiane. In the morning, Pacifique decided enough was enough. He said to his family, "I will go to Congo. If I die, that will be it. Life means nothing to me anymore. If you die, that's how God will have wanted it. If we all stay alive, we will meet again" (GIS20).

Pacifique then approached Jeanne d'Arc to ask for her help. Jeanne d'Arc responded, "No problem. Come, and I'll take you." Jeanne d'Arc instructed Pacifique to wear shorts and go barefoot, so he looked like a poor, young boy. She told him, "We will tell everyone that I am your grandmother." When they left together on foot, Jeanne d'Arc gave Pacifique a washbasin to carry. Her adult daughter found the pair en route and walked with them. Along the way, Jeanne d'Arc's daughter seethed at her mother, "Where are you taking this Tutsi?" Then she nagged, "Why don't you leave him so that they kill him?" They passed numerous roadblocks along the way, some manned by Interahamwe and local men recruited from the neighborhoods, others staffed by policemen or soldiers. When asked, Jeanne d'Arc told the men Pacifique was her grandson. Her daughter dared not contradict her. As they walked, they saw dead bodies strewn on the sides of the road.

When they neared the police barracks at the border, Jeanne d'Arc instructed Pacifique to pass through the nearby fields and wooded areas, pointing out the path near the Goma airport. From there, Pacifique found his own way to safety in Congo. Once he had crossed the border, he looked back at his home country: "When I reached Goma, I stood in the Goma airfield and turned to look at Rwanda. In my heart, I felt anguish, believing I could never return because of everything I had seen there" (GIS20). He then continued to his aunt's home in Goma. A few days later, Jeanne d'Arc helped Pacifique's younger brother cross the border in the same way. Feeling emboldened, she carried the ten-year-old child on her back through the official border crossing into Congo and all the way to the home where Pacifique was staying. She told the men at the roadblocks along the way that her grandson was sick. In early July, she brought Pacifique's youngest sister in the same way.

Pacifique's mother, Verdiane, remained in the family's home in Gisenyi. Interahamwe and Impuzamugambi militiamen continued to arrive at the house to beat and rape her. When she begged them to shoot her, they responded, "We cannot waste our bullets. We will beat you down until you die. . . . You will serve as a pillow for our father Habyarimana." In mid-July, as RPF troops advanced and the battle approached the city, leaders of the interim government and the wealthy businessmen who had funded the Hutu extremist media and militias began fleeing to Congo with their families. Many Hutu civilians followed them. A neighbor warned Verdiane, "If you do not leave tonight, the Interahamwe will kill you in the morning." She left at midnight. The roadblocks were now abandoned because the local guards feared the approaching RPF troops. Verdiane found her way across the border through the brush. In the end, she saved herself.

Pacifique and his siblings survived thanks to Jeanne d'Arc's empathy, courage, and kindness. Like many rescuers, Jeanne d'Arc was intimately connected to genocide perpetrators, like her sons, sons-in-law, and grandsons. Her male kin reported for duty at the roadblocks or night rounds and likely participated in killing or, at least, handed people over to soldiers or militiamen. Even her daughter supported the state's genocidal project and could not understand her mother's empathy for the Tutsi neighbor children. Nonetheless, Jeanne d'Arc saved them by guiding or literally carrying them across the border.

Pacifique recounted Jeanne d'Arc's story to me nearly twenty years later, in 2013. Jeanne d'Arc dared not confront the militiamen and police who came to attack her neighbors' family, but she helped the children later. Thanks to her heroism, Pacifique had grown up, completed his education, found a good job, married, and had children of his own. He never forgot the terrible things he experienced in 1994: his father and older brother's kidnapping and presumed deaths, his mother's pleading with the Interahamwe militiamen who repeatedly attacked the family, the night spent lying silently in his sister's blood.

He also remembered, vividly, Jeanne d'Arc's courage.

When I asked to meet Jeanne d'Arc, Pacifique happily obliged, although he warned us she was so old and frail she did not remember the details of what she had done. When we arrived at her family's simple house of adobe bricks covered in cement and topped with a tin roof, one of her adult granddaughters, who was doing the laundry, greeted us. She went to call Jeanne d'Arc from inside the house. Jeanne d'Arc hobbled to the doorway and sat on the grass mat her granddaughter spread for her. She greeted us and hugged Pacifique, even though she was, at first, unsure who he was. He reminded her, and she exclaimed, "Oh, yes, my son! Thank you for coming to see me. And thank you for bringing these visitors." We chatted briefly, and then I extended my hand to her with a few hundred francs tucked inside and said, "We brought you some banana beer." She cackled with glee and thanked us profusely.

Jeanne d'Arc and Pacifique's story illustrates several important factors related to rescue and the border.

First, the border's proximity to Gisenyi town offered an enormous opportunity for rescue. Thousands of people near the border found safety by escaping across it on their own or with the help of others.

Second, many rescuers were ordinary Rwandans living in poverty who used the simple means at their disposal to help others. Jeanne d'Arc's gender and status as a family elder protected her. In the Rwandan gender cosmology, grandmothers are due respect from kin, community members, or strangers (Burnet 2012). Her own daughter railed against her privately but did not dare do so publicly. As a poor, elderly woman, Jeanne d'Arc was inconsequential to the militiamen, soldiers, police, and border guards. Nonetheless, her grandmotherly authority discouraged any detailed questions. Jeanne d'Arc used her social invisibility to save her neighbor's children. Ismael Mugenzi, whose story opened this book, saved the lives of his neighbor's wife and brother-in-law in the same way, by paddling them across Lake Kivu in his common fishing boat.

Third, rescuers were not able to help everyone. Jeanne d'Arc never confronted the militiamen, police, or soldiers. Neither she nor the other neighbors intervened when the militiamen apprehended Étienne and his son. She did, however, ferry Pacifique and his siblings across the border to Congo—resisting genocidal violence and state sovereignty indirectly.

Finally, many acts of rescue happened in the open. Twice, Jeanne d'Arc crossed the border at the official checkpoint with one of Pacifique's siblings strapped to her back. This intimate act, and the bureaucratic fact that children were registered on their mother's identity cards by law, made Jeanne d'Arc's lies to border guards and roadblock monitors, that the children were her grandchildren, plausible. And her status as a poor, elderly woman made her seem innocuous to the border guards, who could never imagine this woman was a hero risking her life to save Tutsi children.

For Jeanne d'Arc and those children, the border was salvation, but it could also be a snare for those targeted by genocidal violence attempting to flee. The national security forces and militias erected a network of roadblocks across the country to identity Tutsi for extermination. They used the border to ensnare people at official border crossings and along clandestine smuggling routes. Nonetheless, many used the border to escape; some Hutu helped people cross it as well. The border emerged as a polyvalent actor-network component enlisted in a multiplicity of assemblages to produce genocidal agency at times and rescuer agency at others.

This chapter examines the opportunity for rescue in the city of Gisenyi created by the proximity of Rwanda's western border with the Congo. In Gisenyi, the city's dense urban topography made it relatively easy for local authorities who supported the genocide and the Interahamwe and Impuzamugambi militias to quickly establish and effectively maintain a monopoly on the use of force. State sovereignty became synonymous with genocidal violence. As a result, hiding people from attack squads became extremely risky early in April 1994, and moving Tutsi refugees or smuggling them across the border without detection was very difficult. Nonetheless, the border, as the boundary of the genocidal state's sovereignty, offered some Rwandans, like Jeanne d'Arc, a relatively low-risk opportunity to assist people being targeted.

Merchants, traders, and businessmen, who had experiential knowledge of the border from moving goods across it, through both legal and extralegal channels, also had special capacity to move people across the border.[1] Unlike Jeanne d'Arc, whose power rested in her social invisibility, for these businessmen, opportunity to rescue arose from the confluence of their special knowledge of the border's porousness with their patronage ties to the government, military, and MRND and CDR parties. Because of the history of Islam in Rwanda and the overrepresentation of Muslims in business and trade, these individuals were disproportionately Muslim.

Thus, during the genocide, the border simultaneously induced genocidal agency and acts of rescue, depending on local topographies, histories, politics, authority, multigenerational cycles of reciprocity, or social cohesion. In the genocide's gray zone, the border simultaneously constituted an assemblage itself and an assemblage component that facilitated various kinds of agency.

The Border as Actor-Network and Assemblage Component

Many scholars in anthropology and geography have analyzed borders, government policies and enforcement strategies around borders, and the implications of those strategies for human migration and trade.[2] Several of these scholars have explored the duality of the border as both a geopolitical abstraction and a material manifestation, applying actor-network theory to elucidate how human agency becomes diffused through the networks of nonhuman assemblage components that constitute it. For example, Biao Xiang and Johan Lindquist (2014) emphasize the need to focus on the infrastructures of borders, border enforcement, and "systematically interlinked technologies, institutions, and actors that facilitate and condition mobility" for labor migration in Asia (124). In tracing the heterogeneous components entangled in the actor-network of US border enforcement at the border with Mexico, anthropologist Jason De León (2015) highlights how nonhuman actors, including the harsh terrain of the Sonoran Desert, animals, weather, physical barriers, drones, sensors, and policy come together with human actors, including US Immigration and Customs Enforcement agents and US politicians and policy makers, to kill thousands of extralegal border crossers each year. As De León explains, "agency is relational and produced as part of a human-induced chain reaction. Once set in motion, humans and nonhumans as political actors cannot be separated, even if the former have more obvious intentions" (2015, 61). Rwanda's border with Congo, as an actor-network, produced similar effects. The border combined with topographical features, human and nonhuman political actors, and border enforcement by national security forces and Interahamwe militiamen to deliver opportunities to wreak, resist, or escape genocidal violence.

For people living in spaces cleaved by geopolitical abstractions materialized in border fortifications, surveillance technology, and border enforcement, the practicalities of everyday life require daily border crossings and contending with enforcement mechanisms. These realities create specific assemblages related to the practices associated with negotiating the border and border enforcement. Margath Walker's (2018) examination of Mexico's southern border with Guatemala highlights the international, national, regional, and hyperlocal policies and practices that induce particular kinds of agency among ordinary people. The militarization and fortification of Mexico's southern border over the past twenty years transformed people's interactions with the border and their strategies of evasion. Even with high-tech border enforcement and fortifications, extralegal border-crossing channels operate within plain view of the state because local, regional, and national economies depend on them (Walker 2018).

Similarly, before the coalescence of the specific local assemblages generated by the genocide, people living near the border between Rwanda and Congo embodied the everyday practices associated with negotiating the border and its enforcement, engaging with the border simultaneously as a geopolitical abstraction and a material manifestation. In 1994, Gisenyi was home to approximately twenty-two thousand residents (Republic of Rwanda 1994, 33). The city had grown up since the German colonial period as a commercial outpost on the western edge of Rwanda; a sizable Muslim population had long called Gisenyi home (see chapter 3).

People at all levels of the socioeconomic hierarchy contended with the border daily, even if it had little fortification and no high-tech enforcement in 1994. Those who had the required papers or who transported goods legally made their way through two official border crossings, the Grand Barrière (Large gate) and the Petite Barrière (Small gate). Located near the lakeshore and equipped with a paved road, the Grand Barrière handled heavy cargo trucks and commercial traffic. The Petite Barrière primarily handled foot traffic, including the hundreds who crossed the border daily for work or trade, or to visit friends and relatives. People who did not have the necessary papers or wanted to avoid customs fees or taxes found other ways to cross the border, often under the gaze of state agents charged with border enforcement.

Like border towns all over the world, Gisenyi formed a single metropolitan area with its mate across the border, in this case Goma in Congo, and the economy of the combined metropolis focused on cross-border commerce. Rwanda is one of the major land routes from the eastern Congo to seaports in Mombasa and Dar es Salaam. Raw materials from the eastern Congo, including timber and minerals, pass through Rwanda on their way to export elsewhere. Manufactured goods from Kenya and Uganda return to the Congo through Rwanda in the other direction (see map 4).

While much of Gisenyi's (and Goma's) economy is focused on this legal flow of trade, as at most borders around the world, a great deal of cross-border trade occurred through extralegal channels. This extralegal flow was facilitated in the early 1990s by the openness of the border in and near Gisenyi. The border there was an imaginary line passing unmarked through the fields, woods, and forest separating the two countries. Some private residences built on the border had gates that opened onto the other side of the border, effectively creating extralegal, but not clandestine, border crossings (see figure 1). Security forces sometimes patrolled these areas, but because they had no regular controls, these unofficial access points offered ample opportunities to cross the border outside legal channels. In fact, Rwandan security forces were often aware of the extralegal cross-border trade passing along these routes. Sometimes their commanders ordered them to monitor and facilitate this extralegal commerce. At other times, soldiers used the extralegal trade as an opportunity to make extra income by independently facilitating the movement of goods along these routes. Although security at official crossing points was very tight during the genocide, these unofficial crossings remained open, offering an enormous opportunity for rescue for those who dared try.

The politics and history related to the border and human mobility across it induced particular forms of agency embedded in the heterogeneous components that comprised the actor-network at the border. That agency, and the actor-network that produced it, persisted during the genocide to some extent. Manifestations of state power at the border limited ordinary people's choices during the genocide, but these manifestations of state power arose from a history that produced embodied practices in ordinary citizens. Restrictions on mobility in the country dated to the colonial era (see chapters 3 and 4). The postcolonial government vowed to remove such restrictions, but the government instead periodically reimposed them, for national security reasons or to quell internal political dissent.

One such reimposition came in the immediate aftermath of the RPF's initial incursion into the country in October 1990, when the state severely curtailed

FIGURE 1. A gate in a wall on the Rwanda-Congo border. Photo by the author.

both internal and external movement (Sebarenzi 2009, 52, 62). Internally, people were required to have national identity cards and a permit signed by local authorities or the national police to leave their communes of residence (52, 62). Government officials, civil servants, and NGO workers could secure papers that authorized them to move between their communes of residence and work, but they were not allowed to go elsewhere without special authorization (62–63).

Movement across national borders was even more tightly controlled because the Habyarimana government feared both that people would flee to join the RPF rebels and that RPF operatives would enter the country as spies or "infiltrators" (62). Rwandans of all ethnicities needed special authorization, beyond a passport, to cross. Tutsi found it difficult, if not impossible, to get the required authorizations. As Tuyisingize, a large-scale importer-exporter, explained, "[The passes] were issued at the police station. . . . Tutsi could not cross to Goma. If they wanted to try, they had to have a very serious reason [for going]. . . . A few Tutsi could get [the passes], but most of them could not" (GIS41). These restrictions on mobility remained in place until 1994.

Confronted with these material manifestations of state sovereignty and the border, businessmen and traders who frequently traveled between Rwanda and Congo sought to ease their movement across the border by securing dual nationality (GIS41). But, again, Tutsi businessmen found it nearly impossible to secure dual nationality after the civil war started in 1990 (GIS41). Throughout this period, Tutsi especially faced intense scrutiny of their identity papers at security checkpoints because national security forces suspected them of being RPF infiltrators. These policing tactics normalized checkpoints and the use of race as a marker of suspicion.

The limits on mobility fed into the strengthening of patronage networks later used to proliferate genocidal violence. To secure Rwandan travel authorizations, businessmen and traders needed patronage ties to influential people in the government, the MRND party (or later the CDR), and the military. This need for patronage linked many businessmen into social networks that became entangled in Hutu extremist politics in the early 1990s. During the genocide, these patronage ties were, like the border itself, bivalent; they simultaneously imposed obligations on clients to support the genocidal intentions of their patrons and furnished the same clients with enhanced power to protect Tutsi and others from genocidal violence.

During the genocide, the restrictions on mobility and security checkpoints became tools to identify Tutsi and political opponents for killing. Rwanda's national borders were effectively closed on April 6, within hours of President Habyarimana's assassination. Rwandan border agents immediately stopped almost all foot and vehicle traffic across the western border. After a few days, they resumed letting civilians with special permits cross, but they intensified their scrutiny of papers and detained anyone who "looked Tutsi" or whom they suspected of being an RPF infiltrator, even people with the correct documents. Border agents consulted lists, sent from Kigali, of opposition politicians and others deemed threats to national security. While some people with influence or connections to influential people were able to cross, the vast majority of Tutsi were stopped at the border and detained or turned away. Even Rwandans whose identity cards indicated they were Hutu risked detention and interrogation by the police, border guards, or other security forces if they "looked Tutsi" or were suspected of membership in opposition political parties. Nonetheless, the border remained open for trade at Cyangugu and Gisenyi. In part, this decision was necessary; the cross-border trade through these two cities was vital to the national economy and people's everyday survival.

As Maurizio Albahari (2016) wrote about Europe's borders, the border comprises a "classical surveillance and security mechanism" and the "threshold of salvation" for those fleeing violence, whether direct or structural (20). Once genocide became national policy on April 12, the border became a trap for Tutsi and others targeted for killing, even as it offered salvation (Straus 2006; Guichaoua 2015b, 235–37). National security forces and militiamen set up roadblocks along the national highways leading to the borders to weed out Tutsi and political opponents trying to flee. In rural areas, security forces and militiamen set up barriers along known smuggling routes or unofficial border crossing points to catch men, women, and children fleeing for their lives. At the same time, Rwanda's international border represented salvation because the genocidal state's sovereignty ended there. Furthermore, in the genocide's gray zone, inanimate elements of the actor-network, like shallow points on the Akanyaru River in southern Rwanda or doors in the walls of residential compounds in Gisenyi that opened into the Congo, took on ambiguous roles; they could be conduits to escape or traps to catch and kill fleeing Tutsi.

The balance between salvation and snare emerged differently at different borders owing to local and regional histories and geopolitics. Each of Rwanda's borders had distinct characteristics that produced different effects. Thus, Rwanda's national borders, intersecting with national, regional, and local assemblages, had polyvalent effects on patterns of genocidal violence and escape.

For instance, the southern border with Burundi most often became a snare. Political tensions between the Hutu-dominated government in Rwanda and the Tutsi-dominated government in Burundi had caused both countries to reinforce the borders with fortifications and enforce restrictions vigorously. The national highway leading from the southern town of Butare to the border with Burundi had twenty to twenty-five roadblocks on it in just twenty-five miles; the one nearest the border was "manned by soldiers, some of them armed with machine guns and grenades" (Des Forges 1999, 463). Men at the roadblocks inspected the identity papers of all Africans who passed, searching for Tutsi among them (463). In Gikongoro Province, border guards and government soldiers stopped approximately one thousand people between April 12 and 15 gathered at the Burundi border from crossing at the official border or by wading across the river (443). As the genocide continued, Interahamwe militiamen, civilian mobs, the national police, and government troops waited at the border to attack and kill Tutsi who tried to flee to safety (376–79, 497–98). Thus, the border became a trap to contain and kill Tutsi refugees, often before the watchful eyes of foreign civilians evacuating from Rwanda in escort convoys traveling the same routes and international aid workers who waited on the Burundi side of the border to help (463–64). Some Tutsi refugees who made it to Burundi were then attacked and killed by Burundian Hutu militias at the very moment they thought they had made it to safety (400). The Burundian military eventually intervened to protect Rwandan Tutsi refugees, and some twelve thousand Rwandans managed to cross into Burundi by April 19 (400, 463). Many more wanted to leave, but they found it impossible to cross at official crossings after April 19.

The eastern border with Tanzania, in contrast, remained largely open, providing a clear promise of salvation to fleeing Tutsi. In eastern Rwanda, the army and government security forces were focused on defeating the RPF, which advanced rapidly in the last two weeks of April (see map 3). The RPF pushed south to take Byumba on April 21, continued to the south and east to take Rwamagana on April 27, and then Rusumo, at the border with Tanzania in the southeast, on April 30 (295). As the RPF advanced, Hutu and Twa civilians, who feared being killed by RPF soldiers, fled to the west as the Rwandan army fell back, or eastward toward Tanzania. An estimated quarter of a million Rwandans, including Tutsi fleeing genocide and others fleeing the RPF, crossed into Tanzania on April 28 and April 29 (636). How many of those refugees were Tutsi or otherwise targeted for killing is unknown.

In Gisenyi, the border with the Congo persisted as both salvation and snare throughout the 101 days of the genocide. Large-scale violence targeting Tutsi began in town within hours of President Habyarimana's assassination and continued until RPF troops arrived in the region in mid-July (chapter 3). The Grand and Petite Barrières immediately became traps for civilians fleeing violence. During the night of April 6, 1994, a top military commander met with local militiamen. He told them, "The enemy is none other than Tutsi," and ordered them to erect a roadblock a few hundred feet from the Grand Barrière.[3] Border guards turned away all Tutsi who tried to cross into Congo, along with opposition political party members and people on preestablished lists. Nonetheless, the border with Congo presented an opportunity and gave people hope. The region's topography, the lack of border fortification, and smuggling routes afforded hundreds—perhaps thousands—the chance to escape.

Urban Topography and Authority: State Sovereignty and Genocide

Genocidal priming in the years leading up to the genocide, the dominance of Hutu Power political elites in local patronage networks, and the supportive stance of local government, military, and political leaders on April 6 predisposed local actor-networks in Gisenyi to genocidal violence (chapter 3). The city's urban topography helped local authorities and the Interahamwe and Impuzamugambi militias monopolize the use of force in support of the genocide and made hiding or protecting Tutsi for long periods of time nearly impossible. Yet the international border with the Congo emerged as a polyvalent force.

In his study of genocide perpetrators in Cambodia, Alex Hinton (2005) identified genocidal priming as a factor that shapes perpetrators' decision making (280). Gisenyi town had been amply primed for genocide. The concentration of Tutsi in a city (12 percent of the population) surrounded by a region with very few Tutsi (less than 3 percent of the population) played into the ethnonationalist narratives of Hutu extremists (Republic of Rwanda 1994, 124–25). The waves of anti-Tutsi violence and subsequent impunity that began in 1959 and continued through 1974 established local patterns that reemerged in the early 1990s.

Even through these recurring waves of anti-Tutsi violence, however, Gisenyi town also served as a gateway into exile for Tutsi fleeing violence, establishing border crossing as a patterned reaction to anti-Tutsi violence. The waves of violence also established patterns of helping in the city. In 1959, the Muslim community in Gisenyi played a special role in protecting Tutsi. Hamis, a Muslim genocide survivor from Gisenyi, explained:

> In 1959, when they were burning Tutsi houses, there were some Muslims who had pity toward Tutsi. In 1959, a group of Muslims, including my father, decided to hide Tutsi in the Swahili camp to smuggle them to Congo later. Tutsi needed the Muslims to protect them. Those [Tutsi] who did not want to leave lived among the Muslims. Some of them did not convert; others did, like the women who married Muslims. The [Kayibanda] government discovered what the Muslims did and decided to kill or imprison those who had hid Tutsi. (GIS21)

Hutu mobs attacked the Swahili camps in Gisenyi, Kigali, and Rwamagana. They pillaged and looted. Government authorities arrested scores of Muslim men suspected of supporting the UNAR party or hiding Tutsi nobles. This history cemented the association between Muslim and Tutsi in the national imagination and ethnonationalist discourse; it also created a pattern of Tutsi seeking refuge or assistance from Muslims. The later waves of anti-Tutsi violence also touched Gisenyi town, but they mostly left Muslims unharmed. After each wave of violence subsided, many Tutsi from rural Gisenyi prefecture or Kibuye prefecture moved to Gisenyi town to escape persecution in the communities where they had been victimized and to seek social anonymity in the bustling urban landscape.

These historic patterns of anti-Tutsi violence reemerged in Gisenyi prefecture immediately after the RPF incursion in October 1990. Daily life in Gisenyi town changed in the wake of the RPF's surprise attack. As Pacifique described it,

> I remember that on October 1, in 1990, it's when the war started. At school, they said that the Inyenzi [RPF rebels/cockroaches] had attacked us. You could see that things were changing; people became bad. For some of our neighbors [*pause*], you could see that their hearts had changed. You might wonder what caused all that. Some of those neighbors had children who were soldiers, and they are the ones who came and told people what had happened. Their children were in Habyarimana's army, they came back and told their families, "We're being attacked by Tutsi." That's what changed them. They thought that their neighbors' relatives were the ones attacking and compromising national security. (GIS20)

Within days of the RPF incursion, scores of Tutsi men and youth were arrested in Gisenyi town as part of a nationwide roundup of "RPF infiltrators" (Des Forges 1999, 49). They were detained in the soccer stadium because the prison was not large enough to accommodate them all. Most were held for weeks or months without being charged.

The creation of local Interahamwe and Impuzamugambi cells in 1992 further increased day-to-day insecurity for Tutsi in Gisenyi town. Pacifique continued:

> They [Interahamwe and Impuzamugambi] started entering people's homes and looting their property. They targeted people with whom they didn't share the same [political] views. In 1991, two groups like that were created in our neighborhood. . . . They started committing acts of violence. . . . That's the kind of life we led. In 1992—you can't mention all the incidents that happened. . . . Many people were killed or arrested in this town. They were accused of being Inkotanyi accomplices. My own

> brother was taken by those militias to the police station and accused of being an Inkotanyi spy. We never saw him again.
>
> In 1993, many bad things happened, and political parties became too many. . . . The MRND, which was the ruling party, the CDR, MDR Power [*pause*]. The MRND and CDR had those they referred to as "the youth." They were so wicked. Whenever they held rallies at the Umuganda Stadium, it was like life had come to a halt in this whole town. When they met any Tutsi [in the street], they would not leave them in peace. That Tutsi person had to run for their life, otherwise they could die right on the spot. The criminals were not brought to justice. They did not face any punishment for their actions. (GIS20)

The cycle of anti-Tutsi violence and impunity, combined with anti-Tutsi propaganda in the media, schools, and workplaces, created a general atmosphere of fear and eroded solidarity within communities and neighborhoods in Gisenyi. The persistent symbolic and physical violence against Tutsi residents conditioned Hutu community members—even moderates—to remain silent, ignore it, and eventually withdraw assistance from their neighbors.

Genocide was also supported in Gisenyi by the city's distinct urban topography, which facilitated genocidal violence once government, military, and political leaders issued orders to find and kill RPF infiltrators and supporters. The density of people in the city landscape meant local authorities who collaborated with militias could easily control space with roadblocks, security patrols, and nightly rounds. Hiding people from attack squads or smuggling them from place to place was extremely difficult because the settlement density made low-tech surveillance, such as neighbors watching each other, extremely effective. The condensed space made it easier for genocidal authorities to maintain a monopoly on the use of force.

Deploying Social Logics in Strategies of Assistance

Muslims in Gisenyi town reacted to the unprecedented circumstances of the genocide much as Rwandans of other religious faiths did (chapter 3). In Gisenyi, many leaders in the Muslim community had dense social and patronage ties to Hutu extremists (chapters 1 and 3). Unlike in Biryogo and Mugandamure, the historical Swahili camp in Gisenyi had been erased from the topography of the city in the mid-twentieth century (chapters 3 and 4). As a result, Muslims in Gisenyi town had spread out to residential neighborhoods through the city, where they lived interspersed with Rwandans of other religions. In addition, the everyday habits of city life reduced residents' reliance on reciprocity with their kin and neighbors. Finally, the Muslim community in Gisenyi town was quite large, constituting an estimated five thousand to eight thousand residents in the early 1990s.[4] These local characteristics of Gisenyi town meant Muslim residents were enmeshed in actor-networks that greatly resembled those of non-Muslim Rwandans.

All these factors rapidly manifested in Gisenyi's trajectory of genocide. On April 7, Tutsi in Gisenyi immediately understood they were in grave danger and sought to hide. Despite the Muslim community's social ties to Hutu extremists, Hutu Muslims were themselves the object of suspicion because of the community's history of helping Tutsi during earlier episodes of violence and intermarriage among Muslims and Tutsi. Furthermore, Hutu Muslims were suspected because they had renounced the racist extremism that had dominated in Gisenyi since at least 1992. As Saidat (GIS16), a Hutu Muslim woman who was in her mid-forties in 1994, described,

> A young man from Mukamira came running to my house. I knew him. I told him, "If you stay here you are going to be killed because they are searching Muslims' houses." I took him to the pigsty, nearby in a small, wooded area. I told him, "Stay here until I come to tell you the coast is clear. If you leave before then, they will kill you." He stayed for a whole night until the next evening. Then, I took him to my house. When I heard people coming to search, I hid him in the ceiling or under the bed. At night he slept on the roof. (GIS16)

After hiding the young man for two months while looking for a way to smuggle him across the border, Saidat helped him join some of his family members in Goma.

One of the most common ways Hutu residents of all religious orientations helped save their neighbors was warning them of approaching attackers. Gracien (GIS35) eked out a living in Gisenyi town by working for a wealthy neighbor as a day laborer on her farm outside of town. When he encountered a group of Interahamwe headed to his employer's house to kill the woman, he ran ahead: "I immediately warned her and told everybody in the compound to say that she left and was no longer here. . . . She hid in the house. And the Interahamwe never came inside because I told them she had fled a long time ago" (GIS35). Gracien's employer survived thanks to his efforts and the misinformation he spread.

Like in Biryogo, some Hutu Muslims in Gisenyi organized to save Tutsi lives. Yaheya (GIS12), a middle-aged man with a wife and eight children, worked as a money changer and merchant in 1994. Along with a small group of Muslim men who were his close friends, Yaheya secretly organized to protect and save their Tutsi kin, neighbors, and friends. They obeyed the commands of local officials to mount security patrols during the genocide, but they used the patrols to save lives rather than kill. For instance, they rescued a young woman fleeing from Byahi, located about eight kilometers outside of town. A group of militiamen discovered the woman walking on side streets through a neighborhood notorious, in the years leading up to the genocide, for violence perpetrated by the unruly youth of the extremist CDR party. Yaheya told the story:

> On that day, I was in charge of the security patrol. They brought the girl to me and said, "She's Inyenzi." I asked them, "How do you know she is Inyenzi? What does an Inyenzi look like?" I explained that we first needed to agree what makes a person Inyenzi. [They said,] "If she came from the forest, then she must be one [Inyenzi]. If not, she's only Tutsi." Then I asked whether we would kill a Hutu who came from the forest. Everybody kept quiet and said nothing. The second in command [who was also a member of the clandestine rescuers] said, "I agree with Yaheya. We have to follow this rule otherwise we will kill our own children because we don't know the Inyenzi from the others." In the group, we became six people in favor of protecting the girl . . . only three who were against, so we won. We evacuated her to Congo. (GIS12)

In his negotiations with the Impuzamugambi, Yaheya mobilized the official government discourse, which described the situation as a war of self-defense against the "Inyenzi" army, meaning the RPF.

"Inyenzi" was not a new term in Rwandan political discourse, but its meaning had evolved over the decades. In the 1960s, "Inyenzi" referred to Tutsi rebels who launched attacks from refugee camps in Burundi against the newly elected, Hutu-dominated government in Rwanda. The rebels called themselves INYENZI, an acronym for *Ingangurarugo ziyemeje kuba ingenzi* (Those who attack first and who have vowed to be the best) (Twagilimana 2016, 114). It was a laudatory acronym, with the additional benefit that its literal meaning, "cockroach," drew on Rwandan folklore that characterizes cockroaches as moving quickly, being masterly at hiding, and operating under cover of darkness. In the 1990s, the Hutu-extremist hate media resurrected the term to remind Rwandan Hutu of these earlier threats to the country's democracy and to redefine the term "in a negative light" by emphasizing the creature's "vile characteristics—a little, sneaky, and contemptible insect that must be crushed and killed" (Twagilimana 2016, 115). Furthermore, "inyenzi," in all its meanings, contrasted sharply with the RPF rebels' Kinyarwanda name, Inkotanyi, meaning "intrepid fighters" (112). During the genocide, the media and government officials used the term Inyenzi and a wide variety of metonyms to describe the enemy. They rarely referred explicitly to "Tutsi." No one, however, misunderstood the true thrust of the messages: Tutsi civilians should be hunted down and exterminated.

Yaheya mobilized the dissonance between the literal and metaphorical messages to save the girl by insisting on the literal meaning of "Inyenzi": rebel soldier. He rejected the metaphorical extension of the term to all Tutsi civilians, subverting the government's genocide policy, which equated Inyenzi, rebel, Inkotanyi, RPF soldier, and Tutsi. He asked the militiamen, "How do you know she is Inyenzi? What does an Inyenzi look like?" When they responded that if she came from the forest then she must be Inyenzi, meaning an RPF infiltrator, Yaheya used their logic against them. He asked whether they would also kill a Hutu coming from the forest. In the end, Yaheya's logic won over the majority of the group and saved the girl's life.

Yaheya's strategies mobilized the social logics of Rwandan rhetorical arts to persuade the group to free the girl. In Rwanda, the rhetorical arts are considered among the highest forms of art and include proverbs, folktales, folk poetry, storytelling, poems and songs dedicated to cattle, autobiographical warrior poems, and the esoteric poetry of the central court's ritual specialists who recorded the dynasty's official history. The art of negotiation and the use of logic to win an argument are also considered within the domain of rhetorical arts.

These rhetorical arts and the linguistic slippage between the words "Tutsi" and "inyenzi," as well as other metonyms for Tutsi, were yet another polyvalent component in the actor-networks that emerged during the genocide. The Hutu extremist media and Hutu Power politicians, military leaders, and government officials used "inyenzi" and related terms to disseminate their genocidal orders in coded language that later made it extremely difficult to prove their culpability in court. The MRND, CDR, Hutu Power extremists, and militias used the same social logics to incite mobs to genocidal violence. Yaheya, however, redeployed this component of the actor-network to save this girl's life. This story illustrates how the moral gray zone of genocide can be manipulated by a few savvy people to rescue instead of kill. More importantly, this example demonstrates that one person who had remarkably little power on his own could deploy the agency within the actor-networks in which he was enmeshed to enlarge his capacity to rescue.

On other occasions, with his collaborators, Yaheya mobilized other components of the actor-networks—his and his collaborators' social capital and Rwandan cultural logics of respect for elders and social status. Yaheya and his two collaborators were middle-aged Muslim men and successful traders who held leadership positions in the mosque and were well respected in the neighborhood. The local band of Impuzamugambi militiamen consisted of neighborhood youth whom Yaheya and his friends had watched grow up. Rwandan sociality required that the militiamen respect the older men as if they were their own fathers. These social logics of fictive kinship were often upended during the genocide, but in this case, Yaheya's and his collaborators' social status helped reinforce them. Yaheya's position was further reinforced by his active participation in the security patrols. Because he and his accomplices went on security patrols, appearing to do their duty to "defend" the (Hutu) nation, the militiamen could not dismiss them as RPF collaborators.

As elsewhere in Rwanda, bribes and "gratuities" were commonly used to help save lives in Gisenyi. Mohamad (GIS28), who has been recognized as an *indakemwa* by Ibuka, negotiated with Interahamwe at a roadblock to release a stranger, asking them, "Are you going to kill this man just because he is tall?" (GIS28). Eventually, the militiamen relented and released the man. They said to Mohamad, "Now that we've let him go, buy us some tobacco." Mohamad gave them 5,000 Rwandan francs ($35 in 1994).[5] Mohamed's "gratuity" after the fact followed the social logics of Rwandan reciprocity and practices of "everyday corruption" embedded in forms of sociality (Blundo and Olivier de Sardan 2006; Olivier de Sardan 1999). During the genocide, bribes often took the form of gifts exchanged as part of kinship or patron-client relations, as had the forms of everyday corruption that facilitated the operation of the state in the years leading up to the genocide. For example, it was standard to "thank" local officials for their help with paperwork or other issues by offering them a "beer," most often given as cash.

In another case, Robert (GIS44), who worked for Bralirwa, the only brewery in Rwanda, kept his wife and children safe through an ongoing reciprocal gift exchange with a coworker in the Impuzamugambi militia. Headquartered in Gisenyi, Bralirwa operated continuously during the genocide because its production was considered an "essential service." In fact, its beer helped fuel the genocidal violence, as leaders often gave militiamen beer to "compensate" them for "their work" at the roadblocks and killing fields. Robert reported to work each day and rode the company shuttle bus that Bralirwa sent to pick up employees. Because of the importance of the business, the shuttle passed the roadblocks without stopping. Robert's wife was Hutu, but she was from eastern Rwanda and had a "Tutsi physiognomy," as he put it (GIS44). Robert feared she and the children would be attacked while he was at work. A friend and coworker at Bralirwa in the Impuzamugambi offered to keep them safe at his father's house. Robert explained how he thanked his coworker for this service: "Given that I worked at the brewery, I could ask for a crate of beer, which I would give him, like once a week. Since he was keeping my wife at his parents' house, he would say things like, 'How are you doing? Make sure you don't go beyond three kilometers out of town.' I made sure that I kept good relations with him" (GIS44). Robert not only acknowledged his friend's direct assistance, but also explained that the friend provided him with information that allowed him to avoid trouble. More importantly, Robert emphasized that he needed to "keep good relations" with his friend through regular gifts of beer and polite conversation. These elements—the service provided and gifts offered in return, all in the context of an ongoing, mutually beneficial relationship—were fundamental to the reciprocity at the heart of all Rwandan social relations.

In responding to the unprecedented context of the genocide, ordinary people with the will to help Tutsi and others targeted by the violence used whatever means they had to assist. Deploying everyday social logics to help people and resist the genocide increased one's capacity to act. These strategies plugged social logics into the actor-networks created by genocide and enlisted those logics, along with other assemblage components, to produce desired outcomes.

Wealth, Social Capital, Patronage, and Rescue

Patronage networks predisposed many Hutu, regardless of their religion, to genocide violence, but they also increased the capacity of some people to rescue. Businessmen and traders experienced in moving goods back and forth across the border had both specialized knowledge they could deploy to help people cross the border and extensive connections to patronage networks they could use to amplify their capacity. For the remainder of this chapter, I focus on the rescue efforts of one man, Tuyisingize, who used his wealth, social capital, and patronage ties to President Habyarimana's inner circle to increase his ability to rescue people (GIS41). His story contrasts with Jeanne d'Arc's, the poor, elderly woman whose efforts were recounted at the beginning of the chapter. Unlike Jeanne d'Arc, who used the invisibility conveyed by her elderly status and poverty to rescue her neighbor's children, Tuyisingize flaunted his social ties to power, prominence as a former soccer star, wealth, and knowledge of the border to save dozens of lives.

In 1994, Tuyisingize (GIS41) was in his early forties and married with four children. In 2013, he described himself as an independent trader "of all kinds of things" specializing in cross-border trade all over East Africa, including in eastern Congo. Tuyisingize was reluctant to go into detail about the various things he traded. He owned several buildings in Gisenyi's central commercial district and at least two private homes, including one that sat not far from the Grand Barrière border crossing. Over the course of the interview, Tuyisingize gradually revealed that an important aspect of his business was moving goods across the border through extralegal channels—smuggling.

When violence erupted on the morning of April 7, Tuyisingize organized a neighborhood self-defense effort against the roving bands of Interahamwe and Impuzamugambi militiamen.

> TUYISINGIZE: In our neighborhood, nothing [bad] happened because we established our own defenses. . . . I called the [neighborhood's] young men [*abasore*], and I told them, "Since we do not have weapons, let's use stones." I had an old car. We placed it in the middle of the road, so no car could pass. . . .
>
> Q: I know that during the genocide, the Interahamwe, soldiers, the police . . . established roadblocks, too. Was your roadblock like those ones? Or did people know that your roadblock was different?
>
> TUYISINGIZE: We set it to protect the people who were in our houses and keep them from being removed. It was only a car we put there. [The militiamen] used minibuses and trucks to carry people where they would eventually kill them. We put that car there to prevent those vehicles from getting on our streets, because many people sought refuge in our homes, in my home. We put [the roadblock] there so that they would believe that we were fellow Interahamwe [manning the roadblock]. [This impression] kept them from searching our neighborhood. They came to attack me once. So, we added stones near that car. . . . We only lost one person [in our neighborhood], a woman. She left her hiding place, so they found her in her home. (GIS41)

As a former professional soccer player, Tuyisingize had great influence over the youth in his neighborhood; young men looked up to him and relied on his wisdom and patronage. His status as a middle-aged Muslim man with a wife and children and a successful businessman further enhanced his stature with them. He embodied a particular kind of Rwandan masculinity that amplified his capacity to organize young men—both Muslim and non-Muslim—to defend the neighborhood where his family lived.

Beyond his actions to protect the neighborhood, Tuyisingize hid and protected more than forty people, with the help of his wife. They also smuggled dozens of people—those they were sheltering and others—across the border. Tuyisingize succeeded in his efforts because of his intimate knowledge of the border and smuggling routes and the location of his second house near the Grand Barrière. As he explained, "I used that house to import or export things clandestinely; things from Congo or things from Rwanda. They would go via that house. I worked with Congolese soldiers" (GIS41). The house was located only a few blocks from the major roadblock erected by the Impuzamugambi militiamen at La Corniche hotel. However, Tuyisingize could avoid the roadblock and arrive at the house via secondary streets. Tuyisingize also owned a house in Goma, in which his sister lived. In peacetime, he used the house in Goma as a depot; during the genocide, he took people who did not have relatives on the Congolese side of the border to his sister so she could protect them.

Thus, Tuyisingize deployed the powerful components of his actor-network to rescue: his social ties, reputation, and wealth. Tuyisingize used his social ties to important people to reinforce his own power. From his soccer career, Tuyisingize was close friends with Protais Zigiranyirazo, governor of Ruhengeri prefecture from 1974 until 1989 and President Habyarimana's brother-in-law. Although Zigiranyirazo officially resigned from politics in 1989, he remained at the nexus of power surrounding his sister, First Lady Agathe Kanziga, and her husband, the president. It is unclear what role Zigiranyirazo may have played in the organization and implementation of the genocide. A 1993 report by the Fédération Internationale des Ligues des Droits de l'Homme had implicated Zigiranyirazo in the organization of massacres of between three hundred and one thousand Bagogwe in Ruhengeri and Gisenyi prefectures (38). Bagogwe were historically pastoralists, eventually considered a subgroup of Tutsi. In 2008, the International Criminal Tribunal for Rwanda convicted him of genocide and extermination as a crime against humanity and sentenced him to twenty years imprisonment, but the ICTR appeals court overturned his conviction and acquitted him of all charges in 2009. Zigiranyirazo's proximity to power would have made it extremely difficult, but not impossible, to avoid participation in crimes of genocide. Whether or not he was complicit in the genocide, Zigiranyirazo engaged in acts of rescue. He protected and then evacuated his wife, who was Tutsi, their children, and some of his in-laws, as well as two children he had out of wedlock and their Tutsi mother.[6]

In addition, Zigiranyirazo helped his friend Tuyisingize to protect people and smuggle them across the border. In late April 1994, Zigiranyirazo arrived at Tuyisingize's house accompanied by his bodyguards, who were government soldiers. Zigiranyirazo had come seeking Tuyisingize's help to smuggle his wife and other Tutsi family members to safety in Goma. Tuyisingize quickly agreed to help him, but first he leveraged Zigiranyirazo and the soldiers to reinforce his own authority.

> TUYISINGIZE: He came to my house with soldiers. . . . The first thing I did was to drive around town, to show people that I had Zigiranyirazo in my car. I went to the customs offices, where [*he pauses without finishing the thought*]. No one stopped us because he was an important person. Do you understand? I drove around town with those people

in my car. We even reached the border. It was the first time [I tried to drive to the border], so I wanted to see [what would happen].

Q: So, you wanted to show people that you weren't doing anything [suspicious]?

TUYISINGIZE: Yes. And that I was a supporter of the government—to prevent suspicion. I owned the vehicle, a van. I was with Zigiranyirazo and the soldiers in charge of his security. We left his car at my house. He sat in front with me, and the soldiers were in the back. No one could stop me. They knew that I was working with the boss. (GIS41)

Once Tuyisingize publicly established that he was connected to the interim government's power at the highest level, he could move freely through Gisenyi. The militiamen and soldiers manning the roadblocks throughout the city allowed him to pass without closely inspecting his minivan or its contents. This freedom allowed him to transport people. He explained how he concealed them: "I would bring about five people at a time—because I had my Hi-Ace [van]. I would put them in steel drums and say that I was going to fetch water. We had no [running] water in town, so you had to go draw it at certain places. Once I arrived at my compound [the house near the Grand Barrière], I would take them out of the drums" (GIS41). Tuyisingize unloaded the refugees behind closed gates so neighbors did not see them. He then hid the people in the house until nightfall, when he guided them across the border on foot along a smuggling route.

The day after our interview, Tuyisingize invited my research partner, Dr. Hager El Hadidi, and me to his house near the border to meet his family and see how things worked. The family received us outside in the yard, where Tuyisingize again described how he entered the compound with his vehicle and unloaded people behind the walls. His family then welcomed us inside. In 2013, the living room was sparsely furnished, with only a few stools, and the dining room was stacked floor-to-ceiling with new mattresses, large sacks of what appeared to be food, and other merchandise. Obviously, the house was being used more as a depot than a residence. Tuyisingize then took us outside to show us the smuggling route he had used during the genocide. We walked between some houses and rounded a corner. He pointed at a small path through the grass that continued up the hill. "The Congo is just up there around the corner," he said (GIS41). The path was well worn, indicating that the unofficial route across the border was still in use in 2013.

The smuggling route was not the only way Tuyisingize moved people across the border during the genocide. He also hid people inside steel drums normally used to transport water and then drove them in his van across the border at the Grand Barrière crossing. To facilitate his import-export business, Tuyisingize had secured two national identity cards, one for Rwanda and one for the Congo. During the genocide, his dual nationality continued to help him cross the border quickly and without hassle from border agents on either side. His visit to the customs office at the Grand Barrière with Zigiranyirazo had clarified to Rwandan border agents that he had support at the highest levels of government power. Consequently, they allowed him to cross without closely inspecting his loads or interrogating him. This example illustrates how borders become a resource, another component in the actor-network that confers advantage or disadvantage, depending on the circumstances.

When it was too dangerous to move people, Tuyisingize and his wife hid them in the buildings on their various properties around the city. His wife cooked food and found clothing for all the people they hid. I asked Tuyisingize how he found the people he helped. He responded, "Most of them were brought to my home by other people. Sometimes, someone would come and tell me, 'There is a person [hiding] somewhere. They have no food.' I would go get the person and bring them home" (GIS41).

Tuyisingize's character and reputation identified him to others as someone to be trusted, and his influence largely protected him from threat.

> TUYISINGIZE: I didn't fear anything, and [the people I was helping] knew I was a brother to them so they didn't fear me. It's true I was always known as a good person here. Even the Interahamwe liked me because I used to give them money before the war [meaning the genocide]! That's who I am. I wasn't afraid because at that time, Tutsi were the ones being hunted, not Hutu. I was also a member of the MRND party.
>
> Q: Did you know that the MRND party was planning the genocide?
>
> TUYISINGIZE: I really didn't. Things came just like that, and people changed. After they killed Habyarimana, everything changed. I don't know the person who planned it. The thing is, you could not go to Congo if you were not a member of MRND. The only person who was able to cross was the one with the MRND card. (GIS41)

Here, Tuyisingize clarified that he joined the MRND party to facilitate his business and not because he was interested in politics. He added that he regularly gave money to the Interahamwe and Impuzamugambi chapters in his neighborhood for the same reasons. His gifts both demonstrated his generosity and ensured that the militia members were indebted to him, invoking the social logics of reciprocity.

At one point, those regular contributions saved his and his family's lives. During the genocide's first two weeks, Interahamwe militiamen arrived at Tuyisingize's main residence wanting to search the property. Tuyisingize's family had already hidden about forty people in their eight properties around the city. Tuyisingize recounted what happened:

> They came to my house because that's where Tutsi were [hiding]. The Interahamwe leader, who was called Kiguru, came together with other people. . . . They had guns; they had Kalashnikovs. . . . [The Interahamwe] caught me. I called to some men [nearby] and asked them to call other militiamen to come and rescue me. I called the ones who were on the hill; a young man called Ngerageze. He was strong, he was a former soldier. Ngerageze came. When he came, my young men came as well. They were many as well. Then they [the Interahamwe] said, "Come, we need to talk to you." They took me aside. They told me, "We know you have Tutsi." So we negotiated. Then I gave them money. I gave them 400,000 Rwandan francs [about $2,800 in 1994]. (GIS41)

Tuyisingize's support of the local Interahamwe and Impuzamugambi chapters meant that their members were loyal to him. Their intervention and willingness to confront the militiamen loyal to Kiguru created the opportunity for a negotiated settlement instead of the murder of the refugees in his house. By standing with Tuyisingize, they forced Kiguru to pursue other options than violence and the use of force. Then, Tuyisingize's wealth made it possible for him to pay off Kiguru, who distributed the money among his militiamen after taking his own cut. Shortly after this incident, Tuyisingize mobilized his friendship with Protais Zigiranyirazo to reinforce his power by showing he had Zigiranyirazo's protection.

Although journalists have often characterized the Interahamwe and Impuzamugambi militias as acting at the command of government and military officials, "leaders of the militia represented a force with its own base of power" (Des Forges 1999, 230). Thus, although they were "generally responsive to directives from civilian and military authorities," the militias often operated according to their own leaders' orders and desires (230). For instance, militiamen sometimes used their strength to settle personal scores or to commit opportunistic crimes against wealthy Hutu. Furthermore, their brutality and the productive nature of their violence fueled further violence and brutality that sometimes spilled over onto Hutu civilians. Tuyisingize described the unruly and unpredictable nature of the militias: "[In 1994], it was as if Interahamwe had taken over the country. Even Zigiranyirazo feared them. They didn't fear anyone; it's like they are the ones who ruled. Wasn't Protais Zigiranyirazo among the country's owners? Yet even he was scared of them. No one commanded them. I gave them money to placate them. You know with my business . . . and everything" (GIS41). Many other interviewees in Gisenyi echoed these statements.

The force and unruliness of the militias surprised even the Hutu extremists in the interim government and military command, who could no longer control them by early May 1994. In response, Rubavu commune officials and military leaders called a public meeting at the city's soccer stadium. They sought to calm the situation, reestablish the social order, and clarify the targets of violence: RPF infiltrators and RPF sympathizers.[7] For a few weeks, relative calm reigned in the city as the militiamen became more disciplined and followed the commands of government officials and military commanders. However, in late May, as the government army lost ground to the advancing RPF, the interim government issued a decree reorganizing the militias. The decree gave local militia leaders the "power of life and death over any member of the population deemed wanting or hesitant in 'defense of the endangered homeland'" (Guichaoua 2010, 289). In the wake of this administrative order, the militias engaged in another wave of continuous violence against both Tutsi civilians and any Hutu civilians who appeared hesitant to aid in "self-defense" efforts. In the wake of this change, those Hutu assisting, hiding, or protecting Tutsi civilians faced dramatically increased risks.

Even with Zigiranyirazo's protection, Tuyisingize eventually encountered additional threats against his life. He recounted:

> The Interahamwe feared me because of Zigiranyirazo. He had conferred a lot of power on me. Unfortunately, [someone] told his friend that I had helped his wife make it to Goma. The friend told the Impuzamugambi, the CDR militiamen. They came to attack me. Actually, the Impuzamugambi told soldiers, and they came to attack me at home.
>
> A lieutenant named Bukasa came to my home [with other soldiers]. He accused me of taking Tutsi to Congo. He threatened me. He said he was going to have me killed. Then I went to Zigiranyirazo and told him about what had happened. . . . Zigiranyirazo took me with his bodyguards to the lieutenant's place. He told Bukasa, "This young man is a friend. He is a brother. Look at all the things he is carrying to Goma for me. Those people are lying. He is not taking any Tutsi [to Goma], it was just his relative [that he took]." . . . Then, the lieutenant took me outside, and he told me, "I will forgive you, but go and bring me $200 [US]." I said, "No problem." I had money back then, so I gave him $400. . . .
>
> After I gave him that money, what I actually wanted was for him to get in my car so that I could go in town where people could see me with him. He was a notorious killer. I wanted to drive around with him for a

while where everyone would see me and know that he had forgiven me so that it would dissuade anyone else from pursuing me. That's what I wanted to do. That's how I rescued so many people. (GIS41)

Once again, Tuyisingize used his wealth, social stature, and connections to people in positions of power during the genocide to save himself and others. The lieutenant asked Tuyisingize for $200, but Tuyisingize doubled the amount. In so doing, he indebted the lieutenant to him according to the social logics of reciprocity, because his gift exceeded the lieutenant's act of clemency. As a result, when Tuyisingize asked the lieutenant to ride around town in his car, the lieutenant could not easily refuse. In turn, by showing the soldiers and militiamen at the various roadblocks and checkpoints around town that he had the support of a "notorious killer," Tuyisingize enlisted the lieutenant and his authority as additional components in his actor-network, amplifying his own social capital and authority.

The Will to Help: The Beginning but Not the End of Rescue

While the stories of Tuyisingize and Jeanne d'Arc do not adequately represent the diverse ways people helped Tutsi cross the border during the genocide, they reveal some important common features of successful rescue. First, Tuyisingize and Jeanne d'Arc had the will to help people. Because of her advanced age, Jeanne d'Arc could not explain why she chose to help Pacifique and his siblings, even though her daughter scorned her for doing it and her sons reported for duty at the roadblocks or joined the militias. Tuyisingize explained his reasons for helping:

> First of all, our religion, Islam, had forbidden us to kill. And it also depends on a person's heart. That's the reason why most people would go to a person they knew had a good heart.
>
> I can't say anything else; that's all. Besides, my own mother was a Tutsi, but that's not the reason why I saved people. I did it because of my heart.
>
> Thanks to God's help, my efforts were effective. I think everyone had their own way of getting people out, but that was my way. I never told anyone [how I did it]. Only my driver Abdu knew my secret; he is the only one who accompanied me. (GIS41)

In his explanation, Tuyisingize identifies at least five factors that influenced his actions: his religion, Islam's teachings against murder, his "good heart" or conscience, his kinship with Tutsi through his mother, and God's grace that allowed his efforts to bear fruit. He acknowledged the many other factors that contributed to his actions: his friendship with Zigiranyirazo, his patronage to the militiamen in his neighborhood, his knowledge of the border, his wealth, his houses, his wife, his sister in Goma, his faithful driver Abdu, and the secrecy surrounding his actions. Tuyisingize's explanations resonate with those of other rescuers, regardless of their religion. The common theme of having a "good heart" arose in almost all explanations of rescuer actions. Yet having the will to assist was merely the starting point for rescue. Many others who began by helping abandoned their efforts for fear of negative consequences or joined the militiamen and attack squads.

A second common element between Tuyisingize's and Jeanne d'Arc's acts of rescue was their use of social logics to support their efforts. Jeanne d'Arc used her poverty and age to make herself invisible to militiamen and security agents. Rwandan social logics disguised her courage as ordinary, grandmotherly acts of care. Tuyisingize, in contrast, used his wealth, social capital, and patronage ties to powerful people to save Tutsi. His bravado before the militiamen and soldiers at roadblocks disguised his courage as support for the genocidal state and its program of genocide. While Jeanne d'Arc and Tuyisingize each deployed different social logics, they both mobilized their social intelligence to increase their capacity to help.

Third, chance—or luck—helped Tuyisingize and Jeanne d'Arc succeed in saving lives. Jeanne d'Arc was lucky her ruse of playing grandmother to her neighbors' children worked three times. By chance, she never encountered someone at a roadblock who recognized her or the children or questioned her honesty. Tuyisingize was also lucky. The military officer, Bukasa, was greedier than he was duty-bound. The Impuzamugambi militiamen from the neighborhood respected the loyalty they owed Tuyisingize for his donations. Chance also kept Tuyisingize's clandestine smuggling routes open during the genocide.

The theme of luck repeatedly arose in survivor and rescuer accounts. Accounting for luck as a rational factor structuring rescue is impossible. Historian Jacques Sémelin (2019), speaking of rescue during the Holocaust in Vichy France, wrote,

> What can the historian, searching for rational explanations rather than random causes, do with luck? . . . Yes, these people were lucky, because at any moment in any situation they, too, could have been arrested. But it was not only a matter of chance, just as the high rate of survival of Jews in France cannot only be explained as a being a matter of individual luck. . . . No one was safe, whether from a denunciation or a slip-up. Death was always lurking in the shadows, until the very last moment,

> until the very last soldier from the occupying forces had left France. (277–78)

In conceiving of agency during genocide—whether enacted in genocidal violence or rescue—as an emergent effect of actor-networks, luck, chance, and fate also become emergent effects of assemblages and their arrangement and transformation over time. From this perspective, chance is simultaneously random (and irrational) and patterned by the dynamic interchanges between assemblage components. In other words, actor-networks and their effects make successful rescue more or less likely, depending on their arrangement.

Finally, the border was another common denominator between their stories. Tuyisingize and Jeanne d'Arc both used their knowledge of the border to help them succeed. Jeanne d'Arc's embodied knowledge of the border arose from her frequent crossings to Goma to buy or sell things or to visit friends. Tuyisingize's experiential knowledge arose from his occupation as an importer-exporter and smuggler. He had deep experience combining the official power of dual citizenship documents and customs forms with the unofficial power of expediting goods back and forth across the border through extralegal channels. The border is itself an assemblage, constituted through people's knowledge of its terrain and their embodiment of it through crossing. During the genocide, Jeanne d'Arc and Tuyisingize, along with many others, both escaping Tutsi and rescuers, enlisted the border as the boundary of the state's genocidal sovereignty and thus transformed it into a tool that facilitated rescue.

The border offered salvation elsewhere in Rwanda, too. In each place, the border, and its role in the genocide, were linked to local topographies, distinct regional histories, and different everyday engagements with it. The next chapter examines Rwanda's water border with the Congo and explores how rural people in Gisenyi prefecture engaged with it. The chapter presents the case of Nkora, a rural hamlet on the shores of Lake Kivu. In Nkora, fishermen and farmers helped evacuate kin, neighbors, or orphans across Lake Kivu to safety. Congolese traders, fishermen, and farmers who came to the various markets on the shores of Lake Kivu also evacuated Tutsi.

6

AT THE MARGINS OF THE STATE

As long as I had the power or means to help a persecuted person, I used it. As for other people, Satan entered their hearts, and they started slaughtering their brothers. . . . They failed to understand that we are all the same, created by God.

—Ramazani, a Muslim fisherman who saved people (NKO25)

In 1994, Ramazani (NKO25) was thirty years old and married with several young children. He made his living as a fisherman working the large, hand-paddled fishing boats on Lake Kivu. His wife cultivated the few small fields they owned near the lakeshore. They lived in Nkora, a small hamlet with a significant Muslim population on the shores of Lake Kivu in Kayove commune, Gisenyi prefecture. Around sunset on the evening of April 6, Ramazani set off as usual with a fishing crew to spend the night trawling for *sambaza*, the small fish ubiquitous in the methane-infused waters of Lake Kivu. As dawn approached, the men drew in their remaining nets and turned the boat to paddle the three hours to the fish market in Gisenyi town, eleven miles from Nkora. When they approached the methane station near Nyamyumba, eight miles from Nkora, soldiers asked them, "Where are you going?" Ramazani recounted:

> We told them, "We're taking the sambaza to Projet Pêche [Fish project] in Gisenyi." The soldiers told us to hurry. So we kept paddling until we got there. When we arrived, we found no one—not a single customer. The only person who was there was the supervisor. . . . He asked us, "Didn't you hear the news on the radio?" We replied, "We didn't. We spent the entire night on the lake fishing." "*Kinani* died!" he said. Kinani was what they used to call the president, [Habyarimana].[1]
>
> We went uphill to look for food in town, and we saw that roadblocks had been erected. They [the men at the roadblock] asked us where we were coming from and where we were going. We told them that we were

> coming from Nkora, that we had brought our catch [to sell] and that we were looking for food, since we had spent the night on the lake fishing. They told us, "Go eat but hurry! Don't even spend twenty minutes!" Then we went back home. When we got here, we didn't find any problem here. (NKO25)

Ramazani returned home and discovered that his wife had not yet heard the news. He learned the details from neighbors who had been listening to the radio. The situation soon changed dramatically. On April 9, Ramazani learned that "young men" had come down from the highlands to the lakeshore to "hunt down Tutsi."[2] They had attacked people in the Nkora commercial center less than a mile from his home. Ramazani continued: "We saw them coming. They were carrying machetes, scythes, pruning blades, sticks, and clubs. We knew what they were coming to do because the radio, Radio Rwanda and the RTLM, said 'Tutsi killed the president: the people you share food with, the people you live with, who are right next to you.'" Ramazani and his wife were Muslim and Hutu. Their neighbors were Muslim, Catholic, Adventist, agnostic, or practiced indigenous spirit worship cults. Most of them were Hutu, but there were a few Tutsi among them. Despite Nkora's diversity, residents perceived the assailants from the highlands as outsiders who had come to attack the entire community. "We all worked together. Those issues of race were not there. They only appeared after the president died. . . . We knew what they [the men from the highlands] were coming to do. We knew they were coming to hunt down the ones we shared the fishing profession with and our other people. So, we started hiding them [Tutsi]. When we saw them [attackers], we warned each other, 'They're coming for this person. If they catch him, it will be a problem'" (NKO25).

In the midst of the chaos, fishing crews continued to take their boats out, and farmers tended to their fields. One day when Ramazani's fishing crew returned to the docks near Nkora, they saw a mob approaching. Two of their crew members were Tutsi, so the fishing crew feared they could be killed. Ramazani described what happened:

> As the boat was approaching the shore, people were coming with clubs and other weapons. We immediately guessed what they were after. . . . Those boats we use are very large, and there is a smaller, spare canoe on the side. We sent those two young men in the canoe to that island over there [pointing], Gishamwana. . . . The killers did not know how to use a boat. They didn't even know how to paddle! Also, they could not know how to steer the large fishing boat we use. . . . Sailing it requires eight people; one or two people cannot move it by themselves, so the attackers could not follow them.

The fishing crew docked their boat as if everything was normal. The militiamen and others who had come to kill did not find any Tutsi among them, so they left. After the mob moved on, Ramazani and some other crew members swam to Gishamwana island. "We went to tell [our colleagues] that the threat had passed and that they could come back.... We didn't want them to stay there [on Gishamwana], just in case those who were hunting them down found a way to get there. So, we swam there, and then we paddled back with them in the canoe."

Ramazani and his wife hid the two men in their homestead for two days. The Interahamwe searched for them intently. If the men were found in their house, Ramazani and his wife feared the Interahamwe might kill them all or force them to kill the young men. Ramazani decided to evacuate the men to Congo.

> I got those two young men a small boat for two people, down here from a place . . . called Mwiza. During the daytime, I went to steal them a boat. Then, I brought it near my house during the night. I only had one paddle, so I asked this old man, Hamed, "Could you please lend me a paddle?"... He lent it to me and helped me send the fishermen on their way.
>
> We put them in the boat and gave them some food to take with them. We told them, "God willing, we will meet again." The young men wanted to go to Kibuye [in Rwanda], but we told them they must go to Congo, where they would be safe. They heeded our warnings and went to Congo. They are alive now.

Ramazani also went to great lengths to hide and eventually evacuate his Hutu neighbor's Tutsi wife.

Ramazani's story illustrates many important aspects of the agentive effects of topography and local histories of authority, religion, and violence at the margins of Rwanda. The mountainous topography of Kayove commune, its remoteness, and the long shoreline of Lake Kivu positioned residents at the literal and figurative margins of the state and its sovereignty. The commune was very rural and largely inaccessible over land because it lacked paved roads. There were no towns, only a few commercial centers: near the commune office in Kayove sector, the Saint Pierre Catholic Church in Biruyi, or Nkora hamlet along the lakeshore. Its rural residents lived in homesteads dispersed across the hills and along the lakeshore. Although Rwanda's central government administration penetrated deep into the countryside, ordinary rural residents had long employed a variety of tactics to avoid state impositions of authority. These traditions dated to the precolonial period. When state sovereignty became synonymous with genocidal violence in 1994, many Nkora residents used these same tactics to evade the state's genocidal project or help its intended victims escape death.

Unlike in Gisenyi town, where the political border with Congo represented the boundary of the genocidal state's sovereignty (chapter 5), the border's imaginary line in the middle of Lake Kivu's watery expanse created a liminal space where state authority rarely penetrated past the shoreline even during peace times. Out on the lake doing their nightly business, Ramazani and the fishing crew were unaware of the president's assassination. Only when they returned to shore in Gisenyi did they learn the news. Once genocidal violence began in Kayove, the lake and the water border with the Congo was a polyvalent assemblage component that facilitated both acts of genocide and acts of rescue, as did the land border in Gisenyi town.

Ramazani's story reveals how earlier episodes of anti-Tutsi violence in Kayove commune shaped anti-Tutsi violence that reemerged in the 1990s. Roving bands of Hutu men from the highlands (where very few Tutsi lived) went down to the lakeshore (where many Tutsi lived) to attack, pillage, and destroy. In 1994, the only difference was that most attacks ended in killings. These historic patterns of violence in the region produced several, interrelated dialectics around identity: highlands versus lowlands, farmers versus cattle owners, highlands versus lakeshore, (male) farmers versus boatmen. These dialectics on the one hand reinforced a shared Hutu identity among highlanders who lived primarily from subsistence agriculture (a nexus of "highlands," "farmer," and "Hutu") and social cohesion among the more racially and occupationally diverse communities in the lowlands along the lakeshore (fishermen, coffee farmers, merchants, traders, cattle owners, Hutu, and Tutsi). Ramazani's fishing crew included Hutu and Tutsi and people of many religious faiths.

In a stark contrast to the situation in Gisenyi town ten miles away (chapter 5), attackers in Kayove did not establish a new political order, or genocidal sovereignty, evenly spread over the geographic space around Nkora. The terrain was too rugged, the homesteads were too dispersed, and residents were adept at shirking state-imposed duties. The material manifestations of state sovereignty—roadblocks, identity card checks, and other forms of policing—were ineffective strategies in Kayove. Instead, bands of Interahamwe and mobs recruited from the local population roamed the hills looking for victims to kill and property to pillage. This situation created dynamics in the region around Nkora where fleeing and hiding from perpetrators proved an effective rescue strategy in the short term. The persistent return of attack squads—as well as collaborators in the local community who joined in the attacks or denounced people in hiding—increased the risks attached to these rescue strategies as the genocide continued for more than a hundred days. People feared the repercussions of being discovered hiding or helping others. Thus, the lake and the border offered enormous opportunities for escape to those who could cross it.

Fishermen, like Ramazani, and others on the lakeshore who knew how to swim, paddle canoes, or pilot the fishing boats had special capacity to help Tutsi flee to Congo. The lake created a political, physical, cultural, and spiritual boundary that assisted their efforts. In the middle of the lake, Rwanda's political border with Congo demarked the margin of the genocidal state's sovereignty and a "threshold of salvation" for those fleeing the genocide (Albahari 2016, 20). The lake and its shore constituted a physical and cultural boundary because most Rwandans do not know how to swim unless they were born into a lineage experienced with boatmanship. Rwandan parents often warned children away from bodies of water, citing material and spiritual dangers. The material dangers of waterways varied by region. Near Lake Kivu, the principal danger was the infrequent eruption of methane gas from the lake, which could suffocate anyone near the lake's surface (Doughty 2017, 1; 2020, 23). In many lineages, family lore told of multigenerational curses that made crossing water—whether in a boat or by swimming—incredibly dangerous. This spiritual threat reinforced many Rwandans' inability to swim because they dared not tempt fate to try to learn. With their specialized knowledge, Ramazani and his crewmates took advantage of the multivalent boundary of the lakeshore to escape the mob who had come to attack their Tutsi crewmates.

This chapter examines Rwanda's water border with the Congo and the ways rural people engaged with the lake, the border, and the imposition of the state's policy of genocide at the physical and symbolic margins of the state. The watery expanse of Lake Kivu offered a potential escape route for people fleeing genocidal violence. It also constituted a trap for those who reached the shoreline but could not swim to escape the attackers chasing them. In many places, genocide perpetrators used boats to continue pursuing their targets. This chapter presents a case study of the 1994 genocide at the literal and figurative margins of the state. Kayove commune in Gisenyi prefecture was physically distant from the centralized power of the national government, largely inaccessible by road, and on the country's national border. Even though genocidal violence began in Kayove by April 8, 1994, the mayor and other government officials did not initiate it. Instead, a small cadre of local elites with ties to Hutu extremists overthrew the mayor and other local officials to establish a new genocidal political order. These local power dynamics, combined with rural Rwandans' long-term strategies of evading government authority and state demands, produced a genocidal actor-network that made open (as opposed to passive or clandestine) resistance to the genocide possible at certain moments but not at others. This examination of the genocide in Kayove commune engages with the question of authority, genocide, state sovereignty, and what Scott Straus (2006) called the "order of genocide." In

Nkora hamlet, local dialectics of social identities going far beyond the Hutu-Tutsi distinction predisposed Hutu residents to social cohesion and opposition to the genocide. Islam's local history and socio-religious practices contributed to this social cohesion but were not solely responsible for it. Religion was a significant assemblage component but not a singular causal factor.

Local Histories of Authority, Religion, and Violence

The unique histories of political authority, migration, and religion in Kayove commune merged with the region's mountainous topography, lakeshore, and remoteness to produce patterns of engagement with and escape from state sovereignty on its geographic margins. Kayove was also at the symbolic margins of state power, given its history of rebellion and the contemporary reality that President Habyarimana and others in the inner circles of state power hailed from neighboring districts. Kayove's position primed Hutu in the commune's highlands to accept the ethnonationalist narratives of Hutu extremism, but it predisposed others to evade state mandates imposed by local authorities. These entrenched patterns shaped the reemergence of anti-Tutsi violence in the region in the 1990s and conditioned residents' reactions.

The rural hamlet of Nkora sits on the shores of Lake Kivu, where the mountains of western Rwanda descend from the Congo-Nile crest precipitously into the lake. In 1994, Nkora was in Ngabo sector, very near the boundary with Vumbi sector, in Kayove commune, Gisenyi prefecture.[3] Nkora's commercial center included a fishing port and a small settlement of merchants, civil servants, and rural professionals (like teachers and agricultural extension workers). Nearby, the Maziba mosque sat on a small peninsula overlooking the Nkora commercial center and fishing docks.[4] The commercial center, fishing docks, and mosque were surrounded by farmsteads dispersed across the hills, which rose quickly to the highlands where the Kayove commune office stood, seventeen kilometers away over winding, mountainous, and poorly maintained dirt roads. People in the region lived primarily from fishing, farming, livestock husbandry, and trade with communities around the lake, including in Congo. Coffee grew well at the lower elevations near the lakeshore. Those who had sufficient land for coffee plantations were wealthy by rural standards, meaning they had plenty to eat, owned cattle, were able to send their children to school, and could buy clothing and occasional luxury items like transistor radios. The 1989 collapse of the International Coffee Agreement, which had stabilized coffee prices for decades, caused prices to plummet (Bates 1998). Coffee growers in the region, feeling the pinch, diversified their economic activities into fishing, livestock, and other crops. Twice-weekly markets (on Tuesday and Saturday) in Nkora attracted fisherman, traders, and farmers from across the region, as well as from Iwawa island in the middle of Lake Kivu on the Rwandan side of the border, nearby Idjwi island on the Congo side, and the lake's western shores in the Congo.

Kayove commune encompassed several sectors along the shores of Lake Kivu—Kigeyo, Ngabo, Vumbi, Kinunu, Boneza, Busanza, Musasa, and Murama. It also included sectors in the highlands along the Congo-Nile crest—Kayove, Gishwati (synonymous with the old-growth montane rain forest that covered much of the sector), Mushonyi, Gihumba, Rugamba, and Gihinga.[5] The lakeshore sectors of Kigeyo, Ngabo, and Vumbi encompassed both lowlands and highlands. Local histories of migration, settlement, livelihood, and political authority shaped the demographics of Kayove commune in significant ways. Tutsi were 6.8 percent of the population in Kayove commune in 1994, which distinguished it from the rest of Gisenyi prefecture, where Tutsi were less than 3 percent of the population (Republic of Rwanda 1994, 124; Mahy 1989).[6] Local histories of migration and Kayove's highly varied topography and microclimates made certain sectors of the commune favorable for cattle husbandry and others for farming. Thus, in the lowlands along the shores of Lake Kivu, Tutsi were more than 24 percent of the population, while in the highlands near the Kayove commune office, there were only eight Tutsi residents (0.2 percent of the population) (Mahy 1989). These geographic concentrations of Tutsi in the lowlands and Hutu in the highlands shaped the historic patterns of anti-Tutsi violence in the region.

The political history of northwestern Rwanda inclined Hutu in Gisenyi prefecture to accept the ethnonationalist founding narrative promoted by Hutu extremists at the time of decolonization and again in the 1990s. At the dawn of the colonial period, the kingdom of Bugoyi encompassed a portion of what later became Gisenyi prefecture, including most of Kayove commune.[7] The landowning lineages (*abakonde*) of Bugoyi had a reputation for being fiercely independent. Up until the early nineteenth century, landowning lineage heads in Bugoyi—the majority of whom were Hutu—had served as local chiefs known as *abahinzi* (Des Forges 2011, 12). Although the *abahinzi* were brought under the authority of the central court through military campaigns in the early nineteenth century and paid tribute to the court, they still exercised a great deal of autonomy in Bugoyi (18–20). In the Gishwati rain forest, which bordered Bugoyi, lived nomadic pastoralists known as *Bagogwe*. They spoke Kinyarwanda and interacted peacefully with the *abakonde* lineages in the region. Although eventually considered a subcategory of Tutsi, people in the region still recognized Bagogwe as distinct from Hutu and Tutsi through the twentieth century. Under Mwami Rwabugiri, the central court imposed new taxes and sent emissaries to Bugoyi to replace the *abahinzi* chiefs with the system of chieftancies and land tenure system employed in the south (Burnet 2003). Shortly after Mwami Musinga took the throne, Hutu people in Bugoyi and many other areas in the north openly revolted against the Nyiginya dynasty and its representatives (Des Forges 2011, 20). In response, the central court led a devastating military campaign against the people of northern Rwanda and Bugoyi. The mwami's troops pillaged and looted indiscriminately, regardless of whether specific lineages had participated in the revolt (Des Forges 2011, 20). The central court relied on military reinforcement from the German Protectorate Forces stationed at Gisenyi to maintain its control over the region in the early colonial period (17–19). As a result, the people of Bugoyi—Hutu, Tutsi, Bagogwe, and Twa—retained a mistrust of Banyanduga (southern Rwandans), which persisted through the postcolonial period.

By 1994, the region around Nkora had a sizable Muslim population, a rarity in much of rural Rwanda. The Maziba mosque was the only religious institution physically present nearby. The closest church was the Biruyi Parish Saint Pierre Catholic Church, located more than two miles away via mountainous footpaths or three and a half miles over poorly maintained dirt roads that required heavy-duty, four-wheel-drive vehicles. The particular history of this Muslim community in the predominantly Christian countryside generated social cohesion and solidarity among Muslim residents that also influenced the broader community, including non-Muslims.

Given that Islam had largely flourished in towns and along trading routes, rural Muslim outposts dating to the mid-twentieth century like the one at Nkora were relatively rare in Rwanda in 1994. Islam had arrived in Nkora via Gisenyi town's large Muslim community. According to Hamim, an imam interviewed in 2013, Seremani, Faziri Sebutabaruka, and Seifu Ndeze all migrated from Gisenyi town to Nkora to farm coffee or fish, bringing Islam to the region.[8] Sued, an elderly Muslim in his eighties, explained that Seifu Ndeze had converted many people near Nkora to Islam: "Seifu previously lived in Gisenyi. When he moved to Maziba he started fishing. His name became famous as a fisherman, and that is how I knew him. . . . Seifu had love and showed compassion to people. He helped the poor. His actions attracted people, and that is how I was attracted [to Islam]" (NKO32). The earliest mosque in Nkora was built in 1943, of wattle-and-daub walls and a thatched roof (NKO11). Nkora's first imam, Nassin Ayaba, came from Gitarama (NKO11). Moshi Gipanga, a local man, eventually replaced him, becoming the second imam of Maziba mosque. In 1959, Seifu's son, Haj Muhammad, donated the parcel of land for a new mosque made with adobe bricks and a galvanized tin roof (NKO32). It was the same mosque that stood on the site in 1994.

Despite the social cohesion among Nkora residents, the topography, demographics, and local history of authority in Kayove commune had primed the region for anti-Tutsi violence during the decolonization movement and postindependence period. In 1959, mobs of Hutu men came down from the highlands to attack the Tutsi population living in the lowlands (in Kinunu, Busanza, and Boneza sectors). Mugisha (KAY40), a Tutsi genocide survivor and elder from Boneza, described what happened in 1959: "We saw them coming; they pillaged, they burned houses, they killed. But, back then, they didn't kill many people. They burned their houses, took their cattle and . . . everything. They killed few people at that time. . . . They spent a whole week burning houses. . . . It was in November, almost in 1960" (KAY40). Local government officials gave their tacit approval to the anti-Tutsi violence by failing to intervene to stop it. Instead, they arrested Tutsi and UNAR supporters. They arrested and detained Sued, the Muslim man from Nkora, for three months. He was Hutu, but authorities assumed he supported UNAR, the Tutsi monarchist party, because he was Muslim and his mother was Tutsi. During the colonial period, Muslims, like Tutsi, had been exempted from the corvée labor known as *uburetwa*, which had reinforced the association between Muslim and Tutsi among Hutu in northwestern Rwanda (C. Newbury 1988, 112–13; NKO13).

Waves of anti-Tutsi violence continued in 1960, 1963–1964, and 1972–1973. They were particularly acute in Gisenyi prefecture as a whole, as well as in Kayove commune. After the initial wave of violence in 1959, Tutsi in Kayove lived in fear. As Mugisha, a genocide survivor and elder, explained in a 2013 interview, "The war went on; it didn't really stop. In 1960 people fled. You cannot say that there was a time when we were living peacefully. In 1973, they came and burned houses again. Everything was gone, and we had to start over like we had in 1959. They even took all the cattle and all our belongings" (KAY40). When President Habyarimana took power in 1974, he brought an end to anti-Tutsi violence. Then, Tutsi in Kayove lived in relative peace until 1990, even though their attackers were never brought to justice and they were never compensated for their stolen or destroyed property.

Impunity for this violence established local patterns that emerged once again immediately after the RPF incursion in October 1990. During the civil war, Tutsi in Kayove commune faced constant harassment and threats to their lives. Uwimana, a Tutsi woman and genocide survivor, explained: "In 1990, they started attacking us, saying that we were relatives of Inkotanyi [the RPF rebels], . . . that we were the ones who were supporting them. They would come to your house at night [to pillage], so we would spend the night in the bush. In 1992, things became worse, they started cutting people down [killing them]" (KAY43). In 1992, a local mob gruesomely murdered Uwimana's grandparents, not far from where Uwimana lived in her father's compound. A group of men arrived at her grandparents' home and ordered the elderly couple to leave the house so they could destroy it. When the couple refused, the men burned them alive in their own home. "We thought things would improve because they caught the people who did this and imprisoned them. But then, after only two months, they released them" (KAY43). Thus began, for Uwimana and her family members, a regular pattern of hiding from attackers, first at their Hutu neighbors' homes and later, when their neighbors "refused to help them," in the bush (KAY 43). The cycle of anti-Tutsi violence and impunity in these communities, combined with anti-Tutsi propaganda in the media, schools, and workplaces, created a general atmosphere of fear and eroded solidarity within communities. As Uwimana explained, "At first, our Hutu neighbors helped us. They would keep our children for us at night. At some point, they refused. They started to say things like, 'Living with the Inyenzi [literally cockroaches, referring to RPF rebels] is like living with a broken bicycle!'" (KAY43).

The impact of these historic patterns of anti-Tutsi violence and their reemergence in the 1990s in Kayove commune shaped highland residents' reactions in much the same ways as they did in Gisenyi town. The persistent symbolic and physical violence against Tutsi residents from 1990 until 1994 conditioned many Hutu residents in the lowlands of Kayove commune to ignore the violence, to remain silent, and eventually to withdraw assistance from their neighbors. As in Gisenyi town, these processes predisposed many Hutu community members to inaction in the face of rising terror, demonstrating that genocidal priming shapes more than only perpetrators' decision making (Hinton 2005, 280). Genocidal priming lays the foundation of genocide's gray zone by conditioning people to "obsequiousness" (Levi 1989, 37).[9] In Kayove commune, genocidal priming paved the way for rural elites to launch large-scale violence against Tutsi in the region and circumvent local government authorities who initially opposed the genocide.

Yet Muslims in Nkora and the tightly knit community near the Maziba mosque reacted differently. Of the fifty or so homesteads near the Maziba mosque, not a single family was Tutsi, although a few Tutsi women had married into Hutu Muslim families. Many but not all families among these homesteads practiced Islam. When the RPF attacked Rwanda in October 1990, day-to-day life near the Maziba mosque did not change. Given the community's very rural character, distance from Gisenyi town, and minimal intrusion of Hutu propaganda since the RTLM radio broadcasts did not reach them, Nkora residents did not view the war as being between Hutu and Tutsi. Rather, they understood it as a distant conflict between government troops and the RPF rebels. Fatuma, a Tutsi woman originally from Kinunu sector, had married a Muslim man from Ngabo sector in 1990. They lived on a hill overlooking Lake Kivu and Gishamwana island not far from the Maziba mosque. In a 2013 interview, Fatuma explained that life did not change after the RPF's attack. "They used to tell us that there was a war. On the radio they said that it was far from here. They said it would not reach us" (NKO27).

Rural Topography and Authority: Genocide at the Margins of Sovereignty

In Kayove commune, genocidal violence targeting Tutsi began a day or two after President Habyarimana's assassination and continued until RPF troops arrived in the region in mid-July. Like in Gisenyi town, the genocide in Kayove lasted for approximately one hundred days. Despite these important similarities, commune and sector-level authorities in Kayove and Nkora, in contrast to their counterparts in Gisenyi town, adopted different stances regarding genocidal violence. Local government officials in Gisenyi town organized and commanded genocidal violence in the hours immediately after the presidential plane crash (as discussed in chapter 5). In Kayove, a small segment of rural elites, which included civil servants, hospital staff, teachers, and merchants, circumvented local government authorities to instigate anti-Tutsi violence. This cadre of rural elites then recruited Hutu men from across the community—those closed out of social adulthood owing to extreme poverty (Sommers 2012)—to join in pillaging, destroying, and killing Tutsi residents. Faced with this challenge to their authority, commune, sector, and cell-level officials adopted a variety of stances, ranging from active collaboration in the genocide to complicity or resistance. The region's topography and dispersed settlement patterns interacted with the margins of state sovereignty differently from in urban Gisenyi town. These assemblage components produced distinct patterns of genocidal agency and unique opportunities for resistance or escape.

In Kayove commune, the MRND remained the dominant party during the political liberalization of the 1990s. The CDR and MDR parties had only "marginal support" in Kayove (Straus 2006, 72). Unlike in many other places in Rwanda, in Kayove commune local MRND leaders did not initiate or organize the genocide (interviews by author, 2013; Straus 2006, 72).[10] Indeed, the Kayove mayor had actively intervened to stop attacks on Tutsi and Bagogwe in the commune in December 1992 in the days after Leon Mugesera's infamous speech incited massacres in the surrounding region (Fédération Internationale des Ligues 1993, 38–39). In 1994, "a rural elite working with [the MRND] party and other aggressive youth" initiated genocide violence against Tutsi and intimidated "anyone who tried to stop them" (Straus 2006, 72–73). Once they had launched the genocide in Kayove, the mayor did not openly oppose the violence and thus appeared to have "tacitly accepted the attacks" (Straus 2006, 74). Once under way, the mobilization in Kayove commune was extensive. One of the main organizers of the initial attacks in Kayove "led a group that ranged in size from three hundred to five hundred people" that rampaged through the sector near the commune office in the highlands, killing all Tutsi residents in a few weeks (Straus 2006, 64). These mobs roamed the hills looking for targets and descended to the sectors along the lakeshore to attack the Tutsi residents concentrated there.

Genocidal violence in Ngabo and Vumbi sectors on the shores of Lake Kivu, far from the commune office near Nkora, was organized and initiated by Gaetan Ndorerimana. Gaetan had grown up in Ngabo sector, and his extended family still lived there; but he had moved to Kigali, where he worked as a civil servant. An MRND party activist, Gaetan arrived in Ngabo on April 8 or 9 with truckloads of MRND activists and Interahamwe militiamen from Kigali (NKO10, NKO14, NKO29). When he arrived, he called residents to a meeting (NKO10, NKO14, NKO29). Zacharia, a farmer from Ngabo sector and convicted genocide perpetrator, explained, "[Gaetan] told us that in Kigali they started killing people and that we had to start killing, too" (NKO10). Gérard, the *responsable* of Rugaragara cell, elaborated, "After the news of [President] Habyarimana's death, Gaetan was the one to go after the first victims. Crowds of people went to see what was happening" (NKO14).

The patterns of violence at Nkora and in surrounding sectors illustrate the highly localized nature of genocidal violence that played out across the country during the genocide. As in Nyanza and Mugandamure (discussed in chapter 4), these patterns of violence were significantly influenced by regional settlement patterns, topographical features, and previous instances of communal violence. A key difference between these cases is that in Nkora, community insiders were instrumental in launching the violence and directing it according to the plans of Hutu extremists, whereas in Mugandamure and Nyanza, community outsiders initiated the genocide. According to interviewees, Gaetan Ndorerimana and a local man nicknamed Brosse (Brush, in English), who led the mobs attacking Tutsi in Vumbi sector (NKO10, NKO16, NKO29), took advantage of the chaos created by President Habyarimana's assassination to usurp the authority of local state officials. Ndorerimana and Brosse established themselves and the Interahamwe as the new authorities in Ngabo and Vumbi sectors by demonstrating their monopoly on the use of force. Once genocidal violence began, ordinary Rwandans in these communities improvised—drawing on social scripts, prior experiences of communal or ethnic violence, and social relations—to choose a course of action at any given moment.

On April 9, 1994, Gaetan Ndorerimana led a large mob, which included the trained Interahamwe militiamen who came with him from Kigali and local youth recruited from Ngabo sector. They descended from the highlands in Ngabo down toward the Nkora commercial center on the lakeshore. Zahara (NKO41), a Muslim genocide survivor, described what she saw: "The Interahamwe came from Ngabo. They were wearing banana leaves, and they were brandishing blades [machetes, scythes, etc.]. In fact, they were looking for Nkurunziza and my mother because they were the only Tutsi in Nkora center" (NKO41).[11] Nkurunziza was a local merchant who ran a store in Nkora and was wealthy by rural standards. He lived in Nkora with his wife and children. The mob eventually rounded up Zahara's mother, Nkurunziza and his wife, and Carine (NKO30), a Tutsi woman married to a Hutu man. The crowd included militiamen, local men who had joined them, and onlookers who had followed the mob as it descended from Ngabo. Following the cultural logics of Rwandan community justice, the crowd grew ever larger as it roamed. In Nkora center, residents, merchants, fisherman, and others came to see what was happening. The militiamen surrounded Nkurunziza, his wife, Zahara's mother, and Carine, pushing and jeering at them. Carine recounted:

> They were about to stab me in the hip when a Muslim man in the mob—he was my son's godfather—stopped them. Then, many of the Interahamwe took me to the back of the house and started beating me with a steel rebar. Then they took me to the plaza in the center of Nkora. They kept beating me all over my back with the iron rod. Then they put me in a cistern, where there was some water, but not much. They told the children [who were watching] to get more water [to drown us]. (NKO30)

Carine, Zahara's mother, and Nkurunziza and his wife cowered in the cistern, trapped by the mob. They waited as the children brought containers of water to fill the cistern as Gaetan had ordered.

The people we interviewed in Nkora—whether Hutu, Tutsi, Muslim, Catholic, other Christian, local leaders, genocide survivors, confessed perpetrators, bystanders, or rescuers—agreed that Gaetan and his gang of Interahamwe from Kigali had initiated and organized genocidal violence in the region. They disagreed, however, on the actions and stances of local government officials vis-à-vis the genocide. Gérard, who was the *responsable* of Rugaragara cell, initially described the genocide in Ngabo as an uprising of civilian youth in the Interahamwe: "People with machetes went immediately on the roads on April 7, 1994" (NKO14). In his testimony, he emphasized that the Interahamwe overwhelmed government authorities, such as himself. In his telling, Gérard claimed that local government officials had no authority over the Interahamwe: "After the plane crash, there was no more political power, only killing everywhere. The Interahamwe were in command" (NKO14). Gérard later described these so-called

Interahamwe as local degenerates and thugs who were always getting into trouble for stealing or other petty crimes in the years leading up to the genocide. Gérard insisted that genocidal violence in Nkora was initiated by Gaetan. "Gaetan was the one to go after the first victims. And crowds of people went to see what was happening."

In his testimony, Gérard claimed that he had opposed the genocide and rescued many Tutsi from death. Like most local government officials in Kayove commune at the time, he was an MRND member. He insisted that he received no government orders after the downing of the president's plane. He also said that the MRND party leadership did not issue any instructions related to killing Tutsi. Genocide survivors from Nkora, however, implicated Gérard, as well as the *conseiller* of Ngabo sector, whom we also interviewed, and other local officials in the genocide. They made their accusations quietly, carefully, and often indirectly. No one explained how or why they tiptoed around the Ngabo *conseiller* or Gérard. A Tutsi genocide survivor from Nkora, Veneranda, described the actions of local government officials during the genocide: "All of them were not alike. Some did not try to save those who were being hunted down, while others fought for them to fend off the killers. It defeated them, but at least they had tried. I didn't see many leaders supervising, since it was the killers who killed" (NKO29). As she made these statements, she implicated Gérard by motioning with her eyes and then her fingers toward him; he was lingering outside the building where we were conducting interviews. Although Veneranda did not see leaders supervising the killing, she clearly believed they had, at a minimum, supported anti-Tutsi violence because they did not intervene to stop it. Gérard never faced charges for genocide crimes in the Gacaca courts. Likely he had connections to powerful people who protected him or some other leverage that spared him in the Gacaca courts.[12]

Whether Gérard was complicit or directly involved in the genocide, he did assist people by hiding them or evacuating them to Congo. As he explained it, "As a local authority I was able to save some people and showed them where they could hide." Over the course of the genocide, Gérard helped five Tutsi hide or evacuate to Idjwi island. He said that he took these actions "with great risk. . . . One day they were going to kill me not because I was from that ethnic group [Tutsi] but because I smuggled people" (NKO14). In mid-July, as RPF troops advanced in the region, most Hutu civilians—whether they had participated in the genocide or not—fled to Congo. Gérard initially went to Iwawa island, still in Rwanda but four hours away by canoe. When he arrived there, genocide perpetrators from Vumbi and Ngabo caught him. They beat him "because [he] helped Tutsi escape." Then "they ordered me to dig my own grave. I would dig, then they would make me check to see if I could fit in the hole." Gérard's friend and neighbor, who had also retreated to Iwawa island, "negotiated with the Interahamwe" for his release and gave them 60,000 Rwandan francs (or $422 US).[13]

Gérard's actions during the genocide illustrate the interactions of heterogeneous actor-network components at the physical and symbolic margins of state power. Gérard never faced charges of genocide crimes, but clearly many community members thought he was guilty. Gérard's tacit acceptance, complicity, or active participation in the genocide likely increased his capacity to rescue. His demonstration of solidarity with the Interahamwe and those men who joined them—or at a minimum his apparent acquiescence to their new authority—shielded him from attack for a period. Second, people who engaged in acts of rescue—even those like Gérard who may have been complicit or actively participating in the genocide—faced increasing risk over time. Third, the length of the genocide in Kayove—over one hundred days—made some strategies of rescue more or less likely to succeed. In Nyanza and Mugandamure, the shorter length of the genocide made hiding and protecting Tutsi a successful strategy in many cases. In Kayove, the long length of genocidal violence joined with other actor-network components to render evacuation to Congo the best means of saving Tutsi lives. Yet, as the Rwandan army, interim government, and genocide perpetrators fled to Congo, they exported genocidal violence with them and continued to attack and kill survivors and those who attempted to help them (Umutesi 2000, 2004). Finally, Nkora's topography, including the lakeshore and the political border with Congo, delivered opportunities for evasion, escape, and rescue that people like Gérard were equipped to use. The region's topography interacted in unexpected ways with local government officials' authority, state sovereignty, and the new political order and Hutu men recruited to their genocidal enterprise.

The distinct stances of local leaders in Kayove commune interacted with the community's topography to produce local patterns of violence during the genocide. The concentration of Tutsi residents along the lakeshore and Hutu in the highlands—and the historic patterns of anti-Tutsi violence—coalesced once again in 1994 into roving bands of attackers descending from the highlands to pillage and kill in communities near the lakeshore. In addition, the distribution of people and homesteads across the hills in habitation patterns dating to the precolonial period meant that political authority over space was also dispersed—state sovereignty could not be manifested in all places at all times. This situation contrasts sharply with Gisenyi town, where local authorities who collaborated with the Interahamwe and Impuzamugambi could easily control space with roadblocks, security patrols, and nightly rounds because of the population density of the urban landscape (chapter 5). The condensed space made it easy for genocidal authorities to maintain a monopoly on the use of force in Gisenyi town. Rural Rwandans, however, had long lived at the margins of the state and adeptly evaded state demands (Crépeau 1985; Gravel 1968; Thomson 2013). In Kayove, the cultural logics and embodied practices regarding state authority encouraged many residents to evade the new, genocidal state authority established by the local elites who had wrested power from the mayor and others. In Rwandan cultural logics, political authorities can be disobeyed if they do not have the power to enforce their authority by punishing a person (Crépeau 1985, 167–89). Rural Rwandans had long engaged with the Rwandan state through oblique disobedience patterns that dated to the precolonial period. Ordinary rural people escaped the state's demands by ignoring them or complying minimally when forced to through the threat of some negative consequence. Having long lived at the margins of the state, dispersed across a landscape whose mountainous topography and remoteness made control more difficult, people in Kayove had regularly escaped state authority.

Even though Gaetan, Brosse, the Interahamwe, and their mobs established themselves as the new authorities, they could not necessarily ensure compliance with their orders at all times and in all places. The dispersed settlements on the lakeshore and throughout Kayove commune gave Interahamwe militiamen and roving attack squads plenty of opportunity to pillage and destroy property and find Tutsi where they were hiding and kill them. Nonetheless, some Hutu residents, including Muslims, Adventists, Catholics, and others, resisted these attacks and assisted Tutsi kin, neighbors, coworkers, or strangers despite the increasing risks of their actions as the genocide continued.

Religion, Social Cohesion, and Resistance to Genocide in Nkora

As related in Ramazani's story at the beginning of this chapter, Nkora residents living in the lowlands near the Maziba mosque and Nkora commercial center shared a distinctive social cohesion that united them across racial, religious, and occupational distinctions. This social cohesion emerged from the unique local history of Islam in the community and from the communal aspects of Muslim religious practices at the Maziba mosque. As a result, many Nkora residents perceived the onslaught coming from nearby hills as an attack on the entire community.

The Muslim community in Nkora had remained relatively small over the decades. It grew through local people converting to Islam—primarily women from the region marrying into Muslim families. Sometimes these women's brothers also converted to reinforce affinal ties between the families and access economic benefits through Muslim social networks, such as employment or apprenticeship in a trade like fishing. As a result, Muslims in Nkora had dense kinship ties with local lineages and families of various religions. In this way, the community resembled Rubona hill near Nyanza and the Muslim community in Mugandamure (chapter 4). Because the first Muslims who came to live in Nkora were boatmen, fishermen, coffee farmers, and merchants, Muslims continued to be overrepresented in these occupations in the mid-1990s. As a result, many Muslims had experiential knowledge of transporting people and goods around Lake Kivu and across the border to Congo. They also had access to the infrastructure needed to evacuate people during the genocide. Furthermore, Nkora residents involved in these occupations had dense social ties to Muslims. As the only religious institution physically present within a three-mile radius of Nkora, the Maziba mosque had an outsize influence on the community as a whole.

Muslim teachings and practices directly and indirectly shaped non-Muslims' attitudes, beliefs, practices, and expectations in the region. The local Muslim community's generosity, openness, and communal ritual practices attracted converts and also generated goodwill among non-Muslims. Thierry (NKO23), a Muslim man who lived near the Maziba mosque, described why he converted to Islam as an adolescent:

> I became a Muslim in 1976, I think. I used to be Catholic, but I abandoned it. They convinced me to convert to Islam in 1976. I will even tell you why I liked Islam. . . . When there were ceremonies, like when they were closing the fasting period, they would give us rice, sweets . . . when we came here. You could see them hugging, socializing, and it made you happy. But when I attended Mass, I never saw or felt those things. When I joined Islam, the love increased and came to me, that's how I came to love Islam. . . . When we came to Maziba [mosque], they would give us food. All the children together without dividing us [between Muslim and non-Muslim]. Then, everybody, we would play together. They would show you everything they have without hiding anything or saving it for later. In other religions, sometimes people feed their own children after the other children have left. [In Islam], you see someone coming and say, "My child, have another sweet potato." That's the reason why we liked Islam. . . . because we could get food and eat until we were satisfied.

The receptivity and generosity of the Maziba mosque continued to be evident in 2013 when we conducted interviews there.

We arrived in Nkora a few days after Eid al-Adha, the Feast of the Sacrifice. Through informal ethnographic interviews, we learned that the Muslim community had welcomed all community members, regardless of their religion, to join in the festivities and share in the distribution of meat that is part of the celebration. These ongoing social and ritual practices, reinforced by Islamic doctrine, generated social cohesion among all Nkora residents, as well as among Muslims who lived throughout the region. Nkora residents hardly felt the influence of churches in their daily lives because they were physically distant.

The social cohesion of the community around Maziba mosque persisted during the genocide. While Hutu men from the hills of Vumbi and Ngabo sectors joined the killing squads and rampaged through Kayove commune, residents near Maziba remained unified. This unity emerged from their kinship and social ties, but religion—specifically Islam—also played a role. As Fatuma, the Tutsi Muslim woman, recounted,

> Given that Islam is a religion which makes things easy for people and which loves people, you could say that there was not much genocide here. We didn't really have it in us. People who came from elsewhere or even Christians from near here—the ones called Interahamwe—they are the ones who went to get people from faraway places, like from Murama, Kinunu or Busanza, and then kill them here. Otherwise, there was no genocide here. . . . You could see that the ones who came from elsewhere seeking refuge are the ones who faced problems from those Interahamwe, but no one from here in Maziba committed genocide. (NKO27)

Although Fatuma portrays the community's unity as the obvious result of Islam's teachings, this apparent effect emerged from heterogeneous actor-network components—Islam's history in Nkora, kinship and social ties among families both Muslim and non-Muslim, the communal orientation of Muslim celebrations in Nkora, the mufti's statement against racial division, and the local imam's teachings. The imam of the Maziba mosque, Hamim, had actively preached against racism and divisionism in the years leading up to the genocide, in line with the policies of AMUR (NKO11). During the genocide, Hamim advised the Muslim population to oppose the killings and to protect people. Other Hutu male leaders in the mosque also preached against the genocide. For example, Gatebuke, a fisherman, advised Muslims and others to resist the killing (NKO17). He also admonished people to avoid complicity in the genocide by refusing to buy lumber pillaged from Tutsi homes (NKO17). Perhaps the clearest evidence of the impact of Islam on genocidal agency in Nkora is that Muslims rose up to oppose the first attack in the commercial center on April 9.

During Gaetan's attack on April 9, a local merchant and influential Muslim man, Hamed, mounted a defensive counterattack. As Carine, Nkurunziza and his wife, and Zahara's mother stood trapped in the cistern, Hamed called the

Muslim men from Nkora, the cell- and sector-level government officials and the local police, to intervene. He also recruited other people from Nkora and Maziba to oppose the Interahamwe mob. Zahara recounted what she saw:

> Hamed had a large store in the neighborhood. He called the Muslims and other people, "Come! We're being attacked! This mob will kill them." He opened his store and brought out many machetes. He said, "Come, let's fight them! They may kill us. We may kill them, but we can't sit back and let them take these people." . . . The people came, the men, they were eager to fight the Interahamwe and keep them from attacking that center. They set their defense on the road; I will show you where [pointing]. When the Interahamwe saw people from Nkora waving machetes, they got scared. They turned and went back. (NKO41)

Hamed described the same incident:

> There on that hill [pointing], Ngabo, there were men who came from Kigali. They riled up Ngabo's people. We saw all of them running mad. The *conseiller* of Ngabo, the tall old man you interviewed yesterday, he was with them. . . . They came here and were joined by a group of young men [*abasore*] from here [near Nkora]. It was a big group; they started attacking people. We called the police to help. The police came and scared them away. All the Muslims, we had all stood up [against them], but because we didn't have weapons, we called the police. They [the police] shot into the air, which made the attackers climb back up their hill. We hid the ones we had to rescue; that's how it went. (NKO24)

With their solidarity and collective action in this moment, the Muslims of Nkora repelled Gaetan's attack coming from Ngabo. According to Rwandan cultural logics, the Muslims of Maziba mosque demonstrated their authority over the Nkora commercial center through these actions. They were able to do so because the local government officials present acted in different ways—some supporting, at least tacitly, the attack and others actively opposing it. For example, Hamed implied that the Ngabo *conseiller* supported the attack. Yet the communal police and local authorities in Nkora opposed the attack. Authority, in this instance, came down to demonstration of force. After this initial confrontation, the attack squads from the highlands of Kayove continued to rampage, searching for Tutsi or others they identified as RPF infiltrators. Yet small attack squads dared not openly confront the Muslim community in Nkora in the same way after Muslim residents had manifested their physical power (embodied in the residents who arrived to defend themselves) and symbolic legitimacy (materialized through the arrival of communal police and authorities to back the local leaders). This small amount of protection allowed Muslims to organize to protect, hide, and evacuate people across the lake to safety in Congo.

After this initial attack, community leaders organized a resistance to protect the homesteads near Maziba mosque. Hamim explained, "[In 1994], I was head of a five-member youth security committee here. We did not allow the killing of Tutsi to happen here. I was head of the patrol. We refused any entry to outside people. I was still young" (NKO11 speaking during NKO32's interview). The Interahamwe never arrived on the hill around the mosque because the security patrol kept them out (NKO32). Thierry described their tactics: "Our neighborhood was not a place you could just enter. The people who lived there were united and got along very well. An old man would pass and tell you, 'I'm warning you, don't leave home.' Another one would say, 'Don't leave this place. Let's stay together and let those ones who are killing do their things.' You know, where we lived, we were a little more than fifty houses. No one died there, we actually saved people" (NKO23). While organized resistance was effective in these two small locales, that wasn't the case elsewhere. Nkora was unique. In many other lakeshore communities, Hutu fishermen and boatmen joined in genocidal violence and used their boats to pursue people trying to escape death (Doughty 2020, 27).

Like in Nyanza and Mugandamure, the majority of Hutu near Nkora—regardless of religion—initially reacted to the genocide's onslaught with offers of assistance to kin, godparents and godchildren, friends, neighbors, or business associates. As in many other cases, kinship played a significant role in shaping rescue. Beyond kinship ties of blood and marriage, kinship based in religious practice was also important. Mathias (NKO16), a Catholic man who was in his late thirties in 1994, described how he protected his godson:

> I had [a] close relationship with the child's family. . . . When I heard stories about the killing on April 7, 1994, I went to their house and took the child home with me. It was a way of helping the mother, so that she could hide without being worried about her child.
>
> Yet I was interrogated many times. The accusers said that I knew where the mother was hiding since I had the child with me. One day, I sold a goat to get some money to pay someone to take her across to the Congo. . . . I gave them 6,000 Rwandan francs [$42 US], including the money we got from selling the goat.[14] Other people also contributed. I don't know exactly how much money we put together. The mother went to the Congo and stayed there. When the genocide ended, she returned home, and she is still alive today. In the end, the Interahamwe failed to kill anyone in that family. (NKO16)

In Rwandan practices of sociality, the kin ties of godparenthood in the Catholic and other Christian churches reinforced other social ties between lineages. As Mathias said, "I had [a] close relationship with the child's family." Parents often selected godparents from outside their own lineages to ensure parental-like support to their child as well as to formalize their own affective ties with friends.

According to doctrine, Islam does not recognize godparenthood, since all family and community members are obligated to supervise a child's religious education. In Rwanda, however, many Muslims engage in relationships they described as godparent-like, thus incorporating Rwandan cultural logics of sociality. Gatebuke, the Muslim fisherman, was forty years old in 1994. He had completed only three years of primary school, but he owned his own boat and made a decent living fishing and selling his catch at the fishing cooperative in Gisenyi town. He described how he helped save his godson:

> I overheard a group of Interahamwe saying that they were going to kill a young man who was at Kivumu center. While I was in the dry goods shop, I heard Interahamwe plotting to go and kill people uphill. They said when they came back, they would go kill my godson. When the Interahamwe left, I waved the bag of salt I had in my hand so that [my godson] would approach me, and I could speak to him. My cousin and I told him that we would look for a way to evacuate him. . . .
>
> Like a godparent in the Roman Catholic Church, I had initiated that young man to Islam. I did not want him to stay at my house because people would know easily where he was hiding since I was his godfather. So I asked my cousin to hide him. My cousin took the young man here [*pointing*] to Hamed's house close to the mosque, because the Interahamwe knew that he was at my cousin's [and so they might look for the young man at his house]. Hamed was [my cousin's] father-in-law. (NKO17)

Thanks to Gatebuke, his cousin, Hamed, and others who helped smuggle the young man to Congo, he survived the genocide. This ephemeral assemblage emerged from their social ties grounded in the kinship of religion and marriage, from their luck in evading the militiamen who were distracted by more lucrative targets, from the dugout canoe used to evacuate the young man to Congo, and from the imaginary line of the geopolitical border in the lake.

Among rescuers in Nkora, many had participated in protecting Tutsi during previous waves of violence, or they had witnessed their parents or grandparents protecting them. The local histories of violence and patterns of rescue form another component in the actor-network that predisposed some people to acts of rescue. A young Muslim woman from Nkora, Sherifa, and her husband saved the lives of several people by first hiding them in their home and then helping them find passage across Lake Kivu in canoes. Before they had married, Sherifa's husband had helped hide and protect his Tutsi neighbors and friends when there were killings of Tutsi in their community in 1993. Sherifa explained how they hid a child in their home in April and May 1994: "We had guessed that they could attack us on that day, so we had taken the child and put her in the hole for ripening bananas. We kept an eye on them and took turns guarding the girl. Whenever my husband left, I would stay home to keep anyone from seeing the child" (NKO26).

After the initial, collective resistance organized by Hamed in the Nkora commercial center and Hamim near Maziba mosque, other Nkora residents opposed to the genocide shifted strategies to assist Tutsi and others targeted by the violence. Instead of collective, public opposition to the genocide, they mobilized ephemeral networks of individuals who worked together only briefly to evacuate people across Lake Kivu under cover of darkness or via clandestine smuggling routes. These strategies avoided the vengeance of the Interahamwe and roving mobs whose authority and danger grew as the genocide continued.

Ephemeral Networks of Assistance and Rescue

As the genocide continued in Nkora, open and collective opposition to the Interahamwe and other genocide perpetrators was no longer a viable option. Hiding Tutsi and other potential victims became too dangerous. To illustrate this growing danger, let me return to Carine's escape from the mob at the Nkora market. After Hamed organized the confrontation with Gaetan's mob to rescue Carine and the others from the cistern, he took her and her family into his home to protect them. Carine recounted what happened next: "I could not stay at Hamed's because he was married to my husband's niece. The Interahamwe would suspect we were hiding in his home. Hamed's family took us to their friends who live in the hills, about a thirty-minute walk from here. The Interahamwe learned I was hiding there, so they came to attack us that first night. I heard them coming before they reached the house. I jumped out the window with our youngest child on my back" (NKO30). Carine then walked all night to her Hutu brother-in-law's home. Her brother-in-law, his wife, and their children offered her refuge for a few days. "They knew where my husband and children were hiding and helped me reunite with them" (NKO30). Yet again, the Interahamwe attacked them. Even though Carine's husband and her brother-in-law's family were Hutu, the Interahamwe sought to kill them all. Carine, her husband, their five children, and Carine's in-laws fled as the Interahamwe approached the homestead. They ran to hide in the reeds along the lakeshore. Carine watched as the Interahamwe found and killed her two sisters-in-law. She and the others managed to stay hidden all day in the reeds. Then,

> The Interahamwe left to go pillage. My husband and I decided to return home. If the Interahamwe decided to kill us, let it be. We were scared to go directly to our own house, so we returned to Hamed's [for the night]. . . .
>
> Early in the morning, my husband went home and, by a miracle, found two oars. My husband decided to get a boat and cross the lake to Congo. We left our house and went back to Hamed's. He gave us some food: dried fish and *ugali* [thick cassava porridge]. My husband and I took the boat and went to Congo. (NKO30)

Like so many Tutsi who escaped death, Carine and her husband saved themselves and their children through a combination of their own efforts, help from others, and sheer luck. Near Nkora, most successful rescue attempts emerged from similar networks of individuals that coalesced momentarily and then cleaved based on changing circumstances. Individuals in these ephemeral networks improvised their actions to protect or evacuate people to Congo.

In the ordered chaos of genocide, coffee farmers and merchants, fishermen, and traders near Nkora had knowledge and experience moving goods across Lake Kivu and the border. Their knowledge, the physical infrastructure of their work (boats, coffee wash stations, fish-drying cooperatives, storage sheds, and vehicles), social ties forged through commerce, and the spatio-temporality of trade sited in periodic market days at locations around the lakeshore on both sides of the border enmeshed these people in actor-networks primed for rescue. Given the local history of Islam, Muslims were overrepresented in these occupations. The imbrication of Muslim solidarity, Islamic teachings against racism and polarizing politics, their social ties, and the heterogeneous assemblage components tied to their work helped induce acts of rescue during the genocide.

The fisherman Ramazani used his experiential knowledge to protect his Hutu neighbor's Tutsi wife. When genocidal violence began near Nkora, the woman went into hiding. Ramazani and his wife kept her at their house for fifteen days. The Interahamwe and people who had joined in the genocidal violence watched the woman's husband all the time. "They used to say, 'Let's keep an eye on that man. We will learn where the wife is. And she will be killed.' . . . They always followed him, wherever he went. I am the one who used to tell him where his wife was hiding. I did it secretly. He did not speak directly to her until after she returned [from Congo]. We told our friends that she had died" so that people would stop searching for her.

Fearing the Interahamwe might find her at their home, Ramazani took her in his boat under cover of darkness with the help of a friend to her relative's home a couple of miles away. A week or two later, the man who was hiding the woman approached Ramazani at the Nkora market. He told Ramazani, "It is bad there in my area. They [Interahamwe] are destroying houses, looking for people. Though they do not yet suspect my place. I am afraid that they might find her there, which would be very bad for me." Ramazani went in his boat with a friend and brought the woman back to Nkora, but he did not hide her in his house "because the Interahamwe had already searched my house three times. They suspected I might be involved in those acts [of rescue]. So, I took her to my friend's house not far from here." Ramazani found some friends who were willing to evacuate the woman to Congo, but she refused because she did not trust them. "She said that she would only go if I was the one taking her, because then she would know she would get there safely." With the help of another friend, Ramazani paddled her across Lake Kivu to Congo during the night. He did not even tell his wife he was leaving or where he was going. He stayed in Congo for a month before returning to his home, because he feared being attacked by the Interahamwe for saving the woman.

Hamed, the Muslim merchant who had organized the initial resistance to the first attack on the Nkora commercial center, helped dozens of people escape the killers. Hamed ran numerous commercial enterprises in the region, in addition to being a coffee farmer and fisherman. During the genocide, he used the physical infrastructure of his many occupations, his wealth, and his social stature to help Tutsi survive. He also took advantage of the periodic market days when he normally conducted business as opportunities for action. Over the course of months, he paid Congolese coffee merchants to smuggle dozens of people out of Rwanda. He described how they did it:

> They were traders who came to buy coffee at the Nkora market to take to Kituku or to Goma to sell. . . . I negotiated with the Bashi [Congolese] who bought coffee from me. I gave them 2,000 [Rwandan francs, $14 US]. Then, they would put the person in a [coffee] sack, that's how they used to leave. . . . They would hide under the sacks of coffee and would come out only after they were in the middle of the lake. It was a simple sacrifice. Money had no value then anyway. When you can save a life—people are more valuable than money. (NKO24)

At one point, Hamed stole a fishing boat in order to smuggle several boatloads of people to Congo. He later paid the owner 70,000 Rwandan francs [$492 US] for the boat because it never returned from its last trip.[15]

Not all rescuers in Nkora were wealthy or powerful like Hamed. As elsewhere in Rwanda, ordinary people, like Gatebuke the fisherman, or the poor farmer

Ismael Mugenzi whose words inspired the title of this book, risked their lives to try to help Tutsi. They acted in a variety of ways. Gatebuke helped save many other people. He lent his boat to an acquaintance named Mbonyinshuti so that he could take his mother and several other Tutsi to Congo. The son of a Hutu father and Tutsi mother, Mbonyinshuti lived in neighboring Boneza, a sector densely populated with Tutsi. Mbonyinshuti asked Gatebuke for the loan of his fishing boat so that he could evacuate his mother, her relatives, and some Tutsi friends and neighbors. Gatebuke agreed, having no idea when Mbonyinshuti might return the boat—Gatebuke's only livelihood. Mbonyinshuti stayed away for an entire month because he feared the Interahamwe might kill him for having evacuated Tutsi to Congo. Beyond helping Mbonyinshuti, Gatebuke saved a young Muslim man who worked on the same fishing team with him. Gatebuke explained, "I told the Interahamwe he was not Tutsi. The Interahamwe insisted he was Tutsi because of his narrow nose. I tried to convince them that not all people who have that kind of nose are Tutsi. I told them that I knew he was Hutu" (NKO17). His lies worked, and his teammate continued to work the fishing boats unharmed until the genocide ended.

On one occasion, Muslims in Nkora gathered money and bought beer and soft drinks for an Interahamwe mob to placate them and distract them from searching for people to kill (NKO41). On another occasion, the Muslims collected donations so that they could negotiate for the release of a Muslim man detained by Gaetan and his gang. In Kayove, near Nkora, a Muslim woman helped her husband bribe attackers to keep them from killing her co-wife, who was Tutsi (KAY16). In this way, Muslims from Maziba mosque protected not only fellow Muslims who were Tutsi but also others from the community. These kinds of payments and bribes were a common rescue strategy everywhere in Rwanda.[16]

Not all rescuers in Nkora were Muslim. Roger, who was seventeen years old in 1994, described how his Catholic family helped a ten-year-old girl. She had fled ten kilometers to their house under cover of darkness after her family was attacked and killed in their home. She sought their assistance because Roger's parents and hers had been close friends. At a roadblock manned by Interahamwe, she explained that she was going to visit her older sister. She arrived at the family's home just before sunrise. Roger described what happened next:

> She arrived at our door. She knocked. We saw her and told her to come in quickly so that nobody could see that a person in danger [meaning a Tutsi] was entering our house. About ten minutes later, an Interahamwe came and asked for her, saying he had sent her to us. We replied that she wasn't there, that nobody was there. He threatened to bring more Interahamwe to search for her. My father offered to buy him a drink at

> the nearest cabaret. My father pleaded with him in the cabaret and gave him 2,000 francs, and some more beer to carry out. The next day he came again, asking for the girl. My father gave him another 2,000 francs, and he left. (NKO18)

Roger's family hid and protected the girl until the genocide finally came to an end in mid-July when the RPF arrived.

The most striking aspect of the Nkora case is that successful rescue was achieved through the collaboration of many people: no rescuer acted alone. Keeping secrets and limiting the number of people involved in assisting any person or group of people were also vital to success. Ramazani, for example, never worked alone in his rescue attempts. His crewmates, his wife, and his friends helped him at different times. In addition, he kept secrets, limited the number of people involved, and hid from those involved who else had helped. These strategies were vital, because the more people who learned of rescue efforts, the more likely someone could denounce a hiding place or rescuer. The interaction of these two factors meant that ephemeral and constantly changing networks of people came together to assist people in danger. Ramazani's wife knew about and assisted his crewmates in hiding and then escaping, but she did not know where Ramazani had hid the neighbor's wife or that he left to escort her across the lake to Congo. When asked why he did not tell his wife, Ramazani stated that it would have been dangerous for her to know. A final significant factor illustrated by Ramazani's story is that in the genocide's gray zone, successful rescue often required people to act immorally. To help evacuate his crewmates to Congo, Ramazani stole a boat. As a fisherman, this act violated not only the law and social contract, which prohibited theft in general, but also the boatmen's unstated code of honor. To protect his neighbor's wife, Ramazani spread rumors that she had already been killed. When Interahamwe attack squads came to search his house, he and his wife lied to them.

While Hamed was central to many actor-networks, he always had assistance from other people as well as the nonhuman actors like the border, Lake Kivu, his boats, and his social relations. Gatebuke described Hamed's actions: "Hamed did so many kindly acts [great deeds, mitzvahs]. There were many people hidden at Hamed's and here in Maziba. Then Hamed and my cousin tried all ways possible to smuggle these people out of the area with Hamed's boat. I would say that it was usually through the collaboration of five to ten people that victims survived" (NKO17). Hamed's stature in the community increased his ability to organize residents to action regardless of religion. Thus Hamed was involved in dozens of acts of rescue and central to many of them, but he never acted alone. Furthermore, many rescue efforts in Nkora did not involve him.

The constant and unpredictable menace of the Interahamwe militiamen and roving mobs of genocide perpetrators created an ever-changing landscape of threat and possibility. Navigating this treacherous terrain required potential victims and potential helpers to make decisions repeatedly and adapt to the perpetual dynamism of the situation. Successful rescue most often emerged from actor-networks enmeshing many people, their actions unfolding over time, and nonhuman actors that coalesced and then receded to reemerge in new forms. These dynamics were common to successful rescue outcomes all over Rwanda, even though distinct local histories and assemblage components produced different patterns that rendered rescue more likely in certain places, like Nkora. The social cohesion among Muslims and their non-Muslim neighbors in Nkora, the reinforcing ritual practices of feast days and food sharing, and the imam's explicit teachings against racism and political polarization predisposed local assemblages to rescuer agency. Expertise in moving goods across the border via Lake Kivu and opportunities presented by the periodic market days at sites around the lakeshore coalesced into actor-networks primed for rescue. The local Muslim community's observance of Muslim holy days, and their lack of social, economic, and political ties to Hutu Power extremists set them apart from Muslims in Gisenyi town. Lake Kivu and Rwanda's water border with Congo provided enormous opportunities for escape and rescue to those with the capacity to exploit it. The case of Kayove commune illustrates that genocidal state sovereignty did not create a uniform layer over geographic space.

The next chapter examines cases of people who lost their lives while trying to help save others. The will to help was the beginning, not the end of rescue. As the genocide continued—in some places for more than one hundred days—the risk of assisting Tutsi increased. Many Hutu who started out helping their Tutsi kin, friends, or neighbors abandoned their efforts in the face of the rising danger. Yet some refused to abandon their efforts and paid the ultimate price by sacrificing their own lives or the lives of their loved ones.

7

ALTRUISM, AGENCY, AND MARTYRDOM IN THE GRAY ZONE

Never hand over to the hunter quarry that sought refuge in your home.

—Rwandan proverb (Jacob 1985, 272)

Greater love has no one than this: to lay down one's life for one's friends.

—John 15:13

Whoever kills a[n innocent] soul . . .—it is as if he had slain mankind entirely. And whoever saves one—it is as if he had saved mankind entirely.

—Qur'an Surah Al-Ma'idah 5:32

On April 21, 1994, two buses full of people singing religious songs arrived at the municipal cemetery on the outskirts of Gisenyi town. Most of the people on the buses were Tutsi. The Interahamwe and Impuzamugambi militiamen had rounded them up earlier in the day at the Saint Pierre Pastoral Center, a religious retreat facility. But Sister Félicité Niyitegeka, a sixty-year-old Catholic lay minister who managed the Saint Pierre Center, was Hutu.[1] For two weeks, she had protected scores of people who sought refuge at the center, along with dozens of young women who were in a religious retreat when the genocide began. From Saint Pierre, she had smuggled dozens of Tutsi refugees across the border to safety in the Congo. On April 21, Félicité accompanied the Tutsi refugees on the bus, even though she had a clear idea of the fate that awaited them.

On April 12, Félicité's brother, Colonel Alphonse Nzungize, who commanded a military camp several miles from Gisenyi town, had sent two soldiers to warn her that the militias were planning an attack on the center. The soldiers had been instructed to escort her to safety. Félicité refused their assistance and wrote a letter to her brother to explain her decision:

Dear brother,

Thank you for trying to save me. But, it is no good to survive if I must abandon 43 children who risk death. I would rather die with them. Please pray for us, that we may be delivered to God. Also, say goodbye to our mother and siblings. I will pray for you when in Heaven! Farewell and thank you for remembering me.

Your sister,
Félicité Niyitegeka

Postscript: In case the Lord saves us because of our faith in Him, I will see you tomorrow. (UC Louvain Portraits of the Righteous 1994)

With this letter, preserved for posterity, Félicité documented her opposition to the genocidal violence unfolding around her. Its every line reflected her piety: "pray for us," "be delivered to God," "I will pray for you when in Heaven," the postscript, and her use of the word "children," shorthand for "children of God," for the adult refugees in her care. Those who knew her also understood what she left unsaid. Having preached messages of peace and racial reconciliation for years, she refused to become complicit in the genocide or to participate in racial division, even to save herself. She would not abandon those who sought her protection.

Just nine days after Félicité wrote her letter, the Interahamwe forced their way into the compound to "search for inyenzi" (cockroaches / RPF rebels / Tutsi) and "ibyitso" (accomplices) they said were hiding inside (African Rights 2002, 269). In the compound, they rounded up anyone they knew to be Tutsi, believed to be Tutsi based on appearance, or believed to be RPF sympathizers because of personal relationships with Tutsi or membership in opposition political parties. They forced them onto the waiting buses. Félicité pleaded with the militiamen to free those on the buses. When she failed to convince them, she boarded a bus to join the refugees. The militiamen asked her to get off. She refused. One survivor, Eugénie, described the confrontation: Félicité told the militiamen, "'No, I need to know where you are taking these people.' They replied, 'We are taking them to the commune office'" (GIS56). Félicité, who had been hearing for weeks about massacres at Catholic institutions around the country, did not believe them. She again refused to disembark.

As the bus pulled out of the compound, Félicité sought to calm those onboard. "She started singing and leading us in prayer," Eugénie recounted (GIS56). Félicité also asked everyone to "pray for [the] *génocidaires* because they don't know what they are doing," echoing the words of Jesus in Luke 23:34 (African Rights 2002, 269). Eugénie continued:

> Along the route, I saw that civilians, not soldiers or police, manned the roadblocks. We traveled through two roadblocks. At each one, they checked who was on the bus. . . . On the way to the cemetery, when we were stopped at the second roadblock, I heard them say that they would kill us all. . . . Then, I realized that those were our last moments that we would spend on earth. . . . I looked at Félicité and I asked, "Won't it destroy the diocese if you come with us?" She did so many things for the church. . . . She was a pillar of the parish. I wanted to convince her to get off the bus, to not follow us so that she could live. I begged her . . . but she refused. She replied, "No. I will accompany you so that you can arrive in peace. I know you are all innocent." (GIS56)

When the buses arrived at the cemetery, the refugees saw the large crowd that had assembled there and militiamen armed with machetes. "We saw the mob of all kinds of people, women, men, youth, children. They had come there, as if they had come to the movies or to see a performance" (Kayitesi 2009, 119). When the buses stopped, a man who was about thirty years old jumped off and tried to run. Militiamen immediately chased him down and killed him with machetes (120). Eugénie recounted,

> When we arrived at the cemetery, there was already a pit dug. It was not as deep as a real grave. It looked more like a hole to ripen bananas. . . . At the cemetery, there was a dedicated group of killers wielding clubs, machetes, and scythes. There was another group that watched the killings. First, they made us undress. The bystanders were in charge of undressing the victims. There were women, old people, [*pause*]; they laughed at us. . . . They took my watch, my rings, my clothing. . . . Then they ordered us to kneel down [near the pit]. They began shooting. I fell to the ground so that I could not see their guns pointed at me. I waited for my turn. (GIS56)

The Interahamwe rarely shot victims at the Commune Rouge, as the municipal cemetery—the town's largest killing field—came to be known during the genocide; government soldiers needed the ammunition to fight the RPF rebels. Instead, they used machetes, clubs, pruning knives, and scythes. On this day, however, the militiamen used guns to kill the refugees more quickly, because they feared Colonel Nzungize (African Rights 2002, 269). Amid the gunfire, Félicité stood praying and begging the militiamen to spare them all (269). They shot Félicité last and threw her body into the shallow grave with the others.

This chapter focuses on the symbolic potency of martyrdom—specifically narratives about people like Félicité who sacrificed their lives in their attempts to save others—and the politics around who becomes recognized as a martyr and who is ignored. The number of Rwandans—of all religions—who gave their own lives to save kin, neighbors, and strangers from death is unknown. The stories of a few of them have been lifted up by the postgenocide government, churches, or other faith communities. These portrayals of martyrdom herald these select people as the prototypical rescuers: unblemished heroes, pious, the ultimate examples of altruism. Martyrdom easily fits the two key assumptions underpinning most studies of rescue in mass violence: that rescuers are morally superior individuals who act solely out of moral compulsion, and that religious piety increases the likelihood that individuals will engage in acts of rescue.

It may appear at first glance that "martyr" is a straightforward classification, a simple addition to the classic genocide typology of victim, perpetrator, bystander, and rescuer. Yet those killed while resisting the genocide operated in the same moral gray zone as others. Like people who engaged in a range of actions—rescue, complicity, genocide, witnessing, nonintervention—those held up as martyrs engaged in moment-by-moment, incremental decision making and improvisation. Furthermore, the vast majority who died while engaging in rescue have gone unrecognized. How and why are certain cases of martyrdom recognized while others are ignored? What actor-networks in the wake of genocide produce martyrs as stable signifiers?

In the national imagination, those people codified as martyrs wield great symbolic power. Death renders them neutral symbols embodying the morally pure ideal of the righteous rescuer. Death forecloses scrutiny of their motivations or actions, making them useful tools of the government or faith communities. In the political discourse of Rwanda's postgenocide government, Hutu who died while rescuing are the prototypical altruists or "good Hutu." In the country's memory politics, Hutu martyrs exemplify the potential good of Hutu members of the body politic. Their utility is increased because in death they are silenced. They do not offer counternarratives. They do not talk about the complex empirical realities in the genocide's moral gray zone. Furthermore, Hutu martyrs cannot critique the current government or the RPF ruling party.

This chapter interrogates the assumptions that rescuers are morally exceptional people, and that religious piety increases the likelihood that people will become rescuers, by exploring cases where Hutu died trying to save Tutsi and comparing these martyrs with other rescuers. This chapter examines the cases of Sister Félicité Niyitegeka at the Saint Pierre Pastoral Center in Gisenyi and Hamza Habimana and Mohamed Hakuzimana at a mosque in Kibagabaga on the outskirts of Kigali.[2] Félicité protected scores of Tutsi at the center and helped dozens flee over the border to Congo. Ansar Allah Muslims rescued Tutsi from Interahamwe killing squads and gave refuge to hundreds at the sect's headquarters in the Kibagabaga mosque.

Like the Ansar Allah Muslims in Mugandamure (chapter 4) and Mabare (Viret 2011a), the Muslims in Kibagabaga had broken with the Muslim Association of Rwanda (AMUR) because they understood Islam prohibited participation in politics and other doctrinal matters. These constituted actor-network components that induced distinct actions among the Ansar Allah Muslims in Kibagabaga, as they did in Mugandamure and Mabare. Hamza Habimana and Mohamed Hakuzimana openly opposed the orders of a Rwandan military officer and placed themselves in the line of fire when soldiers attacked the mosque. The stories of Félicité Niyitegeka, Hamza Habimana, and Mohamed Hakuzimana illustrate the significance of martyrs in the postgenocide memoryscape.

Through these case studies, the chapter explores how and why some people persisted in their rescue efforts and refused to compromise their moral values in the face of almost certain death. In postgenocide narratives, people recognized as martyrs—whether by the national government or faith communities—are those who refused moral compromise and died alongside those they tried to help. In the gray zone of genocide, moral rectitude posed particular problems when confronting the heterogeneous assemblages that produced genocidal violence. To categorically oppose the Interahamwe or state security forces often precipitated a forceful, violent reaction to maintain the "order of genocide," as Scott Straus (2006) described it. Those who refused moral compromise when faced with impossible choices sometimes paid for their courage with their lives. This investigation yields three interrelated conclusions.

First, these case studies show that martyrdom, like rescue, is the outcome of incremental decision making, in an unforgiving context. Those who later became martyrs did not set out to sacrifice their lives. Like perpetrators, victims, bystanders, and rescuers, martyrs made many small decisions as events unfolded and genocide became state policy. These smaller, individual decisions led them to their fates.

Second, the dynamic unfolding of events that constituted the genocide and the actor-networks that comprised local histories, social relations, individual dispositions, and moral orientations often limited the available choices. When faced with choiceless choices, many people who succeeded in rescuing Tutsi were forced to compromise their moral values. For example, Father Eros turned Tutsi adults away from the Centre Saint Antoine orphanage to protect the children he sheltered (chapter 4). Postgenocide narratives about martyrs emphasize that those people who sacrificed their lives to save others during the genocide persisted in doing moral good (and renouncing evil) even in the face of death.

These narratives oversimplify the complex moral conundrums forged in a genocide's gray zone and ignore the role of luck, fate, or chance in successful rescue. Unknown numbers—quite possibly in the thousands—of Rwandans died resisting the genocide or defending people who sought their help. Many of these people died simply because they had the bad luck of being caught.

Third, the case studies presented in this chapter illustrate the potential power of religious piety within the gray zone of genocide. Félicité Niyitegeka, Hamza Habimana, and Mohamed Hakuzimana were clearly motivated by their deeply held moral conviction that racial discrimination and the killing of innocents were wrong. What is much harder to assess is whether their religious piety made them more willing to lay down their lives in their rescue attempts. Eyewitnesses, many of whom were part of the same religious community and practice as these rescuers, emphasized two significant things in their testimony. First, they underscored Niyitegeka's, Habimana's, and Hakuzimana's religious faith and gave numerous examples illustrating it. Second, witnesses stressed the rescuers' repeated decisions to continue in their rescue attempts even in the face of direct threats and opportunities to save their own lives. However, these retrospective accounts do not make it possible to discern their motivations nor to measure the depth of their religious conviction. After all, defenders of faith communities widely contend that only positive attributes such as compassion, peacemaking, or reconciliation are part of their so-called "true" faith. For example, Pope John Paul II issued a letter to Rwandan bishops in 1996 that stated, "The church in itself cannot be held responsible for the misdeeds of its members who acted against evangelical law" (Winfield 2017).[3] Although most churches described their pastor or members implicated in the genocide as lacking faith or piety, Timothy Longman (2009) demonstrated that racial discrimination was integral to churches in Rwanda and not an anomaly inconsistent with religious teachings. Thus, depth of religious faith or conviction cannot explain the role of religion in rescue, martyrdom, or any other potential action during genocide.

Most importantly, this chapter considers the immense symbolic potency of martyrs in the aftermath of genocide. As symbols, martyrs serve important political ends. Their deaths render them politically neutral, making them easy subjects of the postgenocide government's commemoration practices, and foreclose further scrutiny of their motivations or actions.

Altruism, Rwandan Cultural Logics, and Piety

Samuel and Pearl Oliner (1988) were among the first to identify altruism—meaning sacrificing one's self-interests to benefit others—as a significant personality trait among Holocaust rescuers. In the body of social psychological research growing out of the Oliners' initial study, researchers understood altruism to be "a form of social action" where "the actor aims to increase the resources of another person at the expense of" their own, and where the primary motivation is not self-interested but "an interpretation of right and wrong" (Pessi 2009, 185). Or, as psychologist and Holocaust survivor Ervin Staub (2003) put it most simply, altruism is "caring about and helping others" (145).

Social psychologists have debated whether altruism is innate or learned. Oliner and Oliner (1988) concluded that altruism arises from an individual's personality traits: "Rescuers did not simply happen on opportunities for rescue; they actively created, sought, or recognized them where others did not. Their participation was not determined by circumstances but their own personal qualities" (142). Others have concluded that environmental factors and childhood experiences teach or encourage the development of altruistic tendencies.[4] Staub (1993) concluded that social norms and cultural traits can augment or discourage altruism among all actors during genocide. In the Rwandan genocide, altruism—or the will to help others—was the starting point of rescue (chapter 5); other actor-network components merged with it to produce agency and shape outcomes. In some cases, the compulsion to help eventually materialized as the ultimate act of altruism: self-sacrifice.

The concepts of altruism and self-sacrifice are difficult to discern in Rwandan culture, but the value of martyrdom for the nation (*ubucengeri*) dates back to at least the fourteenth century: "Ubucengeri can be defined as martyrdom for the nation or the act of 'offensive liberation' whereby it was regarded as an honour to offer oneself, shed blood or die for Rwanda to become recognized as *Umucengeri* [martyr]. An act of Ubucengeri was believed to be divinely ordained and blessed to succeed by *Imana* (God), for the selfless act in essence meant the preservation of the sanctity of God's own home (Rwanda)" (Rusagara 2009, 6). Becoming an umucengeri began with a divination ceremony by the central court's ritual specialists, during which the specialists selected a member of one of the royal lineages to sacrifice themself on the enemy's territory (Nsanzabera 2019).

The concept of ubucengeri was closely tied to the emergence of a central state under the sovereignty of the mwami, the queen mother, and nobles. Because ubucengeri interwove patriotism and self-sacrifice with divine ordination and the noble lineages, it became a key feature in the state-centric history of the Nyiginya monarchy recounted in the epic hero poetry (*ibitekerezo*) of the central court. Many of these epic poems laud the heroism and sacrifice of the nation's martyrs (*abacengeri*, pl.).

The sovereignty of the Nyiginya dynasty was limited to a relatively small region in modern-day central Rwanda. Yet people who spoke Kinyarwanda (Banyarwanda) inhabited a much larger region and lived under heterogeneous political systems based on kingships, chieftaincies, or kin-based lineage systems.[5] Banyarwanda practiced diverse ancestor spirit cults, spirit medium cults, and spirit possession cults resembling the religious practices of many Bantu peoples in the African Great Lakes region (Berger 1982). Although precolonial Rwanda was not politically unified, Banyarwanda shared a common culture (de Lame 2005, 88; D. Newbury 1991, 276; Ntezimana 1980, 15). This shared culture formed a cohesive worldview despite the heterogeneity of religious practices and spirits venerated.

Christopher Taylor (1992) and Alexis Kagame (1952) described the religious rituals of the central court and their interior logic based on the flow of "fecundity fluids" through the mwami, the land, cattle, and humans (Taylor 1992, 26–27). Anthropologist Danielle de Lame (2005, 85) demonstrated the links between the central court's magical ideology and rituals to ensure "fertility of the land, cattle, and women" and broader cultural practices and beliefs tied to ancestor spirit cults and the strict regulation of everyday life through dense systems of taboos, customs, and rituals described by Aloys Bigirumwami (2004). "Compliance with taboos," "subordination to one's superiors," and the symbolic and material system regulating the "circulation of people, cattle, and food" among ordinary Rwandans relied on the same cultural logics as the rituals and magic of the central court (de Lame 2005, 85).

The central court rituals focused on the mwami as "the earthly avatar of *Imaána* [*sic*]" (Taylor 1992, 32). In precolonial Rwanda, *imana* referred to "a powerful quality, a dynamic principle of life and fertility" that flowed through the universe (Coupez and d'Hertefelt 1964, 460).[6] Imana suffused "certain trees and plants, royal residences and tombs, animals and objects used in divination, and protective talismans" (Taylor 1992, 26) that virtually every Rwandan man, woman, or child wore at some point during their lives (Bigirumwami 2004; de Lame 2005). Although imana was the supreme creator of all things, it was quite different from Jewish, Christian, or Muslim conceptions of God.[7] In the epic poetry of the royal court, imana was not anthropomorphic or personified and thus was agender. Imana took no interest in the personal affairs of humans.

Owing to the influence of missionaries, early colonial accounts of Rwandan spiritual beliefs and religious practices often depicted imana as an anthropomorphic deity rather than an amorphous life force flowing through the universe. Christian missionaries in Rwanda adopted the word "Imana" to refer to the Christian God in Kinyarwanda. Thus, by the mid-twentieth century most Rwandans conflated imana, a dynamic life force, and Imana, God in Christianity and Islam (Taylor 1992, 27).

Given precolonial Rwandan conceptions of imana, the universe, and the role of ancestor and other spirits in daily life, altruism and self-sacrifice did not fit in Rwandan religious and moral frameworks. Altruism, as defined by psychologists and social scientists, relies on moral judgments predicated on the notion of a supreme arbiter of good and bad, embodied by God in Christianity and Islam.[8] Yet imana, as a dynamic life force, did not provide humans with a code of conduct (Crépeau 1985, 166). Instead, moral decision making was guided by human-to-human and human-to-spirit interactions, situated in the hierarchical, social context of the lineage, the ancestors and other spirits, and the hill as both a community and a political entity (de Lame 2005; Freedman 1984). Whether an act was judged to be morally good or bad depended on the social and political circumstances in which it was performed (Crépeau 1985, 168). In short, the Rwandan view of morality—judging right from wrong—was "essentially fatalistic, pragmatic, relativistic, and individualistic" (170).

In this context, martyrdom for the nation (ubucengeri) was logical, but martyrdom to save other people was senseless. As Rwandan historian Jean de Dieu Nsanzabera (2019) put it, "In Rwandan history, no one rescued another [person] from death for any reason. The saviors (*abacunguzi*) died for the nation to save the innumerable people who live in it," but not for any specific people. Sacrificing one's own life or one's self-interest for the benefit of another person was considered irrational in the precolonial Rwandan worldview. Kinyarwanda has no word for altruism, and no proverbs that laud self-sacrifice.

Many conditions influenced a person's moral values in Rwanda, including innate characteristics or personality traits, parental influence and upbringing, and habits, whether good or bad (Crépeau 1985, 166–67). At the root of Rwandan morality was the idea that all individuals are responsible for their own actions and must suffer their consequences (167–68). Rwandans recognized two sources for social control: laws and edicts from chiefs or the mwami and magico-religious laws (168). Acts in and of themselves were not deemed morally good or bad; rather, acts were deemed useful or risky because of their potential consequences for the person doing them (168). Chiefs' orders could be ignored as long as they were eluded intelligently so as to avoid being caught and punished (Kagame 1956, 399). Thus, "Lying, theft, adultery, and murder [were] not wrong per se but only due to the problems that they might create for their perpetrators"; those "problems" might include official punishment by public authorities, social consequences from the community, or supernatural consequences from the ancestors or other spirits (Crépeau 1985, 168). Thus "the morality of an act [was] decided, ultimately, based on a meticulous calculation of interests where the pros and cons [were] carefully weighed, taking into account all the circumstances which surround[ed] not only the act itself but also the moral judgment which might follow it" (170).

Rwanda's precolonial worldview contrasts sharply with those of Christianity and Islam, both of which categorize certain acts as absolutely, morally wrong—in short, as sins. The Christian and Muslim conceptions of God position him as the ultimate moral judge of human actions that all believers must consider if they hope to merit heaven. Both Christianity and Islam promote altruism and self-sacrifice as noble behaviors. Consider Surah Al-Ma'ida 5:32 from the Qur'an: "Whoever kills a[n innocent] soul . . . —it is as if he had slain mankind entirely. And whoever saves one—it is as if he had saved mankind entirely" ('Usmānī 2020). This surah captures the sin of murder and the virtue of saving the lives of the innocent. In the Bible, John 15:13 explicitly states the virtue of self-sacrifice: "Greater love has no one than this: to lay down one's life for one's friends" (New International Version).

Such theological endorsements of self-sacrifice are foreign to precolonial Rwandan morality. This chapter opens with a Rwandan proverb that may appear, to non-Rwandan readers, to encourage altruism: "Never hand over to the hunter quarry that sought refuge in your home" (Jacob 1985, 272). But that interpretation misreads the proverb. Instead of promoting protection or altruism, the proverb encourages a person to take advantage of another's misfortune. The proverb's meaning is hidden in what is left unsaid: "Never hand over to the hunter quarry that sought refuge in your home *so that you can slaughter and eat it yourself*." Rwandans still use this proverb to justify taking advantage of others' misfortunes. With the exception of parental sacrifice for the benefit of children, the Rwandan worldview promotes the pursuit of self-interest whenever the risk of being caught and punished is deemed reasonable. For example, ignoring or disobeying orders from public authorities was understood as normative in precolonial Rwanda, and the practice continues today. Christianity and Islam, in comparison, promote altruism and self-sacrifice as core to their theology.

Over the course of the twentieth century, European colonialism and the introduction of Christianity and Islam transformed local understandings of the universe, imana, God, morality, rituals, customs, and taboos. The Missionaries of Africa, commonly known as the White Fathers, "sought to dismantle" the rituals and traditions that they perceived at best as "pagan" and at worst as consorting with the devil (Freedman 1984, 17). Although the German and Belgian colonialists did not concern themselves with religious traditions such as the ancestor cults or various spirit cults, the White Fathers categorically forbid Christian converts from practicing them (Freedman 1984, 52).[9] In 1994, almost 90 percent of the population was Catholic or other Christian, while Muslims were less than 2 percent (Republic of Rwanda 1994, 127). Nonetheless, "bits and pieces of rituals, especially rites terminating mourning and those for divining and sacrifices, were still practiced at the end of the 1980s" (de Lame 2005, 82–83). Various illnesses were healed through divination, magic, sorcery, or interactions with various spirits (Taylor 1992). In short, colonialism and conversion to Christianity or Islam transformed many aspects of religious belief and practice in Rwanda, but they did not completely replace the symbolic system underlying the entire cultural system, indigenous beliefs in magic, the power of spirits, or moral orientations emphasizing the nested hierarchies of social relations among humans—whether living or dead. In essence, two cosmological systems coexisted alongside each other, and both shaped human action.

Given this history, it is perhaps unsurprising that the vast majority of Rwandan rescuers explained their motivations in Rwanda cultural terms rather than religion: they said their actions were based on empathy, compassion, or a sense of shared humanity with Tutsi and others who were targeted. Nearly unanimously, genocide survivors, rescuers, community members, and even perpetrators said that what set rescuers apart from the others was having "a good heart" (*umutima mwiza*). The few studies of rescuers in Rwanda published to date have focused on this explanation of rescuer behavior, echoing the focus in Holocaust studies on altruism.[10]

In Kinyarwanda, the heart is the seat of the mind and the emotions. "The heart [*umutima*] is the unifying center of a person where their main psychological values—knowledge, love and friendship, hope and inner joy—reside" (Crépeau 1985, 245). It is "the fundamental harmony of a person . . . it is where a person's personality is found, it is the person themselves and not another" (Nothomb 1965, 24). When Rwandans speak of "the heart" in this way, they are evoking the notion of a conscience. A person may have a "good heart" or a "bad heart."[11] Sylvestre (BIR18), a Catholic genocide survivor, invoked this notion to explain why some people killed in the genocide while others helped: "It depends on the person's heart. It's the heart of the person which tells him that he must not kill, that he must save." By contrast, the Interahamwe and civilians who joined in the killing were described as having "bad hearts" or having been led astray by greed. Valence (KAY27), a Hutu Pentecostal from Kayove who protected Tutsi in the genocide, explained, "People do not share the same heart. . . . Those who participated did so because of the bad nature they were born with or because they embraced the bad lessons taught them. It's like in class; children do not learn in the same way. . . . The ones who participated [in the genocide] had a bad heart, and those who didn't participate had a good heart." In short, most Rwandans identified moral conscience as the foundation of people's actions during the genocide. Yet, many of them also acknowledged that other factors shaped the options available to people and the decisions they made.

Whether they are called "moral conscience" or "altruism," such inner traits cannot fully explain who chooses to rescue and whether the rescue succeeds. In his study of Jewish survival and French assistance during the Holocaust in Vichy France, Jacques Sémelin (2019) writes,

> Having trained as a psychologist, I have profound reservations about the idea that personality was a determining influence on the behavior of those who came to the aid of Jews. Certainly there will have been some individuals by nature inclined to defy convention and predisposed to behave in a certain way in such circumstances. On the whole, however, those we call "rescuers" were not necessarily people who were intrinsically good or instinctively inclined to help others. In some cases, their motives were unclear; they may even have been collaborating in some way with the regime when they ended up helping someone without ever having planned or intended to do so. The context of a specific situation tends to outweigh personality. (265)

Altruism and personality traits explain little about why people risked their lives in the Rwandan genocide. Successful rescue emerged from complex assemblages comprising human impulses, local histories, social relations, chance, and other factors. Rarely were people's motives morally pure.

Even when altruism is the beginning of rescue, many other actor-network components coalesce to produce agency that may end in successful rescue. Sémelin's conclusions and my research demonstrate that rescuers were not necessarily morally superior to others. Rather, they are entangled in the same complex and dynamic context as those who perpetrate genocide. Not infrequently, they are the same people. In some cases, people who succeeded in saving lives simply had better luck than those who failed in their efforts.

Religion may be one component of that actor-network. Indeed, many Hutu Muslims who engaged in acts of rescue during the 1994 genocide explained their motivations in religious terms. They cited Islam's prohibition of murder or its teachings denouncing racism and promoting Muslim unity. The institutional stance of AMUR and its elected leader, the mufti of Rwanda, against divisive politics, racism, and hatred helped ensure Muslims had moral clarity (see appendix 1). When explaining their actions, many Hutu Muslim rescuers mobilized the verses cited in the mufti's statement against racial division, including Surah Al-Ma'ida 5:32, or the local imams' preaching against political polarization in the years leading up to the genocide (chapters 3 and 4).

Many Christians, for their part, were left to divine the morality of the situation on their own. Roman Catholic priests and Christian pastors failed to speak out clearly and with unity on these issues. As a result, the "churches were a key factor in encouraging public involvement" in the genocide because they helped "make participating in the killing morally acceptable" (Longman 2009, 306) by failing to take a stance on racism and racist killings during the civil war or to issue "a prompt, firm condemnation" of the killing (Des Forges 1999, 246). Still, several Hutu Christians described their acts of rescue in religious terms. The Adventist brothers in Rubona, Abel and Ezekiel, explained that they had the courage to risk their lives because, as Ezekiel explained, "It is God's commandment that killing is a sin" (chapter 4). Likewise, Father Eros, the Italian Catholic priest in Nyanza, perceived his actions in religious moral terms of good versus evil and actively used Catholic religious theology and practice to maintain solidarity among the children in the orphanage (chapter 4).

Thus, religious piety did not play a determinative role in all rescue, but it did play a role for some people, some of the time. Piety mingled with other aspects of religious belief, practice, and community, alongside other actor-network components, to make collective rescue possible on Rubona hill, in Mugandamure hamlet, and at the Centre Saint Antoine orphanage in Nyanza. In Mugandamure and Nkora (chapter 6), the Muslim community's social cohesion emerged from shared religious belief and ritual practice, but local histories of settlement, topographical features such as Mugandamure's colonial-era secret passages, and geographical features such as Lake Kivu and the border were also enmeshed in the actor-networks that produced rescue.

In other instances, genocide survivors and the people who helped them attested to their religious faith and prayer as sources of courage that helped them persist while facing great adversity.[12] Martyrs represent perhaps the most significant example of piety's role in the gray zone of genocide. For people motivated by religious principles or moral piety, their gradual decision making in the genocide's gray zone pushed them to take ever more dangerous steps. For these people, religion provided not only moral clarity but also a model of martyrdom, whether based in Christian or Islamic theology. For a few, piety and moral rectitude led them to sacrifice themselves rather than become complicit in the genocide.

Safe Harbor in the Storm: Kibagabaga Mosque and the Saint Pierre Center

The dramatic scene of Félicité Niyitegeka's martyrdom at the municipal cemetery was neither predetermined nor unimaginable at the outset of the genocide in the early morning hours of April 7, 1994. Her act of self-sacrifice emerged from actor-networks encompassing her deeply held moral convictions and religious piety, as well as her social ties, the location of the Saint Pierre Center compound on the political border with Congo, and the local unfolding of violence between the start of the genocide on April 7 and her death, among many other factors. Likewise, the acts of genocide resistance, rescue, and martyrdom of Ansar Allah Muslims at the Kibagabaga mosque in Kigali materialized from heterogeneous actor-network components. Previous chapters detailed the unfolding of the genocide in Gisenyi town and the assemblage components that fueled genocidal violence and facilitated rescue there; here I will describe the important actor-network components that influenced Kibagabaga residents.

Kibagabaga and the Ansar Allah Mosque

In 1994, Kibagabaga was a quiet, peri-urban community just outside of Kigali. Set on a large hill with a relatively wide plateau, it was surrounded on three sides by valleys filled with marshes and agricultural fields. Even though Kibagabaga sat less than two miles from the parliament building, which was located on one of the city's main boulevards, only one mile from the new Amahoro National Stadium in Kimironko, and a little less than two miles from the Gregoire Kayibanda International Airport, the community was physically isolated from the city by a lack of paved roads or public transportation (KIB21). Several clusters of residences interspersed with small commercial buildings were scattered across the plateau. "There were forests everywhere, and only a few people lived here" (KIB21). Many residents still subsisted on farming activities, although the plateau was more densely settled than most rural communities. In the late 1980s, Kibagabaga's inexpensive land and housing had begun to attract people who worked in Kigali as drivers, mechanics, domestic workers, and laborers. They commuted on foot a mile or so to Kimironko, where they could catch a bus to other parts of Kigali. The majority of Kibagabaga residents were among the working poor. The community's topography, physical proximity to Kigali's urban core and sites that became critical during the genocide, rural layout and character, and social and economic ties to the city became significant assemblage components that shaped the unfolding of the genocide there.

Kibagabaga was embroiled in the political and anti-Tutsi violence in the wake of the RPF's initial attack on Rwanda in October 1990, largely because of the proximity to the new stadium, opened in 1989. The soccer matches and political rallies held at the stadium, which attracted Interahamwe and Impuzamugambi members, brought mob violence to Kibagabaga in the years leading up to the genocide. After the events, the militia members would pour into the streets looking to harass people. Alphonse, a long-term Kibagabaga resident, described the result: "We saw [political] parties' violent demonstrations where CDR and MRND members beat people—especially tall people and anyone they believed to be Tutsi. They went after people based on their race" (KIB37). To describe the situation in the early 1990s, Alphonse, a middle-aged Hutu man whose wife was Tutsi, explained that the Interahamwe and Impuzamugambi relied on physical stereotypes to identify Tutsi, "tall people."[13] Gakuba, who was a Tutsi Muslim genocide survivor and long-term Kibagabaga resident, explained, "Whenever there was a political rally, they would force us to give them money, and they would beat us. They would go around chanting, '*Tubatsembatsembe!* Let's massacre them!'" (KIB31). In 1994, Gakuba was in his early thirties. His age, physical appearance, race, and religion made him a frequent target of their attacks.

In 1992 and 1993, groups of Interahamwe and Impuzamugambi burned houses in Kibagabaga and murdered Tutsi and members of opposition political parties (KIB36). André, a Tutsi resident of Kibagabaga, explained: "Some innocent people were accused of being [RPF] accomplices and imprisoned. [The local authorities] claimed that unknown murderers killed those victims. They never investigated those murders, which later became more frequent" (KIB36). The militias acted with impunity. Several prominent members of the local government had joined the CDR and recruited local men to the Impuzamugambi. Those same officials ensured no one was ever prosecuted for the attacks on Kibagabaga residents. André continued, "Yet the public knew who had done it. Anastase Semurima, the *responsable* for the cell; Joseph Ndekezi, a member of the cell council; and also Bernard Bizimana and Nasibu Simba were among the killers. They were the local authorities, so nobody had the power to punish them" (KIB36). These local authorities commanded the Interahamwe and Impuzamugambi to attack Tutsi and political opposition members in April 1994, and they organized Hutu residents of Kibagabaga to help them.

An assemblage component that coalesced collective resistance to the genocide was the Ansar Allah mosque. Residents of Kibagabaga were religiously diverse; Kibagabaga was home to a Roman Catholic church, an Anglican church, a small Pentecostal church, and a mosque. The mosque had been built in the early 1980s by "a Muslim man, Makera. . . . It originally served as his residence and a mosque at the same time. AMA—the Africa Muslims Agency—provided funds to build the bigger mosque" (KIB30). Because there was no other nearby, the Kibagabaga mosque drew worshippers from the surrounding communities (KIB23). Suleiman, who was the imam in 1994 and in 2013, when we interviewed him, explained, "In 1994, about five hundred Muslims came from surrounding areas, like Kimironko, Goropima, Nyagatovu, Nyabisindu, and Kibagabaga, to regularly attend the Kibagabaga mosque. Most of them belonged to Ansar Allah in Rwanda" (KIB21b). As explained in chapter 4, Ansar Allah is a distinct sect of Islam founded in Rwanda in the 1980s. When Ansar

Allah officially split from AMUR in 1990, the Kibagabaga mosque became its headquarters (KIB01, NAT02).

Although Ansar Allah started as a youth movement within AMUR, tensions eventually led Ansar Allah to break with AMUR. A significant contributor to the conflict was the two groups' different stances on political parties and the growing polarization between parties. Despite AMUR and Mufti Ahmad Mugwiza's statement against racism and anti-Tutsi violence issued in 1992, Ansar Allah members interviewed in 2011 and 2013 said AMUR's leadership was collaborating with the state. They said AMUR's statement did not go far enough, because it did not forbid Muslims from joining political parties. AMUR was, according to Ansar Allah members, "100 percent on the side of power," meaning it supported President Habyarimana's government and its growing Hutu extremism (NAT03). They explained that AMUR encouraged Muslims to join the Islamic Democratic Party, which was allied with President Habyarimana's MRND party.

Ansar Allah, in contrast, specifically forbade its members from joining political parties or participating in any form of racism because these acts were un-Islamic (KIB01). Like AMUR, Ansar Allah had preached unity (*ubumwe*) and brotherhood among Muslims throughout the early 1990s. At times, Ansar Allah explicitly opposed government policies and the racist rhetoric of some political parties. Malek (KIB23), who was among the male youth of Ansar Allah in 1994, explained, "Three months before the genocide began, Ansar Allah had made announcements about how to behave in troubled times like those that we were in the midst of"—alluding to the extremist politics and ethnic hatred (KIB23). Hassan, another young male member of Ansar Allah, elaborated: "In 1994 just before the genocide occurred, Ansar Allah fought against it. The association sent statements to authorities, telling them that what they were doing was wrong. Ansar Allah leaders knew that this action could get them killed, but they said, 'We must go against it, even if we die because of that'" (KIB01).

Ansar Allah members played a decisive role in organizing resistance to the genocide in several rural communities around Rwanda, including Kibagabaga, Mugandamure (chapter 4), and Mabare in eastern Rwanda (Viret 2011a). This open opposition made all Ansar Allah members, regardless of race, potential "enemies of Rwanda" in the rhetoric of the Hutu extremists. The sect's statements reinforced its adherents' resolve against racism and political violence, but they also made Ansar Allah Muslims targets of political violence. In Kibagabaga, Ansar Allah Muslims' direct opposition to violence perpetrated by Interahamwe and Impuzamugambi in the years before the genocide and their vocal criticism of the local officials who protected these perpetrators set the stage for the dramatic confrontation that was to come during the genocide.

Kibagabaga's physical proximity to several critical sites further shaped the actor-networks that emerged during the genocide. It was located near the airport, where President Habyarimana's plane was shot down; the parliament building, where an RPF battalion was garrisoned as part of the Arusha Peace Accords; and the Amahoro National Stadium, where the UN Assistance Mission for Rwanda (UNAMIR) peacekeeping forces were headquartered.

As a result of its proximity to these key sites, the community was immediately plunged into the rapidly unfolding chaos after the president's plane went down, on the night of April 6, 1994. Mbabazi, a Tutsi man who was thirty-three years old in 1994, was out with friends, watching the semifinals of the 1994 Africa Cup of Nations soccer tournament. He described that night:

> I was in Kibagabaga that evening. I was drinking some beer with others, when we suddenly saw fire in the sky. It's not very far from the airport. Then we heard on the radio that the president's airplane had just crashed. People started looking at each other with suspicion. They had unanswered questions, such as "Who did it? And how did it happen?" We went home immediately with those troubling questions on our minds. The next morning, radio broadcasts announced that everyone must stay home. Things deteriorated that morning; some families were attacked on accusation of being Inkotanyi accomplices. They accused Tutsi [of] doing those things [killing the president]. People became uneasy and suspicious of each other. They started categorizing each other [by race and political persuasion]. (KIB25)

Gunshots punctuated the darkness throughout the night of April 6 (KIB21). Most people in Kibagabaga were confused, lacking information about what was happening. "Ordinary people, like us, did not understand what was going on. We went to talk with neighbors to see what they knew. Some soldiers passed by and threatened us. They said, 'We were expecting to find Inyenzi-Inkotanyi here. Instead, you stand here lazily and disappoint us'" (KIB23). In the morning, on April 7, gunshots began to ring out from the direction of the airport and the parliament building (KIB01, KIB23, KIB25, KIB36). A battle had broken out between government troops and the RPF rebel soldiers stationed inside.

At the Kibagabaga mosque, "Muslims came for the morning prayer [around 4:50 a.m.]. Afterwards, the radio broadcast the presidential airplane accident and the death of the ex-president. Some Muslims stayed at the mosque, and others went back home to bring their families, because we realized that war had become imminent. In the evening [April 7], the number of people seeking refuge [at the mosque] increased. We all spent the night there" (KIB21). Between the morning of April 7 and the night of April 8, roving bands of militiamen in

Kibagabaga attacked Tutsi and anyone else accused of being RPF "accomplices," usually meaning they held membership in opposition political parties or had close relationships with Tutsi. André described those first days:

> On April 8, systematic killings began on the side near Kimironko, but [the attackers] met some resistance. They moved uphill and came to this area and killed at least five people. The public was not fully aware of what was going on. They launched a campaign to explain that Tutsi were the targets; that Hutu will live better after the extermination of Tutsi. Anastase Semurima, head of the cellule, was in charge of this campaign in collaboration with some other Hutu. April 9 was the day that widespread killings began because the public knew who the targets were. (KIB36)

Anastase Semurima's sons were leaders of the local Impuzamugambi. They had begun harassing, beating, and extorting Tutsi in the area in 1992 and 1993. This pattern continued during the genocide, now with the open backing of the army and police.

As the killing escalated, more people fled to the churches and mosque in Kibagabaga, seeking safety. Kayitesi, a woman who was in her mid-thirties in 1994, lived in Kibagabaga. Her husband was a mason; the eldest of her six children had just started primary school. She fled to the Pentecostal church with her children, while her husband hid. She explained, "The morning after Habyarimana's death, we all came to the Pentecostal church not far from where the hospital is today. That was the last time I saw my husband, at the primary school. Males went into hiding in the forest and marshes, and we [women and children] stayed at the primary school playground" (KIB38). The pattern Kayitesi describes was fairly common in the early days of the violence. People sought refuge in the churches and government buildings where they had found safety in previous episodes of anti-Tutsi violence. They assumed that Tutsi men, more likely perceived as RPF infiltrators or security threats, were in the greatest danger. The men hid in the forest to reduce the threat of violence against the women and children. As the battle between Rwandan government troops and the RPF garrisoned in the parliament building intensified, refugees from Nyarutarama and Remera fled toward Kibagabaga, increasing the numbers sheltered in churches and the mosque.

The Ansar Allah mosque in Kibagabaga—and its mosques elsewhere in Rwanda—remained open during the genocide, unlike most mosques managed by AMUR. AMUR's imams closed their mosques and instructed their members to pray together in their homes to prevent large numbers of refugees from gathering.[14] This action helped ensure that mosques did not become massacre sites, but it also meant they did not provide protection to large numbers of refugees. In Kibagabaga, in contrast, the imam encouraged people, regardless of religion or ethnicity, to gather at the mosque for solidarity and self-defense. Following this call, Ansar Allah Muslims of all races left their homes on April 7 or 8 to stay at the mosque. Many Christians and others from the neighborhood surrounding the mosque also sought refuge there. They had observed that the Muslims in Kibagabaga eschewed politics, rejected racism, and encouraged friendship among Christians and Muslims.

Saint Pierre Pastoral Center and the Unfolding Violence in Gisenyi

The gathering of refugees at the Saint Pierre Pastoral Center in Gisenyi began under different circumstances from those at the Kibagabaga mosque. The Saint Pierre Center was fortuitously located near the Grand Barrière border crossing between Gisenyi and Goma. The center's founder, Félicité Niyitegeka, was the first African member of the Auxiliaries of the Apostolate (Auxiliaires de l'Apostolat), a Roman Catholic lay ministry for women founded in 1917 by Cardinal Mercier in Brussels, Belgium. Born to two early Catholic converts in 1934 in Vumbi in southern Rwanda, Félicité was baptized shortly after her birth, which was unusual at the time (Dusengumuremyi 2015, 23). In 1950, she went to study at the École Secondaire de Save, a Catholic secondary school on the site of the Catholic Church's first mission in southern Rwanda. Niyitegeka studied to become a teacher (Dusengumuremyi 2015, 23). When she was teaching at a school in southern Rwanda, she discerned her calling to serve the church as a lay minister with the Auxiliaries of the Apostolate. Monsignor Aloys Bigurumwami, the bishop of Nyundo diocese and the first Rwandan priest to become a bishop, sent Félicité to study theology in Lourdes, France, for six years in the 1960s. She then spent the next thirty years serving the Nyundo diocese as an Auxiliary of the Apostolate. Félicité managed the center with the help of her colleague Marie Nathalie Icyimpaye—Sister Nathalie—also a member of the Auxiliaries of the Apostolate.[15] Félicité and Nathalie regularly organized prayer retreats for people at the Saint Pierre Center. They also educated women seeking to join the Auxiliaries during their journeys of discernment.

On April 3, 1994, a group of women in training to join the Auxiliaries gathered at the Saint Pierre Center for a religious retreat. The prayer retreat started like any other, despite the tense situation that reigned in the country (Kayitesi 2009, 107–8). The postulants learned of President Habyarimana's assassination on the morning of April 7, when a visiting priest announced it before the start of morning Mass (108). After Mass, Félicité gathered the young women together and asked them to pray for the country. All day long, Félicité received phone calls informing her of the killings of "priests, nuns, friends, acquaintances, and also of the massacres taking place all over Rwanda" (109). The next day, refugees began arriving at Saint Pierre seeking shelter. Many Tutsi Catholics who lived nearby fled to Saint Pierre (GIS50), believing that the center would not be attacked, since people had not dared to desecrate Catholic institutions in previous episodes of anti-Tutsi violence (GIS48). Some of them "hoped to cross the nearby border" or "were attracted by Félicité's presence" (GIS56). Some believed Félicité's religious vocation and her brother's position in the Rwandan military would protect them. "People thought that no one would dare attack the center for fear of Col. Nzungize" (African Rights 2002, 265).

Félicité's character, religious faith, and prior actions created a strong foundation for the choices she made during the genocide. Félicité had taken a vocal stand against the rising Hutu ethnonationalism in the early 1990s and had advocated for peace and a resolution to the war between the government forces and RPF. One of Félicité's students, Eugénie, explained her response to racist propaganda: "She told us, 'Do you not see that people have begun to scrutinize each other's noses? As Christians, it is a sin to distinguish a Hutu nose and Tutsi nose. In Christ, [there is] no Hutu, no Tutsi, no white foreigner'" (GIS56). Félicité's actions went beyond preaching to those who gathered at the Saint Pierre Center; they also included peace activism and public opposition to racist violence. She had helped organized a peace march at the Amahoro National Stadium in Kigali on January 1, 1994, to protest the massive distribution of arms throughout the country (GIS 56). Félicité's religious faith, opposition to ethnic division and hatred, activism, and relationship with her brother, the colonel, constituted actor-network components that produced certain types of agency during the genocide. These attributes were the anchors that strengthened her resolve and gave her courage as she faced the violent storm.

By April 9, "there were many refugees [at Saint Pierre]. We were here waiting for what was going to happen. We heard a lot of noise, gunshots and bombs" (GIS50). As the number of refugees increased, "Félicité went to the authorities to request food assistance for them. The authorities replied that they would try to solve the problem" (GIS56). As the situation in Gisenyi town deteriorated and killings became more widespread, Félicité tried to calm everyone's fears. "Priests and nuns had been killed in Nyundo and in Gisenyi town. It was Félicité who gave us this information. Nevertheless, she continued telling us to have courage" (African Rights 2002, 265). She also sought to conceal the presence of the refugees, to avoid attracting the attention of the militia. "Félicité warned people at the center not to go outside. She did her best to hide the fact that so many refugees were there" (GIS56). Nevertheless, rumors circulated in town that Tutsi were hiding at Saint Pierre.

Several factors predisposed Félicité and the Ansar Allah Muslims to oppose the genocide. Yet their acts of martyrdom were not predetermined when anti-Tutsi violence began around them in the early morning hours of April 7. The Ansar Allah Muslims and the Auxiliaries of the Apostolate, Félicité in particular, had established reputations for opposing racism and Hutu ethnonationalism. They were perceived as "loving everybody" regardless of race, economic class, occupation, or religion (African Rights 2002, 260; interviews by author in Gisenyi and Kibagabaga, 2013). The Saint Pierre Center and the Kibagabaga mosque were religious institutions with track records of social solidarity and diverse congregations in prayer. In addition, their leaders had explicitly addressed political polarization, Hutu ethnonationalism, and anti-Tutsi violence in their preaching prior to the genocide. By explicitly condemning these ideologies and actions as sins, they had unified their members in resisting or opposing them. These actor-network components attracted refugees—both Hutu and Tutsi—who were fleeing the violence and predisposed the people gathered at the Kibagabaga Mosque and the Saint Pierre Center to offer shelter and help. These assemblages eventually propelled these people to resist the genocide and directly oppose national security forces who ordered them to sort themselves according to race.

Becoming a Martyr: Incremental Decisions and Improvisation

> **Intwari iboneka ruremye (Heroes reveal themselves in combat).**
>
> —Rwandan proverb

Like Father Eros in Nyanza, the Ansar Allah Muslims and Félicité did not decide at the outset of the crisis to welcome refugees seeking shelter or protect people from the death squads. They arrived at these actions through a long series of incremental decisions and improvisations in the exceptional, dynamic circumstances of the genocide. Their eventual martyrdom emerged from this decision making, the morally impossible situations forged in the genocide's gray zone, and the collective memory of their actions in the wake of the genocide's ordered chaos. Félicité's, Hamza's, and Mohamed's unwillingness to compromise their moral code led them to confront the state's genocidal sovereignty directly. Christian or Muslim models of martyrdom may also have encouraged, or driven, their final decisions.

Saint Pierre Center

Many events and decisions, both large and small, preceded the dramatic scene of Félicité's self-sacrifice at the municipal cemetery. In the first days of the genocide,

Tutsi Catholics who regularly prayed at Saint Pierre began arriving at the center seeking shelter. Félicité and Nathalie welcomed them. At first, they did their best to hide them from the postulants in training, other people hiding at the center, and people outside the compound gates. They hoped the crisis would pass quickly and that they could protect people by hiding them. As anti-Tutsi violence became a nationwide policy of genocide on April 12, that strategy became infeasible. Refugees continued to come. As their numbers increased, Félicité asked some of the postulants, who were Hutu and not otherwise in danger, to return home to their families (African Rights 2002, 262). Most of them did. One Hutu postulant, Josephine, who was twenty-six years old in 1994, stayed at Saint Pierre to help cook and care for everyone sheltering at the center.

Félicité, Nathalie, and the other sisters had agreed on April 7 that only Félicité, Nathalie, or Hutu sisters would respond to visitors at the compound gate or open it to allow people inside (Kayitesi 2009, 114). Tutsi sisters, postulants, and refugees stayed carefully out of sight whenever the gate was opened. Tutsi refugees continued to arrive, either on their own or brought there by local government officials or by militiamen who were helping particular people even while participating in the violence. The refugees were traumatized by what they had witnessed outside the walls of Saint Pierre. Some had themselves survived attacks, and several arrived wounded (Kayitesi 2009, 111).

The refugees grew so numerous that they ate in shifts in the retreat center dining room. "We couldn't be sure of the exact number of people living at the center because of the way the groups alternated in the canteen. But there were certainly some who never went out and who spent their days either in the bedrooms or even in the ceiling" (African Rights 2002, 263). Many of them were Catholic; some were Muslim or Pentecostal (GIS50). Most of them were Tutsi or well-known representatives of opposition political parties. As the killings continued, Félicité sent Hutu Auxiliaries of the Apostolate to check on the families of those hiding at Saint Pierre (Kayitesi 2009, 112–13). When they found someone alive, they smuggled them to Saint Pierre.

Making use of the center's proximity to the Grand Barrière, Félicité smuggled Tutsi refugees across the border to Goma. Josephine explained, "Every night, Félicité took people a few at a time to Congo. I don't know exactly how she did it. . . . We did not know anything about it" (GIS50). Another postulant, Eugénie (GIS56), described the evacuations:

> Félicité spoke to each person individually and discreetly to explain the plan to cross to Congo. The crossing took place between three and four in the morning through a door in the compound's back wall. First, they would meet in either the bungalow or chapel [in the garden]. They

> waited there silently. Two policemen, who had been sent by her brother [the colonel], were responsible for Félicité's safety. They would keep lookout. When it was safe, they [the policemen] would throw a pebble on the roof of the chapel. When people heard this signal, they would open the door and go out. (GIS56)

Once outside the compound, the refugees walked the short distance to the Grand Barrière, where Félicité had arranged with the border guards who worked the night shift to allow them to cross into Goma (African Rights 2002, 266).

These incremental decisions—hiding Tutsi Catholics who sought shelter, welcoming other Tutsi refugees, asking Hutu postulants who were not in danger to return home, accepting refugees brought by government officials and militiamen, and smuggling people across the border—transformed the assemblages within which Félicité was operating. Each action had implications, each decision produced repercussions, even if they were subtle and unnoticed. Each decision took courage to make and increased Félicité's resolve to continue.

Events elsewhere in Gisenyi town and the decisions of local government officials emerged as significant actor-network components that eventually imperiled the refugees at Saint Pierre Center. Around April 15, an Interahamwe-led mob attacked a Catholic boarding school not far from the Saint Pierre Center. "The Interahamwe killed a lot of people at Saint Fidèle secondary school. We could hear the gunfire at the center. All the survivors ran to Saint Pierre" (African Rights 2002, 265). Some of the refugees who arrived at Saint Pierre had deep machete wounds, injuries from clubs, and even gunshot wounds. "Among the refugees there was a Saint Fidèle student, a girl, who had lost her leg. Félicité took care of her" (GIS56).

Félicité and Nathalie went to the hospital to ask for medical supplies to care for people's injuries. Crossing the city and navigating the many roadblocks erected by the militias endangered the sisters themselves and the people hiding at Saint Pierre. At each roadblock, the sisters had to negotiate their safe passage. Although their status as Auxiliaries of the Apostolate and older Hutu women offered them protection, each encounter risked reminding the militiamen of Saint Pierre Center and its close proximity to the Grand Barrière. Thus, the sisters' search for medical supplies risked arousing suspicion that they were hiding Tutsi.

Félicité and Nathalie returned to Saint Pierre safely with the medical supplies, but their efforts were not without cost. Local government officials became aware that Saint Pierre Center was sheltering refugees. On April 18, these officials brought a large group of refugees to the center. The refugees "had first taken shelter at the Meridien Hotel [a luxury hotel on the lakeshore]" (GIS56). Local authorities eventually relocated them to the MRND party headquarters. This decision, however, proved advantageous for the Interahamwe. With the refugees housed in their party headquarters, the militiamen could simply enter the building and select Tutsi victims to kill (GIS56). Government officials eventually decided to move the refugees to the Saint Pierre Center, with a police escort (GIS56). The gendarmes and communal police who escorted that group of refugees remained to keep everyone safe and bar militiamen from entering. However, the guards left after two days (GIS56).

Aware of the rising tensions, Félicité had planned for everyone at the center to escape the night of April 20, but that night the gendarmes' "all clear" signal never came (GIS56). The next day, a large mob of Interahamwe militiamen led by Omar Serushago forced their way into the compound.[16] They searched the grounds and rounded up everyone they knew to be Tutsi or who looked Tutsi. A few refugees who were fortuitously unseen or well hidden remained at Saint Pierre with the Hutu Auxiliaries of the Apostolate, postulants, and schoolgirls while the buses departed for the cemetery with Félicité and over two dozen Tutsi of all ages. Sister Félicité's final steps toward martyrdom were characterized by courage in the face of death, piety, and grace toward the militiamen who killed them all.

Kibagabaga

In Kibagabaga, the Interahamwe and Impuzamugambi militias began killing people who had taken refuge at the churches on April 7 and 8. Groups of militiamen forced their way into the compounds and grabbed five to ten Tutsi men at a time. They beat them and then took them outside to kill them. When it became clear Tutsi and Hutu members of opposition parties were the targets, many Hutu refugees left the church grounds. Then, on April 9, with the backing of government soldiers, the militiamen perpetrated large-scale massacres. Kayitesi described what happened at the Pentecostal church:

> Habyarimana's soldiers and Interahamwe came for us. Most of us were inside the church. They ordered us to go outside and ordered us to sit down in the playground. They worked with Interahamwe and picked the people they wanted, including women and children. They [the soldiers] picked the first hundred people and supervised the Interahamwe, who started killing the victims using clubs and machetes. I was not among those who were picked. The selection process continued for several rounds. They also took groups of victims to the Catholic church playground to kill them there. I was selected almost ten times, but, God willing, they never killed me. [Each time] they returned me to

> the primary school playground. The vast majority of refugees who came from Kibagabaga, Nyarutarama, Gihogere, Remera, Migina, Kimironko, and Gishushu died at those churches. All the victims who were killed at that location were beaten and cut with machetes. (KIB38)

Kayitesi's testimony here emphasizes a few key points. First, many people, Hutu and Tutsi alike, fled to Kibagabaga from several neighboring hills, where a battle between government soldiers and the RPF rebels began on April 7.[17] The civilians fleeing this battle took refuge in Kibagabaga's churches, mosque, and schools. Second, when government soldiers surrounded these locations, they asked the Hutu refugees to leave. Third, once the soldiers and Interahamwe had concentrated Tutsi in these locations, the militiamen—and not the soldiers—killed them, working slowly and systematically while the soldiers continued to pursue Tutsi hiding elsewhere. The same pattern unfolded at the Catholic and Anglican churches (KIB01).

At the Kibagabaga mosque, the imam and other leaders organized a defense to keep militiamen and other intruders out. Suleiman, the imam, explained:

> We tried our best and collected weapons from the neighbors of the mosque, because it was visible that we would be attacked. . . . We organized the fighters, dividing them into three groups. One group [was] armed with stones so that they could keep enemies at distance before they could reach us. The second group was armed with traditional weapons so that they could fight with any groups who arrived near us. The third group guarded the wives and children inside the buildings so that they [the wives and children] would not flee and fall in battle. (KIB21b)

Hutu men took responsibility for defending the perimeter of the mosque grounds. Tutsi men stayed inside the compound, out of sight, and guarded the entrances to the buildings where the women and children stayed. The Hutu men stationed outside the compound wall erected a roadblock about three hundred yards from the compound gate to prevent militiamen or soldiers from reaching the mosque.

The numbers of refugees grew quickly. "Many people went to the mosque when they saw that those who were there were safe. . . . People who heard that the Interahamwe hadn't come to the mosque would sneak out during the night and go to the mosque" (KIB01). Among the refugees at the mosque "there were different people: children, women and elders; Christians and Muslims. In all, we were between seven hundred and eight hundred people" (KIB21b).

Beyond their defensive efforts, the Ansar Allah leaders organized basic needs for everyone. Inside the compound, they distributed the work needed to support the growing crowd. “We divided tasks among ourselves, Muslims and non-Muslims. Some people cooked, others fetched water, others went to harvest food in the fields, and some people stood guard at the gate” (KIB22). Food was an overriding concern. “We had a problem of finding food, but we escorted people who had food at home so that they could bring it [to the mosque], and sometimes we took food from Interahamwe; like sweet potatoes that they harvested from the fields of people who were with us. We had Muslims who had skills in catering for many people at a time. They cooked, and all of us shared that food so that none would go without” (KIB21b). They also assigned sleeping quarters to everyone: “The men slept outside so that the women and the children [slept] inside the mosque and the classrooms” (KIB01).

Between April 8 and 11, the Ansar Allah members and the refugees at the mosque had several confrontations with Interahamwe mobs. In each confrontation, Ansar Allah Muslims risked their lives by directly opposing the state’s genocidal sovereignty, delegated to the militias and civilians recruited to a genocide disguised as national self-defense. Each of the confrontations with the militiamen reinforced the Ansar Allah Muslims’ resolve to defend innocent human lives, as they understood the Tutsi among them—regardless of religion—to be.

On the morning of April 8, a mob pursued a victim near the mosque. The mob “came from Nyagatovu with great noise like hunters after an animal. They passed by the mosque, crossed the road, and killed the man at Maximilien’s house. On their way back, they said that there were people in the mosque they wanted to take. We told them to leave or we would fight them if necessary” (KIB21b). The same day, Ansar Allah Muslims intervened when mobs attacked households near the mosque. Thérèse, a Catholic woman, explained, “Muslims rescued us from the first Interahamwe attack against my family. Interahamwe came down to our house, surrounded the house, and threw stones and grenades. Muslims came to our rescue in a group and took us to the mosque. They continued protecting us” (KIB27). Hamza Habimana was among the Hutu Muslims who volunteered to leave the relative safety of the mosque compound to join these rescue efforts.

In these first confrontations, the Ansar Allah Muslims primarily negotiated with potential attackers. “We would try to reason with them. We would tell them, ‘We all come from Adam and Eve. Which of them is a Tutsi? Which a Hutu? All the people here are Rwandans. We won’t allow you to kill any of them.’” (KIB01). On the morning of April 9, the arrival of a very large Interahamwe mob at the mosque forced a change of strategy. The situation grew increasingly tense as the mob became enraged by the Muslims’ defiance of the new political order. This time, the defensive group outside the compound gates engaged the mob by throwing stones at them (KIB21b). The mob eventually withdrew after many of them sustained injuries.

The success in repelling the mob on April 9 arose from the unity of those gathered at the mosque—between Hutu and Tutsi, Muslim and Christian—their numbers, and their organized defense. After this attack, however, sentiments inside the mosque began to change. Some Hutu questioned whether remaining in the mosque was wise. Imam Suleiman explained:

> Some people inside the mosque did not share our views. They started to discourage others by saying that the mosque was about to be burned down. Many people wished to leave since they were Hutu and were not persecuted. They did not want to be killed with the others [Tutsi]. An Ansar Allah leader, Hamza Habimana, who was well respected, insisted that everyone should stay so that no one could betray those who were inside. When I discovered this dangerous spirit of mistrust and fear had developed, I appealed to everyone, saying that anybody who wanted to leave—whether Hutu or Tutsi—should go. Then, some [Hutu] chose to leave, and those who stayed were ready to fight against attackers. (KIB21b)

Here again, Hamza distinguished himself as fully committed to the defense of Tutsi civilians and opposition to the genocide, no matter the risks.

After several more clashes in which Ansar Allah Muslims defended the mosque, the Interahamwe sought assistance from government soldiers. On the afternoon of April 11, a squad of four or five soldiers arrived at the mosque to search for RPF rebels or infiltrators. The militiamen had told them that the Muslims were harboring "Inyenzi" (KIB01, KIB21b). Hamza Habimana and Mohamed Hakuzimana, who were among the men standing guard at the mosque roadblock, refused the soldiers entry. The commanding officer demanded to speak with the person in charge. Despite protests from other Ansar Allah leaders, who thought it was too dangerous, Imam Suleiman left the compound to speak with the soldiers in the road. Suleiman described what happened next:

> The soldier asked me why I refused to allow people to go and help the others [search for and kill Tutsi], especially since they had been ordered to help. I replied that I had no right to offer people to go and kill as they had been commanded. He then stepped back a bit to talk to his partner. I took the opportunity to retreat inside. When he turned around, he didn't see me anymore. He commanded Mohamed and Hamza to clear the way. "Remove that tree and get everyone out! Come up here on the road!"
>
> Hamza and Mohamed looked at each other speechless. Then, Hamza yelled, "Allah Akbar [God is great]!" Then, Mohamed added, "You,

> soldier! If your only purpose here is to kill, then it is better for us to shed our blood first before that of the people we are protecting. Do whatever you want, we will not move it." The soldiers' commander abruptly yelled, "Shoot!" They all opened fire. They shot Hamza in the abdomen. Mohamed was riddled with bullets, and an RPG [rocket-propelled grenade] tore his head apart. . . . They continued firing for five minutes, but miraculously no one else was shot because it was impossible to separate Hutu from Tutsi with bullets. (KIB21b)

The soldiers then retreated. The gunfire produced panic among the hundreds of people at the mosque. Some immediately fled downhill behind the mosque enclosure to hide in the valley and marshlands below. Suleiman and the other Ansar Allah leaders brought Hamza into the classroom behind the mosque, where others tended to his wounds. Then they collected Mohamed's remains and buried him behind the mosque in the garden. The remaining Muslims and refugees spent a troubled night in fear of what would happen next.

Why did Hamza and Mohamed confront the soldiers directly and with such ardor? What drove them to these acts, which ended in self-sacrifice? In our interviews in Kibagabaga, the research team learned very little about these two men, their backgrounds, or their occupations. In his official testimony about the events at the mosque, Imam Suleiman wrote,

> Mohamed Hakuzimana was a carpenter. I don't know his parents and where he was born. He died at the age of 32 years. He was a Hutu who lived at Nyagatovu of Kimironko. He left a wife and one daughter, who died of illness after genocide.
>
> Hamza Habimana, son of Zachariah and Kanyange, was a mason born at Gati in Kibungo. He died at the age of 38. He left a wife and 3 children. They are all alive. He was Hutu. (KIB21b)

We were not able to interview Hamza's or Mohamed's family members. All we know about them comes from the testimony of Ansar Allah members who witnessed these events and characterized the two men as martyrs. While no one can say with certainty why these men did what they did, eyewitnesses among the Ansar Allah Muslims cited the men's piety, their rejection of racism in accordance with their faith, and Ansar Allah teachings against Muslim involvement in the country's political conflict as factors that influenced their actions.

In their testimony, Ansar Allah members emphasized Mohamed's and Hamza's religious piety and identified them as *shahid*, understood in Islam to mean martyrs for faith (Cook 2012). The term is most often applied to people who risk their lives bearing witness to their Islamic faith and are killed for it (Habib 2014,

395–96; Habib 2017). For example, Dr. Hager El Hadidi asked Malek, who was among the Ansar Allah youth in 1994, about Mohamed and Hamza:

> Q: Do you believe Mohamed Hakuzimana and Hamza who were killed because they defended the others were shahid [martyrs]?
>
> MALEK: Yes, I testify to that. They were killed in the course of defending the truth. The [government] soldiers said they were searching for Inyenzi-Inkotanyi [RPF rebels or infiltrators]. Mohamed and Hamza were committed to protect everyone [inside the mosque]. They said, "We are all the descendants of Adam. There is no race here. We stand here without any doubt. We are not afraid. We know that we are fighting for the truth."
>
> Q: What do you think of the others who were killed here? Are they also shahid?
>
> MALEK: I would call them innocent victims. What happened to them is different from people like Mohamed who said, "This is injustice, and we are committed to stand against anyone willing to commit injustice," which triggered the soldiers' gunshots that killed them both. (KIB23)

Malek's explanation places Mohamed and Hamza's actions within the Islamic framework of shahid. First, they died on the basis of their religiously motivated moral convictions. Second, Mohamed and Hamza consciously put their lives on the line. Imam Suleiman also portrayed Hamza and Mohamed in terms that fit the Islamic concept of shahid. He described them as "fearless," "willing to kill or be killed" in defense of the truth, and "unforgettable heroes who accepted to shed their blood as sacrifice for others" (KIB21b). He also explicitly linked their acts of bravery to their duty as Muslims: "Their duty was to preach others to follow one God." He painted their last acts as the embodiment of this principle.

While the Ansar Allah eyewitnesses emphasized the men's piety, they also implicitly invoked a Rwandan cultural difference: Hamza and Mohammad's direct confrontation with the soldiers—and thus the state's sovereignty—ran counter to traditional Rwandan social norms. Under those conventions, soldiers were automatically accorded great respect and deference as representatives of the state. In general, civilians were expected to obey soldiers' orders without questions or to cast their opposition indirectly.[18] Additionally, Hamza and Mohamed declared their opposition in a religious idiom, "Allah Akbar." Their use of Islam's universal declaration of faith predicated their moral stand on the principles of Islam. By grounding a confrontation that defied social norms in religion and refusing to cede their moral posture, Hamza and Mohamed collapsed the two systems, simultaneously manifesting both Islamic martyrdom and a deeply Rwandan notion of bravery, captured in the proverb, "A hero is not the one who shoots arrows in combat but the one who begins the fight" (Crépeau and Bizimana 1979, 270). The provocation, suddenly merging the actor-networks in which Hamza, Mohammed, and the soldiers all found themselves, elicited the officer's order to shoot.

A key commonality between these men and Félicité is their direct opposition to the state's genocidal sovereignty and their refusal to compromise their core moral values. These commonalities also distinguish them from previously discussed rescuers, who engaged in ethical pragmatism and subverted the state's genocidal sovereignty through deflection, dissimulation, avoidance, negotiation, and feigned compliance. Religious models of martyrdom and strong moral cores gave Hamza, Mohamed, and Félicité courage and induced them to self-sacrificial agency.

Yet they were not the only ones who risked their lives to save people from genocide at the Saint Pierre Center or the Kibagabaga mosque. In fact, from the perspective of ethical pragmatism, their self-sacrifice may not have been the best moral choice. In her letter to her brother, the colonel, Félicité could have implored him to intervene to save the refugees at Saint Pierre instead of resigning herself to her fate. Extant records and testimony from that period do not make it clear whether she appealed directly to her brother for protection. As Catherine Coquio wrote about Félicité's death, "This gesture was not a sacrifice and it erased all ambiguity: no one was saved by her death, which was predicated on an ethically pure refusal of ethnic division" (Coquio 2009, 41). In other words, for Coquio, Félicité's death was not "a sacrifice" because her death saved no one. Her moral rectitude impeded pragmatic efforts to save lives through moral compromise. Arguably, Félicité could not have saved more lives even if she had chosen to abandon the others and save herself. Nonetheless, Nathalie and the surviving Auxiliaries of the Apostolate continued to hide the Tutsi who had escaped detection by the militiamen and were left behind when the buses pulled away.

Similarly, the remaining Muslims at the Kibagabaga mosque continued in their rescue efforts. The morning after Hamza and Mohamed's shooting, another squad of government soldiers arrived at the mosque and surrounded it. The commander demanded to speak with the imam. Suleiman described the encounter: "He told me that I had caused the death of those young men because I refused to give them the people they were asking for. He aimed his gun at my ribs as he spoke. . . . Then, some soldiers came dragging a man, Saleh Bapfakurera, a Tutsi from Kibagabaga. A soldier said, "This man was hiding in the toilet." The commander then suddenly moved the gun from my ribs and shot Saleh dead" (KIB21b). The commander then trained his rifle back on Suleiman and ordered all the men out of the mosque compound and into the road. The Hutu men who had been standing guard or were ready to fight off attackers exited. They dared not oppose the commander for fear that he would kill the imam. The commander ordered the men to hand over their weapons and sit in the road while his men searched the mosque. "They entered the classrooms and the mosque and went to search people's bags for military weapons. They also looked for Inkotanyi, but they couldn't find any" (KIB01). "They ordered us to get out of the buildings and to show our identity cards. They said that we were mostly Inyenzi [RPF rebels] because the majority of us were Tutsi" (KIB30). The commander then ordered the men of the mosque to go out and join in the killing. "They ordered us to take our personal belongings out of the mosque and to go help other people look for enemies. We obeyed their orders and went inside to pick up our belongings" (KIB30). In the midst of this confrontation, a large Interahamwe mob arrived at the mosque and quickly divided up the confiscated weapons. "It was clear that they [the militiamen] were working with the military commander" (KIB21b). Then, "the soldiers left with local government officials who carried their ammunition for them" (KIG52).

After the soldiers had left, the Interahamwe entered the compound "and started doing their 'work.' . . . They sorted people. They said, 'You, go this side! You, go that side!'" (KIB01). They "looted our property and pillaged" (KIB21b). "Then, they told the Hutu, 'Go home!' and they started killing the Tutsis" (KIB01). Chaos erupted as the killing began, "as Interahamwe chased people who tried to escape" (KIG52) and "everyone began to run away. . . . They ran this way [motioning to the back of the mosque] and that way [the other back corner of the mosque]. Back then, there wasn't a wall there, it was open onto the forest" (KIB33). The Interahamwe killed at least fifteen people in the mosque and many others whom they pursued into the forest. Still others were killed in their homes, after the militia forced them to unlock the houses so they could steal. Many Ansar Allah members fled toward the homes of congregation members, hoping that they would be hidden and protected by them. Virtually all Tutsi Ansar Allah members who survived had been helped, protected, or hidden by Hutu Ansar Allah Muslims. The Ansar Allah Muslims in Kibagabaga who refused to abandon Tutsi refugees to the death squads saved hundreds of lives.

Suleiman, along with the mosque's muezzin and a few other Ansar Allah leaders, collected the bodies of the dead from the mosque's grounds and buried them.[19] The next morning, April 13, the *responsable*, Anastase Semurima, arrived at the mosque with some Interahamwe and ordered the Muslims to go out and search for the bodies of their dead where they had fallen. He commanded them to bring the bodies back to the mosque and bury them. In the process, the Muslims discovered a handful of survivors who were gravely injured. They brought the injured people back to the mosque, pretending they were dead, and hid them in a classroom to tend their wounds. They kept most of these refugees alive for a week, until the Interahamwe discovered them and killed them on April 20.

Later the same day, the survivors of the massacre heard heavy artillery and gunfire very near Kibagabaga as the RPF rebels and government forces fought a fierce battle. Those who had not already fled remained in their hiding places through the night. In the morning, the RPF captured Kibagabaga, saving those who had managed to survive (KIB21a). The arrival of the RPF army in the region saved the lives of those who had managed to survive the massacres in Kibagabaga and neighboring hills. They survived thanks to the Ansar Allah leaders, to Hamza and Mohamed, who sacrificed their lives at the mosque's gate, and to the other Hutu Ansar Allah members who refused to abandon them to save their own lives.

The Symbolic Potency of Martyrs in the Wake of Genocide

Félicité Niyitegeka's work at the Saint Pierre Center and death at the municipal cemetery in Gisenyi constitute one of the most thoroughly documented cases of martyrdom in the Rwandan genocide. The actions and deaths of Hamza Habimana and Mohamed Hakuzimana at the Kibagabaga mosque, in comparison, have been less thoroughly documented. These cases and their contrasting treatment illustrate the impact of politics on public memory.

In postgenocide Rwanda, politics have limited what can be said about the "events of 1994," including both the genocide and the concurrent civil war (Burnet 2009, 2012; Longman 2017; Thomson 2013). This silencing of some narratives began immediately after the genocide and included the erasure of rescuers from public discourse. In the genocide's aftermath, many survivors wanted to recognize the people who helped save their lives, but they soon understood that doing so was risky. As a national representative of Ibuka, the genocide survivor's association, explained, "There have been moments when it has been impossible to talk about rescuers during the genocide. Immediately after, many of us tried to [publicly] recognize the people who saved us, but we discovered it wasn't wise. The government didn't want to hear about it" (NAT24b). When I conducted research in Rwanda in the late 1990s, few people talked openly about the 1994 genocide (Burnet 2012, 79). While the reasons for their silence were numerous, Hutu who had engaged in acts of rescue feared attracting attention that could lead to accusations of genocide crimes.

Beginning in 1995, the national genocide commemoration ceremonies featured Hutu rescuers each year, but this formulaic public recognition contained and controlled public discourse about Hutu opposition to the genocide (Burnet 2012; Longman 2017). The RPF-led government sought to establish a single, dominant narrative about the genocide: the international community had abandoned Rwandans to genocide, and the RPF alone saved them from it. Public recognition of Hutu who had opposed the genocide or saved Tutsi risked complicating this message. Sometime in 1995, the new government scuttled UN-sponsored efforts to recognize Hutu who saved Tutsi during the genocide (Gourevitch 1998, 245). Around the same time, the government created an ad hoc commission to develop criteria for designating national heroes and determine the date for an annual national heroes celebration (Republic of Rwanda 2017, 7). The commission's recommendations and report were delayed for many years. In the meantime, the new government observed National Heroes Day each year on October 1. The day marked the RPF's initial invasion of Rwanda and the start of its liberation struggle. The original National Heroes Day lauded RPF soldiers who had fallen during combat and honored soldiers with decorations for courageous acts.

Among the first stories of rescue to become well known internationally was that of Paul Rusesabagina, the hotel manager whose story was first told by journalist Philip Gourevitch (1998). During the genocide, Rusesabagina took over management of the five-star Hotel de Mille Collines when the Belgian manager was evacuated. Wealthy Rwandans began seeking shelter in the hotel, which was located next to Kigali's central business district. Over time, the numbers of refugees in the hotel swelled; the hotel stopped charging guests. Rusesabagina negotiated with Interahamwe militiamen and plied Rwandan military officers with food and drinks to keep the refugees safe. He used the hotel's fax machine to plead for help from diplomats, foreign leaders, and human rights activists around the world and to protect the civilians in the hotel from certain death at the hands of the militias (Gourevitch 1998, 132–33). Between May 27 and 31, 1994, the refugees were evacuated behind the RPF rebel lines in a prisoner swap brokered between the Rwandan army and RPF rebels by UNAMIR (Bizimana 2020).

In early 2001, Ibuka began research to identify rescuers who should be recognized as heroes (Coquio 2009, 46). The government commission completed its work later that year. The commission defined three categories of heroes: *Imanzi*, "supreme heroes" who demonstrated outstanding achievements in service to the nation; *Imena*, those who died in outstanding service to the nation; and *Ingenzi*, the living who did great works for the nation (Musoni 2013). It designated February 1 as National Heroes Day and recommended an initial list of heroes to be recognized. The prime minister's office and President Kagame approved the commission's report and named the first set to be honored at a National

Heroes Memorial, which was built next to the Amahoro National Stadium in Kigali. Major General Fred Rwigema, the Tutsi RPF commander who died in October 1990 during the initial battles in Rwanda, was named as *Imanzi*, along with the Unknown Soldier, a symbol representing all the unknown RPF soldiers who fell in the liberation struggle. Prime Minister Agathe Uwilingiyimana, who was Hutu and among the first victims of the genocide, and Félicité Niyitegeka were named as *Imena*. Two girls who were killed at the Nyange secondary school in 1998 by armed combatants who had infiltrated Rwanda were also named as *Imena*. The girls and their classmates had refused to divide into groups of Hutu and Tutsi students as their assailants commanded. The classmates who survived the attack were recognized as *Ingenzi*. Outside of the National Heroes Memorial and the annual genocide commemoration ceremonies, little public space was dedicated to recognizing rescuers.

African Rights' *Tribute to Courage*, published in 2002, featured seventeen Rwandan heroes, including Félicité Niyitegeka, and two expatriates who saved hundreds of lives. This publication became the basis for public recognition of rescuers inside Rwanda. Félicité Niyitegeka, Father Célestin Hakizimana, and Sula Karuhimbi, who were profiled in the book, have also appeared in the Kigali Genocide Memorial exhibits and in the Campaign against Genocide Museum.[20] The African Rights volume privileged the stories of rescuers who were dead. Since African Rights' first days operating in Rwanda during the genocide in 1994, the organization maintained close ties with the RPF political party and military wing (Reydams 2016). Thus African Rights' publications about Rwandan often served RPF or Rwandan government interests (Reydams 2016). Privileging dead martyrs served an important state purpose. Death rendered martyrs as unambiguous symbols by fusing signifier with signified: a (Hutu) hero was someone who martyred themselves for the nation, like Agathe Uwilingiyimana, or to save Tutsi lives, like Félicité Niyitegeka and the Nyange schoolgirls.

The focus on dead martyrs followed a general government strategy of reifying connections between categories of people and roles in the genocide. For instance, in the wake of the genocide, the Rwandan government followed a policy of maximal prosecution—pursuing every single genocide crime, from mass murder and sexual torture down to looting property (Waldorf 2006). This policy produced a system in which all Hutu were suspected of genocide crimes (Chakravarty 2016). The national genocide commemorations, memorials, and museums promoted this view with a discourse that blamed all Hutus for the genocide (Burnet 2012). In the logic of the government's discourse, rescuers were (Tutsi) RPF soldiers who saved people by stopping the genocide or Hutu who died trying to save people. Innocent victims were the hundreds of thousands of Tutsi who died. (Tutsi) genocide survivors were victims, but they were often suspected of complicity in the genocide. Living Hutu and Twa were presumed to be, at best, complicit bystanders or, more likely, genocide perpetrators. Martyrs did not disrupt the central presumption that all Hutu were guilty of—or at least complicit in—the genocide (Burnet 2012, 110–11).

The case of Paul Rusesabagina illustrates the ongoing implications of this discourse. In 2004, the movie *Hotel Rwanda* brought the story of Rusesabagina to a much broader international audience than Gourevitch's 1998 book had. At the film's debut in Kigali in May 2005, President Kagame told the film's director, Terry George, that the film exposed the genocide's many horrors (George 2006). A year later, at the twelfth national genocide commemoration ceremony, President Kagame condemned Rusesabagina, saying, "He should try his talents elsewhere and not climb on the falsehood of being a hero, because it's totally false" (George 2006). In 2004, Rusesabagina had begun to criticize President Kagame's government at high-profile public events, saying that the 2003 national elections were not democratic. He then began organizing an opposition political party in exile.[21] In response, the Rwandan government, prominent genocide survivors, and journalists both Rwandan and foreign participated in a smear campaign against him that grew over two decades.[22] Edouard Kayihura (2014) recounted in a memoir that Rusesabagina began demanding that refugees in the hotel pay for their food and rooms when he arrived and took over the hotel's management. The book jacket included endorsements from important Rwandan government officials, General Roméo Dallaire, and others. Rusesabagina continued his political organizing in exile by founding the Rwandan Movement for Democratic Change in 2017 (Fiorentino 2021). In August 2020, Rusesabagina landed at the Kigali International Airport on a chartered jet. The Rwandan intelligence services duped him into believing he was traveling to neighboring Burundi. Upon arrival he was arrested and then promptly charged with "murder, abduction, armed robbery, financing terrorism, and being involved in the creation of an irregular armed group" (Hammer 2021). The Rwandan government alleged that Rusesabagina advocated for a series of violent attacks by the National Liberation Front rebel group when he urged supporters to use "any means possible to bring about change in Rwanda" in a 2017 video (Fiorentino 2021). In September 2021, the Rwandan court hearing his case, which began on February 17, 2021, found him guilty of all charges and sentenced him to twenty-five years in prison (Robertson 2021; Sabiti 2021).

The treatment of Paul Rusesabagina is an extreme case, but Hutu rescuers are often viewed suspiciously in Rwanda. For this reason, many avoid public recognition of their actions during the genocide. Even the genocide survivor association Ibuka's efforts to identify indakemwa (righteous) assessed candidates not only for their actions during the 1994 genocide but also after. The final criterion for designation as indakemwa requires that a person testified truthfully before the courts about the genocide and has not spread genocidal ideology (Kayishema and Masabo 2010, 22–24). In these ways, hegemonic discourse about rescue during the 1994 genocide actively denied the empirical reality of the moral gray zone arising from the genocide machine.

Despite posing fewer complications, not all martyrs' stories are widely known. Although Félicité's martyrdom is widely known in both Rwanda and internationally, the cases of Hamza and Mohamed are familiar only to Ansar Allah members. Why is one story so well known, while the other is not?

One factor is the comparative reach of the religious institutions involved. Félicité's story was first publicized by Catholic missionaries to an international audience less than five months after her death. In September 1994, the White Fathers published a few stories of rescue from Rwanda in their missionary newsletter under the title "Light in the Darkness" (Fortin 1994). The report presented Félicité's story as an example of Catholic heroism. The author, Father Michel Fortin, concluded, "What is certain is that if demons wander in Rwanda, angels walk there too. Most often, they are Rwandan. Whether ordinary Christians, priests or nuns, they work to build a society without insurmountable ethnic opposition" (Fortin 1994).

Fortin mobilized Félicité's story to fit a specifically Catholic and possibly neocolonial understanding of the genocide. He (wrongly) asserts that "ordinary Christians, priests, or nuns"—presumably by virtue of their Christian faith—were opposed to racism and the genocide. The Catholic Church's institutional complicity in the genocide, and the participation of priests and nuns, had not yet come to light outside Rwanda in 1994 (Longman 2009 307–15). In the same story, Fortin quoted extensive eyewitness testimony from Father Wenceslas Munyeshyaka, a Rwandan priest who collaborated with the Interahamwe at the Sainte-Famille Church in Kigali and was later accused of genocide crimes, including rape.[23] Fortin's use of Munyeshyaka's testimony ignored the priest's complicity (and alleged participation), which Fortin perhaps could not have imagined. Thus Félicité's story emerged on the international stage linked to the murky politics of the Catholic Church and its ambivalent role in the genocide. As Coquio put it, "The 'missionaries,' who published her [Félicité's] letter, were caught up in the total confusion of their Church" (Coquio 2009, 40). Nonetheless, Félicité's story gradually became the archetype of a "good Hutu" rescuer inside Rwanda, as well. The global reach of the Roman Catholic Church, its institutional strength in Rwanda, and its ongoing influence in postgenocide Rwanda ensured her story's wide dissemination.

By contrast, Islam's minority status in Rwanda and the conflict between AMUR and Ansar Allah limited the dissemination of Hamza and Mohamed's story in Rwanda. In the aftermath of the genocide, AMUR, PDI, and Muslim RPF supporters promoted stories of Muslim opposition to the genocide and acts of rescue. The prominence of these stories improved the perception of Islam and Muslims in Rwanda. At the same time, Islam grew in the country in part because some Christian survivors converted to Islam, seeking refuge from their churches' institutional failures and clergy's complicity and participation in the violence with a religion they perceived as morally superior.

As the Muslim community grew, AMUR leaders sought to consolidate the association's control over the community and ensure that it remained the sole official Islamic religious entity in Rwanda. AMUR did not want to publicize Hamza and Mohamed's story because doing so would give attention to rival Muslim association Ansar Allah. Mufti Saleh Habimana, elected as the head of AMUR in 2001, sought reconciliation with Ansar Allah. Under his leadership AMUR worked with researchers from CDA Collaborative Learning Projects to document Muslims' roles in the 1994 genocide (Doughty and Ntambara 2005).[24] The final report acknowledged the importance of Ansar Allah in Muslim resistance to the genocide and their rescue efforts. Mufti Habimana emphasized Rwandan Muslims' unity and faith as the roots of their resistance to the genocide in 1994: "In Rwanda we practise pure Islam. There is no fundamentalism, no terrorism. In the Holy Koran it says if you save one life, it is like saving the universe. If you kill one person, it is like killing everyone. The Holy Koran forbade us to partake" in the genocide (Kingstone 2012). Under Mufti Habimana's leadership from 2001 to 2011, AMUR stopped interfering in Ansar Allah's religious activities. The muftis who followed him, however, reinforced the rift between AMUR and Ansar Allah through legal battles over mosques and other property. Additionally, AMUR leaders lobbied against Ansar Allah's attempts to register as a religious organization, as required by a law passed in 2008 and revised in 2012. The conflict between AMUR and Ansar Allah has continued. As a result, Ansar Allah Muslims know Hamza and Mohamed's story well, but Muslims who pray in mosques controlled by AMUR have rarely heard detailed accounts of their actions.

A factor that may have limited the Rwandan government's interest in spreading Hamza and Mohamed's story relates to allegations of RPF killings of civilians in Kibagabaga made by French journalist Pierre Péan (2009).[25] My research in Kibagabaga in 2011, 2013, and 2014 controverts Péan's account of events (Péan 2009, 178–90).[26] Péan claims that the RPF controlled Kibagabaga as of April 9 (Péan 2009, 182) and killed Hutu at these sites beginning on April 7 (192–94). In the testimony we gathered, witnesses stated that the RPF took Kibagabaga on the night of April 20. The massacres of Tutsi at Kibagabaga's churches, schools, and mosques between April 7 and 20, also documented in our interviews, further contradict Péan's timeline. We received no testimony about RPF-perpetrated killings in Kibagabaga. Interviewees may have chosen not to disclose this information for fear of government reprisals, but interviewees in other research sites did mention RPF killings, suggesting that fear was not a serious deterrent to such testimony. Certainly, RPF killings could have taken place in Kibagabaga after the RPF drove the national security forces and militias from the hill on April 20. All interviewees in Kibagabaga—Tutsi and Hutu—indicated they were quickly evacuated by the RPF, first to the Amahoro National Stadium and then to RPF-held territory in northern Rwanda. Regardless of whether the RPF killed civilians in Kibagabaga after April 20, Tutsi were massacred in Kibagabaga between April 7 and April 20, 1994.

A more likely explanation for the relative silence in Rwanda surrounding the martyrdom of Hamza Habimana and Mohamed Hakuzimana is the minority status of Ansar Allah, its ongoing conflicts with AMUR, and the Rwandan government's national security concerns over the potential radicalization of Rwandan Muslims.[27] In addition, Ansar Allah has little reach or influence beyond Rwanda, where the sect began. That Ansar Allah Muslims are the only ones to call for public recognition of Hamza Habimana and Mohamed Hakuzimana's sacrifice reflects the memory politics at play in postgenocide Rwanda. Along with the story of Sister Félicité Niyitegeka, their stories reinforce the assumptions underpinning most studies of rescue during genocide. They appear to be morally superior individuals who acted solely out of moral compulsion, at least insofar as their stories are recounted in local, national, or international venues. According to eyewitnesses who shared their faith, their religious piety and faith in God propelled them to act in the way they did. Whether these observations are accurate representations of how events unfolded or ex post facto narratives is impossible to discern.

Though Félicité's, Hamza's, and Mohamed's stories reinforce common assumptions about altruism, piety, and rescue in genocide, the stories of all the other rescuers at the Saint Pierre Center and the Kibagabaga mosque—Sister Nathalie and the other Auxiliaries of the Apostolate, Imam Suleiman, the muezzin, and the Ansar Allah Muslims who remained at the mosque to defend Tutsi lives from the Interahamwe—demonstrate the complex assemblages that coalesce and cleave to produce rescue, and martyrdom. Furthermore, the many stories of rescue recounted elsewhere in this book demonstrate that successful rescue often requires morally ambiguous action amid genocide's gray zone. The role of luck, chance, or fate must also be embraced, even if it is impossible to quantify in a stable, rational model. And thousands of genocide perpetrators saved or helped some Tutsi while killing others. Those whose lives they saved are grateful for their assistance, even if the survivors recognize that their rescuers were also killers.

Conclusion

I did it because they were human beings.

—Basir, a Hutu Muslim man who rescued dozens of his neighbors (BIR05)

This book began from a simple question: why do some people risk their lives to save others from mass violence? More specifically, I sought to understand why some Rwandans, especially Hutu, risked death to save Tutsi and others targeted for killing in the 1994 genocide. When I began this project, I believed that the beginning and end of rescue was that certain individuals have the moral conviction and courage to oppose genocide. I had unwittingly bought into a common assumption: that rescuers operate from positions of moral clarity, that they make courageous, ethical decisions. I believed these things even though I knew that the ordinary Rwandans who joined in genocidal violence had diverse motivations, experienced unique constraints, and made decisions that led them, sometimes unexpectedly, toward the individual acts of stealing, destroying, denouncing, beating, raping, or murdering that constitute genocide. I knew that Rwandans, regardless of race, faced unimaginable choices during the ordered chaos of the genocide. I had already heard dozens of accounts where ordinary people helped hide, protect, feed, or save Tutsi friends, neighbors, and coworkers, as personal circumstances and political context allowed.

What I discovered, however, is that the will to help is merely the first of many choices that constitute rescue. Acts of rescue emerge from the same extraordinary events, processes, and actions that produce genocide. Genocide emerges from political, economic, social, and ideological structures; racialized political competition over control of the state; armed conflict; racial or ethnic nationalism; and individual and collective actions. Once unleashed, genocidal violence becomes a machine driven by its own internal force. Amid the collective and individual acts that constitute genocide, people often face impossible decisions. Many actions are possible: fleeing, hiding, watching, ignoring, standing guard, denouncing, pillaging, killing, or assisting those who are targeted.

Successful rescue, among these many possible actions, is rare and emerges from actor-networks comprising the rescuer, the rescued, and all the other humans involved, as well as the localized unfolding of events in the context of geography, topography, urban design, opportunity, patronage, histories of reciprocity and gift giving, deference to authority, farming implements and weapons, roadblocks, security patrols, propaganda, crowd dynamics, cultural models of mob justice, social taboos on killing, and other factors.

My assumption that rescuers are morally righteous people who have the courage to risk their lives to help others is not surprising. After all, common sense tells us rescuers are good people who do good things. I came to understand, however, that successful rescue almost always entails morally ambiguous decisions conditioned by the moral gray zone of genocide. A family may refuse help to some so that they can protect others. A neighbor may ignore pleas for help during a violent attack but come to offer assistance after it is over. A friend may refuse to hide adults because of the perceived risks, but they will carry their friends' children to safety. In the moral gray zone of genocide, where genocidal sovereignty deforms the state's protective duties to citizens, few decisions are morally pure. Those rescuers who refuse to adapt their moral values to the situation often find their end by sacrificing their lives (see chapter 7).

At the outset of this project, I inadvertently accepted the premise embedded in genocide studies' classic typology of victim, perpetrator, bystander, and rescuer—that people adopt a single stance during mass violence based on their character or moral orientations and rational, consistent motivations. Even though I had rejected this assumption when analyzing perpetrators and their actions and motivations (along with Fujii 2009, Straus 2006, Thomson 2013, and others), I had to intentionally set it aside to design a research methodology that put rescuers, perpetrators, bystanders, and victims "on equal ontological footing" following the methods of actor-network theory (chapter 2; Müller 2015, 30). Actor-network theory clarifies that acts of genocide and rescue emerge amid the same complex assemblages that constitute genocide, including hundreds of thousands of discrete individual acts entangled with national policy, political ideologies, propaganda, social ties, cultural scripts, geographical features, and human and nonhuman actors.

In the context of genocide, where "individuals generally tend to obey a regime in power . . . resistance is not expected, and thus constitutes an exception"

(Andrieu 2011, 495). In these regimes, genocide is a machine designed to produce actions in line with genocidal policy and to inhibit actions against it. Compliance with state demands—with the machine—is life-preserving for those not targeted for killing. In Rwanda, once it was unleashed, the genocide machine rampaged, consuming people and communities in violence (see chapter 1). Nonetheless, rescuer behavior was widespread in the first days of the genocide in Rwanda. As the killing continued, resistance to the genocide machine posed ever greater risk. Many peopled stopped helping. They asked the Tutsi they had sheltered to leave, or even handed them over to militiamen. Even so, they sometimes continued to offer momentary assistance, what Jacques Sémelin (2019) called "small gestures of support," such as information about which direction to flee, food or water, clothing, or a place to sleep for one night. While those small gestures of support may have helped some Tutsi survive for a day or a week—long enough to find another small help—these small helpers who also participated in the genocide could no longer qualify as rescuers. Their complicity in the genocide precluded it. At best, they were bystanders; at worst, they were perpetrators. A single, swift decision could turn a rescuer into a "killer-rescuer," as Lee Ann Fujii (2011) called them.

Actor-network theory provides a way to understand how people navigate these terrible decisions and how the machine of genocide steers them toward some actions or away from others. Conceiving of agency during genocide as a function of actor-networks, an emergent feature of heterogeneous assemblages of people, institutions, and physical and social environments, allows us to see how the same collectivities produced both killing and rescue apart from the morality of particular actions. Actor-network theory disrupts the classic genocide studies' typology, which assumes that individuals behave in only one way during genocide. Actor-network theory also removes the moral judgment implicit in the typology, providing a structure that accommodates the ambivalence of a "killer-rescuer" or a "victim-perpetrator" and helps explain the morally dubious decisions required of ordinary people who rescued without participating in genocide.

The application of actor-network theory underscores the limitations of positivistic social science approaches exploring universal rules or principles of social structure, social forces, or human behaviors. Structure and agency operate in co-constituting dialectical, iterative processes. Furthermore, micro-level factors such as local histories or geography play an equally important role in shaping agency as do broadly applicable macro-level factors. Holistic approaches that combine positivistic social science research design with the long-term ethnographic fieldwork, cultural knowledge, and linguistic competence of the humanities yield more accurate understandings of the world.

At the Nexus of Macro-, Meso-, and Micro-Level Factors

Actor-networks emerge from the intersection of various forces operating at different levels—from individual contexts to large-scale cultural currents. The case studies in this book demonstrate that macro- and meso-level structural factors consistent across the country still produced local variability in the progress of the genocide because they intersected in different ways with micro-level factors, such as local configurations of power, the effects of Rwanda's gender cosmology on individuals' opportunity to rescue, local histories of relations between people, specific geographical features, and the diverse influences of political parties in different areas (see chapter 1). These constellations of local, regional, and national assemblage components coalesced in distinct actor-networks that at times facilitated each other to produce genocidal violence and at others generated "friction" (Tsing 2015) that enabled rescue. These intersecting forces produced different genocide timelines around the country, significantly affecting the potential for successful rescue at any given time in any given place. In particular, the timing of the onset and end of genocidal violence shaped rescue in different locations, as did the local and national details of genocide policy, which varied over time and across space. These findings highlight the limitations of normative social science research that seeks to establish scientific explanations for social behavior and determine predictable and testable patterns of behavior that can be generalized beyond specific cases. While I have identified discernible patterns and pinpointed factors that shaped behavior and outcomes, the complexity of genocide as a process and the entanglement of multiple factors at all levels make it impossible to establish universal principles.

Genocide Policy and Timelines

Where genocide started early, rescue was more dangerous—thus less likely—from the outset. In Kigali, Gisenyi town, and other communities where killings began on April 7, 1994, Tutsi and political opponents of the Hutu Power movement faced immediate threats to their lives. So did people who offered assistance to those targeted by this early violence. In these communities, acts of rescue rarely went beyond small gestures of assistance, because people feared helping would result in their own or their loved ones' deaths. The principal strategy of successful rescue in these contexts was the mobilization of ephemeral networks of helpers who had limited knowledge of other helpers. This strategy reduced the chances of being caught or of one member of the network revealing the identity of others.

By contrast, in communities where the onset of genocidal violence was delayed, many Hutu kin, friends, and neighbors offered shelter to Tutsi.

The end date of genocidal violence in local communities also made a difference. Where the RPF rebels quickly took control, acts of rescue, including the many small gestures of assistance, were more likely to succeed and had greater impact.[1] For example, in Rwamagana in eastern Rwanda, genocidal violence began early, on April 7, but ended quickly, when the RPF secured the town on April 27 (Guichaoua 1995, 528).

The genocide machine required ordinary Rwandans to make difficult decisions and "choiceless choices" with little or no notice and limited information. People who rescued improvised their actions, just as those who joined in the killing did. People's strategies responded directly to the violence and the changing assemblages that constituted actor-networks within the genocide. Rescue was not an accident, nor was it random, but it was also not an obvious choice or predetermined outcome of a particular religious belief or moral disposition. The interactions between what other researchers have called "structural factors" or "situational constraints" shaped human agency in profound ways that are difficult to discern.[2] Those forces and their role in people's decisions and actions may be traced with actor-network theory.

In communities where genocidal violence continued for months, many people who first engaged in ongoing rescue efforts abandoned them as the risks of discovery or punishment increased. In other locations, the duration of the violence shifted power structures, making rescue impossible. In Butare Province in southern Rwanda, government administrators and many local elites continued to resist the genocide even as it wore on. Tutsi and others who feared attacks by the Interahamwe and Impuzamugambi fled to government buildings, churches, and schools, where they were protected by government officials and local police. But these courageous acts of resistance led to devastating massacres after the interim government replaced the governor on April 19 and mayors adopted genocide as local policy. Collected in easily identified buildings, Tutsi were easy to find and kill in large numbers.

The local details of genocide policy, whether local officials immediately adopted it or resisted its implementation, further shaped rescue efforts. In Nyanza, regional and local officials at first refused to implement the national policy of genocide. They kept the state's genocidal sovereignty at bay for two weeks. Once massacres started around Nyanza, cell-level officials in places like Rubona hill and Mugandamure continued to interpret central government orders literally and limited searches to target only RPF combatants, excluding Tutsi residents. In places like Kayove in northwestern Rwanda, these containment efforts were quickly overcome by competing local elites who sided with the

Hutu Power movement and interim government (chapter 6; Straus 2006, 72–73). Once the tipping point was reached, few people resisted the genocidal onslaught in Kayove commune.

Geographical Features and the Built Environment

Geographical features also structured genocidal violence and affected opportunities for rescue, constraining them at some times and places but expanding them at others. Borders were a particularly significant feature. In Gisenyi town, the international border with the Congo offered salvation to Tutsi who could find a way across. Some businessmen and smugglers familiar with the clandestine routes used to move goods across the border applied their expertise to rescue dozens of Tutsi. In Nkora, fishermen and traders transported Tutsi across Lake Kivu to safety in the Congo, often at great risk to themselves.

Elsewhere, features of the built environment facilitated rescue. In Mugandamure in southern Rwanda, the layout of the hamlet facilitated community efforts to harbor fleeing Tutsi and keep out potential assailants by limiting access to the community. Likewise, the design of the former Swahili camp Biryogo, in Kigali, enabled rescue efforts. In both historically Muslim communities, small passages between compounds further aided escape from Interahamwe, soldiers, or police search parties who gained entry to the communities. These features often intersected with the social histories of the area. At Mugandamure, Biryogo, and Rubona hill, local settlement patterns and social histories had reinforced kinship and other social ties among residents. This history coalesced into social cohesion that inclined residents to protect Tutsi community members and others seeking refuge.

Gender, Social Position, and Opportunity

Rwanda's gender cosmology and an individual's social position shaped rescue and rescuer behavior in several ways. These factors had particularly strong effects in rural areas, where gendered expectations of behavior were the strongest. Rwanda's gender cosmology is structured by life stage and position in the kin group just as much as by whether an individual is male or female (Burnet 2012). In addition, people at certain life stages, such as a woman beyond her reproductive years or a newborn baby, are often treated as not having a gender or as having honorary male status and the privileges that come with it. A person's position in the household, lineage, kin group, or community also produces gendered effects. All these factors interacted to make rescuer behavior more or less possible for specific individuals.

For example, unmarried Hutu male youth and married Hutu middle-aged men faced specific pressures to join in genocidal violence.[3] Hutu men between the ages of nineteen and thirty constituted the majority of the Interahamwe and Impuzamugambi militias' membership. These young men were the first to initiate anti-Tutsi violence in the wake of President Habyarimana's assassination. Once genocide became nationwide policy, Hutu male youth across the country faced intense pressure to join the militias. Likewise middle-aged men as heads of household were expected to represent their families at security meetings and participate in night rounds (*amarondo*). The state's gentle coercive power guided many ordinary Hutu men to participate in these everyday activities—the duties of married male citizens—and turned them to ominous ends by using these mechanisms to hunt down and kill Tutsi. Nonetheless, some Hutu male youth and married men resisted this gentle coercion and found ways to help Tutsi escape. Hutu men married to Tutsi women were generally able to protect their wives and children in the first several weeks of the genocide. In mid-May, however, all Tutsi women—even those married to Hutu men—became targets of the genocide (Des Forges 1999, 296). At the same time, children born of mixed marriages faced extermination, and Hutu men in mixed marriages could no longer protect their families.

Most publicly recognized rescuers in Rwanda, as well as the indakemwa identified by Ibuka, were in fact middle-aged men at the time of the genocide. Most often, they were assisted in their rescue efforts by their wives and other household members. According to the cultural logics of patrilineal kinship, all members of a household are assumed to have the same opinions on community issues and operate together as a unit. Thus, Hutu women married to Tutsi men were targeted for killing along with their children as soon as genocidal violence began in a community. Wives, daughters, female household members, and children played significant roles in helping protect people in hiding since women are responsible for drawing water for household use and preparing food. Beyond these acts, they kept their families' dangerous secrets. According to the same cultural logics, married women rarely had the means to help or hide people without their husbands' knowledge or consent. Yet married women did engage in everyday acts of kindness or small gestures of support without their husbands' knowledge. The women sometimes did these things even when their husbands participated avidly in genocidal violence. The few women publicly recognized as rescuers or identified as indakemwa by Ibuka were widows, divorced, or unmarried women such as Sister Félicité Niyitegeka or Sula (Zula) Karuhimbi. Their unique social positions—as women operating outside Rwandan gender norms and patrilineal obligations—gave them the autonomy to help people without answering to male kin for their actions

Polyvalent Social Ties

Social structures are another aspect of the actor-network that shapes responses to genocide. Many researchers have tried to account for social ties—whether based in kinship, religion, patronage, or affinity—as a salient variable in genocidal violence or in rescue. Building on the growing body of empirical research on perpetrator behavior and social ties in the Rwandan genocide, Fujii (2011) and Omar McDoom (2014) found that Rwandans were much more likely to become genocide perpetrators when they had more social connections to perpetrators.[4] My research demonstrates that social ties are polyvalent variables: sometimes they increase a person's likelihood to perpetrate, and sometimes they increase a person's likelihood to rescue.

Comparison of the Muslim communities in Biryogo, Gisenyi, Mugandamure, Kibagabaga, and Nkora illustrates the polyvalence of social ties. As with other groups, Rwandan Muslims' unique political and economic history, ongoing social exclusion, and particular subjectivities conditioned their reactions to the intense violence of the genocide. Despite the common belief that Muslims did not participate in the 1994 genocide, many Hutu Muslims in Biryogo and Gisenyi, especially Muslim men between twenty and forty years of age, were complicit in the genocide or participated actively in killing. In these communities, particular local histories of settlement, migration, urbanization, postindependence politics, patronage, and social relations entangled Muslims in actor-networks that induced acts of genocide.

Muslims in Biryogo and Gisenyi reacted to President Habyarimana's assassination, the coup d'état by Hutu extremists, and the state-backed genocide in the same varied ways as Rwandans of other religious faiths. Some responded immediately to Hutu Power calls to attack Tutsi. Many more initially tried to save their Tutsi neighbors, friends, and kin. Some Muslims persisted in their assistance to those targeted by violence, even as the genocide continued, while others abandoned their rescue efforts. Some Muslims participated directly in the genocide by manning roadblocks or killing people. Others colluded in the genocide by denouncing people in hiding to Interahamwe killing squads.

In contrast, Muslims in Mugandamure, Kibagabaga, and Nkora were less likely to be embroiled in assemblages primed for genocide because of the distinct local histories of Islam in these communities, including historical ties to Tutsi nobility among Muslims in Mugandamure; social cohesion within these communities arising from religious belief and practice; and social cohesion with non-Muslim community members arising from the everyday social practices of these communities. As a minority within a minority, the Ansar Allah sect in Kibagabaga and Mugandamure played an additional role in reinforcing social ties among members. Ansar Allah members' dense social ties, as well as their recent break with the AMUR, reinforced their solidarity. Their exclusion, along with the sect's teachings, increased Ansar Allah members' empathy toward unjustly targeted Tutsi civilians. These cases illustrate the potential power of sermons and religious teachings to influence people's behavior.[5]

Whether Rwandan Muslims acted exceptionally during the 1994 genocide depended not so much on their religion as on local assemblages. Some elements of those assemblages arose from national-level forces, such as colonial apartheid practices, ongoing social and economic marginalization of Muslims, and other large-scale factors. Other elements, such as geographical features and social ties ranging from kinship to patronage, were locally determined. Islamic doctrine, Muslim religious leaders' active role in explaining the morality of multiparty politics and anti-Tutsi violence, religious practices, and the social practices of local Muslim communities also played roles in the genocide's unfolding in specific communities. In some cases, Muslim communities were enmeshed in actor-networks more likely to resist the state's genocidal sovereignty and engage in rescue; in others, Hutu Muslims reacted in much the same way as Hutu of other faiths.

Common Elements of Rescue

The micro-level dynamics of violence; local social, political, and economic histories; and social ties within communities shaped the unfolding of genocide in specific locales and made rescue more or less likely within particular communities. Nonetheless, some common elements of successful rescue can be distilled from this variation. These elements begin with the will to help potential victims, but they also include a range of other factors that may only partially depend on individuals and their moral orientations. For example, being asked for help made a difference in some cases. Another important element was that social logics preceded the genocide and enmeshed people in genocidal violence in some cases while inducing people to resist and help Tutsi in others. Momentary assistance and small gestures of support often increased Tutsi victims' chances of survival immensely. Finally, random chance often determined whether a person lived or died.

The Will to Help

The foundational element of rescue is having the will to help. After President Habyarimana's assassination, a relatively small number of Rwandans, primarily Hutu men, immediately began attacking and killing Tutsi and opposition political party members. They had been primed for action through their membership in the Interahamwe or Impuzamugambi political party youth wings turned militias, military training, political rallies, Hutu Power propaganda, and the impunity with which prior attacks on Tutsi people were met. Most Hutu, however, initially reacted with what political scientist Kristen Monroe (2004) called "the hand of compassion." That compulsion to help is at the core of rescue.

In her study of Yad Vashem–identified rescuers in the Holocaust, Monroe demonstrated that the "impetus for moral action" to provide assistance to Jews arose from a "fellow feeling" of common humanity (2004, 245). That sense of shared humanity also motivated rescuers in Rwanda. As Basir, a Hutu Muslim man who saved dozens of his neighbors in Biryogo, put it, "I did it [hid people] because they were human beings" (BIR05). Ismael Mugenzi, in Nkora, risked his life and livelihood to ferry his neighbor's wife and brother-in-law to safety in the Congo because "they were brothers and sisters, and they were in a difficult time" (NKO12). Even if Mugenzi's Muslim faith supported his convictions, his motivations also arose from his perception of their common humanity.

At its root, this sense of common humanity is a moral characteristic, grounded simultaneously in individual character or self-conception, social ties, and cultural palimpsests. Most Rwandans we interviewed identified rescuers' actions as emanating from their "good heart" or moral conscience. In their studies of indakemwa identified by Ibuka, Daniel Rothbart and Jessica Cooley (2016) and Paul Di Stefano (2016) concluded that this moral conscience arose from moral education or the "influence of positive role models" (Di Stefano 2016, 199). In the Rwandan worldview, "having a good heart" goes beyond these researchers' interpretations. "Having a good heart" can arise from an individual's personality, religious belief and practice, social environment, relationships to other people, and cultural practices like gift giving, sharing milk, and mutual assistance. Mugenzi, for example, cited his Tutsi neighbors' common humanity, his social history with his neighbor's wife who had been his classmate in primary school, and his religious faith as motivations for his actions: "How could I lose heaven and earth in a single lifetime?" he said (NKO12). Yet a sense of common humanity or brotherhood is an insufficient condition to compel all people to action. For example, the killer-rescuer Kabera (chapter 2) killed scores of people who were "like brothers" and who "shared milk" with him. A sense of brotherhood forged in the semi-sacred bonds of sharing milk did not prevent Kabera from killing.

The will to help also arises from sociological factors, such as social ties. Abel and Ezekiel, the Seventh-day Adventist brothers who lived on Rubona hill near Nyanza, had dense social ties to Tutsi; their wives were Tutsi. Those ties compelled the brothers to rescue. Ezekiel explained his actions: "I was not afraid to hide those people because I knew they hadn't committed any crime. If I was killed with them, I was ready to die with them because we were all the same. We had committed no crime. I knew they were innocent neighbors" (NYA28). Asked what moved him to protect people when he knew he could be killed, Abel explained his motivations in terms of his social ties to Tutsi and his belief in God: "My wife was a Tutsi. And my brother-in-law. Ezekiel also had a lot of people he had to protect. . . . When I married in 1970, I did not know my wife's race. We were simply in love. Later, when I learned it, I had to stand between where I am from and my wife [to protect her]. It was not my heroism: it was God's. By His grace, He gave me the strength" (NYA29). But social ties to Tutsi—even through marriage—were not enough to compel all Hutu people to acts of rescue. Many Hutu men with Tutsi wives colluded in the killing of their affinal kin.

Even where the compulsion to help is present, it may be restricted by other factors that contribute to the perceptions of opportunity and risk. Abel's and Ezekiel's capacity to protect people was affected by numerous factors: Rubona's topography and social history, their authority as local officials, and the respect community members accorded them because of their reputations.

For many rescuers, the will to help was united with a strong belief that rescue was the only viable option. With that motivation, rescuers asserted their agency, resisting the genocide. Genocide "joiners," in comparison, typically believed that they had little or no control over the situation and that genocidal violence was inevitable (Fujii 2008, 587). Even those people who initially helped Tutsi found it difficult to persist in their efforts over the long term. As the genocide continued, the state and Interahamwe militias increased pressure on Hutu and Twa to participate in the genocide, even if in minimal ways. When the militias killed Hutu or Twa caught helping Tutsi hide or flee, they terrorized many others who were assisting genocide victims and caused them to stop.

In the dynamic context of genocide, many people are willing to offer help when the perceived risk is low. Few, however, persist in this choice over time in the face of increasing risk. Rescuers persist in their sense of the moral necessity of rescue even as that choice forces them to engage in morally dubious decision making. In fact, it is their willingness to make morally problematic decisions, such as refusing help to some while saving others, that distinguishes successful rescue from martyrdom in the Rwandan context. Future research should investigate whether this is a general rule.

Being Asked

Another potentially important element of rescue is being asked for help. Federico Varese and Meir Yaish (2000, 2005) demonstrated that being asked for help significantly increased the likelihood that non-Jews helped Jews during the

Holocaust in Europe. Nicole Fox and Hollie Nyseth Brehm (2018) identified being asked for help as a decisive "situational factor" in their study of Ibuka's indakemwa.[6]

Our interview data bear out this assertion. Ismael Mugenzi did not anticipate his neighbors' need. Hitimana knocked on Mugenzi's door one night to ask for his help. Without Hitimana's request, Mugenzi might never have understood his neighbors' desperate situation, or he might never have dared to volunteer his assistance. Scholastique and her son Sylvestre, both Catholic, asked her Muslim son-in-law Khassim to protect them (chapter 3). As Scholastique explained, "There was no one else who could have saved us. . . . He held his breath" (BIR19). Being asked for help even provoked acts of rescue among some notorious killers. For example, Kabera in Mugandamure (chapter 2) hid several of his Tutsi neighbors, including a local government official much sought after by the militias, because, he explained, "They came to me and told me their problem" (MUG34).

Again, social ties played a role in this dynamic, although social ties alone are not predictive. Mugenzi, Kabera, and Khassim all had social ties to the people they helped. People asked them for help because they believed them either willing or able to assist. Yet genocide survivors we interviewed recounted dozens of episodes in which they asked for assistance and were denied. A female genocide survivor said, "You could run to a person, then the person would tell you 'Leave, before you have me killed! Find another place to go'" (GIS26). And in other cases, strangers offered assistance, even continuous shelter and protection, simply because they were asked. Thus, social ties as a stand-alone variable explain very little about agency or decision making in genocide because they constitute actor-network components that interact with the entire assemblage to produce agency.

The Rule of Social Logics

In the ordered chaos of the genocide, the state enforced its genocidal sovereignty by mobilizing social logics through security patrols, checkpoints, communal labor (*umuganda*), and the amplified force of mobs modeled on cultural scripts of community justice. Just as social ties created polyvalent forces in the genocide, social logics were ubiquitous on both sides of the equation—rescuers also relied on them to support their efforts.

Jeanne d'Arc, the old woman in Gisenyi (chapter 5), used the social logics around age and poverty as a kind of disguise. She relied on her poverty, her age, and the image of grandmotherly care to make herself appear innocuous to militiamen and security forces as she escorted her neighbor's children across the border to safety in the Congo. The wealthy and well-connected businessman Tuyisingize (chapter 5) used his wealth, his patronage ties to important people in the president's family, his knowledge of smuggling, and his business's infrastructure to evacuate dozens of Tutsi across the border. He used social logics around deference to authority, patronage, and bribes disguised as forms of "everyday sociality" (Olivier de Sardan 1999) to increase his capacity to rescue. Virtually everywhere in Rwanda, people bribed militiamen with money, cigarettes, beer, or other items to induce them to turn a blind eye or spare people's lives. They couched these bribes as gifts, everyday forms of sociality embedded in the logics of negotiation, gift giving, and solidarity that existed during ordinary times.

Beyond these tangible expressions of dominant social logics, people mobilized arguments about the rule of law or state sovereignty to negotiate with security patrols and civilian search parties looking for Inyenzi and ibyitso (RPF rebels and their accomplices). They deployed these arguments to convince searchers that Tutsi civilians were harmless noncombatants who were not part of the RPF insurgency. These negotiations invoked shared ideas about patriotic duty and about which people were dangerous to the country.

Small Gestures of Support

An important factor that increases survival for those targeted in mass violence are the random acts of solidarity and small gestures of support that come from people of all sorts. During the Rwandan genocide, most Hutu or Twa people had the opportunity, even if fleeting, to assist someone targeted for killing. Even though they do not fit the model of the "heroic helper" as Ervin Staub (1993) called them, these small gestures of assistance saved unknown numbers of lives. At the height of genocidal violence, these small gestures were sometimes all people were willing to risk. Sémelin (2019) found that these "random acts of solidarity towards the persecuted" had a significant cumulative effect, increasing the chances of Jewish survival and the numbers of Jews who eventually escaped death in Vichy France (191–257).

These small gesturers are the hardest to document through retrospective research, but they likely had the largest cumulative effect on rescue outcomes because they were so widespread. Future research needs to investigate these small gestures systematically to assess their cumulative effects. Broadening the study of rescue to encompass these small gestures of assistance and momentary acts of help reveals the moral ambiguity of the genocide's gray zone. Acts of rescue were not always heroic or extraordinary, nor were they always morally pure.

Ephemeral Networks of Assistance

As the perceived risk of helping Tutsi escape rose and open opposition to the genocide was no longer a viable option, Hutu who were engaged in rescue shifted their strategies to hide their rescue efforts in diffuse networks of assistance. They created ephemeral networks that coalesced and cleaved as needed to reduce risk in the rapidly changing dynamics of the genocide. The fishing crew member Ramazani, for instance, moved his neighbor's Tutsi wife from his home to a friend's house in another community. He did not tell even the woman's own husband where he had hidden her. He then helped evacuate the woman to Congo with the help of another friend. He left without telling his own wife where he was going, to protect them all from the wrath of the Interahamwe. Likewise, Antoine, who was nineteen years old in 1994, helped hide and protect Tutsi members of their Seventh-day Adventist congregation in Gisenyi town. His family handed refugees off to other Hutu congregant families to evade militiamen and house-to-house search parties. Antoine explained that he had no idea how many households participated in the assistance network because his family knew only two other families involved. The network intentionally limited its members' knowledge to limit the potential damage and danger should a household in the network be discovered.

These ephemeral networks of assistance diffused agency and responsibility throughout the network. No single person or family bore all the responsibility or risk. This strategy helped disguise rescue while it was taking place. In the genocide's aftermath, these ephemeral networks have remained hard to detect. In particular, interviewing indakemwa identified by Ibuka will not reveal these networks. If members of the network do not even know who else is involved, they cannot all be revealed. Thus, these rescuers have most often remained unseen and unrecognized.

Random Chance or Luck

A final common element of rescue is chance—even if it evades rational explanations grounded in science and eludes social science models. Many people escaped slaughter in the genocide out of sheer luck.

René, a Tutsi father of two, twice evaded genocide by chance. He escaped detection when the Interahamwe overran the Saint Pierre Center because he had stepped behind the chapel door as the militiamen entered. The militiamen were distracted by someone outside and did not notice him. Weeks later, after René had left Gisenyi and was making his way to his home region, he encountered a security checkpoint. The soldiers demanded to see his ID card, which was marked "Tutsi." René recounted what happened: "Like in a novel, a man named Laurent who was a teacher and who knew my family appeared. He had been transferred from the Congo-Nile crest [near René's home region] to that place near the [Gishwati] forest. He rescued me from the crowd that had surrounded me and wanted to kill me. As an educated person, he interrogated me while reading my papers. He showed the crowd that he knew my family members" (GIS62). Laurent eventually convinced the mob that René was not an RPF rebel and then escorted him away from the security checkpoint to their home region. In his retelling, René emphasized that the role of chance in his survival baffled him. Although he was a devout Catholic who regularly participated in prayer retreats at Saint Pierre, he did not attribute his survival to his faith or to God. He could not because so many others just like him, whose faith was as strong as his, had perished in the genocide.

Berthe Kayitesi (2009), who witnessed the killing of Sister Félicité Niyitegeka at the municipal cemetery in Gisenyi, also attributed her survival to chance. Although Kayitesi was at the cemetery when Sister Félicité and everyone with her were killed, Kayitesi escaped death because she happened to know the militiaman, Thomas, who drove the bus from Saint Pierre to the cemetery (119–23). Amid the killing at the cemetery, Thomas pulled her from the line of victims. Even while insisting he could do nothing to help her, he ordered her to get back on the bus. Kayitesi offers no explanation for Thomas's actions or her ultimate survival. Mere chance put her and Thomas at the scene together.

Luck also played a role in rescue. Many rescuers succeeded in their efforts, thanks in part to chance. Tuyisingize, the wealthy merchant in Gisenyi, was lucky that the army officer who discovered him helping Tutsi was greedy (chapter 5). In Mugandamure, Nyanza, and Rubona hill, residents benefited from the momentous arrival of the RPF rebel forces before the communities became massacre sites (chapter 4). In Gisenyi, Eugénie escaped death thanks to the courage of a young neighbor and luck. When government soldiers arrived in the neighborhood on April 8, Eugénie and her family ran for their lives: "The young girl saw me, invited me in their house, and camouflaged me in a few seconds behind a pile of firewood. The soldiers interrogated her and even slapped her, but she pretended she had never seen me. She opened the doors for me. They searched the house and did not find me" (GIS56). By chance, Eugénie encountered her young neighbor as she fled for her life. With luck, the soldiers did not see Eugénie hidden in the hastily rearranged pile of firewood.

Yet luck cut both ways during the genocide. Idi, the victim-perpetrator (chapter 1), had the misfortune of being caught by soldiers while he was out with his friend buying sugar. His identity card, marked "Hutu," was not enough to spare him hours of torture or coerced participation in a killing.

Whether called luck, fortune, chance, or fate, it was an emergent effect of the actor-networks at play during the genocide. Chance was both random (and irrational) and patterned by the interactions between assemblage components.

Courage, Moral Ambiguity, and Persistence

A primary conclusion of this study is that acts of rescue are often performed by ordinary people amid the extraordinary circumstances of war, genocide, and mass violence. In the Rwandan genocide, most people's first reaction was to help their kin, neighbors, friends, and coworkers. Like everyone else caught in the genocide machine, rescuers improvised their actions and reactions in response to the unexpected and rapidly changing context of genocide. Over time, many people abandoned rescue efforts as the perceived risks of rescue increased, as rescue attempts failed, and as government security forces and militias adapted their tactics to defeat the compulsion to help.

Broadening the study of rescue to encompass the full spectrum of rescuer behavior reveals the fundamental complexities of human agency and motivation. With the word "complexities," I am invoking the theoretical and methodological framework encapsulated in John Law and Annemarie Mol's (2002) volume, *Complexities.* They write, "complexity and simplicity are not necessarily opposites" (6). Complexity acknowledges (1) the multiplicity of worlds or epistemes that exist simultaneously, join together, and interfere with each other; (2) the erratic "flowing and churning" of time, which does not move in a linear fashion; and (3) the use of lists, cases, and "walks" (as opposed to classificatory systems) to investigate phenomena. This concept is particularly relevant here because of the profound impact of culture on people's actions. Without my decades of ethnographic research in Rwanda, I would have been unequipped to understand the ways gender, social position, social ties, traditions of mob justice, patronage, and kinship influence people's actions in genocide.

People rarely act for singular reasons or purposes. Instead, they often have muddled, even conflicting, motivations. In addition, both motivations and capabilities are conditioned by nested, multiscalar assemblages entangled in power relations. Even if agency appears to be sited in human actors, it emerges from the actor-networks in which humans are embedded. Nevertheless, some shared characteristics do set rescuers apart from those who offered momentary aid, stood by, or participated: courage, the ability to navigate moral ambiguity in the genocide's gray zone, and persistence.

Courage

Successful rescue required the courage to act. Sometimes, this courage arose on the spot, as it did with the young girl who hid Eugénie and kept her secret when soldiers beat her. At other times, this courage was strengthened by social ties to soldiers or militiamen, as it was with Karaha, whose son was in the Presidential

Guard (chapter 3), or ties to leaders of Hutu extremist political parties, as in the case of Haruna, the brother of Hassan Ngeze in Biryogo (chapter 3). Not infrequently, an individual's participation in the genocide gave that person the courage to rescue, like Kabera (chapter 2). In some cases, people's courage led them to make enormous sacrifices, like Évariste, whose sons were killed because he refused to report for duty at the roadblocks (chapter 4), or Félicité Niyitegeka, Hamza Habimana, and Mohamed Hakuzimana, who gave their own lives defending Tutsi and other innocents (chapter 7).

Navigating Moral Ambiguity

Hutu and Twa who assisted Tutsi may have been motivated by many things other than altruism, a belief in their common humanity, or fear of God. Rescue was often morally compromised or morally compromising. Martyrs like Félicité, Hamza, and Mohamed sacrificed their own lives because they were unwilling to compromise their moral rectitude. These cases exemplify the assumption that rescuers are morally exceptional people. Yet those people who succeeded in saving both potential victims and themselves from the genocide often had to make morally ambiguous decisions. Rescue was not necessarily a morally pure act; it could not be, taking place as it did in genocide's moral gray zone, the same gray zone occupied by complicity and some acts of perpetration. Rescuers had to be able to navigate that moral gray zone to achieve good outcomes, facing decisions that were morally ambiguous or impossible.

And those decisions had to be made repeatedly: whether to go to a meeting called by local authorities; whether to participate in "community work projects" (*umuganda*), which were really organized searches for people in hiding; whether to report for security patrols; whether to allow militiamen to search their house; whether to hand over people to police officers or soldiers with warrants. Sometimes rescuers made these decisions daily; sometimes they made them repeatedly throughout the course of a single, exhausting day. Sometimes they made decisions under coercion or a perceived threat to themselves or their kin.

The genocide generated ethical quandaries; no rescuer could save everyone. Sometimes rescuers were forced to choose. For instance, one man explained how his friend helped his children flee Biryogo but refused to take his wife because she "looked too Tutsi and it was risky to take her through roadblocks" (BIR04). At the Centre Saint Antoine orphanage in Nyanza, Fathers Eros and Vito saved more than eight hundred children and many of the Tutsi adults who worked in the orphanage. Yet they were unable to protect the three Tutsi priests from the parish church, and they turned away adults who sought refuge (chapter 3). Jeanne d'Arc escorted her neighbor's children to safety in the Congo, but she did not try to intervene to stop the attacks on the children's mother, nor did she oppose the arrest of their father and his oldest son (chapter 5).

Even when people's decisions to assist Tutsi were morally compromised—as in the case of killer-rescuers—they still saved lives. While saving Tutsi lives in no way morally or legally excuses genocide crimes, those actions of rescue still contributed to good outcomes for some people. Paying attention to these morally dubious acts of rescue is necessary to understand the phenomenon in a holistic sense. Furthermore, it underscores the empirical and theoretical reality that anyone can become a rescuer. These actions are not reserved for altruists, morally exceptional people, or even the most courageous.

Persistence

Rescuer behavior, widespread at the start of the genocide, diminished over time. As Saoudi, a Muslim butcher who rescued people, explained, "That war [*intambara*] was so very hard that everyone was scared while it lasted. Even those who had hidden people got discouraged at some point, and they asked the people they had hidden to leave, because they saw cases of people who were killed for hiding people. They [the militiamen] could tell you, 'Kill them yourself!' That was the reason [many people stopped helping Tutsi]" (MUG21). Successful rescue was not determined by a single decision or a single moment. Moment-by-moment decisions could result in rescue or participation in genocide. The same person might help a person one time and later force the person to flee, or hide a friend or family member at home while killing others at a roadblock, or turn strangers over to the Interahamwe while protecting friends or coworkers.

To begin as a rescuer and remain one required tenacity and courage, expressed in repeated, incremental choices. Dozens—even hundreds—of smaller decisions eventually resulted in rescue. For example, Fathers Eros and Vito did not decide to stay in Rwanda at the beginning of April. Rather, they decided to wait and see how things evolved. Then, as the pressure of anti-Tutsi violence arose around them, the numbers of children in the orphanage increased, and they discovered the numerous Tutsi adults among the orphanage staff members, they decided to stay and protect the children and staff members in their care.

In the best cases, courage and persistence reinforced each other, ensuring that a person continued to follow through on the initial decision to rescue even when faced with increased threat. After all, a single decision could instantly move someone from victim to perpetrator, like Idi at the roadblock (chapter 1), or from rescuer to killer, like the man from Rubona who was forced to kill his sister-in-law to save himself and his brother (chapter 4).

The Difference Religion Makes

For some people, their understanding of their religion's moral teachings and their belief in the goodness of God and heaven reinforced their courage. Religious leaders often contend that compassion and courage are evidence of authentic faith and denounce members who participate in genocide as lacking piety. Social science research, on the other hand, has revealed a more complex picture of the relationship between religion, perpetration, and rescue. Much of this research has focused on religion's potential impact on moral orientations, personality, altruism empathy, or inclusion.[7] Robert Braun (2019), Patrick Cabanel (2011), and Yves Ternon (2011) found that religious minorities are more likely to engage in rescue than members of dominant religions. More recent research has broadened the consideration of religion to include the social relations within religious communities and between people of different religious communities (Braun 2019; Longman 2009). In this project, I systematically compared Muslim and Catholic communities. I found that religion does affect resistance to genocide and rescue, but depth of faith is not a key factor.

Religion cuts across internal, external, and sociological factors because it is multifarious: it is an ideological system that shapes moral orientations, a set of rules for living by, and a set of practices that create and reinforce social ties and produce cultural palimpsests. It has the potential to create boundaries between groups that can generate social marginalization for minorities, such as Muslims in Rwanda.

Religion writ large, including moral teachings, shared convictions, and social bonds, motivated people to help and, perhaps more importantly, sustained them as they persisted in their increasingly risky opposition to genocide. The cases explored in this book demonstrate that religion can facilitate rescue. In these cases, moral religious teachings, unity founded on shared beliefs and practices, faith in God and the promise of heaven, and religious leadership all contributed to successful rescue. The tiny religious minority of Jehovah's Witnesses in Rwanda have been recognized for their members' refusal to participate in the genocide and their acts to protect their Tutsi Jehovah's Witness brethren (Seminega 2019). Yet depth of faith alone does not fully explain the collective rescue efforts in these cases. The social ties forged within these religious communities, religious teachings, moral orientations, and experiences of social marginalization among religious minorities all played roles as well. In addition, depth of faith—or the lack of it—cannot account for the significant involvement of Muslims from Biryogo and Gisenyi or Catholic priests, nuns, and church members in the genocide. Like social ties, religion—and its constituent elements—were polyvalent components in the assemblages that coalesced and dissolved over the course of the genocide.

The Potential Impact of Rescue Stories

Without a doubt, rescuers had a direct impact on the lives of the people they saved. Beyond these immediate effects, stories about rescue have the potential to contribute to individual and collective healing, peace building, and reconciliation in the aftermath of genocide or mass violence. For the first decade after the 1994 genocide, the Rwandan government largely suppressed or contained narratives about rescue. The lack of public testimony about rescue—of all varieties—supported the dominant narratives that cast Hutu or Twa as genocide perpetrators or bystanders. Once the government opened a limited public dialogue about martyrs in 2001 (chapter 7), stories of rescue began to emerge as the genocide survivors' association, Ibuka, began systematically identifying indakemwa.

Survivor testimonies about rescue promoted healing from psychosocial trauma for some survivors. The potential therapeutic effects of bearing witness to traumatic experiences have long been recognized in trauma recovery. Eugénie, who gave us her eyewitness testimony of Félicité Niyitegeka's courageous acts, spoke for nearly four hours straight when I interviewed her. Repeatedly, she exhorted me to tell Félicité's story so that people would know of her selfless acts, good deeds, and the sacrifice she had made. In the time I spent with her, it became clear that telling her story of survival and Félicité's story of sacrifice helped her regain a sense of control over her harrowing memories.

Based on the entirety of my research in Rwanda since 1996, genocide survivors who were helped by people during the genocide have a more positive outlook on life, their fellow Rwandans, and the country's future. Their positive experiences amid the horrors of genocide allowed them to imagine a past and a future where at least some Hutu and Twa are good (Mieth 2020; Shapiro-Phim 2020; Zucker 2020). This tentative finding warrants systematic investigation in the future.

Many survivors have maintained ongoing friendships or kin-like ties with their rescuers. Pacifique, the young boy Jeanne d'Arc escorted across the border in Gisenyi, continued to visit the elderly woman for decades after the genocide (chapter 5). As Pacifique explained, he treated her as if she were his grandmother who had perished in the genocide. He brought her gifts of banana beer and clothing, gifts with important symbolism in Rwandan culture. They were emblematic of an adult son or grandson's care. Recounting their stories of survival and the people who saved them helps genocide survivors reconnect to the world of the living by forging social ties and distinguishing the past from the present.

Rescuers' stories can help restore some hope and the potential to trust others. Genocide survivors who were not helped by others during the genocide understandably tend to have very negative views of their fellow Rwandans. They often distrust people and avoid developing transracial relationships. Nonetheless, hearing stories of rescue, especially those told by other survivors, opens new possibilities for some. For Tutsi who were not in Rwanda during the genocide, or people born after the genocide, rescue stories can help them recognize the good in other people. All Rwandans, regardless of race, were exposed to evidence of atrocities in the aftermath through courts, media coverage, discovery of remains, and so on. Often this repeated exposure to narratives about the genocide and past crimes committed against Tutsi confirmed bias against Hutu and Twa Rwandans. Stories of rescue can counteract this bias as they help society members envision a new future and rediscover empathy (Kahn 2020). For Hutu, Twa, and Rwandans of mixed marriages, rescue stories can allow them to see themselves and their families in a new light. These stories can also provide role models that allow them to imagine themselves acting in a different or new way.

Beyond modeling empathy or restoring hope to survivors, adding stories of rescue to the dominant narratives in the wake of mass violence is a form of diversifying narratives. Peaceful coexistence requires the equitable distribution of narratives so that many points of view can be heard while still accounting for empirical facts (Gordon 2020). In Rwanda, genocide survivors were the only ones who could give testimony publicly in the early years after the genocide. This situation impeded peaceful coexistence by publicly erasing the wrongs suffered by Hutu victims of the genocide or those suffered by Rwandans of all ethnicities at the hands of the RPF forces or the new government (Burnet 2012). Creating spaces where people with diverse experiences of the civil war, the genocide, and its aftermath could speak about what had happened and be heard by others helped build empathy and trust (Burnet 2012; King and Sakamoto 2015). The dual process of speaking and being heard was the key to helping individuals find a way forward and building new relationships. Adding narratives about rescue, including the morally ambiguous choices people faced, opens new avenues of hope.

Sharing the stories of rescue in genocide is also important within genocide studies education. When taught and contextualized in the history of a specific genocide, stories of rescue can illustrate the impossible choices people often faced and demonstrate that there were still choices about how to behave. One of the most prominent examples is the Facing History and Ourselves (Facing History) program, which supports secondary school teachers in the "moral, character, or civic education" of students by exploring their own thinking and "others' choices in relation to incidents of social injustice" (Barr 2005, 145–46). As part of its original historical case study of Germany in the 1920s and 1930s, Facing History systematically introduces the genocide studies' typology of perpetrators, "victims, bystanders, collaborators, opportunists, rescuers," and resisters as a way for students to talk about the choices people faced in the past and have today (147).

Presenting this diversity of viewpoints helps students develop critical thinking skills when analyzing historical examples and their own behavior.

Finally, recognizing the good—no matter how small or fleeting—that occurred amid the evil and unimaginable horrors of genocide reminds us of every human's capacity for both good and evil.

Appendix

ASSOCIATION DES MUSULMANES DU RWANDA (AMUR) STATEMENT ON POLITICAL PARTIES

Message from the Muslim Association of Rwanda Directorate about Rwandan Political Parties

Note: The following is the author's translation with assistance from an interpreter.

In the name of God, the merciful.

Most Rwandans are wondering what the Muslim Association of Rwanda' position is regarding the multiparty system which was adopted by our country and even about the activities of political movements in Rwanda. They also speculate on the Muslim opinion about the transitional government which was established on December 30, 1991, and about the many protests which followed its establishment. They also ask themselves what the Muslim position is regarding the Arusha peace negotiations and about the negotiations between the leaders of Christian churches and of political parties. Those negotiations were followed by different actions between political parties which have proven that they have many partisans. In response, His Excellency the President of the Republic created the council of direction whose charge is to work together to establish a new transitional government where all the political parties will be represented and that will reinforce democracy in our country and in the mind-set of the Rwandan people.

This special assembly of the AMUR Directorate, held from February 22, 1992, to March 1, 1992, publicly proclaims that the Muslim community in Rwanda does not take part in political issues, as stated in its charter, article 2, first paragraph, which says, "AMUR is an apolitical association, its main concerns are the Muslim religion and promoting the people's welfare." Given that our country's laws give every citizen the right to join the political party of their choice or to create one, and given that Rwandan Muslims are also concerned by that law; the association directorate has decided that they also have the right to join the party of their choice, as long as their partisanship does not interfere with their faith—this point is very important. The AMUR Directorate asks political parties not to interfere in AMUR's affairs. For that reason, all association leaders at the commune level or the prefecture level, those who are at the headquarters, members of the Association's two commissions, the Sheiks Commission and the Experts Commission, and the Association missionaries are not allowed to be elected as representatives at any level of any political party.

The AMUR Directorate fully supports all kinds of negotiations which seek to restore peace in the country. The Directorate reminds all Rwandans that without peace and security, we will never be able to reach the Democracy we are advocating for. The AMUR Directorate supports negotiations between different political parties and the council representing the Government of Rwanda to establish a new transitional government with all political parties. That is the government all Rwandans impatiently await because it is the one they hope will help solve the difficult problems our country is facing. For this reason, the Directorate asks Rwanda's various leaders in different political parties and the council members to be willing to sacrifice some of their parties' demands so that they can quickly establish a transitional government that suits everybody's needs because that will strengthen the unity of all Rwandans.

AMUR takes this opportunity to remind everyone that each and every Rwandan has a right to life. That no one must be a victim of their race [*ubwoko*] or because they come from a certain region. No race is above the other, as the God Lord says in the Qu'ran, chapter 49, verse 13, "O mankind, We have created you from a male and a female, and made you into races and tribes, so that you may identify one another. Surely the noblest of you, in Allah's sight, is the one who is most pious of you. Surely Allah is All-Knowing, All-Aware" ['Us̱mānī 2020].

Notes

PREFACE

1. For more details on the numbers of dead and their politicization see the discussion in chapter 1 Straus (2006, 51), Meierhenrich (2020), and Guichaoua (2020).

2. See Fujii (2008, 2009, 2013, 2017); Hogg (2010); McDoom (2013, 2014); Straus (2006); and Verwimp (2005, 2006).

3. See Donà (2018); Fujii (2009, 2011); Rothbart and Cooley (2016); Viret (2011a); and Waldorf (2009).

4. Hassan Ngeze, Omar Serushago, Mikaeli Muhimana, and Yussuf Munyakazi.

5. See D. Hoffman (2011); Lubkemann (2008); and Nordstrom (1997, 2004).

6. To protect the anonymity of research participants, I do not name the specific communities in which I conducted long-term fieldwork.

7. The research protocol, questionnaire, and procedures for human subjects' protection were reviewed and approved by both the University of Louisville Institutional Review Board for the Use of Human Subjects in Research and the Rwandan Ministry of Education's Directorate for Research. The Georgia State University Institutional Review Board monitored the project from 2015 until all data were anonymized in 2018.

8. These designations come from the administrative units created in 2005 through "Law N° 29/2005 of 31/12/2005 Organic Law Determining the Administrative Entities of the Republic of Rwanda," which amended the prior province, district, and sector boundaries created in 2000 through Law N° 47/2000. In 1994 when the genocide took place, Rwanda was organized into prefectures, communes, sectors, and cells (from largest administrative unit to smallest). Maps 1 and 2 show these different boundaries and the locations of research field sites.

9. For details on the methods for conducting ethnographic interviews see Spradley (1979) and Weller (2015).

10. The Gacaca courts were courts composed of judges elected from the local population who were not lawyers or jurists. These courts tried the vast majority of genocide suspects in communities across Rwanda.

11. Throughout this book, I use they/them/their as nongendered singular pronouns.

12. I developed the technique of deep empathy by drawing on Ruth Behar's (1997) concept of the vulnerable observer.

13. Twa was a less flexible category since most Twa people lived apart from Hutu and Tutsi and pursued distinctive livelihoods, especially hunting, foraging, and making pottery.

INTRODUCTION

1. Pseudonym. Unless otherwise noted, all interviewees' names have been changed to protect their privacy.

2. See Krebs and Van Hasteren (1992), Monroe (1996, 2004, 2008), Monroe and Martinez (2009), Oliner et al. (1992), Pessi (2009), and Seidler (1992).

3. See Browning (1992, 2000), Charnysh and Finkel (2017), Fujii (2009), Hinton (2005), Kalyvas (2006), and Straus (2006).

4. See Fujii (2009), McDoom (2005), Straus (2006), and Verwimp (2005, 2006).

5. See the collection edited by Sémelin, Andrieu, and Gensburger (2011), Fogelman (1994), Fujii (2011), Jefremovas (1995), Monroe (1996, 2004), Oliner and Oliner (1988, 1995), Oliner et al. (1992), Staub (2003), Straus (2011), and Varese and Yaish (2000).

6. See Monroe (1996, 2004), Oliner and Oliner (1988, 1995), Oliner et al. (1992).

7. See the collection edited by Sémelin, Andrieu, and Gensburger published in French in 2008 and in English in 2011.

8. See Braun (2019), Fujii (2011), Kerenji (2016), Varese and Yaish (2000), and Viret (2011a).

9. On the roles of social norms or cultural traits see Staub (2003); on social ties, Casiro (2006), Fujii (2008, 2009), and McDoom (2013, 2014); on political ideologies and religious beliefs, practices, or communities, Braun (2019), Fogelman (1994), Longman (2009); on membership in minority groups, Braun (2019) and (Viret 2011a); on ambiguity, Latané and Darly (1970) and Staub (2003); and on collective action, Kerenji (2016) and Varese and Yaish (2000).

10. See Arendt (1963), Browning (1992), Fujii (2008, 2009, 2011), Hinton (2005), Hilberg (1992), Monroe (2004), Staub (1993, 2003, 2014), and Straus 2006.

11. See Fox and Nyseth Brehm (2018), King and Sakamoto (2015), Luft (2015), and Staub (2019).

12. Those ordinary Rwandans who reported for security patrols or duty at roadblocks were found guilty of genocide crimes when their actions led to deaths.

13. I use the term *resistance* to refer to active or passive refusal to participate in the genocide. This use differs from that of the Rwandan government, which defines *genocide resistance* solely as the use of defensive violence to oppose the genocide. The most famous case of genocide resistance as defined by the government was at Bisesero hill in Western Province, where a few hundred genocide survivors fled to a forested hilltop and held off attackers for months. My use of the term encompasses both this type of defensive violence and much more common forms of passive resistance.

14. The term and concept of a "founding narrative" come from Straus's (2015) deft analysis.

1. DYNAMICS OF VIOLENCE IN THE GRAY ZONE

1. Readers seeking a detailed history of the genocide or its causes should see Des Forges (1999), Guichaoua (2010, 2015b), Prunier (1997), or Thomson (2018). For analysis of the organizational and social aspects of the genocide's violence see Fujii (2008, 2009, 2011), McDoom (2013, 2014), and Straus (2006, 2015). For analysis of its consequences see Burnet (2012), Ingelaere (2016), Longman (2017), Reyntjens (2004, 2011), and Thomson (2013).

2. Estimates of how many people died in the 1994 genocide range from five hundred thousand (Des Forges 1999, 15) to one million (Republic of Rwanda 2004, 21). For more on the numbers of dead and their politicization see Scott Straus (2006, 51), Jens Meierhenrich (2020), and Guichaoua (2020).

3. In a special forum in *Journal of Genocide Research*, numerous social scientists from a range of disciplines and using diverse quantitative approaches independently reached a surprising consensus of five hundred thousand to six hundred thousand deaths in the 1994 genocide (Meierhenrich 2020, 75; Armstrong, Davenport, and Stam 2020; de Walque 2020; Guichaoua 2020; McDoom 2020; Tissot 2020; Verpoorten 2020). In 2004, the Ministry of Local Government undertook a census of genocide victims that identified 1,074,017 Rwandans who had been killed (Republic of Rwanda 2004, 21). In the study, genocide victim was defined, according to Law 08/96, as "every person who was killed between 1 October 1990 and 31 December 1994 because he was Tutsi or looked Tutsi, had family ties

with a Tutsi, was the friend of or had particular relationships with a Tutsi, or had political thoughts or relationships to people with political thoughts that opposed the extremist politics from before 1994" (cited in Republic of Rwanda 2004, 17).

4. Organized in Uganda in the late 1980s, the RPF recruited from the Rwandan exile community in Uganda, Burundi, the Congo (then Zaire), Tanzania, and elsewhere in the diaspora. It also recruited inside Rwanda and collaborated with internal opponents of Habyarimana's regime (Golooba-Mutebi 2013, 8).

5. See Guichaoua (2015b, 143–47), Prunier (1997, 213–17), Reyntjens (2010), Straus (2006, 44–45).

6. This understanding draws from the growing body of empirical research on the Rwandan genocide and relies heavily on the frameworks set forth by French sociologist André Guichaoua (2010, 2015b) and American political scientist Scott Straus (2006, 2015).

7. Even while it was the site of a fierce battle, the parliament provided a safe haven for Tutsi trying to escape slaughter in Kigali.

8. In 1994, the administrative structure started at the level of the nation, then prefecture (n=11), commune (n=145), sector, cell, and *nyumbakumi*. In 2001 and then again in 2006, the government reorganized the administrative structure. As of 2006, the administrative structure goes from largest to smallest unit: nation, province (n=4), district (n=30), sector (n=416), cell (n=2,148), and village (n=14,837).

9. See Prunier (1997, 5). These statistics were also reported in the US Central Intelligence Agency World Factbook until 2010, https://www.cia.gov/the-world-factbook/. Race was removed from the Rwanda entry in the 2011 edition of the CIA Factbook online.

10. Nearly all (91 percent) of the population relied on agriculture, livestock, fishing, or hunting for their living, according to the 1990 census (Republic of Rwanda 1994, 116).

11. Smeulers (2015) highlights the roles of women as "administrative and supporting personnel in instances of mass violence" ranging from the Holocaust, the Cambodian genocide, the Rwandan genocide, and the conflict in Sierra Leone.

2. AGENCY AND MORALITY IN THE GRAY ZONE

1. Kabera's explanation has been corroborated in formal research by scholars, including Fujii (2009, 2011), Straus (2006), and Verpoorten (2012a, 2012b).

2. See Fujii (2009), McDoom (2005), Straus (2006); on social ties see Fujii (2008), McDoom (2014); on the economic profile of low-level perpetrators see Verwimp (2005); on the use of firearms versus machetes in the genocide see Verwimp (2006).

3. See Burger (2014); Einwohner (2014); Ent and Baumeister (2014); Haslam, Reicher, and Birney (2014); Miller (2014); Overy (2014); Reicher, Haslam, and Miller (2014); Staub (2014).

4. This description is based on my eyewitness account of mob justice meted out in a rural community in southern Rwanda in 2001.

3. MUSLIM EXCEPTIONALISM AND GENOCIDE

1. In 2013, Imam Abdul Karim was a regional leader in the Muslim Association of Rwanda (AMUR, Association des Musulmans du Rwanda).

2. Prosecutor v. Ferdinand Nahimana, Jean-Bosco Barayagwiza, and Hassan Ngeze, Case no. ICTR-99-52-T, Judgment ¶ (December 3, 2003), International Criminal Tribunal for Rwanda.

3. See Doughty and Ntambara (2005); Longman (2009, 196); Prunier (1997, 253); Viret (2011a).

4. See Doughty and Ntambara (2005); Viret (2011a); chapters 4, 5, 6, and 7 of this book.

5. Interviews by El Hadidi in Biryogo, Kigali, August and November 2013, and in Gisenyi, October and November 2013. Interviews by the author in Biryogo, Kigali, February and March 2014 and in Gisenyi, October 2013 and February 2014.

6. See Doughty and Ntambara (2005); Viret (2011a); chapters 4, 5, and 6 of this book.

7. I borrow the term "mythico-historical" from Malkki (1995).

8. Most often I heard Karuhimbi's story recounted without any mention of her name or specific geographic location. She is among the "heroes" recognized in the Gisozi Genocide Memorial Centre's exhibit.

9. Direct observation by author in 2009 and 2011. In 2019, the display had been relocated within the museum and reduced to four examples, two of them Muslim.

10. See Hammer (1995); Lacey (2004); Hebblethwaite (1994).

11. See appendix 1 for the complete text of the statement.

12. Translation by Muḥammad Taqī ʻUs̠mānī (2020).

13. See Carney (2016); Des Forges (2011); Kagabo (1988); Linden (1977); Longman (2009); Vansina (2005).

14. For example, AMUR raised money to build its own school, the Intwari Primary school, in Nyamirambo. When the building was complete, the government took the school and gave it to a Protestant church (KIG05).

15. Beginning in the late 1980s, a few Muslim leaders received scholarships from Libya, Egypt, Saudi Arabia, or the United Arab Emirates to continue their studies in Islamic universities abroad (Kasule 1982, 138–41).

16. The rural communities of Mabare in eastern Rwanda and Nkora in western Rwanda are notable exceptions; these were places where Muslims organized to collectively protect and assist Tutsi during the genocide.

17. Until 1994, non-Rwandan Africans who married Tutsi women were perceived as Hutu.

18. For an exploration of Rwandan cultural logics of reciprocity, mutual assistance and cooperation, and deep social ties see de Lame (2004, 2005).

19. Prosecutor v. Protais Zigiranyirazo, Case no. ICTR-01–73-T, Judgment ¶ (December 18, 2008), p. 57. Des Forges (1999, 199) confirms this account.

20. Prosecutor v. Protais Zigiranyirazo, Case no. ICTR-01–73-T, Judgment ¶ (December 18, 2008), 58.

21. In February 1994, only two weeks before the genocide's start, the Hutu extremist magazine *Kangura* published an article describing the RPF's "Final Attack" and plan to take Kigali (*Kangura*, no. 57, February 1994, p. 4, cited in Des Forges 1999, 167). The article claimed that RPF soldiers were hiding in Biryogo and warned that "all who are concerned by this problem" should be on alert.

22. His real name, because he was convicted of genocide crimes.

23. After the genocide, Karekezi was prosecuted for genocide crimes and found guilty; he died in prison.

24. More of Eugénie's story is related in chapter 6.

25. Kagabo does not cite his source.

4. RESISTANCE, RESCUE, AND RELIGION

1. In the country's 2020 administrative organization, Rubona hill is in Nyanza cell, Busasamana sector, Nyanza district, South Province. In 1994, it was in Nyanza cell, Busasamana sector, Nyabisindu commune, Butare prefecture.

2. His real name. Because the case of Father Eros and the Saint Antoine Orphanage is widely known, hiding his identity is impractical. The quotations in this chapter are used with Father Eros's consent.

3. Habyalimana, who had attended the ceremony, was arrested the next day. He was later executed, and his family was killed by civilian mobs (Des Forges 1999, 265).

4. Presidential Guard soldiers had visited Nyanza in the days after the president's assassination and had gone "around checking on the names of owners of various houses" (Des Forges 1999, 439).

5. For much of the late twentieth century, national radio broadcasts of the news served as a political barometer in countries across Africa. In any coup d'état, the national radio was a key resource to control. Thus, as long as the news broadcasts continued at their usual times, listeners assumed the government was still in control.

6. Catholic missionaries had tried to fight Muslim influence in the country since the missionaries' first arrival in Rwanda (Kagabo 1988, 35).

7. Another interviewee related the same story (MUG01). I doubt that Rudahigwa purchased the land. He likely had the authority as mwami to transfer use rights to Muslims, since the land would have fallen under customary land tenure law at the time.

8. Djumapili was his real name. He had earned the title "Hadji" by completing the hajj, the pilgrimage to Mecca required of all Muslims at least once in their lives.

9. Ugirashebuja was indicted for genocide crimes in Rwanda in the 2000s, but as of September 2018 he lived in the United Kingdom, where he has successfully fought extradition twice (Government of Rwanda v. Nteziryayo and Others, Approved Judgment).

10. Government of Rwanda v. Nteziryayo and Others, Approved Judgment.

11. In 1959, 1961–1964, and 1973–1974, Tutsi had fled their homes and found safety with friends, hid in forests, or fled to churches, schools, or government buildings. In 1994, the genocidal government used this behavior to consolidate Tutsi so it could kill them more easily.

12. As of 2018, Ansar Allah was a Muslim sect that operated separately from the dominant Sunni community organized under AMUR. Ansar Allah retained control over its mosque in the Kibagabaga neighborhood of Kigali but had relinquished its other mosques in legal fights with AMUR.

13. In 2013 interviews in Mugandamure, most Muslim residents minimized the contributions of Ansar Allah and its members to the community's resistance to the genocide. In the early 2000s, the conflict between Ansar Allah and AMUR had intensified. AMUR took legal action to seize all mosques in the country and wrest them from Ansar Allah control. Under new laws requiring registration of religious organizations, Ansar Allah faced an uphill battle as powerful and politically connected AMUR members lobbied against them. AMUR imams preached against Ansar Allah and labeled the association and its members blasphemous. As a result, remaining Ansar Allah members in Mugandamure began to pray in their homes and to meet separately on Fridays for prayers in other members' homes.

14. In 2002, the ICTR indicted Father Hormisdas for his roles in killing Nyanza parish priests and other crimes related to the genocide, although the court found him not guilty in 2009, citing insufficient evidence to substantiate his role in these crimes (United Nations International Criminal Tribunal for Rwanda 2009).

15. Straus (2006) has documented this "tipping point" as a nationwide phenomenon corresponding to different dates (7–9).

16. As Father Eros noted, even more children may have been saved: "We had the names of all those children. It's possible that there were more, but that we didn't have the names of those ones" (NYA38).

5. THE BORDER AS SALVATION AND SNARE

1. Following Nordstrom (2004), I use the term "extralegal" rather than "illegal" to refer to this trade. As Nordstrom notes, "'extra-state' exchange systems . . . are fundamental to war, and . . . are central to processes of development" (11). As she puts it, "much of this trade passes across boundaries of il/legality" (2004, 11).

2. See Andersson (2016); De León (2015); Sandberg (2009); Walker (2015, 2018); Xiang and Lindquist (2014).

3. Prosecutor v. Protais Zigiranyirazo, Case no. ICTR-01–73-T, Judgment ¶ (December 18, 2008), pp. 57–58.

4. According to the national census conducted in 1991, Muslims accounted for 1.4 percent of Gisenyi prefecture's 734,658 residents, or an estimated 10,285 people (Republic of Rwanda 1994, 127). A total of 22,159 residents in Gisenyi prefecture lived in "urban zones" (1994, 58). Only 0.7 percent of the rural population nationwide was Muslim, so almost all Muslims lived in urban zones. Hence my estimate of five to eight thousand, slightly more than one-third of the population.

5. Although this may seem like a tiny amount of money, it was a significant sum, equal to the expected contribution to sponsor a wedding celebration or to support the costs of a funeral.

6. His son, Jean-Marie Vianney Makiza, shot and killed three Tutsi police officers at a roadblock near the family's second home in Giciye commune in rural Gisenyi prefecture, where the family had fled when they left Kigali in mid-April. Testimony before the court indicates Zigiranyirazo and police commanders did not approve of Makiza's actions. Prosecutor v. Protais Zigiranyirazo, Case no. ICTR-01–73-T, Judgment (December 18, 2008), pp. 61, 92, and 95.

7. Based on interviews by the author.

6. AT THE MARGINS OF THE STATE

1. The word *ikinani* in Kinyarwanda means "talisman" and evokes supernatural powers tied to magic. In Rwandan warrior poems, *ikinani* means "invincible person" or "formidable opponent" (Jacob 1983, 2:377).

2. In recounting his story, Ramazani avoided using the word "Interahamwe" and instead used the words "young men" (*abasore*), "attackers," or "killers" (*abicyanyi*).

3. In the 2019 administrative organization, Nkora cell is in Kigeyo sector, Rutsiro district. The Nkora commercial center lies near the boundary between Mushonyi and Kigeyo sectors in the 2019 administrative boundaries.

4. The mosque was in Rugaragara cellule, Vumbi sector, in 1994 (now Rutsiro district, Mushyoni sector, Kaguriro cellule, Rugerero village).

5. All these former sectors sit in Rutsiro district following the administrative reorganization of 2006.

6. Tutsi were 6.8 percent of the population in Kayove commune, Hutu 92.7 percent, and Twa less than 1 percent in 1989 (Mahy 1989).

7. The neighboring kingdom of Bwishaza lay to the south of Bugoyi, and Bugara to the northeast.

8. These are their real names since they are all deceased.

9. See the full discussion of the gray zone in chapter 2 and Levi's (1989) definition of it as the moral "ambiguity which radiates out from regimes based on terror and obsequiousness" (37).

10. In fact, many people we interviewed in Nkora were MRND party leaders and local government officials at the time of the genocide. In most other research sites, we could not locate many MRND party leaders or local government officials from 1994 to interview

because most of them had fled the country and never returned, been killed by RPF soldiers, died in prison facing charges of genocide crimes, or were still imprisoned, serving their sentences for genocide crimes.

11. Zahara's testimony was confirmed by many other interviewees who witnessed the events.

12. For a discussion of the many ways local politics influenced the operation of the Gacaca courts see Chakravarty (2016).

13. This is an enormous sum of money in rural Rwanda. According to World Bank data, Rwanda's gross national income per capita was $310 in 1993. Annual household income in rural Rwanda was well below this figure.

14. This amount of money was an enormous sum for a farmer in rural Rwanda to raise.

15. Even for Hamed, this was a significant sum of money. For an average farmer in Nkora, it was an unimaginable amount.

16. While many Muslims from Nkora resisted the genocide and helped potential victims, a few Muslims joined the killing squads, as they did in Biryogo, Mugandamure, and Gisenyi (chapters 3 and 4). Hamada, a Muslim man from Nkora, reported for duty at roadblocks where people were killed. Even though he killed no one himself, he was prosecuted for genocide crimes and found guilty.

7. ALTRUISM, AGENCY, AND MARTYRDOM IN THE GRAY ZONE

1. Her real name.

2. Their real names.

3. In 2017, Pope Francis reversed the church's position, acknowledged its institutional responsibility for the genocide, and begged forgiveness for the "sins and failings of the church and its members" (Winfield 2017).

4. See M. Hoffman (1981); Krebs and Van Hasteren (1992); Staub (2003); Pessi (2009, 188).

5. These include Kinyaga in southwestern Rwanda (C. Newbury 1988), Rukiga in northern Rwanda and Uganda (Freedman 1984), Gisaka in southeastern Rwanda, Ndorwa in northern Rwanda, and many other polities.

6. I use lowercase imana to refer to the notion of a dynamic life force or a "good omen" (de Lame 2005) and uppercase Imana to refer to an anthropomorphic Christian or Islamic God.

7. Here I have used a gender-neutral pronoun for Imana. In Kinyarwanda, the word is agender, as it belongs to the ninth class of nouns, which begin with the prefix *i-* (sing. and pl.). By the late twentieth century, most Rwandans conceived of Imana as male; it is impossible to know to what extent this conception derives from the influence of Christianity or Islam.

8. Crépeau explains that Rwandan morality "was not based on the imperatives of an absolute and vigilant moral master" (1985, 166).

9. British colonizers in Uganda who administered the Rukiga region inhabited by Kinyarwanda speakers outlawed the Nyabingi spirit medium cult and vigorously pursued spirit mediums and priests for imprisonment (Freedman 1984, 31).

10. Rothbart and Cooley depict the importance of having a good heart and conclude that "influential adults" shaped the moral education of these people during their upbringing (2016, 87). Di Stefano similarly concludes that rescuers had the "influence of positive parental roles models" and "an ethnically blind worldview grounded in a 'common humanity'" (2016, 199). Both of these studies rely on extremely small sample sizes, which weakens the generalizability and validity of their conclusions. Rothbart and Cooley interviewed thirty-three "self-identifying rescuers" located with the help of two Rwandan

genocide survivor organizations (77). Di Stefano relies on "thirty-one testimonials from Hutu rescuers" from "written testimonials gathered by Aegis Trust, the London-based organization responsible for creating the Genocide Memorial Centre in Kigali" and his own interviews (195).

11. In their extensive dictionary of Rwandan proverbs, Crépeau and Bizimana (1979) identified twenty that speak of the heart.

12. Beyond the accounts in this book see also the memoirs by Seminega (2019) and Ilibagiza and Erwin (2009).

13. According to the racialized stereotypes, Tutsi are "tall and thin, with aquiline features" and "light complexions." Hutu are "shorter and more muscular with a broad nose and dark skin." Twa are very short with more body hair (Burnet 2012, 47).

14. The imam closed the El Fath mosque near ONATRACOM for this reason (BIR03, BIR15, BIR24). The imam at the Biryogo mosque closed the mosque on April 9, 1994, because of the threat of the nearby roadblock controlled by the CDR and Impuzamugambi (BIR05). The Qadafi mosque in Nyamirambo was closed later in April 1994, after the Interahamwe entered and killed a couple of people hiding there (BIR06). At the Rwampara mosque in Biryogo, Hutu Muslims protected some Muslim and Christian Tutsi who hid (BIR06).

15. African Rights (2002) incorrectly recorded Marie Nathalie Icyimpaye's name as Anatalie (262). Kayitesi (2009) recorded Nathalie's full name (99).

16. Serushago led the Interahamwe in Gisenyi. In 1999, he pleaded guilty to four of the five charges against him in the ICTR. He was sentenced to fifteen years in prison. Prosecutor v. Omar Serushago, Sentencing Judgment, ICTR Trial Chamber I, ICTR 98–39-S (February 5, 1999).

17. RPF units based in the parliament building engaged with government forces in an effort to capture the nearby airport and secure a supply route via the national highway leaving the capital city toward the east.

18. Thomson (2013) describes in detail Rwandans' indirect opposition to state power in the postgenocide period.

19. A muezzin is the person who recites the Adhan, or call to prayer, five times each day.

20. Direct observations by the author in 2011 and 2019.

21. Direct observations of the author in 2004 and 2005.

22. See Melvern 2011.

23. Father Munyeshyaka was never prosecuted. He fled to Europe, where he was initially protected by the Catholic Church. In the end, the French government dropped the case against him (Tabaro 2018).

24. "CDA Collaborative Learning" is the operating name of the organization.

25. Péan was charged with racial defamation in Rwanda for his controversial account of the Rwandan genocide in an earlier book (2005), which blamed the RPF for provoking the genocide and alleged that the RPF waged a "counter genocide" (*L'Obs* 2008). Even scholars critical of the RPF, such as Reyntjens, have noted that Péan's inflammatory accusations should be read with caution (*L'Obs* 2008).

26. Péan misrepresents the geographic realities of Kibagabaga. In the book, he presents a map, not drawn to scale, that marks Kibagabaga "village," as he calls it, as a single point near Kimironko along a large road (Péan 2009, 184). The map implies that Kibagabaga was of strategic importance, and the accompanying text emphasizes its geographic centrality in relation to several military and police installations. The map and the text, however, do not reflect the state of the area in 1994. The map depicts large roads from Remera through Kibagabaga and from Kagugu to Munini, but these roads were poorly maintained dirt tracks in 1994. In addition, Kibagabaga was inhabited by the working poor and tradesmen of all races, rather than "a concentration of Tutsi" (Péan 2009, 191). Although Kibagabaga

was centrally located near strategic locations, the poorly maintained dirt roads and footpaths that connected it to these places limited its accessibility.

27. For more on the Rwandan government's national security concerns see the *International Religious Freedom Report* for Rwanda (US Department of State 2018).

CONCLUSION

1. RPF soldiers killed unknown numbers of RAF soldiers, militiamen, and civilians in the territories they seized. Sometimes they summarily executed militiamen and genocide perpetrators, but they also killed unarmed Hutu civilians in their sweeps (Des Forges 1999, 702–22).

2. See Monroe (1996, 2004); Rothbart and Cooley (2016); Sémelin (2019); Sémelin, Andrieu, and Gensburger (2011); Varese and Yaish (2000, 2005).

3. Nyseth Brehm, Uggen, and Gasanabo found that most perpetrators prosecuted by the Gacaca courts were men between the ages of nineteen and forty years at the time of the genocide (2016, 726).

4. See Fujii (2008, 2011); Longman (2009); McDoom (2005, 2013, 2014); Straus (2006); Verwimp (2005, 2006).

5. McClendon and Riedl (2019) demonstrated the potential impact of sermons on citizens' political participation in sub-Saharan Africa.

6. Because of the limitations of their sample, Fox and Nyseth Brehm's analysis considers only what rescuers say about their own actions retrospectively and does not triangulate with other people's observations of rescuers' actions.

7. See Barnett (1998); Fogelman (1994); Longman (2009); Monroe (1996); Monroe and Martinez (2009); Oliner (2004); Oliner and Oliner (1988); Seidler (1992); and Viret (2011a).

References

Abu-Lughod, Lila. 1991. "Writing against Culture." In *Recapturing Anthropology: Working in the Present*, edited by Richard G. Fox, 137–62. Santa Fe, NM: School of American Research.

Adler, Reva N., Cyanne E. Loyle, and Judith Globerman. 2007. "A Calamity in the Neighborhood: Women's Participation in the Rwandan Genocide." *Genocide Studies and Prevention* 2 (3): 209–33. https://doi.org/10.3138/gsp.2.3.209.

African Rights. 1995. *Rwanda Not So Innocent: When Women Become Killers*. London: African Rights.

——. 2002. *Tribute to Courage*. London: African Rights.

Albahari, Maurizio. 2016. *Crimes of Peace: Mediterranean Migrations at the World's Deadliest Border*. Philadelphia: University of Pennsylvania Press.

American Anthropological Association. 1971. "AAA Statement on Ethics." Past AAA Statements on Ethics. https://www.americananthro.org/ParticipateAndAdvocate/Content.aspx?ItemNumber=1656.

——. 1998. "Code of Ethics of the American Anthropological Association." *Anthropology News* 39 (6): 19–20. https://doi.org/10.1111/an.1998.39.6.19.2.

——. 2009. "Code of Ethics of the American Anthropological Association." Past AAA Statements on Ethics. https://www.americananthro.org/ParticipateAndAdvocate/Content.aspx?ItemNumber=1656.

——. 2012. "Principles of Professional Responsibility." AAA Ethics Forum. November 1, 2012. http://ethics.americananthro.org/category/statement/.

Amsterdamska, Olga. 1990. "Surely You Are Joking, Monsieur Latour!" Edited by Bruno Latour. *Science, Technology, & Human Values* 15 (4): 495–504. https://www.jstor.org/stable/689826.

Andersson, Ruben. 2016. "Hardwiring the Frontier? The Politics of Security Technology in Europe's 'Fight against Illegal Migration.'" *Security Dialogue* 47 (1): 22–39. https://doi.org/10.2307/26293583.

André, Catherine, and Jean-Philippe Platteau. 1998. "Land Relations under Unbearable Stress: Rwanda Caught in the Malthusian Trap." *Journal of Economic Behavior & Organization* 34 (1): 1–47. https://doi.org/10.1016/S0167-2681(97)00045-0.

Andrieu, Claire. 2011. "Conclusion: Rescue, a Notion Revisited." In *Resisting Genocide: The Multiple Forms of Rescue*, edited by Jacques Sémelin, Claire Andrieu, Sarah Gensburger, and Cynthia Schoch, translated by Emma Bentley, 495–506. New York: Columbia University Press.

Arendt, Hannah. 1963. *Eichmann in Jerusalem: A Report on the Banality of Evil*. New York: Viking.

Armstrong, David A., Christian Davenport, and Allan Stam. 2020. "Casualty Estimates in the Rwandan Genocide." *Journal of Genocide Research* 22 (1): 104–11. https://doi.org/10.1080/14623528.2019.1703251.

Asad, Talal. 1986. *The Idea of an Anthropology of Islam*. Washington, DC: Center for Contemporary Arab Studies.

Barnett, Victoria. 1998. *For the Soul of the People: Protestant Protest against Hitler*. New York: Oxford University Press.

Barr, Dennis K. 2005. "Early Adolescents' Reflections on Social Justice: Facing History and Ourselves in Practice and Assessment." *Intercultural Education* 16 (2): 145. https://doi.org/10.1080/14675980500133556.

Bates, Robert H. 1998. "The International Coffee Organization: An International Institution." In *Analytic Narratives*, edited by Robert H. Bates, Avner Greif, Margaret Levi, Jean-Laurent Rosenthal, and Barry R. Weingast, 194–230. Princeton, NJ: Princeton University Press.

Berger, Iris. 1982. *Religion and Resistance: East African Kingdoms in the Precolonial Period*. Tervuren, Belgium: Musée Royal de l'Afrique Centrale.

Bernard, H. Russell, and Gery W. Ryan. 2010. *Analyzing Qualitative Data: Systematic Approaches*. Los Angeles: SAGE.

Bernard-Donals, Michael. 2016. *An Introduction to Holocaust Studies*. New York: Routledge.

Bigirumwami, Aloys. 2004. *Imihango n'imigenzo n'imizilirizo mu Rwanda: Yerekeye ku Bantu bazima n'abandi Bantu bazima: Yerekeye ku Bantu bazima n'abandi Bantu bazimu*. 4th ed. Nyundo, Rwanda: Diocèse de Nyundo.

Bizimana, Jean Damascène. 2020. "Evacuation of the Refugees from Hotel Des Mille Collines and the Death of Capitain Mbaye Diagne of UNAMIR." National Commission for the Fight against Genocide. May 30. https://cnlg.gov.rw/index.php?id=87&tx_news_pi1%5Bnews%5D=4228&tx_news_pi1%5Bcontroller%5D=News&tx_news_pi1%5Baction%5D=detail&cHash=8002ec2378ccad737d580afddc4d7e60.

Blundo, Giorgio, and Jean-Pierre Olivier de Sardan. 2006. *Everyday Corruption and the State: Citizens and Public Officials in Africa*. New York: Zed Books.

Booh-Booh, Jacques-Roger. 1994. "Communiqué de presse No 30/94." Kigali, Rwanda: UNAMIR Bureau d'Information, d'Éducation et de Presse. 20476. France Génocide Tutsi. https://francegenocidetutsi.org/BIEP30.html.en.

Bourke, Joanna. 2014. *The Story of Pain: From Prayer to Painkillers*. New York: Oxford University Press. https://doi.org/10.1891/1062-8061.25.1.180.

Braun, Robert. 2019. *Protectors of Pluralism: Religious Minorities and the Rescue of Jews in the Low Countries during the Holocaust*. New York: Cambridge University Press. https://doi.org/10.1017/9781108633116.

Browning, Christopher R. 1992. *Ordinary Men*. New York: HarperCollins.

——. 2000. *Nazi Policy, Jewish Workers, German Killers*. New York: Cambridge University Press.

——. 2005. "'Alleviation' and 'Compliance': The Survival Strategies of the Jewish Leadership in the Wierzbnik Ghetto and the Starachowice Factory Slave Labor Camps." In *Gray Zones: Ambiguity and Compromise in the Holocaust and Its Aftermath*, edited by Jonathan Petropoulos and John K. Roth, 26–36. New York: Berghahn Books.

Bueger, Christian. 2013. "Actor-Network Theory, Methodology, and International Organization." *International Political Sociology* 7 (3): 338–42. https://doi.org/10.1111/ips.12026_3.

Burger, Jerry M. 2014. "Situational Features in Milgram's Experiment That Kept His Participants Shocking." *Journal of Social Issues* 70 (3): 489–500. https://doi.org/10.1111/josi.12073.

Burnet, Jennie E. 2003. "Culture, Practice, and Law: Women's Access to Land in Rwanda." In *Women and Land in Africa*, edited by Lynne Muthoni Wanyeki, 176–206. New York: Zed Books.

——. 2009. "Whose Genocide? Whose Truth? Representations of Victim and Perpetrator in Rwanda." In *Genocide: Truth, Memory and Representation*, edited by Alex Laban Hinton and Kevin O'Neill, 80–110. Durham, NC: Duke University Press. https://doi.org/10.1215/9780822392361-004.

——. 2012. *Genocide Lives in Us: Women, Memory, and Silence in Rwanda*. Madison: University of Wisconsin Press.

——. 2015. "Genocide, Evil, and Human Agency: The Concept of Evil in Rwandan Explanations of the 1994 Genocide." In *Evil in Africa: Encounters with the Everyday*, edited by William C. Olsen and Walter E. A. Van Beek, 75–90. Bloomington: Indiana University Press.

——. 2019. "Uwilingiyimana, Agathe." In *Oxford Research Encyclopedia of African History*. New York: Oxford University Press. https://doi.org/10.1093/acrefore/9780190277734.013.487.

Cabanel, Patrick. 2011. "Protestant Minorities, Judeo-Protestant Affinities and Rescue of the Jews in the 1940s." In *Resisting Genocide: The Multiple Forms of Rescue*, edited by Jacques Sémelin, Claire Andrieu, Sarah Gensburger, and Cynthia Schoch, translated by Emma Bentley, 383–94. New York: Columbia University Press.

Callon, Michel, and John Law. 1995. "Agency and the Hybrid Collectif." *South Atlantic Quarterly* 94 (2): 481–507.

Carney, J. J. 2016. *Rwanda before the Genocide: Catholic Politics and Ethnic Discourse in the Late Colonial Era*. New York: Oxford University Press.

Casiro, Jessica. 2006. "Argentine Rescuers: A Study on the 'Banality of Good.'" *Journal of Genocide Research* 8 (4): 437–54. https://doi.org/10.1080/14623520601056281.

Chakravarty, Anuradha. 2016. *Investing in Authoritarian Rule: Punishment and Patronage in Rwanda's Gacaca Courts for Genocide Crimes*. New York: Cambridge University Press. https://doi.org/10.1017/CBO9781316018804.

Charnysh, Volha, and Evgeny Finkel. 2017. "The Death Camp Eldorado: Political and Economic Effects of Mass Violence." *American Political Science Review* 111 (4): 801–18. https://doi.org/10.1017/S0003055417000296.

Clifford, James. 1988. *The Predicament of Culture: Twentieth-Century Ethnography, Literature, and Art*. Cambridge, MA: Harvard University Press. https://doi.org/10.2307/j.ctvjf9x0h.

Collins, Patricia Hill. 1990. *Black Feminist Thought: Knowledge, Consciousness, and the Politics of Empowerment*. Boston: Unwin Hyman.

——. 1998. "Intersections of Race, Class, Gender, and Nation: Some Implications for Black Family Studies." *Journal of Comparative Family Studies* 29 (1): 27–36. https://doi.org/10.3138/jcfs.29.1.27.

Cook, David. 2012. "Martyrdom (Shahada)." In *Oxford Bibliography of Islamic Studies*. New York: Oxford University Press. https://doi.org/10.1093/OBO/9780195390155-0124.

Coquio, Catherine. 2009. Preface in *Demain ma vie: Enfants chefs de famille dans le Rwanda d'après*, edited by Berthe Kayitesi, 7–50. Paris: Éditions Laurence Teper.

Coupez, André, and Marcel D'Hertefelt. 1964. *La royauté sacrée de l'ancien Rwanda*. Tervuren, Belgium: Musée Royal de l'Afrique Centrale.

Crenshaw, Kimberlé. 1991. "Mapping the Margins: Intersectionality, Identity Politics, and Violence against Women of Color." *Stanford Law Review* 43 (6): 1241–99. https://doi.org/10.2307/1229039.

Crépeau, Pierre. 1985. *Parole et sagesse: Valeurs sociales dans les proverbes du Rwanda*. Vol. 118. 8. Tervuren, Belgium: Musée Royal de l'Afrique Centrale.

Crépeau, Pierre, and Simon Bizimana. 1979. *Proverbes du Rwanda*. Tervuren, Belgium: Musée Royal de l'Afrique Centrale.

Davenport, Christian, and Allan Stam. 2014. "Troop Movements without Violence." GenoDynamics. 2014. http://genodynamics.weebly.com/data-animations.html.

de Lame, Danielle. 2004. "Mighty Secrets, Public Commensality, and the Crisis of Transparency: Rwanda through the Looking Glass." *Canadian Journal of African Studies / Revue Canadienne des Études Africaines* 38 (2): 279–317. https://doi.org/10.2307/4107302.

——. 2005. *A Hill among a Thousand: Transformations and Ruptures in Rural Rwanda*. Madison: University of Wisconsin Press.

De León, Jason. 2015. *The Land of Open Graves: Living and Dying on the Migrant Trail*. Berkeley: University of California Press.

Des Forges, Alison. 1995. "The Ideology of Genocide." *Issue: A Journal of Opinion* 23 (2): 44–47. https://doi.org/10.2307/1166506.

——. 1999. *"Leave None to Tell the Story": Genocide in Rwanda*. New York: Human Rights Watch.

——. 2011. *Defeat Is the Only Bad News: Rwanda under Musinga, 1896–1931*. Edited by David S. Newbury. Madison: University of Wisconsin Press.

de Walque, Damien. 2020. "Relative Measures of Genocide Mortality: Benefits and Methodological Considerations of Using Siblings' Survival Data." *Journal of Genocide Research* 22 (1): 112–15. https://doi.org/10.1080/14623528.2019.1703254.

Di Stefano, Paul. 2016. "Understanding Rescuing during the Rwandan Genocide." *Peace Review* 28 (2): 195–202. https://doi.org/10.1080/10402659.2016.1166755.

Donà, Giorgia. 2018. "'Situated Bystandership' during and after the Rwandan Genocide." *Journal of Genocide Research* 20 (1): 1–19. https://doi.org/10.1080/14623528.2017.1376413.

Doughty, Kristin. 2017. "Converting Threats to Power: Methane Extraction in Lake Kivu, Rwanda." In *Governance in the Extractive Industries: Power, Cultural Politics and Regulation*, edited by Lori Leonard and Siba N. Grovogui, 95–114. New York: Routledge.

——. 2020. "Carceral Repair: Methane Extraction in Lake Kivu, Rwanda." *Cambridge Journal of Anthropology* 38 (2): 19–37. https://doi.org/10.3167/cja.2020.380203.

Doughty, Kristin, and David Moussa Ntambara. 2005. "Resistance and Protection: Muslim Community Actions during the Rwandan Genocide." Steps toward Conflict Prevention Project. Cambridge, MA: CDA Collaborative Learning Projects. http://live-cdacollaborative.pantheonsite.io/wp-content/uploads/2016/01/Resistance-and-Protection-Muslim-Community-Actions-During-the-Rwandan-Genocide.pdf.

Dusengumuremyi, Jean d'Amour. 2015. *No Greater Love*. Lake Oswego, OR: Dignity.

Einwohner, Rachel L. 2014. "Authorities and Uncertainties: Applying Lessons from the Study of Jewish Resistance during the Holocaust to the Milgram Legacy." *Journal of Social Issues* 70 (3): 531–43. https://doi.org/10.1111/josi.12076.

Ent, Michael R., and Roy F. Baumeister. 2014. "Obedience, Self-Control, and the Voice of Culture." *Journal of Social Issues* 70 (3): 574–86. https://doi.org/10.1111/josi.12079.

Fédération Internationale des Ligues des Droits de l'Homme. 1993. "Violations massives et systématiques des droits de l'homme depuis le 1er octobre 1990." *La Lettre Hebdomadaire de la FIDH* 2 (162). https://www.fidh.org/fr/regions/afrique/rwanda/14463-rwanda-violations-massives-et-systematiques-des-droits-de-l-homme-depuis.

Fiorentino, Michael. 2021. "'Hotel Rwanda' Brought Praise, Now He Faces Terrorism Charges." *NBC News*, March 20, 2021. https://www.nbcnews.com/news/world/he-was-praised-after-movie-hotel-rwanda-now-paul-rusesabagina-n1261533.

Fogelman, Eva. 1994. *Conscience and Courage: Rescuers of Jews during the Holocaust*. New York: Anchor Books.

Fortin, Michel. 1994. "Lumière dans les ténèbres." *Africana Plus* 4 (September). http://africana.mafr.net/APlusFra/rwa1.html.

Fox, Nicole, and Hollie Nyseth Brehm. 2018. "'I Decided to Save Them': Factors That Shaped Participation in Rescue Efforts during Genocide in Rwanda." *Social Forces* 96 (4): 1625–48. https://doi.org/10.1093/sf/soy018.

Freedman, Jim. 1974. "Ritual and History: The Case of Nyabingi (Rite et histoire: Le cas de Nyabingi)." *Cahiers d'Études Africaines* 14 (53): 170–80. https://www.jstor.org/stable/4391287.

——. 1984. *Nyabingi: The Social History of an African Divinity*. Tervuren, Belgium: Musée Royal de l'Afrique Centrale.

Fujii, Lee Ann. 2008. "The Power of Local Ties: Popular Participation in the Rwandan Genocide." *Security Studies* 17 (3): 568–97. https://doi.org/10.1080/09636410802319578.

——. 2009. *Killing Neighbors: Webs of Violence in Rwanda*. Ithaca, NY: Cornell University Press.

——. 2010. "Shades of Truth and Lies: Interpreting Testimonies of War and Violence." *Journal of Peace Research* 47 (2): 231–41. http://dx.doi.org/10.1177/0022343309353097.

——. 2011. "Rescuers and Killer-Rescuers during the Rwandan Genocide: Rethinking Standard Categories of Analysis." In *Resisting Genocide: The Multiple Forms of Rescue*, edited by Jacques Sémelin, Claire Andrieu, and Sarah Gensburger, translated by Emma Bentley, 145–57. New York: Columbia University Press.

——. 2013. "The Puzzle of Extra-Lethal Violence." *Perspectives on Politics* 11 (02): 410–26. https://doi.org/10.1017/S1537592713001060.

——. 2017. "'Talk of the Town': Explaining Pathways to Participation in Violent Display." *Journal of Peace Research* 54 (5): 661–73. https://doi.org/10.1177/0022343317714300.

Geertz, Clifford. 1975. *The Interpretation of Cultures: Selected Essays*. New York: Basic Books.

George, Terry. 2006. "Smearing a Hero." *Washington Post*, May 10, 2006, online edition, sec. Opinion Editorials. http://www.washingtonpost.com/wp-dyn/content/article/2006/05/09/AR2006050901242.html.

Golooba-Mutebi, Frederick. 2013. "Politics, Political Settlements and Social Change in Post-colonial Rwanda." ESID Working Paper, no. 24. http://www.effective-states.org/wp-content/uploads/working_papers/final-pdfs/esid_wp_24_golooba-mutebi.pdf.

Gordon, Matthew. 2020. "The Politics of Resilience in Somaliland: The Contribution of Political Community and Autonomy to Post-conflict Stabilization and Coexistence." In *Coexistence in the Aftermath of Mass Violence*, edited by Eve Monique Zucker and Laura McGrew, 218–43. Ann Arbor: University of Michigan Press. https://doi.org/10.3998/mpub.11302800.

Gourevitch, Philip. 1998. *We Wish to Inform You That Tomorrow We Will Be Killed with Our Families: Stories from Rwanda*. New York: Farrar, Straus and Giroux.

Gravel, Pierre Bettez. 1968. *Remera: A Community in Eastern Ruanda*. Studies in African History, Anthropology, and Ethnology. The Hague: Mouton.

Greene, Joshua M., and Shiva Kumar. 2000. *Witness: Voices from the Holocaust.* New York: Simon & Schuster.

Guichaoua, André. 1995. *Les crises politiques au Burundi et au Rwanda: 1993–1994.* Paris: Karthala.

——. 2010. *Rwanda, de la guerre au génocide les politiques criminelles au Rwanda (1990–1994).* Paris: La Découverte.

——. 2015a. "Box 14. The Interim Government of 8 April 1994." From War to Genocide digital archive. http://rwandadelaguerreaugenocide.univ-paris1.fr/wp-content/uploads/2015/11/From-War-to-Genocide-Box-14.pdf.

——. 2015b. *From War to Genocide: Criminal Politics in Rwanda, 1990–1994.* Translated by Don E. Webster. Madison: University of Wisconsin Press.

——. 2020. "Counting the Rwandan Victims of War and Genocide: Concluding Reflections." *Journal of Genocide Research* 22 (1): 125–41. https://doi.org/10.1080/14623528.2019.1703329.

Habib, Sandy. 2014. "Dying in the Cause of God: The Semantics of the Christian and Muslim Concepts of Martyr." *Australian Journal of Linguistics* 34 (3): 388–98. https://doi.org/10.1080/07268602.2014.898223.

——. 2017. "Dying for a Cause Other Than God: Exploring the Non-religious Meanings of Martyr and Shahīd." *Australian Journal of Linguistics* 37 (3): 314–27. https://doi.org/10.1080/07268602.2017.1298395.

Hammer, Joshua. 1995. "Blood on the Altar." *Newsweek*, September 3.

——. 2021. "He Was the Hero of 'Hotel Rwanda.' Now He's Accused of Terrorism." *New York Times*, March 2, 2021, online edition, sec. Magazine. https://www.nytimes.com/2021/03/02/magazine/he-was-the-hero-of-hotel-rwanda-now-hes-accused-of-terrorism.html.

Haraway, Donna. 1988. "Situated Knowledges: The Science Question in Feminism and the Privilege of Partial Perspective." *Feminist Studies* 14 (3): 575–99. https://doi.org/10.2307/3178066.

Harrison, Faye V. 2007. "Feminist Methodology as a Tool for Ethnographic Inquiry on Globalization." In *The Gender of Globalization: Women Navigating Cultural and Economic Marginalities*, edited by Nandini Gunewardena and Ann Kingsolver, 23–31. Santa Fe, NM: School for Advanced Research.

Haslam, S. Alexander, Stephen D. Reicher, and Megan E. Birney. 2014. "Nothing by Mere Authority: Evidence That in an Experimental Analogue of the Milgram Paradigm Participants Are Motivated Not by Orders but by Appeals to Science." *Journal of Social Issues* 70 (3): 473–88. https://doi.org/10.1111/josi.12072.

Hebblethwaite, Peter. 1994. "In Rwanda, 'Blood Is Thicker Than Water—Even the Water of Baptism.'" *National Catholic Reporter*, June 3, 1994. https://www.proquest.com/docview/215334020/abstract/8D16E3F141364ACEPQ/23.

Hilberg, Raul. 1992. *Perpetrators, Victims, Bystanders: The Jewish Catastrophe, 1933–1945.* New York: HarperCollins.

Hinton, Alexander Laban. 2005. *Why Did They Kill? Cambodia in the Shadow of Genocide.* Berkeley: University of California Press.

Hoffman, Danny. 2011. *The War Machines: Young Men and Violence in Sierra Leone and Liberia.* Cultures and Practice of Violence Series. Durham, NC: Duke University Press.

Hoffman, Martin L. 1981. "The Development of Empathy." In *Altruism and Helping Behavior: Social, Personality, and Developmental Perspectives*, edited by Richard M. Sorrentino and J. Philippe Rushton, 41–64. Hillsdale, NJ: Erlbaum Associates.

Hogg, Nicole. 2010. "Women's Participation in the Rwandan Genocide: Mothers or Monsters?" *International Review of the Red Cross; Cambridge* 92 (877): 69–102. http://dx.doi.org/10.1017/S1816383110000019.

hooks, bell. 1982. *Ain't I a Woman?* London: Pluto.

Horowitz, Sara R. 2005. "The Gender of Good and Evil: Women and Holocaust Memory." In *Gray Zones: Ambiguity and Compromise in the Holocaust and Its Aftermath*, edited by Jonathan Petropoulos and John K. Roth, 165–78. New York: Berghahn Books. http://ezproxy.gsu.edu/login?url=http://search.ebscohost.com/login.aspx?direct=true&db=cat06552a&AN=gsu.9914842063402952&site=eds-live&scope=site.

Ilibagiza, Immaculée, and Steve Erwin. 2006. *Left to Tell: Discovering God amidst the Rwandan Holocaust*. Carlsbad, CA: Hay House.

Ingelaere, Bert. 2016. *Inside Rwanda's Gacaca Courts: Seeking Justice after Genocide*. Madison: University of Wisconsin Press.

Jacob, Irénée, ed. 1983. *Dictionnaire rwandais-français, en trois volumes*. Vol. 1 (A–H). Butare, Rwanda: Institut National de Recherche Scientifique.

——, ed. 1985. *Dictionnaire rwandais-français, en trois volumes*. Vol. 3 (S–Z). Butare, Rwanda: Institut National de Recherche Scientifique.

Jefremovas, Villia. 1995. "Acts of Human Kindness: Tutsi, Hutu and the Genocide." *Issue: A Journal of Opinion* 23 (2): 28–31. https://doi.org/10.2307/1166503.

Kagabo, José Hamim. 1988. *L'Islam et les "Swahili" au Rwanda*. Paris: Éditions de l'École des hautes études en sciences sociales.

Kagame, Alexis. 1952. *La poésie dynastique du Rwanda*. Vol. 22, no. 1. Brussels: Mémoire de l'Institut Royal Colonial Belge, Section des sciences morales et politiques.

——. 1956. *La philosophie bântu-rwandaise de l'Être*. Brussels: Académie Royale des Sciences Coloniales.

Kahn, Leora. 2020. "The Rescuers: The Role of Testimony as a Peacebuilding Tool to Create Empathy." In *Coexistence in the Aftermath of Mass Violence*, edited by Eve Monique Zucker and Laura McGrew, 149–70. Ann Arbor: University of Michigan Press. https://doi.org/10.3998/mpub.11302800.

Kalyvas, Stathis N. 2006. *The Logic of Violence in Civil War*. New York: Cambridge University Press.

Kasule, Omar Hassan. 1982. "Muslims in Rwanda: A Status Report." *Institute of Muslim Minority Affairs Journal* 4 (1): 133–44.

Kayihura, Edouard. 2014. *Inside the Hotel Rwanda*. Dallas: BenBella Books.

Kayishema, Jean-Marie, and François Masabo. 2010. "Les justes rwandais 'Indakemwa.'" December. Kigali, Rwanda: Ibuka.

Kayitesi, Berthe. 2009. *Demain ma vie: Enfants chefs de famille dans le rwanda d'après*. Paris: Éditions Laurence Teper.

Kerenji, Emil. 2016. "'Your Salvation Is the Struggle against Fascism': Yugoslav Communists and the Rescue of Jews, 1941–1945." *Contemporary European History* 25 (1): 57. https://doi.org/10.1017/S0960777315000478.

King, Régine Uwibereyeho, and Izumi Sakamoto. 2015. "Disengaging from Genocide Harm-Doing and Healing Together between Perpetrators, Bystanders, and Victims in Rwanda." *Peace and Conflict: Journal of Peace Psychology*, Collective Harmdoing, 21 (3): 378–94. https://doi.org/10.1037/pac0000078.

Kingstone, Heidi. 2012. "Muslims Move into Mainstream in Rwanda." On Line Opinion: Australia's e-Journal of Social and Political Debate, August 28. https://www.onlineopinion.com.au/view.asp?article=14040&page=0.

Kinzer, Stephen. 2008. *A Thousand Hills: Rwanda's Rebirth and the Man Who Dreamed It*. Hoboken, NJ: John Wiley & Sons.

Kleinschmidt, Jochen. 2015. "Drones y el orden legal internacional. Tecnología, estrategia y largas cadenas de acción." *Colombia Internacional* 84 (August): 17–42. https://doi.org/10.7440/colombiaint84.2015.01.

Krebs, Dennis L., and F. Van Hasteren. 1992. "The Development of Altruistic Personality." In *Embracing the Other*, edited by Pearl Oliner, Samuel Oliner, Lawrence Baron, Lawrence A. Blum, Dennis L. Krebs, and Zuzanna Smolenska, 142–69. New York: NYU Press.

Kuperman, Alan J. 2001. *The Limits of Humanitarian Intervention: Genocide in Rwanda*. Washington, DC: Brookings Institution. https://www.jstor.org/stable/10.7864/j.ctt127xzj.

——. 2004. "Provoking Genocide: A Revised History of the Rwandan Patriotic Front." *Journal of Genocide Research* 6 (1): 61–84. https://doi.org/10.1080/1462352042000194719.

Lacey, Marc. 2004. "Since '94 Horror, Rwandans Turn toward Islam." *New York Times*, April 7, 2004, sec. World. https://www.nytimes.com/2004/04/07/world/since-94-horror-rwandans-turn-toward-islam.html.

Lang, Berel. 2013. *Primo Levi: The Matter of a Life*. New Haven, CT: Yale University Press.

Langer, Lawrence L. 1991. *Holocaust Testimonies: The Ruins of Memory*. New Haven, CT: Yale University Press.

Latané, Bibb, and John M. Darley. 1970. *The Unresponsive Bystander: Why Doesn't He Help?* New York: Appleton-Century Crofts.

Latour, Bruno. 2005. *Reassembling the Social: An Introduction to Actor-Network-Theory*. Clarendon Lectures in Management Studies. New York: Oxford University Press.

Law, John, and Annemarie Mol, eds. 2002. *Complexities: Social Studies of Knowledge Practices*. Durham, NC: Duke University Press.

Lee, Sander H. 2016. "Primo Levi's Gray Zone: Implications for Post-Holocaust Ethics." *Holocaust and Genocide Studies* 30 (2): 276–97. https://muse.jhu.edu/article/630517.

Levi, Primo. 1989. *The Drowned and the Saved*. New York: Vintage International.

Lewin, Ellen. 2006. *Feminist Anthropology: A Reader*. Oxford: Blackwell.

Linden, Ian. 1977. *Church and Revolution in Rwanda*. New York: Africana.

L'Obs. 2008. "Rwanda: La condamnation de Pierre Péan requise." September 26. https://www.nouvelobs.com/societe/20080926.OBS2817/rwanda-la-condamnation-de-pierre-pean-requise.html.

Longman, Timothy. 2009. *Christianity and Genocide in Rwanda*. New York: Cambridge University Press. https://doi.org/10.1017/CBO9780511642043.

——. 2017. *Memory and Justice in Post-genocide Rwanda*. New York: Cambridge University Press. https://doi.org/10.1017/9781139086257.

Lubkemann, Stephen. 2008. *Culture in Chaos: An Anthropology of the Social Condition in War*. Chicago: University of Chicago Press.

Luft, Aliza. 2015. "Toward a Dynamic Theory of Action at the Micro Level of Genocide: Killing, Desistance, and Saving in 1994 Rwanda." *Sociological Theory* 33 (2): 148–72. https://doi.org/10.1177/0735275115587721.

Mahy, Lina. 1989. "Étude alimentaire et socio-économique dans la commune de Kayove." RWA/87/012/DOC/TR/17. Gisenyi, Rwanda: Projet PNUD/FAO. http://www.fao.org/docrep/006/AD177F/AD177F00.htm#TOC.

Malkki, Liisa. 1995. *Purity and Exile: Violence, Memory, and National Cosmology among Hutu Refugees in Tanzania*. Chicago: University of Chicago Press.

Matthäus, Jürgen. 2009. *Approaching an Auschwitz Survivor: Holocaust Testimony and Its Transformations*. New York: Oxford University Press.

McClendon, Gwyneth H., and Rachel Beatty Riedl. 2019. *From Pews to Politics: Religious Sermons and Political Participation in Africa*. New York: Cambridge University Press.

McDoom, Omar. 2005. "Rwanda's Ordinary Killers: Interpreting Popular Participation in the Rwandan Genocide." 77. Crisis States Programme Working Papers Series. London School of Economics Development Studies Institute. http://eprints.lse.ac.uk/28153/1/wp77.pdf.

——. 2013. "Who Killed in Rwanda's Genocide? Micro-Space, Social Influence and Individual Participation in Intergroup Violence." *Journal of Peace Research* 50 (4): 453–67. https://doi.org/10.1177/0022343313478958.

——. 2014. "Antisocial Capital: A Profile of Rwandan Genocide Perpetrators' Social Networks." *Journal of Conflict Resolution* 58 (5): 865–93. https://doi.org/10.1177/0022002713484282.

——. 2020. "Contested Counting: Toward a Rigorous Estimate of the Death Toll in the Rwandan Genocide." *Journal of Genocide Research* 22 (1): 83–93. https://doi.org/10.1080/14623528.2019.1703252.

Meierhenrich, Jens. 2020. "How Many Victims Were There in the Rwandan Genocide? A Statistical Debate." *Journal of Genocide Research* 22 (1): 72–82. https://doi.org/10.1080/14623528.2019.1709611.

Melson, Robert. 2005. "Choiceless Choices: Surviving on False Papers on the 'Aryan' Side." In *Gray Zones: Ambiguity and Compromise in the Holocaust and Its Aftermath*, edited by Jonathan Petropoulos and John K. Roth, 97–106. New York: Berghahn Books.

Melvern, Linda. 2000. *A People Betrayed: The Role of the West in Rwanda's Genocide*. New York: Palgrave.

——. 2011. "Hotel Rwanda—without the Hollywood Ending." *Guardian*, November 17, sec. Film. http://www.theguardian.com/commentisfree/2011/nov/17/hotel-rwanda-hollywood-ending.

Mieth, Friederike. 2020. "And to This New Life We Are Striving: The Role of Imagination in Post-conflict Sierra Leone." In *Coexistence in the Aftermath of Mass Violence*, edited by Eve Monique Zucker and Laura McGrew, 29–52. Ann Arbor: University of Michigan Press. https://doi.org/10.3998/mpub.11302800.

Milgram, Stanley. 1974. *Obedience to Authority*. New York: Harper & Row.

Miller, Arthur G. 2014. "The Explanatory Value of Milgram's Obedience Experiments: A Contemporary Appraisal." *Journal of Social Issues* 70 (3): 558–73. https://doi.org/10.1111/josi.12078.

Mol, Annemarie. 2003. *The Body Multiple: Ontology in Medical Practice*. Durham, NC: Duke University Press.

Monroe, Kristen R. 1996. *The Heart of Altruism: Perceptions of a Common Humanity*. Princeton, NJ: Princeton University Press.

——. 2004. *The Hand of Compassion: Portraits of Moral Choice during the Holocaust*. Princeton, NJ: Princeton University Press.

——. 2008. "Cracking the Code of Genocide: The Moral Psychology of Rescuers, Bystanders, and Nazis during the Holocaust." *Political Psychology* 29 (5): 699–736.

Monroe, Kristen R., and Maria Luisa Martinez. 2009. "Empathy, Prejudice, and Fostering Tolerance." In *On Behalf of Others: The Psychology of Care in a Global World*, edited by Sarah Scuzzarello, Catarina Kinnvall, and Kristen Renwick Monroe, 147–62. New York: Oxford University Press.

Mudimbe, Valentine Y. 1988. *The Invention of Africa: Gnosis, Philosophy and the Order of Knowledge*. Bloomington: Indiana University Press.

Mugwanya, George William. 2011. "The Contribution of the International Criminal Tribunal for Rwanda to the Development of International Criminal Law." In *Prosecuting International Crimes in Africa*, edited by Chacha Murungu and Japhet Biegon, 63–96. Pretoria: Pretoria University Law Press (PULP).

Müller, Martin. 2015. "Assemblages and Actor-Networks: Rethinking Socio-material Power, Politics and Space." *Geography Compass* 9 (1): 27–41. https://doi.org/10.1111/gec3.12192.

Musoni, Edwin. 2013. "Know Your Heroes." *New Times* (Rwanda), January 31, online ed. https://www.newtimes.co.rw/section/read/62418/.

Newbury, Catharine. 1988. *The Cohesion of Oppression: Clientship and Ethnicity in Rwanda, 1860–1960*. New York: Columbia University Press.

——. 1998. "Ethnicity and the Politics of History in Rwanda." *Africa Today* 45 (1): 7–24.

Newbury, David S. 1991. "The 'Rwakayihura' Famine of 1928–1929: A Nexus of Colonial Rule in Rwanda." In *Histoire sociale de l'Afrique de l'Est (XIXe–XXe siècle)*, edited by Université du Burundi Département d'histoire, 269–85. Paris: Karthala.

Nigmann, Ernst. (1911) 2005. *German Schutztruppe in East Africa: History of the Imperial Protectorate Force 1889–1911*. Translated by Robert E. Dohrenwend. Nashville, TN: Battery.

Nordstrom, Carolyn. 1997. *A Different Kind of War Story*. Philadelphia: University of Pennsylvania Press.

——. 2004. *Shadows of War: Violence, Power, and International Profiteering in the Twenty-First Century*. Berkeley: University of California Press.

Nothomb, Dominique. 1965. *Un humanisme africain: Valeurs et pierres d'attente*. Brussels: Éditions Lume Vitae.

Nsanzabera, Jean de Dieu. 2019. "Amaraso y'Umunyarwanda: Intsinzi Ku Gihugu Cye, Icyorezo Ku Mahanga." *Igihe*, February 26, online ed. https://www.igihe.com/umuco/article/amaraso-y-umunyarwanda-intsinzi-ku-gihugu-cye-icyorezo-ku-mahanga.

Nsengiyumva, Dan. 2020. "Inside Campaign against Genocide Museum." *New Times* (Rwanda), July 2, online ed. https://www.newtimes.co.rw/news/pictures-video-inside-campaign-against-genocide-museum.

Ntezimana, Emmanuel. 1980. "Coutumes et traditions des royaumes hutu du Bukunzi et du Busozo." *Études Rwandaises* 13 (2): 15–39.

Nyseth Brehm, Hollie, Christopher Uggen, and Jean-Damascène Gasanabo. 2016. "Age, Gender, and the Crime of Crimes: Toward a Life-Course Theory of Genocide Participation." *Criminology* 54 (4): 713–43. https://doi.org/10.1111/1745-9125.12122.

Oliner, Pearl M. 2004. *Saving the Forsaken: Religious Culture and the Rescue of Jews in Nazi Europe*. New Haven, CT: Yale University Press.

Oliner, Pearl M., and Samuel P. Oliner. 1995. *Toward a Caring Society: Ideals into Action*. Westport, CT: Praeger.

Oliner, Pearl M., Samuel P. Oliner, Lawrence Baron, Lawrence A. Blum, Dennis L. Krebs, and Zuzanna Smolenska, eds. 1992. *Embracing the Other: Philosophical, Psychological, and Historical Perspectives on Altruism*. New York: NYU Press.

Oliner, Samuel P., and Pearl M. Oliner. 1988. *The Altruistic Personality: Rescuers of Jews in Nazi Europe*. New York: Free Press.

Olivier de Sardan, Jean Pierre. 1999. "A Moral Economy of Corruption in Africa?" *Journal of Modern African Studies* 37 (1): 25–52. http://www.jstor.org/stable/161467.

Overy, Richard. 2014. "'Ordinary Men,' Extraordinary Circumstances: Historians, Social Psychology, and the Holocaust." *Journal of Social Issues* 70 (3): 515–30. https://doi.org/10.1111/josi.12075.

Péan, Pierre. 2005. *Noires fureurs, blancs menteurs: Rwanda 1990/1994*. Paris: Fayard.

——. 2009. *Le monde selon K*. Paris: Fayard.

Pessi, Anne B. 2009. "Spirit of Altruism? On the Role of the Finnish Church as a Promoter of Altruism of Individuals and of Society." In *On Behalf of Others: The Psychology of Care in a Global World*, edited by Sarah Scuzzarello, Catarina Kinnvall, and Kristen Renwick Monroe, 147–62. New York: Oxford University Press.

Petropoulos, Jonathan, and John K. Roth, eds. 2005. *Gray Zones: Ambiguity and Compromise in the Holocaust and Its Aftermath*. New York: Berghahn Books.

Prunier, Gérard. 1997. *The Rwanda Crisis: History of a Genocide*. 2nd ed. New York: Columbia University Press.

Raffles, Hugh. 2002. *In Amazonia: A Natural History*. Princeton, NJ: Princeton University Press.

Reicher, Stephen D., S. Alexander Haslam, and Arthur G. Miller. 2014. "What Makes a Person a Perpetrator? The Intellectual, Moral, and Methodological Arguments for Revisiting Milgram's Research on the Influence of Authority." *Journal of Social Issues* 70 (3): 393–408. https://doi.org/10.1111/josi.12067.

Republic of Rwanda (République du Rwanda). 1994. "Recensement général de la population et de l'habitat au 15 août 1991: Analyse des résultats définitifs." Kigali, Rwanda: Service National de Recensement, Ministère du Plan. http://francegenocidetutsi.org/19910815RecensementGeneralPopulation.pdf.

——. 2004. *Denombrement des victimes du génocide*. Report. Kigali, Rwanda: Ministry of Local Government, Communal Development, and Social Affairs. http://www.cnlg.gov.rw/fileadmin/templates/Publications/denombrement_des_victimes_du_genocide_perpetre_contre_les_tutsi_avril_2004.pdf.

——. 2017. "National Policy of Awarding National Orders." Kigali, Rwanda: Ministry of Sports and Culture.

Reydams, Luc. 2016. "NGO Justice: African Rights as Pseudo-prosecutor of the Rwandan Genocide." *Human Rights Quarterly* 38 (3): 547–88. https://doi.org/10.1353/hrq.2016.0041.

Reyntjens, Filip. 2004. "Rwanda, Ten Years on: From Genocide to Dictatorship." *African Affairs* 103 (411): 177–210. https://doi.org/10.1093/afraf/adh045.

——. 2010. "A Fake Inquiry on a Major Event: Analysis of the Mutsinzi Report on the 6th April 1994 Attack on the Rwandan President's Aeroplane." Working Paper 2010.07. IOB Institute of Development Policy and Management Working Paper. Antwerp: University of Antwerp. https://repository.uantwerpen.be/docman/irua/2faab7/1766.pdf.

——. 2011. "Constructing the Truth, Dealing with Dissent, Domesticating the World: Governance in Post-genocide Rwanda." *African Affairs* 110 (438): 1–34. https://doi.org/10.1093/.

Robertson, Geoffrey. 2021. "The Case of Paul Rusesabagina." American Bar Association Center for Human Rights. https://www.americanbar.org/content/dam/aba/administrative/human_rights/trialwatch/rwanda-paul-rusesabagina.pdf.

Rothbart, Daniel, and Jessica Cooley. 2016. "Hutus Aiding Tutsis during the Rwandan Genocide: Motives, Meanings and Morals." *Genocide Studies and Prevention: An International Journal* 10 (2): 76–97. https://doi.org/10.5038/1911-9933.10.2.1398.

Rothberg, Michael. 2009. *Multidirectional Memory: Remembering the Holocaust in the Age of Decolonization*. Stanford, CA: Stanford University Press.

Rusagara, Frank K. 2009. *Resilience of a Nation: A History of the Military in Rwanda*. Kigali, Rwanda: Fountain.

Rutayisire, Emmanuel. 2014. "RDF Defends War Memorial Monuments at Parliament." *New Times* (Rwanda), July 18, online ed. https://www.theeastafrican.co.ke/rwanda/News/RDF-defends-war-memorial-monuments-at-parliament/1433218-2389352-12463aw/index.html.

Sabiti, Daniel. 2021. "FLN Terror Suspects Resume Trial, Plead for Leniency." *KT PRESS*, July 15, 2021, sec. National. https://www.ktpress.rw/2021/07/fln-terror-suspects-resume-trial-plead-for-leniency/.

Sandberg, Marie. 2009. "Performing the Border." *Anthropological Journal of European Cultures* 18 (1): 107–28. https://doi.org/10.3167/ajec.2009.180107.

Sanders, Edith R. 1969. "The Hamitic Hypothesis: Its Origin and Functions in Time Perspective." *Journal of African History* 10 (4): 521–32. https://www.jstor.org/stable/179896.

Sanford, Victoria. 2003. *Buried Secrets: Truth and Human Rights in Guatemala*. New York: Palgrave Macmillan.

Sayes, Edwin. 2014. "Actor-Network Theory and Methodology: Just What Does It Mean to Say That Nonhumans Have Agency?" *Social Studies of Science* 44 (1): 134–49. https://doi.org/10.1177/0306312713511867.

Scarry, Elaine. 1985. *The Body in Pain: The Making and Unmaking of the World*. New York: Oxford University Press.

Schaffer, Simon. 1991. "The Eighteenth Brumaire of Bruno Latour." *Studies in History and Philosophy of Science Part A* 22 (1): 174–92. https://doi.org/10.1016/0039-3681(91)90020-S.

Schoenbrun, David Lee. 1998. *A Green Place, a Good Place: Agrarian Change, Gender and Social Identity in the Great Lakes Region to the 15th Century*. Portsmouth, NH: Heinemann.

Scott, James. 1985. *Weapons of the Weak: Everyday Forms of Peasant Resistance*. New Haven, CT: Yale University Press.

Sebarenzi, Joseph. 2009. *God Sleeps in Rwanda: A Journey of Transformation*. New York: Simon & Schuster.

Seidler, V. J. 1992. "Rescue, Righteousness, and Morality." In *Embracing the Other*, edited by Pearl Oliner, Samuel Oliner, Lawrence Baron, Lawrence A. Blum, Dennis L. Krebs, and Zuzanna Smolenska, 48–66. New York: NYU Press.

Sémelin, Jacques. 2011. "Introduction: From Help to Rescue." In *Resisting Genocide: The Multiple Forms of Rescue*, edited by Jacques Sémelin, Claire Andrieu, Sarah Gensburger, and Cynthia Schoch, translated by Emma Bentley, 1–14. New York: Columbia University Press.

——. 2019. *The Survival of the Jews in France, 1940–44*. New York: Oxford University Press. https://doi.org/10.1093/oso/9780190939298.001.0001.

Sémelin, Jacques, Claire Andrieu, and Sarah Gensburger. 2008. *La résistance aux génocides*. Paris: Les Presses des SciencesPo.

——, eds. 2011. *Resisting Genocide: The Multiple Forms of Rescue*. Translated by Emma Bentley. New York: Columbia University Press.

Seminega, Tharcisse. 2019. *No Greater Love: How My Family Survived the Genocide in Rwanda*. Ashland, OH: GM&A.

Shapiro-Phim, Toni. 2020. "Imagining Alternative Views: Cambodia, Accountability, and Compassion." In *Coexistence in the Aftermath of Mass Violence*, edited by Eve Monique Zucker and Laura McGrew, 71–96. Ann Arbor: University of Michigan Press. https://doi.org/10.3998/mpub.11302800.

Simons, Marlise. 2003. "Rwandan Pastor and His Son Are Convicted of Genocide." *New York Times*, February 20, sec. A. https://www.nytimes.com/2003/02/20/world/rwandan-pastor-and-his-son-are-convicted-of-genocide.html.

Sirven, Pierre. 1984. "La sous-urbanisation et les villes du Rwanda et du Burundi." Doctoral diss., l'Université de Bordeaux III.

Smeulers, Alette. 2015. "Female Perpetrators: Ordinary or Extra-ordinary Women?" *International Criminal Law Review* 15 (2): 207–53. https://doi.org/10.1163/15718123-01502001.

Soares, Benjamin, and Filippo Osella. 2009. "Islam, Politics, Anthropology." *Journal of the Royal Anthropological Institute* 15: S1–23. https://doi.org/10.1111/j.1467-9655.2009.01539.x.

Sommers, Marc. 2012. *Stuck: Rwandan Youth and the Struggle for Adulthood*. Athens: University of Georgia Press.

Spradley, James P. 1979. *The Ethnographic Interview*. New York: Harcourt Brace Jovanovich College Publishers.

Staub, Ervin. 1993. "The Psychology of Bystanders, Perpetrators, and Heroic Helpers." *International Journal of Intercultural Relations* 17 (January): 315–41. https://doi.org/10.1016/0147-1767(93)90037-9.

——. 2003. *The Psychology of Good and Evil*. New York: Cambridge University Press.

——. 2014. "Obeying, Joining, Following, Resisting, and Other Processes in the Milgram Studies, and in the Holocaust and Other Genocides: Situations, Personality, and Bystanders." *Journal of Social Issues* 70 (3): 501–14. https://doi.org/10.1111/josi.12074.

——. 2019. "Witnesses/Bystanders: The Tragic Fruits of Passivity, the Power of Bystanders, and Promoting Active Bystandership in Children, Adults, and Groups." *Journal of Social Issues* 75 (4): 1262–93. https://doi.org/10.1111/josi.12351.

Strathern, Marilyn. 1987. "An Awkward Relationship: The Case of Feminism and Anthropology." *Signs* 12 (2): 276–92. https://www.jstor.org/stable/3173986.

Straus, Scott. 2006. *The Order of Genocide: Race, Power, and War in Rwanda*. Ithaca, NY: Cornell University Press.

——. 2015. *Making and Unmaking Nations: War, Leadership, and Genocide in Modern Africa*. Ithaca, NY: Cornell University Press.

Tabaro, Jean de la Croix. 2018. "French Court Drops Fr. Wenceslas Munyeshyaka's Genocide Case." *KT PRESS*, June 21, 2018. https://ktpress.rw/2018/06/french-court-drops-fr-wenceslas-munyeshyakas-genocide-case/.

Tambiah, Stanley J. 1996. *Leveling Crowds: Ethnonationalist Conflicts and Collective Violence in South Asia*. Berkeley: University of California Press.

Taussig, Michael T. 1984. "Culture of Terror—Space of Death: Roger Casement's Putumayo Report and the Explanation of Torture." *Comparative Studies in Society and History* 26 (3): 467–97. https://www.jstor.org/stable/178552.

——. 1999. *Defacement: Public Secrecy and the Labor of the Negative*. Stanford, CA: Stanford University Press.

Taylor, Christopher C. 1992. *Milk, Honey, and Money: Changing Concepts in Rwandan Healing*. Washington, DC: Smithsonian Institution.

——. 1999. *Sacrifice as Terror: The Rwandan Genocide of 1994*. New York: Berg.

Ternon, Yves. 2011. "The Impossible Rescue of the Armenians of Mardin: The Sinar Safe Haven." In *Resisting Genocide: The Multiple Forms of Rescue*, edited by Jacques Sémelin, Claire Andrieu, Sarah Gensburger, and Cynthia Schoch, translated by Emma Bentley, 383–94. New York: Columbia University Press.

Tevosyan, Hamsik. 2008. "Les pratiques de sauvetage durant le génocide arménien." In *La résistance aux génocides*, edited by Jacques Sémelin, Claire Andrieu, and Sarah Gensburger, 185–204. Paris: Les Presses des SciencesPo.

Thomson, Susan. 2013. *Whispering Truth to Power: Everyday Resistance to Reconciliation in Postgenocide Rwanda*. Madison: University of Wisconsin Press.

——. 2018. *Rwanda: From Genocide to Precarious Peace*. New Haven, CT: Yale University Press.

——. 2019. "Settler Genocide in Rwanda? Colonial Legacies of Everyday Violence." In *Civilian-Driven Violence and the Genocide of Indigenous Peoples in Settler Societies*, edited by Mohamed Adhikari, 241–66. Cape Town: UCT Press.

Tissot, Roland. 2020. "Beyond the 'Numbers Game': Reassessing Human Losses in Rwanda during the 1990s." *Journal of Genocide Research* 22 (1): 116–24. https://doi.org/10.1080/14623528.2019.1703250.

Trimingham, John Spencer. 1964. *Islam in East Africa*. Oxford: Clarendon.

Tsing, Anna Lowenhaupt. 2015. *The Mushroom at the End of the World: On the Possibility of Life in Capitalist Ruins*. Princeton, NJ: Princeton University Press.

Twagilimana, Aimable. 2016. *Historical Dictionary of Rwanda*. Lanham, MD: Rowman & Littlefield.

UC Louvain Portraits of the Righteous. 1994. "Letter from Félicité Niyitegeka to Her Brother Colonel Alphonse Nzungize, April 12, 1994." https://cdn.uclouvain.be/public/Exports%20reddot/cr-cridis/images/Rwabaho_Niyitegeka_Felicite_lettre.png?itok=SFRLtHKw.

Umutesi, Marie Béatrice. 2000. *Fuir ou mourir au Zaïre*. Paris: L'Harmattan.

——. 2004. *Surviving the Slaughter: The Ordeal of a Rwandan Refugee in Zaire*. Madison: University of Wisconsin Press.

United Nations. 1999. "Report of the Independent Inquiry into Actions of the United Nations during the 1994 Genocide in Rwanda."

United Nations International Criminal Tribunal for Rwanda. 2009. "Father Hormisdas Nsengimana Acquitted (Press Release)." United Nations International Criminal Tribunal for Rwanda, November 17. http://unictr.irmct.org/en/news/father-hormisdas-nsengimana-acquitted.

US Department of State. 2018. *Rwanda International Religious Freedom Report*. Washington, DC: US Department of State. https://www.state.gov/wp-content/uploads/2019/05/RWANDA-2018-INTERNATIONAL-RELIGIOUS-FREEDOM-REPORT.pdf.

'U<u>s</u>mānī, Muḥammad Taqī. 2020. *The Noble Qur'ān with Explanatory Notes*. Karachi: Turath.

Vansina, Jan. 2005. *Antecedents to Modern Rwanda: The Nyiginya Kingdom*. Madison: University of Wisconsin Press.

Varese, Federico, and Meir Yaish. 2000. "The Importance of Being Asked." *Rationality and Society* 12 (3): 307–34. https://doi.org/10.1177/104346300012003003.

——. 2005. "Resolute Heroes: The Rescue of Jews during the Nazi Occupation of Europe." *European Journal of Sociology* 46 (1): 153–68. https://doi.org/10.1017/S0003975605000068.

Verpoorten, Marijke. 2020. "How Many Died in Rwanda?" *Journal of Genocide Research* 22 (1): 94–103. https://doi.org/10.1080/14623528.2019.1703253.

Verwimp, Philip. 2005. "An Economic Profile of Peasant Perpetrators of Genocide." *Journal of Development Economics* 77 (2): 297–323. https://doi.org/10.1016/j.jdeveco.2004.04.005.

——. 2006. "Machetes and Firearms: The Organization of Massacres in Rwanda." *Journal of Peace Research* 43 (1): 5–22. https://doi.org/10.1177/0022343306059576.

Viret, Emmanuel. 2010. "Rwanda—a Chronology (1867–1994)." Sciences Po Mass Violence and Resistance. March 1. https://www.sciencespo.fr/mass-violence-war-massacre-resistance/en/document/rwanda-chronology-1867-1994.

——. 2011a. "Social Cohesion and State of Exception: The Muslims of Mabare during the Genocide in Rwanda." In *Resisting Genocide: The Multiple Forms of Rescue*, edited by Jacques Sémelin, Claire Andrieu, Sarah Gensburger, and Cynthia Schoch, translated by Emma Bentley, 481–94. New York: Columbia University Press.

——. 2011b. "Les habits de la foule: Techniques de gouvernement, clientèles sociales et violence au Rwanda rural (1963–1994)." Doctoral diss., Institut d'Études Politiques de Paris.

Wagner, Michele D. 1998. "All the Bourgmestre's Men: Making Sense of Genocide in Rwanda." *Africa Today* 45 (1): 25–36. https://www.jstor.org/stable/4187201.

Waldorf, Lars. 2006. "Mass Justice for Mass Atrocity: Rethinking Local Justice as Transitional Justice." *Temple Law Review* 79 (1): 1–87.

——. 2009. "Revisiting *Hotel Rwanda*: Genocide Ideology, Reconciliation, and Rescuers." *Journal of Genocide Research* 11 (1): 101–25. https://doi.org/10.1080/14623520802703673.

Walker, Margath A. 2015. "Borders, One-Dimensionality, and Illusion in the War on Drugs." *Environment and Planning D: Society and Space* 33 (1): 84–100. https://doi.org/10.1068/d13138p.

——. 2018. "The Other U.S. Border? Techno-Cultural-Rationalities and Fortification in Southern Mexico." *Environment and Planning A: Economy and Space* 50 (5): 948–68. https://doi.org/10.1177/0308518X18763816.

Weedon, Chris. 1987. *Feminist Practice and Poststructuralist Theory*. New York: Blackwell.

Weller, Susan C. 2015. "Structured Interviewing and Questionnaire Construction." In *Handbook of Methods in Cultural Anthropology*, edited by H. Russell Bernard and Clarence C. Gravlee, 343–90. Lanham, MD: Rowman & Littlefield.

Willame, Jean-Claude. 1995. *Aux sources de l'hécatombe rwandaise*. Paris: L'Harmattan.

Williams, Linda Meyer, and Victoria L. Banyard, eds. 1999. *Trauma and Memory*. Thousand Oaks, CA: SAGE.

Winfield, Nicole. 2017. "Pope Begs Forgiveness for Church Role in Rwanda Genocide." Associated Press News Online, March 20. https://apnews.com/article/788a4dd6ee8841b3bfb3a112d012e466.

Xiang, Biao, and Johan Lindquist. 2014. "Migration Infrastructure." *International Migration Review* 48 (1_suppl): 122–48. https://doi.org/10.1111/imre.12141.

Zucker, Eve Monique. 2020. "In the Realms of Ritual and Enchantment: Imagination and Recovery in the Aftermath of the Khmer Rouge." In *Coexistence in the Aftermath of Mass Violence*, edited by Eve Monique Zucker and Laura McGrew, 29–52. Ann Arbor: University of Michigan Press. https://doi.org/10.3998/mpub.11302800.

[illegible]

Index

Page numbers in *italics* indicate maps.